OREGON

CONTRACTOR REFERENCE MANUAL

Prepared by

PROMETRIC

For the

CONSTRUCTION CONTRACTORS BOARD

Eleventh Edition

ISBN 1-931345-24-4

ACKNOWLEDGMENTS

Thank you to the following individuals who volunteered their time and expertise:

CCB Staff:
Administrator James Denno; Education Manager Cheryl Martinis; Licensing Manager Laurie Hall; Licensing Manager Stan Jessup; and Policy Analyst Kathi Dahlin.

Prometric:
Rod Watkins, Client Services Manager; Janice Flores, Client Services Manager; Brooke Kang, Technical Editor; and Stacy Lawson, Team Lead.

Professional and State of Oregon Administrative Agencies:

Chapter 1:   Kathi Dahlin, policy analyst, and other CCB staff

Chapter 2:   Kay Thrash, senior investigator
                  Workers' Compensation Division,
                  Employer Compliance Unit, Salem, Oregon

Chapter 3:   Van White, Attorney
                  Samuels Yoelin Kantor Seymour & Spinrad LLP,
                  Portland, Oregon
                  Melvin Oden-Orr, Attorney
                  Board member, Construction Contractors Board

Chapter 4:   Alan L. Mitchell, Attorney
                  Mitchell Law Office, Portland, Oregon
                  Ed Lohman, Attorney
                  Lohman & Lohman PC, West Linn, Oregon
                  Kathi Dahlin, policy analyst, CCB

Chapter 5:   Michael Sause, CPA, Senior Manager, Construction Division
                  AKT LLP, Lake Oswego, Oregon
                  Kay Del Marshall, Senior Stakeholder Liaison, Small Business &
                  Self-Employed C/L/D, IRS, Portland, Oregon

Chapter 6:   Greg Olson, President
                  Olson & Jones Construction, Inc., Portland, Oregon
                  Brent Schafer, Builder
                  Todd Construction, Tualatin, Oregon
                  The Construction Specifications Institute (CSI) and Construction
                  Specifications Canada (CSC), publishers of the *MasterFormat*™
                  Numbers and Titles used in this chapter with permission from CSI
                  99 Canal Center Plaza, Suite 300, Alexandria, VA 22314,
                  800.689.2900; 703.684.0300; www.csinet.org

Chapter 7:	Andrea F. Simmons, manager, Policy and Technical Services Oregon State Building Codes Division, Salem, Oregon
Chapter 8:	Marilyn Schuster, deputy administrator, OR-OSHA, Salem, Oregon
Chapter 9:	Dottie Boyd, asbestos inspector/natural resource specialist, air quality; Krista Ratliff, natural resource specialist, stormwater; and others. Oregon Department of Environmental Quality
Chapter 10:	Toby C. White, vice president, Forensic Building Consultants, Portland, Oregon
Others:	Bonnie Sullivan, Sullivan's Carpet Service, Inc., Jefferson, Oregon.
Facilitators of Chapter Teams:	Brad Rafish, Partner Talbot, Korvola & Warwick, LLP, Portland, Oregon Liz Brooke, Consultant Talbot, Korvola & Warwick, LLP, Portland, Oregon

Professional and Trade Associations:

The Construction Contractors Board wishes to recognize the value of resources provided by the American Society of Professional Estimators, Associated General Contractors, Construction Specifications Institute, National Association of Women in Construction, Oregon Building Industries Association, Oregon Remodelers Association, Oregon Society of CPAs, and the Oregon State Bar Association.

Prelicense educators:

Many of the educators who provide prelicense training to future contractors reviewed this manual for its content and provided invaluable edits and other assistance.

Mission: *The Construction Contractors Board protects the public's interest relating to improvements to real property. The Board regulates construction contractors and promotes a competitive business environment through education, contractor licensing, dispute resolution, and law enforcement.*

Disclaimer

This manual is for educating and providing reference information for contractors in Oregon. It is not meant to be legal advice and should not be relied on without discussing with an experienced attorney. Legal questions are technical and subject to interpretation by the courts. If your project is located outside of the State of Oregon, seek legal counsel for that state.

John A. Kitzhaber, MD, Governor

Construction Contractors Board
www.oregon.gov/ccb
Mailing Address:
PO Box 14140
Salem, OR 97309-5052
Street Address:
700 Summer St NE
Suite 300
503-378-4621

Sept. 15, 2014

Dear New Oregon Construction Contractor:

Welcome to the Oregon construction industry and community. When you obtain your new contractor license, you will join nearly 35,000 other construction businesses that are licensed and provide Oregonians with quality professional construction services.

Your success as a construction business operating in Oregon is not only important to you – it is of vital concern to the construction industry, consumers, and the people of Oregon. Failed businesses often damage consumers, leave suppliers unpaid, violate health and safety regulations, and harm consumer confidence in the construction industry. Successful businesses not only provide profit to their owners, but also provide quality goods and services needed by consumers and fuel the engine of Oregon's economy.

Your full understanding of all of the factors (including government regulation) that affect your business is essential to the successful operation of your business. This is the reason why the time you invest in this program is so very important.

The Construction Contractors Board (CCB) governs this contractor education and testing program.

The required 16 hours of prelicense education, for which this Oregon Contractor Reference Manual was prepared, will help you establish effective relations with your clients and partners in the construction industry. These relationships will also strengthen and promote the success of your business.

We, the staff of the CCB, wish you and your construction business, prosperity and long life.

TABLE OF CONTENTS

Chapter 1: Construction Contractor Laws and Regulations

Chapter 2: Employer Obligations and Employee Rights

Chapter 3: Contract Law

Chapter 4: Oregon Construction Lien Law

Chapter 5: Taxes, Record Keeping, and Business Practices

Chapter 6: Project Management

Chapter 7: Building Codes

Chapter 8: Oregon Occupational Safety and Health Division And Safety Issues

Chapter 9: Sound Environmental Laws and Practices

Chapter 10: Oregon Building Exterior Shell Training (BEST)

INTRODUCTION

Construction contractors face challenges in today's business world. A contractor cannot succeed simply with tools, sweat, and a handshake. Today, contractors must work smarter and know how to transact as business owners. This requires a working knowledge of business, laws, and rules.

Your success in the construction business is important to the Oregon community. Business failures cause the greatest amount of damage to the consumer market. The State of Oregon and the Construction Contractors Board believe that the information discussed in the *Oregon Contractor Reference Manual* will provide a foundation upon which you can build a successful business in construction or remodeling.

Construction is a highly regulated industry. This manual discusses business and law principles for construction contractors. There are Oregon administrative agencies that enforce many of those principles. Some of those agencies have contributed to the development of this manual as a way of helping contractors to know and understand the laws and rules. Since these laws and rules change and affect business practices and methods in the industry, this manual is updated regularly.

At the beginning of each chapter, you will find a list of objectives, which identify essential information that you should know and understand. The objectives were developed with input from successful Oregon contractors who determined that this information was vital to helping new contractors develop good business practices and avoid potential problems.

Learn as much as you can. We encourage you to read this manual before and after you pass the licensing exam. It will go a long way toward setting you on course for running a successful business.

CHAPTER 1
CONSTRUCTION CONTRACTOR LAWS AND REGULATIONS

Objectives

At the end of this chapter, you will be able to:

1. Describe how to locate copies of statutes and rules that govern construction contractors in Oregon.
2. Explain the composition of the Oregon Construction Contractors Board.
3. Explain who needs to be licensed to act as a construction contractor in Oregon.
4. Describe what business names must be registered.
5. Explain the requirements to operate as an independent contractor.
6. Describe the exempt and non-exempt classes of contractor licenses and identify the class to which particular businesses belong.
7. Describe license endorsements and identify the types of structures or projects that correspond to each endorsement.
8. Describe the special licenses or certifications and when they are required.
9. Identify the surety bond amount and the insurance amount and coverage required for each contractor license endorsement.
10. Explain the requirements for written contracts.
11. Describe the consumer notices and the requirements for their delivery.
12. Explain warranty requirements and maintenance schedules.
13. Explain the dispute resolution process, including:
    a. Types of complaints.
    b. Time limits for filing complaints.
    c. Where and how to file complaints.
    d. Procedures to resolve complaints.
14. Describe the violations of Oregon construction contractor law and how laws are enforced.

Contractor Licensing

Laws and Rules

Oregon law requires individuals or business entities conducting construction activities within the State of Oregon to be licensed with the Construction Contractors Board (CCB). These individuals or entities are "contractors."

Oregon Revised Statutes (ORS)

The Oregon Legislature enacts the laws that govern construction contracting. The legislature first created the CCB, then known as the Builders Board, in 1971. The laws can be found at ORS chapter 701. The laws may be revised every year.

Oregon Administrative Rules (OAR)

As directed by the Oregon Legislature, the CCB adopts administrative rules to carry out legislative directives. The rules can be found at OAR chapter 812. Rules may change more than once a year. Contractors can check the CCB website to stay current.

Construction Contractors Board

The CCB licenses contractors, investigates possible violations of contractor law, and mediates disputes against contractors.

Board Members

The CCB is governed by a nine-member board appointed by the Governor and confirmed by the Oregon Senate. The nine-member board reports to the Governor. The board consists of the following individuals:

- Two contractors who work primarily on residential or small commercial structures.
- One contractor who does residential or small commercial remodeling.
- Two commercial general contractors who work primarily on large commercial structures.
- One commercial specialty contractor who works primarily on large commercial structures, or a residential limited contractor.
- Two public members.
- One elected representative of a governing body of local government.

The Board's duties include:

- Setting policy for the CCB and implementing legislation.
- Overseeing responsibilities of the CCB administrator.
- Adopting administrative rules.
- Considering appeals to CCB proposed orders.

Who Must be Licensed?

A "contractor" is an individual or business entity that, for compensation or with the intent to sell, arranges or undertakes or offers to undertake or submits a bid to construct, alter, repair, add to, subtract from, improve, inspect, move, wreck or demolish, for another, any building, highway, road, railroad, excavation or other structure, project, development or improvement attached to real estate, or to do any part thereof. (ORS 701.005(5)(a)). An individual or entity is a contractor regardless of the type of property involved – residential, commercial, industrial, or publicly owned.

The following are also contractors:
- Those who construct or arrange for the construction of a building on their own property with the intent to sell (unless exempt).
- A school district or community college that has students construct buildings and sells those buildings.
- Those who perform tree services (unless licensed landscape contractors or otherwise exempt).
- A home inspection business.
- Those who clean and service chimneys.

Responsible Managing Individual (RMI)

Contractors must have one Responsible Managing Individual (RMI) on the record at all times. The RMI must be an owner of the business applying for the license, or the license applicant may instead designate an employee.

If the license applicant designates an employee as the RMI, the designated employee must exercise management or supervisory authority over the construction activities of the business.

The RMI completes the training and testing requirement and is named at the time of application or at a change of record. Some RMIs who have worked as contractors for many years are exempt from the training and testing requirements ("grandfathered"). The CCB considers the RMI an important part of the business' operations.

Under CCB law, if a contractor fails in its obligations and has construction-related debt, the RMI as well as the owners will be prevented from obtaining a CCB license until the debt has been cleared.

Contractors Exempt from Licensing

Some individuals or entities are not required to have licenses even if they are acting as "contractors" (ORS 701.010). Those not subject to the licensing laws include:

- Those who construct, alter, improve, or repair personal property.
- Those who construct, alter, improve, or repair a structure located within the boundaries of any site or reservation under the jurisdiction of the federal government.
- Those who furnish materials, supplies, equipment, or finished products but do not perform the construction work or make any arrangements for the performance of the construction work.
- Those who work on one structure or project, under one or more contracts, when the cumulative price of the contracts for labor, materials, and all other items is less than $1,000 and such work is casual, minor, or inconsequential. This does not apply to those who promote or advertise their services as contractors.
- An owner who contracts for work to be performed by a licensed contractor. This does not apply to those who, as a business, construct, remodel, or repair a structure or those who arrange to have a structure constructed, remodeled, or repaired, with the intent to sell. It is presumed that the structure is offered for sale if the owner does not occupy the structure after completion.
- An owner who contracts for one or more licensed contractors to perform work wholly or partially within the same calendar year on not more than three existing residential structures of the owner. This exemption does not apply to an owner contracting for work that requires a building permit unless the work that requires the permit is performed by, or under the direction of, a residential general contractor.
- Those who perform work on a property that they own or who perform work as the owner's employee and individuals who perform work on their residence, whether or not they own the residence. This exemption does not apply to those who perform work on a structure with the intent to sell.
- Those licensed in one of the following trades or professions when operating within the scope of that license:
  - A registered architect.
  - A registered professional engineer.
  - A licensed water well contractor.
  - A licensed sewage disposal system installer.
  - A licensed landscape contracting business.
  - A licensed pesticide operator when not conducting inspections for wood-destroying organisms for real estate sales.
  - A licensed or certified appraiser.

- A licensed landscape contracting business that:
  - Constructs fences, decks, arbors, patios, landscape edging, driveways, walkways or retaining walls
  - Subcontracts to a licensed plumber to install, repair or maintain an irrigation system.
- A person who performs construction work as an employee of a contractor.
- A manufacturer of a manufactured home constructed under standards established by the federal government (when that manufacturer does not install the home by attaching it to real property).
- A person moving:
  - Modular buildings or structures, other than manufactured structures, not in excess of 14 feet wide; or
  - Structures not in excess of 16 feet wide if the person moving the structure is the owner and not otherwise acting as a licensed contractor.
- A commercial lending institution or surety company that arranges for the completion, repair, or remodeling of a structure in which the commercial lending institution or surety company holds a security interest and where one or more licensed contractors perform the work.
- A real estate licensee or employee of the licensee who manages rental real estate when working on a structure that the agent or broker manages under a contract.
- Units of government. However, a school district or a community college district must be licensed if it allows students to construct residential or small commercial structures to learn building techniques and, upon completion, sells the structures.
- A qualified intermediary in a 1031 exchange if the qualified intermediary is not performing construction work.
- Worker leasing companies or temporary service providers that supply workers to licensed contractors to perform work under the direction and supervision of the contractors.
- City or county inspectors or building code inspectors.
- A person performing work for purposes of agricultural drainage, agricultural trenching or agricultural irrigation, or a person constructing agricultural fencing to control livestock.
- A person working on forestland for which a Notice of Operations has been filed.

Business Entities

The CCB licenses both individuals and business entities. When an individual operates a business, the individual does so either as a sole proprietor (sole owner) of the business or in partnership (or a joint venture) with other owners. In addition to these types of individual businesses, Oregon law recognizes other business forms, including corporations and limited liability companies.

Contractors must first determine, and set up, the business entity that it wishes to use before applying for a license.

The choice of a business entity affects tax, workers' compensation, and liability. When selecting a business entity, consider the owner's management experience, financial condition of the business, and liability exposure.

Individuals may wish to consult with an attorney and an accountant to determine and/or set up the appropriate business entity. Chapter 5 discusses the types of business entities and applicable tax considerations.

New License Needed for Business Entity Change

Licenses are not transferable between business entities. If a business changes from one type of entity to another (for example, from a sole proprietorship to a corporation), the new business must complete a new CCB application, pay new fees, and provide a new bond and insurance for the new business entity. Ordinarily, if a partner or joint venturer departs from a contractor that is a partnership or joint venture, the contractor must obtain a new license. However, this requirement does not apply to a contractor that offers securities registered with the Securities and Exchange Commission for sale to the general public.

Business Identification

Assumed Business Name (ABN)

An assumed business name (ABN) is any name that is not the "real and true" name of the owner (for example, sole proprietor or partners) or of the business entity. For individuals, the real and true name consists of first name, middle name or middle initial, and last name. For example, John J. Smith does not need to register the name "John J. Smith Enterprises" as an ABN but must register "John Smith Enterprises," "John's Enterprises," "Smith's Enterprises," "John J. Smith & Company," or "John Smith & Associates." The same applies for partnerships and joint ventures composed of individuals.

Similarly, a business entity may conduct business under its actual registered name without further registration, but must register any other name that is used as an ABN. For example, Tom Jones Construction, Inc. does not need to register the name "Tom Jones Construction, Inc." as an ABN but must register as an ABN "Tom Jones Construction," "Tom Jones Homes" or "TJ Construction."

If an individual or business entity operates under an ABN, the name must be registered with the Oregon Corporation Division, Business Registry, before submitting an application to the CCB. The business will receive a registry number that it must include on the license application.

Registering an ABN lets the public know who is doing business under that name. To obtain an ABN, contact the Oregon Corporation Division at 503-986-2200 or download forms at www.filinginoregon.com/forms. An application fee must be submitted with the ABN registration application.

Workers' Compensation Division Compliance Number; Business Identification Number (BIN); Employer Identification Number (EIN).

If an individual or business entity will hire employees, it must obtain:

- A compliance number from the Workers' Compensation Division
- An Oregon business identification number (BIN) from the Oregon Department of Revenue
- A federal employer identification number (EIN) from the Internal Revenue Service (IRS).

With regards to a partnership, joint venture, limited partnership, limited liability partnership, or corporation, the entity will need workers' compensation insurance coverage and an Oregon BIN if it has more than two partners, members or corporate officers who are not family members. *Family members* includes parents, spouses, sisters, brothers, daughters, sons, daughters-in-law, sons-in-law, and grandchildren. All individuals or business entities with a commercial endorsement must carry workers' compensation insurance. Entities that use workers provided by worker leasing companies may use the workers' compensation insurance provided by the worker leasing company.

Licensees must be Independent Contractors

All licensed contractors must be "independent contractors" and not employees of a business (ORS 701.035(1)).

An independent contractor is an individual or business entity that contracts to perform a specified activity or project. The individual or entity has the right to determine how the specified work will be done to deliver satisfactory results. An employee, on the other hand, works under the right of direction and control of a supervisor or owner, often for an hourly wage or by piecework.

Are You an Independent Contractor?

YES	NO	
1. ☐	☐	You are free from a client's direction and control over the means and manner of providing the services. You are subject only to the right of the client (for whom the services are provided), to specify the desired results of the work.

2. ☐	☐	You will be customarily engaged in an independently established business by:
		
		(YOU MUST CHECK <u>THREE OF THE FOLLOWING FIVE</u> TO QUALIFY)
		
		a. ☐ Maintaining a business location that is separate from the business or work location for whom the services are provided; or that is in a portion of your residence and that portion is used primarily for the business.
		
		b. ☐ Bearing the risk of loss related to the business or provision of services as shown by factors such as:
		
		  ▪ You enter into fixed-price contracts.
		
		  ▪ You are required to correct defective work.
		
		  ▪ You warrant the services provided or you negotiate indemnification agreements or purchase liability insurance, performance bonds, or errors and omissions insurance.
		
		c. ☐ Providing contract services for two or more different persons within a 12 month period, or you routinely engage in business advertising, solicitation or other marketing efforts reasonably calculated to obtain new contracts to provide similar services.
		
		d. ☐ Making significant investment in the business, through means such as:
		
		  ▪ Purchasing tools or equipment necessary to provide the services.
		
		  ▪ Paying for the premises or the facilities where the services are provided; or
		
		  ▪ Paying for the licenses, certificates, or specialized training required to provide the services.
		
		e. ☐ Having the authority to hire other persons to provide or to assist in providing the services and has the authority to fire those persons. Contractors hiring employees must be licensed under the non-exempt class of independent contractor and carry proper workers' compensation insurance to protect subject workers.

3. ☐	☐	You will maintain an active license with the CCB in accordance with ORS Chapter 701 while performing construction services.
4. ☐	☐	You are responsible for obtaining other licenses or certificates necessary to provide the construction services.

Workers' Compensation: Exempt or Non-Exempt

Once an applicant has formed a business entity, the applicant must choose a class of independent contractor. There are two classes of independent contractor: exempt and nonexempt.

Exempt generally means the business will **not** have employees and does not need workers' compensation insurance coverage. The business could perform the work by itself or subcontract work to other independent contractors (licensed businesses). In all these ways, the business is working as exempt.

The following businesses are exempt:

- Sole proprietorships with no employees. Family members are considered employees.
- Partnerships or joint ventures with no employees and only two partners or venturers.
- Partnerships with no employees where all of the partners are immediate family members.
- Corporations with no employees and only two corporate officers.
- Corporations with no employees and more than two corporate officers where all of the corporate officers are family members.
- Business trusts with no employees and no more than two trustees.
- Business trusts with no employees and more than two trustees where all of the trustees are family members.
- Limited liability companies with no employees and no more than two members.
- Limited liability companies with no employees and more than two members where all of the members are family members.
- Limited partnerships or limited liability partnerships with no employees and no more than two general partners.
- Limited partnerships or limited liability partnerships with no employees and more than two general partners where all of the general partners are family members.

Nonexempt means the entity has employees. The business must carry workers' compensation insurance at all times. The following are nonexempt businesses:

- Sole proprietorships with employees. Family members are considered employees.
- Partnerships or joint ventures with employees.
- Partnerships or joint ventures with more than two partners or venturers unless all of the partners or venturers are family members.
- Corporations with employees.
- Corporations with more than two corporate officers unless all of the corporate officers are family members.
- Business trusts with employees.
- Business trusts with more than two trustees unless all of the trustees are family members.
- Limited liability companies (LLCs) with employees.
- Limited liability companies with more than two members unless all of the members are family members.
- Limited partnerships (LPs) or limited liability partnerships (LLPs) with employees.

- Limited partnerships or limited liability partnerships with more than two general partners unless all of the general partners are family members.
- Sole proprietorships, partnerships, corporations, LLCs, LPs or LLPs that lease workers from a licensed worker leasing company.

Any business entity endorsed as a commercial contractor *must* have workers' compensation insurance.

License Endorsements

A contractor must obtain a license endorsement as a commercial contractor, as a residential contractor, or as both. Contractors working on large commercial structures or development projects must obtain an endorsement as a commercial contractor.

A commercial contractor holds an endorsement as one of the following:
- Commercial General Contractor Level 1
- Commercial Specialty Contractor Level 1
- Commercial General Contractor Level 2
- Commercial Specialty Contractor Level 2
- Commercial Developer

Contractors working on residential structures or development projects must obtain an endorsement as a residential contractor. A residential contractor holds an endorsement as one of the following:
- Residential General Contractor
- Residential Specialty Contractor
- Residential Limited Contractor
- Residential Developer
- Residential Locksmith Services Contractor
- Home Inspector Services Contractor
- Home Services Contractor
- Home Energy Performance Services Contractor

Contractors working on small commercial structures or development projects may choose to be endorsed as either a commercial or residential contractor.

Contractors working on both residential structures and large commercial structures must hold both endorsements.

A **residential structure** includes a:
- Site-built home
- Structure that contains one or more dwelling units and is four stories or less
- Condominium or other residential unit

- Modular home constructed off-site
- Floating home
- Manufactured dwelling
- Any appurtenance to the listed structures

A **small commercial structure** is:

- A nonresidential structure with a ground area of 10,000 square feet or less and the structure is not more than 20 feet tall
- A nonresidential unit in a larger structure if the unit is 12,000 square feet or less and the unit is not more than 20 feet tall
- Any appurtenance to (1) or (2), and
- A nonresidential structure of any size if the contract price for all construction is not more than $250,000

A **large commercial structure** is any nonresidential structure that is not a residential structure or a small commercial structure.

Appendix A – Endorsement Summary provides a detailed description of the endorsements together with the requirements for bonds, insurance, experience or education, and continuing education.

Experience Requirements for Commercial Contractors

An applicant for a commercial contractor endorsement must demonstrate that the applicant has or employs persons with sufficient qualifying experience, or education. A commercial general contractor or commercial specialty contractor, level 1 must have one or more key employees with a combined total of eight years of construction experience. A commercial general contractor or commercial specialty contractor, level 2, must have one or more key employees with a combined total of four years of construction experience. The following may substitute for construction experience:

- Completion of an apprenticeship program may substitute for up to three years of experience.
- A bachelor's degree in a construction-related field may substitute for up to three years of experience.
- A bachelor's degree or master's degree in business, finance or economics may substitute for up to two years of experience.
- An associate's degree in construction or building management may substitute for up to one year of experience.

Choosing the Right License and Endorsement for the Work to be Performed

- If a contactor performs work only in preparation for or in connection with residential structures, the contractor needs an endorsement as a **residential** contractor.
- If a contractor performs work only in preparation for or in connection with large commercial structures, the contractor needs an endorsement as a **commercial** contractor.
- If a contractor performs work in preparation for or in connection with small commercial structures, the contractor may obtain an endorsement as either a residential or a commercial contractor.
- If a contractor performs work in preparation for, or in connection with both residential and large commercial structures the contractor needs both endorsements.
- A commercial or residential **general** contractor may perform and subcontract an unlimited number of unrelated construction trades on a job site.
- A commercial or residential **specialty** contractor may perform or subcontract only one or two unrelated construction trades on a job site.

Residential Limited

If the contractor performs work on only residential or small commercial structures and the work does not exceed $40,000 in gross annual volume and each contract is for $5,000 or less, the contractor may obtain an endorsement as a **residential limited** contractor.

Developer

The business may become licensed as a residential or commercial **developer**. A developer is a contractor that owns property and engages in the business of arranging for construction work to improve the property, with the intent of selling the property. A developer may only act in association with licensed and properly endorsed general contractors and may not perform any of the actual construction work on the property.

Maintaining a CCB License

Contractors must maintain their CCB license and provide the CCB information about changes that are made to the business. Often, these changes must be made to the CCB license record by completing a change form. Below are some common business changes that must be reported to the CCB.

Address Changes

Contractors must notify the CCB of any address change while licensed and for one year following the license expiration. The notification must be given within 10 days of the change (ORS 701.117).

Business Entity Changes

A CCB license is not transferable when changing from one business entity to another. Contractors must complete a new license application and be issued a new CCB number.

Endorsement Changes

Contractors must have the proper endorsement for the type of structures on which they work. If a contractor endorsed as a residential specialty contractor decides to bid on a large commercial project, the contractor must change his or her license to carry both endorsements. A residential specialty contractor who wants to perform more than two unrelated building trades for a residential or small commercial project must also change his or her endorsement.

Official Personnel Changes

Contractors must notify the CCB when they add or remove official personnel such as corporate officers, members, or the RMI (see below). This requirement does not apply, however, if the contractor offers securities registered with the Securities and Exchange Commission for sale to the general public.

Responsible Managing Individual (RMI) Changes

Contractors are required to have an RMI designated at all times. If the designated RMI changes, the CCB must be notified.

Inactivating a CCB License

Contractors who stop their contractor work temporarily can inactivate their license. A contractor does not need to maintain a bond or general liability insurance while a license is inactive, but must continue to renew a license every two years to have it remain inactive. Additionally, the business entity registration with the Oregon Corporation Division must be maintained in active status while a license is inactive. A person cannot work, advertise, bid, obtain permits, offer to perform, or perform as a contractor with an inactive license.

Renewing a CCB License

An active or inactive CCB license renews every two years. Contractors can find the expiration date of their license by looking at the license or the CCB website.

Approximately six weeks before a license is due to renew, the CCB sends the contractor a Renewal Notice as a courtesy. It is the contractor's responsibility to make certain the license has been renewed. A person cannot legally work as a contractor with an expired license.

When renewing a license:

- Submit the required application fee. The application fee is the same for both an active and inactive license.
- Renew in either an active or inactive status. If renewing in the inactive status, the contractor does not need to maintain the bond or insurance.
- If the license is currently active or the contractor wants to reactivate an inactive license, the following must be on file in order to renew:
  - A current bond in the proper amount. A bond is good until it is cancelled. As long as premiums are paid and the bond company has not cancelled the bond, it should still be valid. If a contractor purchases a new bond, the contractor must immediately send the original bond to the CCB.
  - A current Certificate of Insurance in the proper amount. Contractors must always send a new Certificate of Insurance at least a week prior to the expiration date of their insurance.
  - A person designated as the Responsible Managing Individual (RMI).
  - Current and valid employer account numbers.
  - An active registration at the Oregon Corporation Division, if using an assumed business name, or are a limited liability company, corporation, or trust.

Continuing Education Requirements

Contractors must complete continuing education to renew their licenses. The amount and kind of continuing education depends on whether the CCB licensee is endorsed as a commercial contractor, residential contractor, or has both a commercial and residential endorsement.

Residential Contractors

The following contractors are exempt from residential continuing education:

- Residential developers
- Residential locksmith contractors
- Home inspection contractors
- Home services contractors

- Home energy performance score contractors
- Plumbing contractors licensed by the Building Codes Division
- Electrical contractors licensed by the Building Codes Division
- Contractors owned by or having an officer who is a registered architect
- Contractors owned by or having an officer who is a licensed professional engineer

Unless you exempt from continuing education, you must satisfy the following residential continuing education requirements:

Licensed *less* than six years and a Responsible Managing Individual with less than six years' experience

Subject Area	Hours
CCB Laws, Regulations, and Business Practices (LRB)	3
Series A courses (Construction business practices, safety and codes)	5
Series A courses (as above) or Series B courses (Trade practices and energy efficiency)	8
Total	**16**

Licensed *six or more* years or a Responsible Managing Individual with six or more years' experience

Subject Area	Hours
CCB Laws, Regulations, and Business Practices (LRB)	3
Series A courses (Construction business practices, safety and codes)	5
Total	**8**

Contractors renewing licenses that lapsed before Jan.1, 2014, are still subject to the Building Exterior Shell Training and building code requirements.

Only approved classes count for credit
The CCB must approve all course providers. It also approves the Series A courses but only registers the Series B courses. Providers report directly to the CCB when a contractor completes a course. A contractor can visit the CCB website to see the type and number of hours it has completed.

All approved courses are listed at www.oregon.gov/ccb in the course catalog. Contractors will not get credit for any course that is not listed in the course catalog even if they are offered by other state agencies or trade associations. The rules are different for commercial contractors.

Commercial Contractors

Contractors with a commercial endorsement must take continuing education hours based upon the contractor's endorsement level and number of key employees the business had at the beginning of the license period. At renewal, the commercial contractor will certify the completed continuing education. The following illustration identifies required commercial continuing education:

Required Commercial Continuing Education

Commercial Endorsement	Number of Key Employees	Number of CE Hours per two-year licensing period
Commercial General Contractor Level 1 (CGC1) or Commercial Specialty Contractor Level 1 (CSC1)	5 or more	80
	4	64
	3	48
	2	32
	1	16
Commercial General Contractor Level 2 (CGC2) or Commercial Specialty Contractor Level 2 (CSC2)	Any number	32
Commercial Developer (CD)		None

Topics may include construction means, methods, and business practices. Construction means and methods include training on topics such as:
- Installation methods
- Best practices
- Product training
- Construction science
- Any other training that provides contractors with information on building better structures or operating a successful business

By law, providers for continuing education can be:
- Community colleges, colleges, universities
- Trade schools
- Trade or business associations
- Professional societies
- Private companies
- Public agencies
- Product manufacturer training
- In-house training

The commercial continuing education requirements do not apply if a contractor is licensed only as a commercial developer. In addition, contractors regulated under certain Oregon laws are not subject to CE requirements. This includes but is not limited to, commercially endorsed contractors who are licensed to work as:

- Electrical contractors
- Plumbing contractors
- Boiler or pressure vessel contractors
- Elevator contractors
- Renewable energy contractors
- Pump installation contractors
- Limited sign contractors

Endorsed as Both a Commercial and Residential Contractor

Contractors having both endorsements must fulfill the continuing education requirements established for each endorsement. A contractor may apply the hours taken for the residential obligation towards the commercial obligation.

Special Licenses and Certification

Contractors performing specific work must hold a special license or certification. These include:

Lead-Based Paint Activities

Lead-based paint activities include inspection, risk assessment and abatement. CCB licenses both individuals and businesses that work in this field. CCB licenses the following individuals:

- Lead supervisors
- Lead workers
- Lead assessors
- Lead inspectors

CCB also licenses the following contractors:

- Lead abatement contractor
- Lead inspection contractor

Certified Lead-Based Paint Renovation (LBPR) Contractor's License

Contractors that perform "renovation" on "target housing" or "child-occupied facilities" must complete an Environmental Protection Agency certification class and obtain a LBPR license from the CCB. The certification is good for five years; the CCB lead-safe license must be renewed annually.

"Renovation" means modifying any existing structure (or portion of the structure) that disturbs the painted surface. Renovation includes, for example:

- Modification of painted or varnished doors
- Restoring building surfaces
- Window repair
- Painting preparation (scraping, sanding)
- Removal of walls, ceilings, plumbing and windows
- Window replacement
- Weatherization projects
- Interim controls that disturb painted surfaces

Renovation does not include "minor repair and maintenance," which means disrupting six square feet or less of painted interior surface or 20 square feet or less of painted exterior surface.

"Target housing" means any housing built before 1978, except:

- Housing for the elderly or persons with disabilities
- Any housing with no bedrooms.

"Child-occupied facilities" means a building, or part of a building, regularly used by the same child under age 6. Child-occupied facilities may include:

- Day care centers
- Preschools
- Kindergarten classrooms
- Restrooms commonly used by children under age 6

Child-occupied facilities likely do not include:

- Sunday school classrooms (used only weekly)
- Supermarkets (visits less than three hours; not same child)
- Hallways in public schools

Locksmith Certification

The CCB certifies an individual as a locksmith. To advertise, offer and perform locksmith work in Oregon (unless exempt), a contractor must have both of these:

- A CCB license
- An owner or employee certified as a locksmith
- A residential Locksmith Services contractor must have an RMI who is certified as a locksmith.

A locksmith is defined as anyone who services, installs, repairs, rebuilds, rekeys, repins or adjusts locks, hardware peripheral to locks, safes, vaults, safe deposit boxes or mechanical or electronic security systems.

Certain exemptions from the certification requirement are allowed for:
- Tow truck drivers performing work for a certified towing business
- A person who duplicates keys at a fixed location as long as the person does not offer other locksmith services
- A licensed construction contractor (and employees) acting within the scope of the CCB license if they are not holding out as a locksmith provider

Oregon Certified Home Inspector

To advertise, offer and perform home inspection work in Oregon (unless exempt), a contractor must have both of these:
- A CCB licensed owner or employee certified as a home inspector
- A Home Inspector Services contractor must have an RMI who is certified as a home inspector.

A home inspector is an individual who, for a fee, inspects and provides a written report on the overall physical condition of a residential structure. A home inspector inspects more than one structural component and provides a written report of his or her findings. The following are structural components:
- Exterior and site
- Roofing
- Plumbing
- Electrical
- Heating/Central air conditioning
- Interiors
- Insulation and ventilation
- Built-in kitchen appliances

Certified home inspector requirements do not apply to individuals acting within the scope of specific licenses such as appraisers licensed under ORS 674 or building inspectors.

Persons performing, or reporting on, the following are exempt from the requirements for certified home inspectors:
- Energy audits
- Forensic evaluations
- Home performance review

Contractor Responsibility to Customers

Bond Requirements

A CCB surety bond is a promise by a bonding agency to provide limited payment to a consumer if a contractor fails to pay a CCB determination. A property owner can file a CCB complaint against a contractor for breach of contract (including failure to complete work) or for negligent or improper work. If the CCB determines a contractor owes money, the contractor must pay as ordered. If the contractor does not do so, the bonding company will pay the money owed up to the amount of the bond. The bonding company will then seek reimbursement from the contractor.

A licensed contractor must provide and maintain a CCB surety bond in the full amount that is required for the license endorsement. If the bonding agency cancels the surety bond and does not reinstate it, the contractor's license will automatically suspend 30 days from the date the cancellation is received by the CCB unless a new bond replaces the cancelled bond.

Bond requirements for new and renewal licenses:

Commercial Contractors	
Commercial general contractor level 1	$75,000
Commercial specialty contractor level 1	$50,000
Commercial general contractor level 2	$20,000
Commercial specialty contractor level 2	$20,000
Commercial developer	$20,000
Residential Contractors	
Residential general contractor	$20,000
Residential specialty contractor	$15,000
Residential limited contractor	$10,000
Residential developer	$20,000
Residential locksmith services contractor	$10,000
Home inspector services contractor	$10,000
Home services contractor	$10,000
Home energy performance score contractor	$10,000

A contractor may hold both a residential and a commercial endorsement at the same time. A contractor with dual endorsements must maintain separate surety bonds for each endorsement.

Insurance Requirements

A licensed contractor must maintain insurance to protect third parties (for example, customers). The insurance provides coverage for public liability, personal injury, property damage, and liability for products and completed operations. Examples of losses might be a contractor's ladder falling and breaking a window or a contractor causing a roof fire with a discarded cigarette.

Insurance requirements for new and renewal licenses:

Commercial general contractor level 1	$2,000,000 aggregate
Commercial specialty contractor level 1	$1,000,000 aggregate
Commercial general contractor level 2	$1,000,000 aggregate
Commercial specialty contractor level 2	$ 500,000 per occurrence
Commercial developer	$ 500,000 per occurrence
Residential general contractor	$ 500,000 per occurrence
Residential specialty contractor	$ 300,000 per occurrence
Residential limited contractor	$ 100,000 per occurrence
Residential developer	$ 500,000 per occurrence
Residential locksmith services contractor	$ 100,000 per occurrence
Home services inspector contractor	$ 100,000 per occurrence
Home services contractor	$ 100,000 per occurrence
Home energy performance score contractor	$ 100,000 per occurrence

Written Contracts

A contractor who performs work for an owner of a residential structure or a zero-lot-line dwelling must have a written contract with the owner if the contract price is more than $2,000. (A "zero-lot-line dwelling" refers to a single family dwelling unit in a group of attached units). The contract must be clear and use words of common understanding. It must contain:

- The contractor's name, license number, address, and telephone number.
- If the contract is for a new home, an acknowledgement of a written offer of a warranty and whether the buyer accepted or rejected the offer.
- An explanation of the property owner's rights, under the contract, including the ability to file a complaint with the CCB and the existence of any mediation or arbitration clause.
- Customer's name and address.
- Address where work is to be performed.
- Description of work to be performed.
- Price and payment terms.

A contract to perform construction on residential property may not contain any provision that limits a person's right to file a complaint for damages with CCB.

Contract cancellation

A property owner who enters into an initial written contract to construct, improve or repair a residential structure or zero-lot-line dwelling may cancel the contract by delivering, to the contractor, a written notice of cancellation any time before midnight of the next business day.

Consumer Notices

Contractors must provide the following notices to residential customers when contracting directly with the owner and when the written contract is more than $2,000.

Information Notice To Owner About Construction Liens

This notice explains to customers Oregon's construction lien laws and identifies the rights and responsibilities of property owners and contractors under the law (ORS 87.093). *See Chapter 4 – Oregon Construction Lien Law.*

Consumer Protection Notice

This notice explains to customers what actions they may take to protect themselves during a construction project (ORS 701.330(1)). The notice addresses contractor licensing, bond, and insurance requirements, warranty requirements, and other information. *See Appendix B.*

Notice of Procedure

This notice describes the procedures that customers must follow to notify contractors about defective work before compelling arbitration, beginning a court action against a contractor, or filing a CCB complaint against a contractor (ORS 701.330(2)). *See Appendix C.*

A contractor must provide the three notices listed above on or before the date the contract is entered into. A contractor must maintain proof of delivery of the notices for a period of two years. The notices may be incorporated into the written contract.

Notice of Compliance with Homebuyer Protection Act (HPA)

This notice is required for the sale of new residential property and the remodel or improvement of residential property costing at least $50,000 that is completed within three months of the sale of the remodeled or improved property (ORS 87.007). The notice indicates the method selected by the contractor to protect the buyer against liens that may be filed. The HPA notice must be provided no later than the date of sale of the residential property. *See Appendix D.*

The Lead-Safe Certified Guide to Renovate Right

This pamphlet must be provided to the owner prior to beginning renovation activities on target housing or child-occupied facilities under Oregon's lead-based paint requirements. The contractor must obtain a written acknowledgement that the owner received the pamphlet, or a certificate of mailing at least seven days prior to the renovation.

Warranties

Residential warranties.

A contractor must offer a warranty against defects in materials and workmanship if the contractor does either of the following:

- Enters into a contract to construct a new residential structure or zero-lot-line dwelling
- Sells a new residential structure or dwelling constructed as a "spec" home

Commercial warranties.

A commercial general contractor who constructs a new, large commercial structure must provide the owner with a two-year warranty against defects in materials and workmanship that covers the building envelope and penetration components. The warranty should provide that the contractor will annually inspect the building. The warranty does not need to cover failures due to improper owner maintenance.

Maintenance Schedules

A contractor who constructs new residential structures or zero-lot-line dwellings must provide a maintenance schedule to the original purchaser or owner of the structure or dwelling. The contractor must provide the maintenance schedule at the same time the contractor offers the warranty. The maintenance schedule must include a description of moisture intrusion and water damage, an explanation of how these may occur, a recommended schedule for maintenance to prevent moisture intrusion, advice on how to recognize water damage, and appropriate steps to take upon discovering water damage. *See Appendix E.*

Dispute Resolution

Who Can File Complaints Against Contractor

How a complaint is filed, when it may be filed, and how it is processed are determined by whether the complaint involves a residential or commercial contractor. A person who files a complaint with CCB is referred to as the *complainant*. The person against whom the complaint is filed is referred to as the *respondent* or *respondent contractor*.

The CCB may only accept and determine damages against licensed contractors. The CCB has the authority to process the following types of complaints:

- **Property owners** can file complaints for breach of contract or negligent or improper work. A complaint may be filed by an owner against a contractor when the contractor was licensed during all or part of the work period.
- **Property owners** can file complaints against a contractor to discharge or recover funds spent in discharging a lien filed by anyone but the respondent contractor. In order to file this complaint, the owner must have paid the contractor for work done and the contractor must have failed to pay the person filing the lien.
- **A general contractor** can file a complaint for negligent or improper work or breach of contract against a subcontractor.
- **A subcontractor** can file a breach of contract based on failure to pay. If the subcontractor performed work that required a contractor's license, the subcontractor must have been licensed at the time the bid was made or the contract was entered into and must have remained licensed continuously throughout the work period. For the complaint to be valid, the respondent contractor must have been licensed during all or part of the work period.
- **An employee** can file a complaint against a contractor for nonpayment of wages or employee benefits. For the complaint to be valid, the respondent contractor must have been licensed during all or part of the work period. The CCB only has jurisdiction over wages or benefits earned while the respondent contractor was licensed.
- **A material or equipment supplier** can file a complaint against a contractor for nonpayment of materials purchased or equipment rented for construction. The CCB only has jurisdiction over amounts for material delivered or equipment rented while the respondent contractor was licensed.

Time Limits for Filing Complaints

The CCB may only process a complaint, including a complaint based on a court judgment or arbitration award, if the complaint is filed in a timely manner. A complaint is filed when it is received by the CCB.

Owner Complaints

The owner of a new structure can file a complaint, including a lien claim, within one year after the date the structure was first occupied or two years after completion, whichever is first. The owner of an existing structure can file a complaint within one year after the date the work was substantially completed.

If a contractor fails to complete the work, the owner of either an existing or new structure can file a complaint within one year after the date the contractor ceased work on the structure. If a contractor fails to start the work, the complaint must be filed within one year of the date the parties entered into the contract.

General (Prime) Contractor Complaints

A licensed contractor can file a complaint against another licensed contractor performing work as a subcontractor on a new structure. This complaint must be filed within 14 months after the date the structure was first occupied or within two years after completion of the structure, whichever comes first.

A licensed contractor can file a complaint against another licensed contractor working as a subcontractor on an existing structure. This complaint must be filed within 14 months after the subcontractor's work on the structure was substantially completed.

If the subcontractor fails to complete the work, the CCB must receive the complaint within 14 months after the date the subcontractor ceased to work on the structure.

Employee Complaints

An employee can file a complaint against an employer who is a licensed contractor within one year after the date unpaid wages were due. For more information, refer to Chapter 2, "Statute of Limitations" under "Wage Disputes."

Equipment or Material Supplier or Subcontractor Complaints

A material or equipment supplier or a licensed subcontractor can file a complaint against a licensed contractor within one year after the date the contractor incurred the debt for the materials, equipment, or subcontractor labor.

Where and How to File a Complaint
Complaints against Residential Contractors

Complaints against a residential contractor may be submitted to the CCB. These complaints are filed on a complaint form and must include, for example, copies of contracts, change orders and invoices, to verify a contractual relationship. CCB will attempt to mediate the complaint. If the parties do not resolve or settle the complaint, the complainant must go to court. If the complainant prevails, CCB will make a determination in favor of the complainant.

Complaints against Commercial Contractors

Complaints against a commercial contractor must first be filed in court or initiated in arbitration. If the complainant prevails, CCB will make a determination in favor of the complainant.

- The person files a complaint in a court. (A person filing a complaint in court is called a plaintiff. The person against whom the court complaint is filed is the defendant.) The plaintiff must also complete and submit a complaint form to the CCB so the agency can determine jurisdiction. (This person may now be referred to as a complainant and the person against whom the complaint is filed as a respondent.)
- The plaintiff/complainant must deliver a copy of the court complaint, together with a CCB complaint form, to the CCB and contractor's surety. Delivery needs to be made by certified mail, return receipt requested, within 90 days of the court filing date but no later than the 14th day before the first day of the trial, or the 30th day before the court issues a judgment.
- The date the CCB receives the copy of the court complaint and the CCB complaint form is the date the CCB uses to establish the priority and timeliness of the CCB complaint.

Similar procedures apply when a matter is subject to arbitration.

Complaints against Contractors Having Both a Commercial and Residential Endorsement

If the complaint is filed against a contractor endorsed as both a residential contractor and a commercial contractor, the complaint is:

- Filed with the CCB if the work involved a residential structure
- Initiated in court (or by arbitration) if the work involved a large commercial structure
- Filed with the CCB or initiated in court (or by arbitration) if the work involved a small commercial structure, as selected by the complainant

Pre-Complaint Notice and Fee

The complainant must satisfy two requirements before and shortly after filing a complaint.

Pre-Complaint Notice

Oregon law requires anyone wanting to file a complaint against a contractor to notify the contractor of his or her intent to file a complaint before filing the complaint. This written notification, usually a letter, must be sent by certified mail to the address listed for the contractor in CCB Licensing records at least 30 days before filing the complaint. When the complainant files the complaint, he or she must attach a copy of the notice and the mailing receipt to the complaint form. No notice is required if the respondent already has actual notice of the complaint as described under CCB rule.

Fee

Oregon law requires that the CCB charge complainants a fee to process a complaint. A $50 fee applies to all types of CCB complaints except those initiated in court or by arbitration. CCB collects the fee after it reviews the filing and determines that it has jurisdiction of the complaint.

Miscellaneous Jurisdiction Issues

Complaints are accepted only when certain relationships exist between the complainant and the contractor. These include:

- A direct contractual relationship between the complainant and the contractor or his or her agents. For example, owners cannot file a complaint against subcontractors or suppliers who provided materials or services to the general contractor.
- An employment relationship between the complainant and the employer. Alternatively, if an employee assigned a wage claim to the Bureau of Labor and Industries (BOLI), BOLI may file the CCB complaint.
- A trustee authorized to receive employee benefit payments from the contractor for the benefit of the contractor's employees.
- A contractor who made repairs to real estate that the complainant purchased if repairs were part of the purchase agreement.

Complaints may be processed only under the following conditions:

- The respondent contractor must have been licensed during all or part of the work period.
- A subcontractor filing a complaint for unpaid moneys must have been licensed at the time the bid was made and throughout the entire work period.
- For material complaints, the contractor must have been licensed when the material was delivered.

- For employee complaints, the contractor must have been licensed when the work was performed.
- Complaints may only be made for work performed within the boundaries of the State of Oregon or for materials or equipment supplied or rented for use upon structures located in the State of Oregon.
- Complaints by contractors or by individuals or businesses furnishing material or renting or supplying equipment to a contractor must be for $150 or more.

Work period means the time period from the date a contractor accepts a payment, offers a written proposal, enters into a contract, or begins construction, whichever comes first, until the date the contractor's work is substantially completed, or if not completed, the date when work ceased.

The CCB may refuse to process a complaint that includes an allegation that is already contained in a complaint previously filed by the same complainant against the same contractor.

Complaint Procedures
Complaint against Residential Contractors
Jurisdiction
Once the CCB receives a complaint form, along with any required documents, CCB reviews the material to determine if the CCB has *jurisdiction* over the complaint

On-Site or Telephone Mediation
CCB then conducts either an onsite or telephone mediation with both parties present. During mediation, CCB may recommend to the contractor such actions as the mediator-investigator considers appropriate to compensate the complainant. The mediation helps the parties reach a voluntary settlement and it allows CCB's investigator to document the problems. CCB investigators help settle more than 70 percent of complaints that go to mediation. If no settlement is reached, the mediator-investigator reports his or her observations about the alleged improper work.

Mediator-Investigator's Recommendation
The mediator-investigator's recommendation may be that the:
- Complaint be dismissed.
- Contractor repair or replace items.
- Contractor pays damages or in some way compensates the complainant.

Settling the Complaint

Settlement normally resolves the complaint with the least amount of time and money incurred by the parties.

Going to Court (or Arbitration)

If the parties do not settle their dispute, the complainant may go to court or, in some cases, initiate arbitration. If the matter involves a dispute of $10,000 or less, the complainant may go to Small Claims Court. If the complainant prevails, the complainant may submit the court judgment to CCB. (An arbitration award will need to be entered as a court judgment.) CCB will then make a determination of the amount of the judgment that is in the CCB's jurisdiction, including court costs and interest. The determination issued by CCB may not include payment of attorney fees awarded in the final judgment.

CCB's determination is an "order in other than a contested case." This means that any person that challenges the determination must do so in Oregon Circuit Court (trial court).

Bureau of Labor and Industries Final Order

If the complaint involves a wage claim, and the parties do not settle their dispute, the complainant may go to the Oregon Bureau of Labor and Industries (BOLI) for relief. If BOLI issues a final order in favor of the complainant, CCB will make a determination in favor of the complainant in that amount.

Surety Challenge to CCB Determination

If CCB makes a determination and the contractor does not pay, CCB forwards its determination to the contractor's surety for payment. The surety may only challenge the determination in trial court.

Complaint against Commercial Contractors

Complainant Files the Complaint in Court or Initiates Arbitration

The complainant must deliver a copy of the court complaint (or documents initiating arbitration) together with a completed CCB complaint form to the CCB and to the contractor's surety. To assure that the court action or arbitration is still being actively pursued, the CCB will request regular status reports from the complainant.

The CCB will then wait for a judgment from the court or a judgment based on an arbitration award. If the court issues a judgment against a contractor, the complainant must deliver a certified copy to the CCB and the contractor's surety. This copy must be delivered within 30 days from the date the judgment was entered by the court.

CCB reviews the judgment to determine jurisdiction and if the complaint can be paid by the surety. If so, CCB makes a determination of the amount of the judgment that falls within the CCB's jurisdiction, along with court costs, interest, and attorney fees awarded by the court. The determination is an "order in other than a contested case." This means that any person that challenges the determination must do so in Oregon Circuit Court (trial court).

Payment of Complaints

The contractor must pay the amount determined by CCB within 30 days or CCB may send its determination to the surety for payment.

The date the CCB sends its determination to the surety for payment depends on the relationship of the complaint to other complaints against the same bond.

Payments from residential surety bonds cover complaints against residential contractors. Payments from commercial surety bonds cover complaints against commercial contractors.

If a surety bond is not adequate to pay all complaints, priority may be given to earlier complaints and the bond amount may be prorated.

The total amount paid from a residential bond for non-owner complaints may not exceed $3,000.

Payments from a commercial contractor's surety bond are satisfied in the following order of priority:
- Complaints by employees for wages and benefits.
- All other small commercial or large commercial structure complaints, except for claims for costs, interest, and attorney fees.
- Costs, interest, and attorney fees.
- The amount of the determination that is not paid by the surety may not be filed as a lien. However, the underlying judgment (if not fully paid) is the basis for a lien.

Violating Contractor Legal Requirements

Violations

Offering to work or working without being licensed

A person not otherwise exempt from the law violates the law if they advertise, bid or otherwise offer to work, or if they in fact work, as a contractor without having a license. Acting as a contractor without a license violates criminal laws and is punishable as a Class A misdemeanor. It also subjects the violator to a civil penalty of up to $5,000. The CCB also reports the identity of violators to the Oregon Department of Revenue, the Workers' Compensation Division and the Employment Department.

Criminal convictions

Certain criminal convictions may result in the denial of a new license, or the revocation of an existing license. The CCB application asks questions relating to criminal convictions. If applicable, the CCB may request additional information regarding the conviction.

Failure to pay debts

If a business, its owner, officer or RMI, or a business connected with the same owner, officer or RMI, fails to pay its construction debts, the CCB may deny the business a new license or suspend its existing license. Construction debts include amounts owed under a CCB order issued to resolve a dispute initiated by a complainant. In addition, the contractor's license may be suspended for unpaid civil penalties, child support, income taxes, employment taxes, and student loans.

Assisting an unlicensed contractor

A contractor may be sanctioned for knowingly assisting an unlicensed person to act as a contractor.

Failing to display contractor's license number

Contractors must include their CCB license number in advertisements, bids and contracts. Specifically, the following must contain a contractor license number:

- Newspaper advertisements
- Written bids and contracts
- Telephone directory ads
- Radio commercials (by audible statement)
- Television commercials
- Website or internet ads
- Business cards, letterhead
- Vehicles that display company information

However, signs that are permanently affixed or attached at the contractor's place of business do not need to display a CCB license number.

Other violations

There are other violations that may also be the basis for a sanction against a contractor's license or a civil penalty. These include:

- Failure to enter into a written construction contract, to offer warranties, to provide recommended maintenance schedules, or to deliver required notices.
- Failure to maintain a list of other contractors or subcontractors performing work for the contractor.
- Failure to notify the CCB of a change in partners or corporate officers.
- Failure to pay a subcontractor, material supplier, or employee, resulting in a lien being filed.
- Knowingly supplying false information to the CCB.
- Working without a construction permit where such a permit was required and work resulted in a complaint filed with the CCB.
- Working with more than two licensed exempt sole proprietors on the same task on the same job at the same time.
- Failure to timely pay persons who supplied materials or labor on public improvements when the contractor has received payment from a public contracting agency.
- Reporting bad faith or false complaints of nonpayment against contractors.
- Hiring employees when the contractor obtained a license as qualified exempt from workers' compensation requirements.
- Violation of other laws, such as building code laws and workers' compensation laws.
- Engaging in conduct as a contractor that is dishonest or fraudulent and injurious to the public welfare.
- Working without the proper endorsement.
- Supplying any governmental entity or person with false information regarding the business activities when the false information results in the person evading taxes, Social Security contributions, workers' compensation premiums, wage and hour laws, safety and health laws, child support, alimony, judgments and garnishments.

Immediate license suspension

The CCB may issue an *emergency suspension* and immediately suspend a license, without a hearing, when the contractor's conduct creates a serious danger to the public welfare. The grounds for such an emergency suspension include failure to maintain a surety bond or required insurance, hiring employees while exempt, and failing to pay construction debts.

Enforcement Process

The CCB Enforcement Section, together with CCB Field Investigation Section, responds to complaints of violations of licensing laws. CCB works with the Oregon Department of Justice, local district attorneys, law enforcement agencies, and other state agencies to investigate and prosecute illegal activity in the construction industry.

This is the process:
- The CCB starts a disciplinary action by issuing a *notice.*
- The contractor may then contest the action by submitting a written request for a *hearing.* If the CCB receives a timely hearing request, it schedules a *contested case hearing.* The hearing is conducted by an Administrative Law Judge (ALJ) from the Office of Administrative Hearings (OAH). OAH is a separate agency, independent from the CCB.
- As an alternative to a hearing, the CCB often offers an opportunity to resolve a disciplinary action through a *settlement agreement.* A settlement agreement might provide that a portion of the penalty may be suspended if conditions of the settlement are met. Conditions may include, for example, becoming licensed with the CCB, making restitution to a victim for damages on a complaint, taking classes, or assuring future compliance with the law.
- After a contested case hearing, the contractor may appeal the order by filing *written exceptions.* The Appeals Committee, consisting of three CCB board members, will hear any exceptions filed.
- Either party can appeal a final order to the Oregon Court of Appeals.

Common Administrative or Enforcement Actions

Warning or Notice of Intent to Take Action

If the CCB determines that a contractor has committed a violation, the CCB may issue a warning or a notice of intent to take action. The action may propose a civil penalty of up to $5,000, to revoke or suspend a license, or to refuse to issue, or reissue, a license. The notice provides information necessary to protect the *due process* rights guaranteed to the contractor, specifically the opportunity for a hearing.

Probation, corrective action

If three or more complaints are filed against a contractor in a 12-month period, the CCB may place the contractor on probation and require the contractor to develop a corrective action plan. The CCB may require the contractor to take training and pass the test required of new contractors.

Increased surety bond

The CCB may require a contractor to obtain a bond of up to five times the amount of the statutory bond if the business, its owner, officer or RMI, or a business connected with the same owner, officer or RMI, fails to pay its construction debts.

Bar from public works contracts

The CCB may list a contractor as not qualified to participate in public improvement contracts if the contractor fails to timely pay subcontractors, material suppliers or laborers when the contractor received payment from a public contracting agency.

Stop Work or Corrective Action Order

If the board believes that a contractor is violating regulations, it may order the contractor to cease the act or take corrective action. . Under certain circumstances, the CCB may order the work stopped immediately if the contractor working on a structure was not licensed when the work started.

Court Injunction

The CCB may apply to the court for an injunction stopping an individual or business from violating the laws governing construction contracting.

Loss of Legal Rights Resulting from Lack of License

Contractors may lose their legal rights to defend themselves or obtain payment for their work if they are not licensed for the entire length of a job. Under ORS 701.131, a contractor must be licensed with the CCB from the time of the bid or when the contract was entered into and licensed continuously throughout the work period in order, for example, to do the following:

- File a complaint against a subcontractor for negligent or improper work
- File a complaint against a general contractor for breach of contract based on failure to pay
- File a construction lien against a property owner for payment on a job
- File a lawsuit in Oregon for any construction work or breach of contract

Unlicensed contractors cannot file counterclaims against customers who sue them.

Appendix A

Endorsement Summary

Endorsement Type	Description	Comments	Bond	Insurance	Experience	Continuing Education per 2-year License	Responsible Managing Individual (RMI)
Commercial General – Level 1	A contractor whose business (including subcontractors) requires the use of more than two unrelated business trades and who undertake or offers to undertake work in connection with small or large commercial structures.	This contractor may also perform work that requires two or fewer unrelated business trades.	$75,000	$2,000,000 aggregate	8 years' experience or qualifying substitute education	Up to 80 hours of continuing education for key personnel	Must have an RMI
Commercial Specialty – Level 1	A contractor whose business requires the use of two or fewer unrelated business trades and who undertakes or offers to undertake work in connection with small or large commercial structures.		$50,000	$1,000,000 aggregate	8years' experience or qualifying substitute education	Up to 80 hours of continuing education for key personnel	Must have an RMI
Commercial General – Level 2	A contractor whose business (including subcontractors) requires the use of more than two unrelated business trades and who undertakes or offers to undertake work in connection with small or large commercial structures.	This contractor may also perform work that requires two or fewer unrelated business trades.	$20,000	$1,000,000 aggregate	4 years' experience or qualifying substitute education	Up to 32 hours of continuing education for key personnel	Must have an RMI
Commercial Specialty – Level 2	A contractor whose business requires the use of two or fewer unrelated business trades and who undertakes or offers to undertake work in connection with small or large commercial structures.		$20,000	$500,000 per occurrence	4 years' experience or qualifying substitute education	Up to 32 hours of continuing education for key personnel	Must have an RMI
Commercial Developer	A developer of property that is zoned for or intended for use compatible with a small commercial or large commercial structure.		$20,000	$500,000 per occurrence	None	None	No RMI
Residential General Contractor	A contractor whose business (including subcontracts) requires the use of more than two unrelated business trades and who undertakes or offers to undertake work in connection with residential or small commercial structures.	This contractor may also perform work that requires two or fewer unrelated business trades.	$20,000	$500,000 per occurrence	None	Up to 16 hours of continuing education for personnel	Must have an RMI
Residential Specialty	A contractor whose business requires the use of two or fewer unrelated business trades and who undertakes or offers to undertake work in connection with residential or small commercial structures	A manufactured dwelling installer is a specialty contractor.	$15,000	$300,000 per occurrence	None	Up to 16 hours of continuing education for personnel	Must have an RMI
Residential Limited	A residential limited contractor performs work on residential or small commercial structures but does not perform work		$10,000	$100,000 per occurrence	None	Up to 16 hours of continuing education for personnel	Must have an RMI

	exceeding $40,000 in annual volume or enter into any one contract to perform work that exceeds $5,000.						
Residential Developer	A developer of property that is zoned for or intended for use compatible with a residential or small commercial structure.		$20,000	$500,000 per occurrence	None	None	No RMI
Residential Locksmith Services	A contractor that operates a business providing the services of locksmiths.	May not provide other services.	$10,000	$100,000 per occurrence	None	None	RMI must be certified locksmith
Home Inspector Services	A contractor that operates a business providing the services of home inspectors.	May not provide other services.	$10,000	$100,000 per occurrence	None	None	RMI must be certified home inspector
Home Services	A contractor that operates a business providing service, repair or replacement through a licensed contractor under a home services agreement.	May not provide other services	$10,000	$100,000 per occurrence	None	None	No RMI.
Home Energy Performance Score	A contractor that operates a business assigning home energy performance scores.	May not provide other services.	$10,000	$100,000 per occurrence	None	None	Needs RMI. Owner or employee must be certified home energy assessor.

Appendix B

For educational purposes. This form may be revised.

Consumer Protection Notice

Actions to help make your project successful

(ORS 701.330 (1))

Oregon law requires contractors to provide the homeowner with this notice at the time of written contract, for work on a residential structure. This notice explains licensing standards, bond and insurance requirements, and steps that consumers can take to help protect their interests.

START OUT YOUR PROJECT RIGHT

1. Make sure your contractor is properly **licensed** before you sign a contract. Visit www.oregon.gov/ccb, and click on the link, **Click on a Contractor's License**, or call our offices at 503-378-4621. To be licensed in Oregon, contractors must take training and pass a test on business practices and law. Licensing is not a guarantee of the contractor's work.

   - **A license also requires the contractor to maintain a surety bond and liability insurance** - The CCB surety bond provides a limited amount of financial security if the contractor is ordered to pay damages in contract disputes. It is not intended to be a safety net for consumer damages. Consumers with large projects may wish to look into performance bonds. Liability insurance coverage provides for property damage and bodily injury caused by the contractor. It does not cover contract disputes, including poor workmanship.

   - **If your contractor is not licensed** - the CCB bond and dispute resolution services will not be available to you.

2. **What you should know about bids, contracts, and change orders:**

   - **Bids** - *Do not automatically accept the lowest bid* - A low bid may make it necessary for the contractor to use lower quality materials and to cut corners in workmanship.

   - **Contracts and Change Orders** - *Always get it in writing.* Your contractor is required to provide a written contract if the contract price is more than $2,000. The CCB recommends that all contracts be in writing.

   - **Contracts should be as detailed as possible -** Some items to include are materials and costs, permits, estimated start and completion dates, debris removal, and arbitration clauses. Make sure the contractor's name, CCB number, and contact information is included in the contract.

   - **Read and understand your contract before signing it** - Don't be pressured into signing your contract without taking the time needed to go through it. Make sure it includes enough details to avoid misunderstandings and to protect you and your property.

3. **Additional contract information you should know:**

   - **A payment schedule** - should be included in the contract. Stick to the schedule and never pay in full for a project before the work is complete.

   - **Special Note on Liens** - Subcontractors and material suppliers that work on your project are often paid by the general contractor. If a general contractor fails to pay, the subcontractor may file a lien on your property. For information on construction liens, visit the CCB's Consumer Help Page at www.oregon.gov/ccb, or contact an attorney.

   - **Warranty on new residential construction** – Contractors must make an offer of a warranty when constructing a new residential structure. Consumers may accepts or refuse the warranty.

4. **If you should have a problem with your contractor** – You can file a complaint with the CCB against a **licensed** contractor within one year of the substantial completion of work on your project. Contact the CCB office at 503-378-4621 for help.

Visit the CCB website at for more information on having a successful project.

www.oregon.gov/ccb

CONTRACTOR:	CCB#: _____	PROPERTY OWNER:	
_____		_____	
Signature	Date	Signature	Date

F:CPN. 4-26-2011.

Appendix C

For educational purposes. This form may be revised.

Notice of Procedure
REGARDING RESIDENTIAL CONSTRUCTION
Arbitrations and Lawsuits
(ORS 701.330)

Oregon law contains important requirements that homeowners must follow before starting an arbitration or court action against any contractor, subcontractor, or supplier (materials or equipment) for construction defects.

Before you start an arbitration or court action, you must do the following:

1. **Deliver a written notice of any conditions that you believe are defective to the contractor, subcontractor, or supplier that you believe is responsible for the alleged defect.**

2. **Allow the contractor, subcontractor, supplier, or its agent, to visually inspect the possible defects and also allow the contractor, subcontractor, or supplier to do reasonable testing.**

3. **Provide the contractor, subcontractor, supplier, or its agent, the opportunity to make an offer to repair or pay for the defects. You are not obligated to accept any offer made.**

There are strict procedures and deadlines that must be followed under Oregon law. Failure to follow those procedures or meet those deadlines will affect your right to start an arbitration or court action.

You should contact an attorney for information on the procedures and deadlines required under Oregon law.

Your contractor is supplying this notice to you as required by Oregon law.

CONTRACTOR: CCB#: _____   HOMEOWNER:

_____   _____
Print Contractor Name (as it appears on contract)   Print Homeowner Name (as it appears on contract)

_____ _____   _____ _____
Signature of Authorized Representative   Date   Signature   Date

F:noticeofprocedure/adopted 12-04-07.

Appendix D

For educational purposes. This form may be revised.

Notice of Compliance with the Homebuyer Protection Act (HPA)(ORS 87.007)

In compliance with Oregon law, the below mentioned **Seller** has selected to comply with the requirements of ORS 87.007.

1. ADDRESS or DESCRIPTION OF PROPERTY		
Address or Location	City, State	Zip Code

2. DATE OF PURCHASE (CHOOSE ONE)

A. ...☐ ORS 87.007 (which includes the provisions listed in part B of this form) does not apply to the sale of the above described **Property**.

B. ...☐ ORS 87.007 applies to the sale of the above described **Property**. **Seller** complied with ORS 87.007(2) by (check which <u>one</u> applies):

    1. ☐ **Title Insurance** as provided for in ORS 87.007(2)(a).

    2. ☐ **Retained in Escrow** not less than 25 percent of the sale price as provided for in ORS 87.007(2)(b).

    3. ☐ **Bond or Letter of Credit** as provided for in ORS 87.007(2)(c).

    4. ☐ **Written Waivers** received from every person claiming a lien as provided for in ORS 87.007(2)(d).

    5. ☐ **Completed Sale After the Deadline** for perfecting liens as provided for in ORS 87.007(2)(e).

3. SELLER INFORMATION

Company Name (if applicable)

_____

Agent of Company or Individual Seller

_____

Title of Company Agent (if applicable)

_____

Signature   Date

_____   _____

4. BUYER INFORMATION
Buyer Name
Agent of Company or Individual Buyer
Title of Company Agent (if applicable)

Signature   Date

_____   _____

F/HPAform2 12-1-2010

Instructions

These instructions are provided to assist sellers of residential property with the Oregon Homebuyer Protection Act (HPA), codified in ORS 87.007. The HPA protects residential property buyers against construction liens filed in county records after the sale of the property where such liens arise out of new construction, additions or remodeling within 90 days of the date of the sale.

Disclaimer
These instructions do not constitute legal advice. For questions, please contact an attorney.

Who must complete this form?
A residential property owner selling –

- A new single family residence, condominium unit or residential building (containing four or fewer dwelling units), or
- An existing single family residence, condominium unit or residential building (containing four or fewer dwelling units) that had at least $50,000 worth of improvements, additions or remodeling completed within 90 days of the date of the sale.

Instructions for Section A
If the property fits the description above, but the seller knows that no person may file a lien against the property, the seller may check the box in Section A of the form.

Instructions for Section B
If the seller knows that it is possible for someone to file a lien against the property, the seller must check Section B of the form and at least one corresponding box that applies to the action the seller took, or will take, to comply with the HPA.

> **Box 1 Title Insurance** – The seller has or will purchase or provide an owner's extended coverage title insurance policy or equivalent that <u>does not except</u> filed or unfiled claims of lien. A standard title insurance or a lender's title insurance policy may not be sufficient. *See* ORS 87.007(2)(a).

> **Box 2 Retain in Escrow** – The seller will arrange to retain in escrow an amount of not less than 25 percent of the sales price of the property. The escrow will pay any claims of lien not paid by the seller filed after the date of the sale. Any unused funds will be released to the seller upon fulfillment of the following conditions:
> - Claims of lien have not been filed against the property **and** at least 90 days have passed since the date the construction was completed.
> - One or more claims of lien were filed against the property, at least 135 days have passed since the date the liens were filed, **and** the liens were released or waived. *See* ORS 87.007(2)(b).

> **Box 3 Bond or Letter of Credit** – The seller has or will maintain a bond or letter of credit. A Construction Contractors Board bond, required for licensure under ORS chapter 701, is not sufficient. *See* ORS 87.007(2)(c).

> **Box 4 Written Waivers** – The seller has or will obtain written waivers from every subcontractor or supplier who claims liens of $5,000 or more. Provide copies of the waivers to the buyer no later than the date of the sale. (The CCB recommends consulting an attorney for assistance with preparing forms for waivers). *See* ORS 87.007(2)(d).

> **Box 5 Completed Sale after the Deadline** – The sale will not be completed until at least 75 days after the completion of all construction. *See* ORS 87.007(2)(e).

Additional Instructions
The seller and the buyer must sign and date the form on or before the closing date of the sale. Both parties should retain a copy of the form. **Compliance with the HPA is the sole responsibility of the seller.**

F/HPAform2 12-1-2010

Appendix E

For educational purposes. This form may be revised.

Moisture Intrusion & Water Damage
Information For Home Owners

Contractors that build new homes must provide special information to homebuyers about moisture intrusion and water damage, and provide a home maintenance schedule in accordance with ORS 701.335. The Construction Contractors Board prepared this information to help contractors comply.

What is moisture intrusion and water damage? "Moisture intrusion" means water – whether liquid, frozen, condensed or vaporized – that penetrates into your home. "Water damage" means damage or harm caused by moisture intrusion that reduces the value or usefulness of your home.

How does moisture intrusion and water damage occur? Some causes of moisture intrusion and water damage are:

- Missing or loose roofing materials or flashing
- Window sills or door frames without adequate caulking or weather-stripping
- Lack of caulking in siding, mortar in masonry, or grout in exterior ceramic tile installations
- Degraded paint on exterior siding or surfaces
- Overflowing or clogged gutters
- Gutter drains or downspouts that are not a sufficient distance from the structure
- Improper drainage slope next to foundation
- Plant materials too close to the structure or foundation
- Sprinklers that overspray onto the structure or foundation
- Non-working interior ventilation systems

How can you tell if your home has water damage? Signs of water damage may include dampness, staining, mildew (blackened surfaces with a musty smell), or softness in wood (a possible sign of dry rot).

What to do if you see signs of water damage: If water damage is discovered, you should investigate its source. Take steps to repair or replace any building parts or materials that allowed the moisture intrusion. You may need to take additional steps, depending on the extent of the water damage.

If you have specific questions about maintaining your new home, ask your contractor. If you need professional assistance in conducting a maintenance inspection, you may wish to contact your contractor or a licensed home inspection business.

(ORS 701.335) (OAR 812-001-0240)

RECOMMENDED MAINTENANCE SCHEDULE FOR HOMEOWNERS (ORS 701.335) (OAR 812-001-0240)

Maintenance Item	Description of Maintenance	How Often	Date	Date	Date	Date	Date	Date
Caulking/Weather-Stripping	Check and repair missing, cracked, or peeling caulking or weather-stripping around window sills, door frames, and in siding gaps.	Twice yearly						
Debris Removal	Inspect gutters for debris blockage. Remove debris (for example, tree needles and leaves) from downspouts and gutters.	Yearly						
Foundation	Check soil around foundation to make sure that it slopes in such a way that water can flow away from the foundation. Fill soil in any area that have settled around the foundation.	Yearly						
Gutters & Downspouts	Inspect gutters and downspouts for leaks. Repair if necessary. Check alignment of gutters, downspouts, and splash blocks to ensure that water is properly diverted away from the structure and foundation. Repair if necessary.	Yearly						
Landscaping Sprinklers	Check landscaping sprinklers to make sure that they are not set so that they will soak siding or form puddles near the foundation. Adjust if necessary.	Yearly						
Mortar	Check and repair missing mortar in exterior masonry.	Yearly						
Paint	Check painted surfaces for cracking, peeling, or fading. Repaint if necessary.	Yearly						
Roof	Check roof for damaged, loose, or missing shingles. Check flashing around roof stacks, vents, skylights, and chimneys and in roof valleys for missing or loose flashing. Repair or replace if necessary.	Yearly						
Trees & Shrubs	Trim back tree branches, shrubs, and other plants to make sure they are not in contact with the structure.	Yearly						
Ventilation Systems	Check to make sure that interior mechanical ventilation systems (such as bathroom, kitchen, and utility room vent fans) are in good working order. Repair if necessary.	Every two months						
Water Stains	Check for water stains in the roof of the attic and in the exterior overhangs or soffits. If water stains are present, locate and repair the cause of moisture intrusion.	Yearly						

Sample Questions

CHAPTER 1

1. **When must a contractor give the *Consumer Protection Notice*?**

   ❑ 1. At the time of the contract for work on residential structures when a written contract is required.

   ❑ 2. Anytime during the residential construction project but before final payment is made.

   ❑ 3. At the time the final payment is received for work on a residential construction project.

   ❑ 4. Within 10 days of the start of the residential construction job.

2. **Which one of the following situations requires the contractor to have a CCB license?**

   ❑ 1. Furnishing materials, supplies, equipment or finished products but do not perform or make arrangements to perform the work.

   ❑ 2. Construction work on your personal property.

   ❑ 3. Bidding and performing construction work for your neighbor.

   ❑ 4. Worker leasing companies supplying workers to licensed construction contractors.

3. **Which of the following is true?**

   ❑ 1. All contractors must take classes about the exterior shell of a structure.

   ❑ 2. All contractors need electives.

   ❑ 3. Residential contractors with six or more years of experience need eight hours of continuing education every two-year renewal period.

   ❑ 4. Commercial and residential contractors must meet the same continuing education requirements.

Answers: 1. [1]

2. [3]

3. [3]

CHAPTER 2
EMPLOYER OBLIGATIONS AND EMPLOYEE RIGHTS

Objectives

At the end of this chapter, you will be able to:

1. Be familiar with Oregon's workers' compensation laws.
2. Describe unemployment insurance.
3. Be familiar with federal and Oregon wage and hour regulations, including minimum wage, overtime, and rest and meal period requirements.
4. Be aware of prevailing wage rate laws.
5. Understand the process for resolving wage disputes.
6. Be familiar with the requirements for employing minors.
7. Comprehend the requirements for employee termination and employment agreements.
8. Know essential employee civil rights and anti-discrimination and anti-harassment laws.
9. Be familiar with employee medical leave requirements.
10. Understand the restrictions and requirements applicable to the hiring process.

Workers' Compensation Insurance

Generally, every business that employs one or more workers must provide workers' compensation insurance coverage. Worker's compensation is a "no-fault" coverage, meaning it provides coverage even if the worker cannot prove the employer was negligent or acted improperly. Workers' compensation covers an employee's medical expenses for on-the-job injuries and disease. It provides payments to employees while they are temporarily or permanently disabled by that injury. Workers' compensation also provides death benefits to dependents if an employee dies as a result of occupational injury or disease.

Commercial contractors who are "exempt" (do not have employees) must carry workers' compensation insurance. A business that does not have employees may obtain a "personal election" policy that covers the businesses' owners.

Summary of Oregon's Workers' Compensation Law

The Oregon Department of Consumer and Business Services (DCBS), Workers' Compensation Division (WCD), administers Oregon's workers' compensation laws. These laws seek to:
- Provide sure, prompt, and complete medical treatment for the employee's job-related injury or disease as well as fair, adequate, and reasonable income benefits to injured employees and their dependents.
- Provide a fair and just administrative system for delivery of benefits to injured employees.
- Restore injured employees quickly to physical and economic self-sufficiency.
- Encourage employers to implement accident studies, and to institute prevention programs that reduce industrial accidents.
- Provide the exclusive source and means for employees to seek and qualify for workers' compensation.

Benefits of Workers' Compensation Insurance

Workers' compensation insurance is good for employees and good for business. If an employee gets hurt, workers' compensation insurance provides the employee with medical treatment, payment for lost time and disability, and even re-employment assistance if it is needed. Workers' compensation insurance also protects employers by providing a fair and equitable system for medical care and income for employees who are accidentally injured on the job. There was a time when employees who were hurt on the job sued their employers for help with their expenses. An employer could risk financial ruin if the worker received a large award in court.

No-Fault Coverage

Workers' compensation replaces legal liability with no-fault insurance. Employees with injuries or diseases caused by work can get treatment quickly, without proving the employer at fault. Employers are protected from lawsuits. Benefits are for actual loss and do not add up to large sums intended to punish the employer or pay for "pain and suffering." As long as the injury or illness resulted from work, the employer or employee can avoid going to court.

Types of Employee Benefits

Employees covered by workers' compensation insurance in Oregon have benefits for work-related injuries that generally include:
- Coverage when required by their employer to temporarily work in another state
- Medical treatment necessary for the job-related injury or disease
- Compensation for lost time
- Compensation for partial or full disability
- Re-training

Workers' Compensation Coverage Requirements

Any business that employs one or more subject workers must provide workers' compensation insurance coverage for its workers. All workers are subject workers unless specifically exempted by law.

The duties of an employer are to:
- Be insured by an Oregon authorized insurer, be certified as a self-insured employer, or arrange for coverage through a licensed worker leasing company before workers are on the job.
- Assure a staffing company has coverage if workers are used on a temporary basis (special situation requiring temporary workers).
- Report workers' compensation claims to its insurer within five days.

Special Conditions Related to Workers' Compensation Benefits

If an employee is an Oregon subject worker, but is required by the employer to temporarily work in another state and is then injured while in the other state, that individual may be entitled to Oregon workers' compensation benefits as if working in Oregon.

If an employee is injured or dies because of the employee's intention to harm or kill himself or herself, no benefits will be paid.

If an employee is injured or dies because of the employer's deliberate intention to harm or kill the employee, the employee or the employee's dependents may not only collect workers' compensation benefits but may also have cause for action in court.

If the employee is injured or dies because of the acts of a third person not employed by the same company, the employee or his or her dependents may seek a remedy through the courts.

Means of Coverage

Workers' compensation insurance coverage is available through:

Self-Insurance

An employer may be able to qualify as a self-insured employer. This option is usually available to large employers because the employer must have resources to pay for major claims. An employer is required to have a substantial security deposit and be certified by the WCD to be self-insured.

Private Insurance Carrier

An employer can obtain workers' compensation insurance from any insurer that is authorized to provide such coverage in Oregon. There are more than 300 insurers authorized to write workers' compensation insurance in Oregon.

Many of these insurers sell policies through agents. Often the agency that handles a business' insurance can also write workers' compensation insurance.

Some insurers will deal directly with the employer; others have special arrangements to provide workers' compensation through business organizations or associations.

Oregon Workers' Compensation Insurance Plan

The Oregon Workers' Compensation Insurance Plan, commonly known as the assigned risk pool, is a safety net for employers who try to obtain workers' coverage but are refused at least once by a private insurance carrier. "Personal election" insurance may also be available only through the assigned risk plan. In an assigned risk pool, the workers' compensation insurance rates are not negotiable and may require a higher premium level than those rates in the voluntary market of private insurance companies.

Employers in the Oregon Workers' Compensation Insurance Plan can seek private coverage after maintaining an injury-free work environment, developing a good payment history, and establishing good job safety records with OR-OSHA.

For more information, contact the Workers' Compensation Ombudsman for Small Business Employers or the National Council on Compensation Insurance (NCCI). See Appendix A for contact information.

Workers' Compensation for Leased Employees

The leasing company will handle payroll, workers' compensation, and most other paperwork for workers hired through a "worker leasing company."

Worker leasing companies must be licensed with the Workers' Compensation Division so you can call that agency to see if a company is properly licensed.

Liabilities for a Non-complying Employer

A non-complying employer is an employer who does not provide workers' compensation coverage as required by law. A business that erroneously classifies a worker as an independent contractor rather than an employee may be a non-complying employer.

The penalty for a first offense of employing without providing coverage is two times the amount of the premium that should have been paid, with a minimum of $1,000.

If an employer continues to employ without coverage, the penalty goes to $250 per day with no limit on the total fine. The Workers' Compensation Division will also request a permanent court injunction to force the employer into compliance. An employer who disobeys an injunction is in contempt of court and is subject to other types of sanctions, including jail time.

In addition, the non-complying employer is responsible for all claim costs that may arise from injury or disease to its workers.

By law, bankruptcy does not remove obligations for noncompliance. Corporate directors, officers, limited liability company members, and managers are personally liable for penalties and claim expenses. An employee can also file a civil suit against a non-complying employer in addition to obtaining payment on a workers' compensation claim.

Claims Procedure

The claims procedure is shown in the Workers' Compensation Flowchart and described in the following paragraphs.

Employer's Responsibility

If an employee files a claim for workers' compensation, the employer has five days to report to the insurer. The report shall include:

- The date, time, cause, and nature of the accident and injuries
- Whether the accident arose out of, and in the course of, employment
- Whether the employer recommends or opposes acceptance of the claim and the reasons why
- The name and address of any health insurance provider for the injured employee
- Any other details the insurer may require

Acceptance or Denial of Claim

Written notice of acceptance or denial of the claim must be furnished to the employee by the insurer within 60 days after the employer receives notice of the claim. The insurer may revoke acceptance and issue a denial at any time for fraud, misrepresentation, or certain other illegal activity by the employee.

Workers' Compensation Flowchart

(This is an overview. Some programs and processes are not covered.)

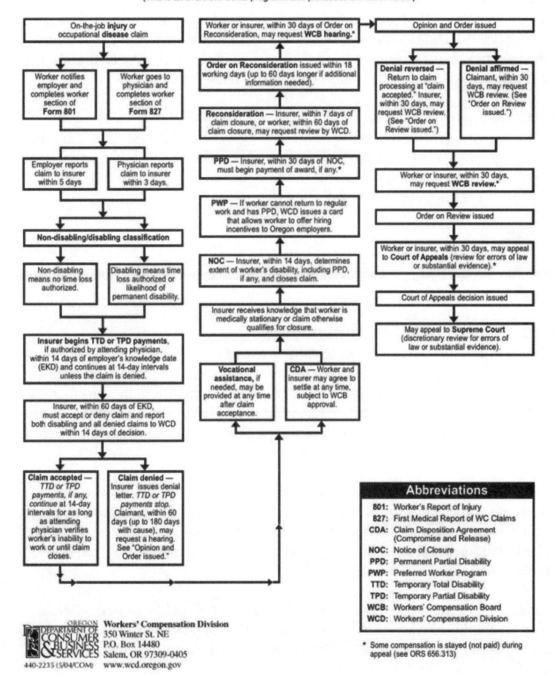

On-the-job **injury** or occupational **disease** claim

| Worker notifies employer and completes worker section of **Form 801** | Worker goes to physician and completes worker section of **Form 827** |

| Employer reports claim to insurer within 5 days | Physician reports claim to insurer within 3 days. |

| **Non-disabling/disabling classification** |

| Non-disabling means no time loss authorized. | Disabling means time loss authorized or likelihood of permanent disability. |

| **Insurer begins TTD or TPD payments,** if authorized by attending physician, within 14 days of employer's knowledge date (EKD) and continues at 14-day intervals unless the claim is denied. |

| Insurer, within 60 days of EKD, must accept or deny claim and report both disabling and all denied claims to WCD within 14 days of decision. |

| **Claim accepted —** *TTD or TPD payments, if any, continue at 14-day intervals for as long as attending physician verifies worker's inability to work or until claim closes.* | **Claim denied —** Insurer issues denial letter. *TTD or TPD payments stop.* Claimant, within 60 days (up to 180 days with cause), may request a hearing. See "Opinion and Order issued." |

| Worker or insurer, within 30 days of Order on Reconsideration, may request **WCB hearing.*** |

| **Order on Reconsideration** issued within 18 working days (up to 60 days longer if additional information needed). |

| **Reconsideration —** Insurer, within 7 days of claim closure, or worker, within 60 days of claim closure, may request review by WCD. |

| **PPD —** Insurer, within 30 days of NOC, must begin payment of award, if any.* |

| **PWP —** If worker cannot return to regular work and has PPD, WCD issues a card that allows worker to offer hiring incentives to Oregon employers. |

| **NOC —** Insurer, within 14 days, determines extent of worker's disability, including PPD, if any, and closes claim. |

| Insurer receives knowledge that worker is medically stationary or claim otherwise qualifies for closure. |

| **Vocational assistance,** if needed, may be provided at any time after claim acceptance. | **CDA —** Worker and insurer may agree to settle at any time, subject to WCB approval. |

| Opinion and Order issued |

| **Denial reversed —** Return to claim processing at "claim accepted." Insurer, within 30 days, may request WCB review. (See "Order on Review issued.") | **Denial affirmed —** Claimant, within 30 days, may request WCB review. (See "Order on Review issued.") |

| Worker or insurer, within 30 days, may request **WCB review.*** |

| Order on Review issued |

| Worker or insurer, within 30 days, may appeal to **Court of Appeals** (review for errors of law or substantial evidence).* |

| Court of Appeals decision issued |

| May appeal to **Supreme Court** (discretionary review for errors of law or substantial evidence). |

Workers' Compensation Division
350 Winter St. NE
P.O. Box 14480
Salem, OR 97309-0405
www.wcd.oregon.gov

440-2235 (5/04/COM)

Abbreviations

801:	Worker's Report of Injury
827:	First Medical Report of WC Claims
CDA:	Claim Disposition Agreement (Compromise and Release)
NOC:	Notice of Closure
PPD:	Permanent Partial Disability
PWP:	Preferred Worker Program
TTD:	Temporary Total Disability
TPD:	Temporary Partial Disability
WCB:	Workers' Compensation Board
WCD:	Workers' Compensation Division

* Some compensation is stayed (not paid) during appeal (see ORS 656.313)

Hearing Request and Response

When an employee requests a hearing on a denied claim that alleges fraud, misrepresentation, or other illegal activity, the insurer must prove the deception. If the insurer accepts a claim in good faith and later obtains evidence that the claim is not compensable, the insurer has two years to deny the claim.

Once an employee requests a hearing, the insurer must prove that the claim is not compensable, or that the insurer is not responsible for the claim. If an administrative law judge, the Workers' Compensation Board or a court sets aside denial of a previously accepted claim, benefits must be paid to the employee starting from the date the benefits were terminated.

Litigation

If an appeals process goes as far as litigation, the insurer will have an attorney. Injured workers will probably retain attorneys. Fees will be paid out of, or in addition to, the compensation award.

Reinstatement of Injured Employees

Oregon law provides certain rights to employees who are injured on the job. Most Oregon employers are prohibited from discriminating against employees because of such injuries. Usually, injured employees must be allowed to return to their former positions when they are able to perform them. In addition, employers are obligated to return employees to suitable positions when the employees are unable to perform their former jobs but can perform in other position(s).

If the former position has been eliminated for legitimate business reasons, the employer does not have to create a job or resurrect the old job but must offer the employee a suitable vacant job (re-employment). A **suitable position** is one that is substantially similar to the former position in compensation, duties, skills, location, duration (full or part time, temporary, or permanent) and shift.

As long as six or more persons are employed, the employer has an obligation to re-employ an employee who is able to return to work, but unable to perform former duties. The employee should be employed in the most suitable vacant position available.

An employee loses the right to reinstatement/re-employment if any of the following occurs:

- The employee is determined to be medically stationary and not physically able to return to the former position (for loss of reinstatement rights) or to any position (for loss of re-employment rights).
- The employee is eligible for and participates in vocational assistance.
- The employee accepts suitable employment with another employer after becoming medically stationary.
- The employee refuses the employer's offer, made in good faith, for doing suitable light duty or modified work employment from the employer before becoming medically stationary.
- Demand for reinstatement is not made by the employee within seven days from the date the employee is notified by the insurer or self-insured employer by certified mail that the employee's attending physician has released the employee to the former position (for loss of reinstatement rights) or for re-employment (for loss of re-employment rights).
- Three years have elapsed since the date of the employee's original injury.
- The employer discharges the employee for reasons not connected with the injury and for which others are or would be discharged.
- The employee clearly abandons future employment with the employer.
- The employee does not report to work as specified in the employer's suitable job offer.

As long as the workers' compensation claim is compensable, the employer may not discipline the employee for any absences that are related to that claim. The employer must pay the benefits if that is what the employer does for other employees. In no instance may an employer provide fewer benefits for an injured employee than for other employees.

Exemptions

Some construction contractors who are "exempt" do not need to be covered by workers' compensation insurance.

- **Sole Proprietors**
  A sole proprietor is exempt from workers' compensation insurance.
- **Partners**
  Two or more members of the same family who are partners may be exempt. The partners must have substantial ownership.
- **Corporate Officers or Limited Liability Company Members**
  Two or more members of the same family who are corporate officers or limited liability members/managers may be exempt. They must have substantial ownership.

NOTE: Construction businesses with a commercial endorsement are required to carry workers' compensation insurance even if they would otherwise be exempt.

There are some general exemptions that may apply.

- **Private Residence Employees**

  A worker who is hired to do gardening, maintenance, repair, or remodeling in or about the private home of the person employing the worker is exempt from workers' compensation insurance. This does not include a worker doing new home construction.

- **Out-of-State Employees**

  If an employer from out of state brings employees into Oregon, the workers' compensation coverage from the home state will usually satisfy Oregon's requirement for those workers temporarily in Oregon. If the contractor hires a worker specifically to work in Oregon, then Oregon-specific coverage is required.

Unemployment Insurance

Definition

Unemployment is a tax used to pay benefits to unemployed employees.

Employees Disqualified from Receiving Benefits

A person is disqualified from receiving unemployment benefits if the person was terminated from a job because of misconduct, or if the person voluntarily left work without good cause. Unemployed persons are disqualified if they fail to apply for available suitable work when they are referred by the employment office or fail to accept suitable work when it is offered.

A person will be disqualified from receiving benefits if he or she is discharged or suspended because of the unlawful use of any controlled substance unless that person is participating in a recognized drug rehabilitation program.

He or she may also be disqualified for being discharged two or more times within a 12-month period for substance abuse. He or she will be disqualified if it is found that the person committed a felony or theft in connection with work, admits the act, and is convicted in a court.

Employees not Disqualified from Receiving Benefits

A person will not be disqualified for benefits if:

- The person quits work or fails to accept work when a collective bargaining agreement is in effect and the employer modifies the amount of wages in breach of the agreement
- The person is laid off
- The person is discharged for other than misconduct or use of controlled substances
- The person voluntarily left work before the date of a good-cause voluntary leaving date
- The actual voluntary leaving occurs no more than 15 days before the planned date of voluntary leaving

Wage and Hour Regulations

Federal Wage and Hour Regulations

The U.S. Department of Labor (US-DOL), Wage and Hour Division, administers the federal Fair Labor Standards Act (FLSA).

Generally, to be subject to the FLSA, a business must have two or more employees and an annual sales volume of $500,000 or more. The FLSA also applies to employees whose work regularly involves them in commerce between states (interstate commerce), regardless of the sales volume of the employer.

Oregon Wage and Hour Regulations

The Oregon Bureau of Labor and Industries (BOLI), Wage and Hour Division, administers Oregon's wage and hour laws. Oregon's wage and hour regulations apply to all private and non-federal public sector employees.

Employee

An employee is any person who is permitted to work or who provides services for an employer who pays or agrees to pay the person at a fixed rate.

Independent Contractor "Economic Realities" Test Check

The laws applied by the US DOL and BOLI relating to independent contractors are slightly different from laws applied by other agencies. BOLI applies a test commonly known as the "economic realities" test to determine if an individual is an employee of a business or an independent contractor.

Generally, the criteria include the:

- Degree of control exercised by the employer
- Extent of the relative investments of the worker and the employer

- Degree to which the employer determines the worker's opportunity for profit and loss
- Skill and initiative required in performing the job
- Permanency of the relationship

The relationship between the worker and the business is considered in light of the "realities of the relationship." For example, it does not matter if the worker signed a contract stating or indicating that he or she is an independent contractor. BOLI (and the courts applying this test) "look behind" the contract to determine if the worker is actually an employee.

Minimum Wage

Most Oregon employers are subject to both federal and state minimum wage and overtime laws. The effect of this dual coverage is that, in cases where both federal and state laws apply, the employer must comply with the most stringent standard. For example, since state law currently requires a higher minimum wage rate than federal law, all Oregon employers must pay the Oregon state rate, unless their employees are exempt under Oregon law.

Federal Minimum Wage

Effective July 24, 2009, the federal minimum wage is $7.25 per hour.

State Minimum Wage

From Jan. 1, 2015, through Dec. 31, 2015, Oregon's minimum wage is $9.25 per hour. Oregon law requires the minimum wage rate to be adjusted annually for inflation by Sept. 30 of each year for the following calendar year.

Minimum Wage Applies to Oregon Employees

Minimum wage applies to all employees in Oregon, unless exempt. For each hour of work time that the employee is gainfully employed, no employer may employ any employee at a lower wage. However, BOLI may approve hourly wage rates lower than the minimum wage for persons who are mentally or physically disabled or who are student-learners.

Minimum Wage Posters

Every employer with employees subject to the minimum wage provisions must post an Oregon, "Minimum Wage Poster," summarizing the requirements of Oregon wage and hour laws. This must be posted in a place which can be accessed easily by employees. Posters can be downloaded from the bureau's website at www.oregon.gov/boli.

Employees are Entitled to Payment for Hours Worked

Employees must receive at least minimum wage for all hours worked, including preparation time, opening and closing times and required meetings. State (and federal) minimum wage laws define "employ" as "to suffer or permit to work." "Work time" includes both time worked and time of authorized attendance.

By this definition, any time spent by an employee in the performance of any duties must be recorded and paid as time worked.

Under state law, you can pay wages by the hour, as a salary, in commissions or at a piece-rate. Whichever method is used, employers must keep accurate time records and the employee's total earnings must equal or exceed minimum wage for all hours worked.

In order to avoid liability for payment, the employer must have and enforce rules prohibiting unauthorized work. For example, assume an employee arrives at work early or stays late because of transportation problems. The employee prefers to work rather than remaining idle, and states that he or she will volunteer the time. Wage and hour laws require that an employer must compensate an employee for all hours worked, whether those hours are authorized or not. If an employee insists on not following an employer's work rules, discipline may be in order.

Employers are responsible for maintaining accurate time records of all hours worked. The records must be kept for at least two years to defend against wage claims and comply with audits.

Overtime Rate Equals One and One-Half Times the Regular Rate

The rate for overtime required by both the federal government and the State of Oregon is one and one-half times the employee's regular rate of pay.

When Overtime Must Be Paid

Unless exempt from overtime, any hours worked over 40 in a workweek must be paid at one and one-half times the employee's regular rate of pay. Whenever overtime is required to be paid on a daily basis, such as public works projects for example, it also must be calculated on a weekly basis. The greater of the two amounts is the amount to be paid. The payment of overtime is required by state and federal law and may not be waived by agreements with employees.

Employers May Establish Workweek

"Workweek" means any seven consecutive 24-hour periods as determined by the employer. The beginning of the workweek may be changed if the change is intended to be permanent and is not designed to evade the state or federal overtime requirements. For purposes of overtime computation, each workweek stands alone.

Overtime Based on the Actual Number of Hours Worked

Wage and hour laws require an employer to compensate an employee for any overtime hours the employee works. If an employee violates the business policy and works overtime without required authorization, the employer may discipline the employee but overtime must still be paid for the hours worked.

Compensatory Time

Compensatory (comp) time, (the provision of time off instead of paying wages for time worked over 40 hours per workweek), is only available to public employees under certain circumstances. Employers in the private sector are not permitted to provide compensatory time in place of overtime payment.

Rest and Meal Periods

Rest Periods

Paid rest periods of 10 minutes must be provided to non-exempt adult employees for every four hours or "major portion thereof" (meaning two hours and one minute through four hours) worked in a work period. The rest period is to be taken approximately in the middle of each work segment. Rest periods may **not** be added to meal periods or deducted from the beginning or end of the employee's work shift to shorten the time worked.

In addition, both state and federal laws require employers to provide reasonable rest periods (not less than 30 minutes) to employees who need to express milk for a child 18 months of age or younger. Employers are also required to make reasonable effort to provide a private location that is reasonably close to the employee's workstation where she can express milk. The location may not be a public restroom or toilet stall and must be free from intrusion by other employees or the public. There are some "undue hardship" exceptions.

Meal Periods

Oregon law requires employers to provide meal periods of not less than 30 minutes to non-exempt employees who work six or more hours in a work period. The meal period is not required to be paid, but the employee must be relieved of all work duties during the meal period. If an employee is not relieved of all work duties during a 30-minute meal period, the employer must pay the employee for the entire 30 minutes.

The scheduling of meal periods depends on the length of the workday. If the work period is seven hours or less (but at least six), the meal break must be between the second and fifth hour worked. If the work period is more than seven hours, the meal break must be taken between the third and sixth hour worked.

When an employer fails to provide an employee with a required meal period, the employer has the burden to show that one of four exceptions applies:
1. An established industry custom providing a meal period less than 30 minutes but not less than 20 minutes
2. An undue hardship to the employer in which employees are provided advance written notice
3. A fourth exception applies only to tipped food and beverage service workers

Regular Paydays

All employers must establish and maintain regular paydays. Paydays may not exceed 35 days after the first day an employee begins work or between paydays.

When an employer has notice that an employee has not been paid the full amount the employee is owed on a regular payday and there is no dispute about the amount of the unpaid wages, then:
- If the unpaid amount is less than 5 percent of the employee's gross wages due on the regular payday, the employer must pay the employee the unpaid amount no later than the next regular payday
- If the unpaid amount is 5 percent or more of the employee's gross wages due on the regular payday, the employer must pay the employee the unpaid amount within three days after the employer has notice of the unpaid amount, excluding Saturdays, Sundays and holidays

If an employer fails to make timely payments to employees, BOLI may require an employer to post a bond to ensure timely payment of wages.

Deductions From Wages

Employers must withhold state withholding tax, federal income withholding tax, Social Security, Medicare, and Workers' Benefit Fund (WBF) assessments from employees' wages in accordance with federal and Oregon tax laws. Employee payroll deductions are discussed further in Chapter 5.

An employer may not withhold, deduct or divert any portion of an employee's wages unless the:
- Employer is required to do so by law, for example, required tax withholdings as described above or a garnishment order (including permitted processing fees);
- Deductions are authorized by the employee in writing, are for the employee's benefit and are recorded in the employer's books;

- Employee has voluntarily signed an authorization for a deduction for any other items (such as charitable contributions), provided that the employer is not the ultimate recipient of the money, and the deduction is recorded in the employer's books;
- Deduction is authorized by a collective bargaining agreement to which the employer is a party; or
- Deduction is made from the payment of wages upon termination of employment and is authorized pursuant to a written agreement between the employee and employer for the repayment of a loan made to the employee if certain conditions are met.

Deductions may **not** be made from the wages of employees for items required by the employer, including the following:

- Uniforms, tools and transportation that are required to do the job (or "draws" for the purchase of such items)
- Deposits for equipment, shortages, breakages, losses or theft
- Meals and lodging, if they are required by the employer

All employers who are required to have workers' compensation insurance must also pay a workers' compensation assessment to the state. This payroll assessment does not have any effect on workers' compensation insurance coverage. The assessment may be split between employees (payroll deduction) and employers, or paid in full by the employer. The workers' compensation assessment pays for specific programs that benefit injured employees and the employers who hire them.

An itemized statement of deductions made from wages must be furnished to employees on their regular paydays at the time payment is made. The statement must show the amount and purpose of each deduction.

The statement may be a part of the paycheck, attached to it, or it may be a separate document. If the employee agrees, and has the ability to print or store the statement, the statement may be provided in an electronic format.

When an employer deducts an amount from an employee's wages as required or authorized by law or agreement, the employer must pay the amount deducted to the appropriate recipient within the time required by the law or agreement. If the time for payment is not specified by the law or agreement, the employer must pay the amount deducted to the appropriate recipient within seven days. Failure to pay the amount as required constitutes an unlawful deduction. An employee may pursue collection of amounts which he or she feels have been unlawfully deducted through a private attorney, in small claims court, or by filing a wage claim with the CCB or Wage and Hour Division of BOLI.

Personnel Records

Personnel records include those records that are or have been used to determine the employee's qualification for employment, promotion, additional compensation, employment termination, or other disciplinary action.

If the employee requests such records, the employer is required to furnish a certified copy of these records or allow the employee to review them within 45 days after receipt of the employee's request. If the employee's personnel records are not readily available, the employer and the employee may agree to extend the time within which the employer must provide the employee reasonable opportunity to inspect the records or furnish the employee a certified copy of the records. After the employee terminates, the employer must keep these records for at least 60 days.

Final Paychecks

If an employee quits employment and has given advance notice of at least 48 hours (excluding Saturdays, Sundays and holidays), the employee's final pay is due on the last day worked. If the employee quits without 48-hours' notice, final pay is due within five days (excluding Saturdays, Sundays or holidays) or on the next regular payday after the employee quits, whichever is sooner.

If an employee who is regularly required to submit time records to the employer quits employment without giving at least 48-hours' notice and fails to submit time records, the employer is required to pay the employee the wages the employer estimates are due within five calendar days after the employee has quit. If the employee subsequently submits time records, the employer must pay any additional wages due to the employee within five days of receiving the time records.

If an employer discharges an employee, or if employment is ended by mutual agreement, all wages earned and unpaid must be paid by the end of the next business day after discharge or termination.

Prevailing Wage Rate

The Prevailing Wage Rate (PWR) law, also known as the "Little Davis Bacon Act," regulates the payment of wages for work performed on public work projects. The following is a brief overview of this state law.

Covered Projects

The PWR law applies to "public works" projects carried on or contracted for by a public agency to serve the public interest. The term public works includes, but is not limited to, the construction, reconstruction, major renovation or painting of roads, highways, buildings, structures and improvements of all types to serve the public interest. Public works may also include:

- Projects for the construction, reconstruction, major renovation or painting of a privately owned road, highway, building, structure or improvement of any type that uses funds of a private entity and $750,000 or more of funds of a public agency or in which 25 percent or more of the square footage of the completed project will be occupied or used by a public agency;
- The construction or installation on public property of any device, structure or mechanism that uses solar energy, regardless of the total project cost or whether the project uses funds of a public agency; and

A **public agency** includes the State of Oregon or any of its political subdivisions, or any county, city, district, authority, public corporation or entity, or any of their legal agencies.

Workers on public works projects subject to the PWR law must be paid no less than the prevailing rate of wage published by BOLI for the trade or occupation in the locality where such labor is performed. Contractors must pay workers employed on projects subject to both the state PWR law and federal Davis-Bacon Act the higher of the applicable state or federal wage rate.

BOLI publishes rates applicable to projects subject to the state PWR law. These rates and a link to the federal Davis-Bacon wage rates are available at http://egov.oregon.gov/BOLI/WHD/PWR/pwr_book.shtml.

General contractors or subcontractors engaged on a public works project that requires prevailing wage rates must post the applicable wage rates in a visible place on the project.

Contractors who have intentionally failed or refused to post and pay the prevailing wage rates are ineligible to receive any contract for public works (except for federal contracts) in Oregon for three years. BOLI may also debar the officers of debarred contractors, and place them on a "list of ineligibles."

Exemptions

Public works projects that are exempt from prevailing wage rates requirements include:

- Projects for which the total project amount does not exceed $50,000.
- Projects that are privately owned, use funds of a private entity, and in which less than 25 percent of the square footage of the completed project will be occupied or used by a public agency and for which less than $750,000 of funds of a public agency are used.
- Projects for which no funds of a public agency are directly or indirectly used.
- Projects for residential construction that are privately owned and that predominantly provide affordable housing as defined by law.
- Contracts of a People's Utility District.
- Projects of the Oregon State Lottery Commission.
- Projects of the Travel Information Council.
- Oregon Department of Corrections' inmate labor work release program assignments.
- Oregon Youth Conservation Corps members.

Contractor Responsibilities

Before a contractor may work on a public works project subject to the PWR law, the contractor must file a $30,000 Public Works Bond with the Construction Contractors Board to be used exclusively for unpaid wages determined to be due by BOLI. Exemptions from the bond requirements include projects that are $100,000 or less or for certified disadvantaged, minority, women and emerging small business enterprises. General contractors are required to verify that any subcontractors have filed a public works bond before permitting a subcontractor to start work on a project.

Contractors and subcontractors are required to submit weekly payroll information and certified statements to the contracting agency by the fifth business day of each month for each week following a month in which workers were employed upon a public work. The contractor may submit a weekly payroll on either a form provided by BOLI or may use a similar form, provided this form has all the same information.

Public agencies and general contractors are required to withhold 25 percent of amounts owed to contractors if certified payrolls are not submitted as required.

If a contract that is initially less than $50,000 later increases to an amount greater than $50,000, the contractor must pay prevailing wage rate wages for the entire project.

The commissioner determines the prevailing wage rates based on annual independent wage surveys. Contractors must reply to wage surveys sent by the commissioner.

Contractors engaged on projects that require payment of prevailing wages must post a notice, in a location frequented by employees, of the number of hours per day and days per week that the employees may be required to work, and the applicable prevailing wage rates for that project. The notice must also contain information regarding any health and welfare or pension plan provided for employees, how and where to make claims, and where to obtain further information.

When overtime must be paid. Every public contract must also contain a condition that no person shall be employed for more than 10 hours in any one day, or 40 hours in any one week, except in cases of emergency or where the public policy absolutely requires it. In such cases, the employee shall be paid at least time-and-a-half pay for all:

- Overtime in excess of eight hours a day or 40 hours in any one week when the workweek is five consecutive days, Monday through Friday.
- Overtime in excess of 10 hours a day or 40 hours in any one week when the workweek is four consecutive days, Monday through Friday.
- Work performed on Saturdays, Sundays, and legal holidays.

Applications of Prevailing Wage Regulations to Types of Work and Contracts

The term "public works" refers to the construction, reconstruction, major renovation, or painting carried on or contracted for by a public agency or privately owned projects that use funds of a private entity and $750,000 or more of funds of a public agency or in which 25 percent or more of the square footage of the completed project will be occupied or used by a public agency.

The type of work performed on a project, not what a contract is called, determines prevailing wage rate coverage. For example, if a project includes covered activities, such as rewiring a major portion of a building, and meets the other jurisdictional requirements of the PWR laws, the entire project is covered.

- Construction includes the initial building of structures and roads.
- Reconstruction includes the restoration of existing buildings and the restoration, rebuilding, or resurfacing of existing roads.
- Major renovation includes any remodeling or alteration of existing structures or roads that cost $50,000 or more.

PWR laws cover the cleanup of hazardous material spills if the project includes some construction or reconstruction. The PWR law does not cover contracts that only include picking up and hauling away hazardous material not in connection with a covered construction project.

PWR law covers demolition work only if it is to prepare for planned construction or renovation. If no construction is planned to replace the demolished property, the demolition is exempt.

General maintenance work, such as sweeping, cleaning, and landscaping is not covered unless it is done as part of a covered construction, reconstruction, or major renovation project. For example, PWR laws do not apply if maintenance landscaping work such as mowing or pruning is performed on the grounds of an existing building where no other work is being performed. If the same landscaping is part of new construction or a major building renovation, then it is covered work.

Persons employed on a public works project who spend more than 20 percent of their time during any workweek performing duties that are manual or physical in nature as opposed to mental or managerial in nature are workers and must be paid the prevailing wage rate. Mental or managerial duties include administrative, executive, professional, supervisory, or clerical duties.

The PWR law does not apply to "owner-operators" of trucks. Drivers who own and operate their own trucks and who are independent contractors are not required to be paid prevailing wage rate wages. Operators of other equipment or motor vehicles are not exempt.

Persons employed on a public work for the manufacture or furnishing of materials, articles, supplies, or equipment are not workers required to be paid prevailing wages unless the employment of such persons is performed in connection with and at the site of the public work. Persons employed on a public work who are employed by a commercial supplier of goods and materials must be paid no less than the prevailing wage for work performed in fabrication plants, batch plants, barrow pits, job headquarters, tool yards, or other such places that are dedicated exclusively, or nearly so, to the public works project.

Employees are not required to be paid prevailing wage rate wages for travel time unless they are traveling between the job site and a dedicated site. Other wage and hour regulations may require that travel be compensated, however. Contact BOLI for more information.

Penalties

In addition to any other penalty provided by law, BOLI may assess a civil penalty not to exceed $5,000 for each violation of any provision of PWR law or any rule the commissioner has adopted. If a contractor fails to comply with the PWR law, the CCB may also order a civil penalty of $1,000 and can suspend the contractor's license until the money required as employee wages or civil penalties assessed is paid in full. BOLI may, as a condition of settling a case, require the contractor to take a training course on PWR laws and ask for a commitment of future compliance.

Any contractor failing to pay prevailing wages owes the amount of underpayment. Employers may also be liable for liquidated damages equal to the amount of unpaid wages and additional civil penalties for the underpayment of wages. For example, if a contractor underpaid an employee by $1,500, the contractor is responsible for the unpaid wages plus an equal amount in liquidated damages for a total of $3,000.

Every contractor on the site is responsible for the posting of all prevailing wage rates that apply to the project. A civil penalty may be assessed and/or the contractor may be debarred from public contracting for failing to post the prevailing wage rates as required.

Wage Disputes

If the employer does not pay an employee wages to which he or she is entitled, the employee may file a claim with BOLI.

Employee Claims

The following paragraphs outline the procedures to be followed by employees who file claims in connection with wage disputes.

BOLI Claims

An employee's first step is to file a claim with BOLI. The wage claim will be reviewed for completeness and to make sure the division has jurisdiction. The employee may be asked to provide additional information and/or evidence to support the claim. BOLI will not accept a wage claim if:

- A private legal action has already begun to recover the wage claims.
- No work was performed in Oregon.
- The claim is against a business in which the employee was a partner, an owner, or had a direct financial interest.
- The claim is against a relative.
- The employee is unwilling to take the employer to court.

CCB Complaints
An employee may also file a complaint with the CCB for nonpayment of wages by a contractor. The CCB will notify the contractor and then investigate the complaint. CCB complaints, if possible, are settled by mediation.

The CCB is not required to accept complaints for amounts less than $1,000. The respondent must be licensed during all or part of the work period.

Payment by Employer of Undisputed Amount
In case of a dispute over wages, the employer must pay, without condition and within the time set by law, all wages the employer agrees are due. The employee retains the right to claim any balance the employee alleges is due by filing an action with the court or a claim with BOLI.

Penalty for Willfully Withholding Wages
If an employer willfully fails to pay an employee final wages when due, the employer is subject to a penalty of the employee's hourly rate for eight hours per day for each day the employee remains unpaid up to a maximum of 30 days. The penalty may not exceed 100 percent of the unpaid wages if the employer pays the wages due within 12 days after written notice of nonpayment is sent to the employer, and the employer has not willfully violated the final pay provisions of the law in the preceding year.

Statute of Limitations for Wage Disputes
Employers are liable for unpaid wages for a period of six years from the date the wages were earned and two years for claims of unpaid overtime. Employees may lose their right to their wages if they fail to pursue claims in a timely manner.

Discriminating Against an Employee
Discharging or otherwise retaliating against an employee because the employee has discussed, inquired about, or filed a wage claim is prohibited.

BOLI Procedures for Processing a Wage Claim
Upon receipt of a wage claim, BOLI will notify the employer of the claim by mail.
- If the employer agrees the amount claimed is due, the employer may issue a check to the claimant and send it to BOLI.
- If the employer agrees that a portion of the amount claimed is due, that amount should be paid promptly.
- If the employer disagrees with the wage claim, the claim will be assigned for investigation to a wage and hour compliance specialist, who will review the employer's records and other relevant information to determine whether wages are owed and if so, the amount of unpaid wages.

- If the employer disputes the compliance specialist's determination, an administrative hearing or court trial may be held.

Employment of Minors

Special rules exist concerning employing minors in Oregon. Some of these are described in the following paragraphs. There are many other rules relating to the employment of minors (under age 18). If you employ minors, we recommend that you consult with an attorney who specializes in employment law or contact BOLI's Technical Assistance for Employers.

Minors Employed in Construction

Minor employees who are ages 16 and 17 may work in construction with restricted use of some machinery and explosives. Minors are not allowed to perform hazardous work activity. Hazardous work includes using motor vehicles and transporting goods (except under limited circumstances for minors 17 years old); use of woodworking machines, battery-powered handheld drills and sanders; operating power-driven hoisting apparatus or power-driven metalworking machines; or being involved in activities like wrecking, demolition, excavation, and roofing. Minors under 16 years of age may not be employed in construction activities.

Annual Employment Certificate

Employers who hire minors must verify the age of the minor and obtain an annual employment certificate. The certificate covers all minors the employer hires. The employer estimates the number of minors that will be employed during the year, lists the job duties they will be performing, and identifies any machinery or equipment they will be using.

Employment certificate applications may be obtained from the BOLI Child Labor Unit, Wage and Hour Division (971-673-0836), or may be downloaded from BOLI's website at www.oregon.gov/BOLI/WHD/CLU. The certificate must be posted in a conspicuous place in the work area where employees may review it.

Minimum Wages for Minors

Under state law, minors must be paid the same applicable minimum wage rate as adult employees. Employees ages 16 and 17 may work at any time with no daily hour restrictions up to 44 hours per week. However, they must be paid time and one-half the regular rate of pay for any time worked over 40 hours in a week.

Rest and Meal Periods for Minors

Paid rest periods of at least 15 minutes must be given to minors during each four-hour period of work. This differs from the requirement for adults, which is 10 minutes. Meal periods of at least 30 minutes must be provided (see section titled "Rest and Meal Periods" above). Exemptions to the meal period requirement do not apply to 14- and 15-year-olds, who must be fully relieved of work duties during this time.

Parental Requirements

Some child labor law exceptions apply for employment by a minor's parent(s). Contact BOLI for specific information.

Employee Rights

Employment at Will and its Exceptions

An employer may not terminate an employee in violation of public policy or for exercising certain statutory rights. For example, an employee becomes disabled and requests an adjustable chair to reasonably accommodate the disability so he or she can resume work. It is illegal to terminate that employee either because of the disability or because he or she asked for a reasonable accommodation.

Exception to Employment at Will: Employment Agreements

An agreement between employer and employee as to terms and conditions of employment, how the employer will handle discipline or termination, and so on, may be binding on the employer. Note that not all such agreements are written.

Exception to Employment at Will: Wrongful Discharge

An employer may be liable for "wrongful discharge" in violation of public policy if the employer terminates the employee for complying with a public duty, or for pursuing a right granted by law.

Examples of such violations are numerous and include an employee who is terminated because he or she:
- Brought a safety concern to the employer's attention
- Had to miss work to serve jury duty
- Reported in good faith what he or she believed to be illegal conduct or activities being committed by fellow employees or supervisors

Employment Agreements

Types of Agreements

Express

An express contract is an actual agreement of the parties, which consists of the terms that are declared at the time it is formed and stated in clear and explicit language, either verbally or in writing. Under certain circumstances, an employee handbook or manual can constitute a contract.

Implied

An implied contract is one that is not formed by an explicit agreement of the parties. Instead, it is inferred from the acts or conduct of the parties that show the existence of an agreement between them.

Collective Bargaining Agreements

Collective bargaining agreements are contracts that have been negotiated between union representatives and company representatives on behalf of the union member.

Employer's Breach

An employer's breach occurs when the employer does not live up to the express, implied, or bargained agreement. A breach could include such actions as not paying an agreed-upon salary, not paying wages in a timely manner, not providing agreed-upon benefits, and not providing workers' compensation coverage.

Remedies for Violation of Employment Agreements

Monetary and other relief may be awarded in an action for breach of an employment contract.

Statutory Protection of Employee Rights

Federal and state laws protect employees from discrimination based on race, sex, and other protected classes.

Discrimination Based on Race, Sex, and Other "Protected Classes"

Federal Law

Title VII of the Civil Rights Act of 1964, as amended, prohibits employers from discriminating against applicants and employees in employment on the basis of race, color, religion, sex, national origin, and genetic information. Title VII applies to employer decisions regarding hiring, promotion, discipline, and discharge or termination. An employee may challenge actions taken by supervisors, co-workers, and even third parties. Further, Title VII prevents retaliation against a person who, in good faith, has made a Title VII complaint or assisted another's Title VII complaint.

The **Age Discrimination in Employment Act (ADEA) of 1967** applies to employers of 20 or more employees. It prohibits discrimination in hiring, employment, or termination against applications and/or employees aged 40 or over, with certain limited exceptions. The ADEA also prohibits retaliation against an applicant or employee who either makes an ADEA complaint himself or herself or who assists with another person's complaint. The ADEA provides discrimination protection to workers, age 40 and older, in companies of 20 or more employees. Interestingly, the ADEA does **not** protect workers who are younger than 40 from being discriminated against by employers who favor older workers. In other words, the ADEA does not protect younger workers from "reverse age discrimination."

Oregon Law

Oregon law parallels Title VII of the Civil Rights Act of 1964 and the federal ADEA in several respects. It prohibits discrimination on the basis of age, religion, race, color, disability, sex, sexual orientation and gender identity, national origin, and marital status. Discrimination because of pregnancy is sex discrimination. A full listing of all protected classes under Oregon law can be found at the BOLI website: www.oregon.gov/boli.

The Oregon Court of Appeals has held that Oregon law provides some protection on the basis of sexual orientation. Note also that this law prohibits discrimination on the basis of:

- Age against persons 18 years and older (as opposed to the ADEA, which prohibits discrimination against persons 40 years and older).
- Association with a person belonging to a protected class.

Workplace Harassment

Harassment of an individual by an employer or by other employees because of the individual's sexual orientation, race, marital status, color, religion, national origin, age, or disability is a form of discrimination.

Refer to BOLI's website at www.BOLI.state.or.us and publications for more information. Appendix C lists resource materials available from BOLI.

Disability Discrimination and Reasonable Accommodation

Federal Law: Americans with Disabilities Act

Since 1994, the Americans with Disabilities Act (ADA) prohibits employers of 15 or more employees from discriminating against qualified individuals with disabilities. An employer with 15 or more employees cannot discriminate against a qualified individual with a disability because of the disability. The ADA applies to discrimination during employment-related activities like job application procedures, hiring or firing, promotions, compensation, fringe benefits, training, or conditions of employment.

Under both state and federal law, a "person with a disability" is any of these:
- An individual who has a physical or mental impairment that substantially limits one or more major life activities
- A person who has a record of such an impairment
- A person who is regarded as having such impairment

Oregon Law

Discrimination against persons with disabilities prohibited. It is against Oregon law for any private sector employer of six or more employees to discriminate in employment because an otherwise qualified person has a disability.

Direct Threat. An employer may require that an employee not pose a direct threat to the health or safety of the employee and/or others in the workplace. Direct threat is defined as a significant risk of substantial harm that cannot be eliminated or reduced with reasonable accommodation.

The employer cannot discriminate in:
- Refusing to hire, employ, or promote
- Preventing or terminating from employment
- Compensation
- Terms, conditions, or privileges of employment

If an employer has prepared a written description before advertising or interviewing applicants for a job, the position description shall be considered evidence proof of the essential functions of the job. A person is considered qualified for the job if he or she can perform the essential functions of his or her job, with or without reasonable accommodation by the employer. Essential functions are the fundamental job duties of the employment position the individual with a disability holds or desires.

A job function may be essential for any of several reasons, including but not limited to:

- The position exists to perform that function
- A limited number of employees are available among whom the performance of that job function can be distributed
- The function may be highly specialized so that the incumbent in the position is hired for his or her expertise and ability to perform the particular function

Reasonable accommodation. The ADA and Oregon's disability law require not only that employers not discriminate based on disability, but that employers provide "reasonable accommodation" to an otherwise qualified person if such accommodation would allow the person to perform the essential functions of the job the person holds or desires. The employer must accommodate such individuals if such accommodation would not create an undue hardship.

Reasonable accommodation is a modification or adjustment that enables a person with a disability to apply for a job (for example, holding a job interview in an accessible location), to perform the essential functions of a position (for example, purchasing an amplifier to allow a hearing-impaired person to talk on the telephone), or to enjoy the same benefits and privileges of employment as other employees (for example, holding a business function in a location accessible to all employees).

Since an employer cannot ask medically related questions of an applicant, the employer cannot discuss reasonable accommodation unless the applicant initiates the discussion. Once a person is hired, if the need for accommodation is obvious (for example, the individual uses a wheelchair), the employer may ask what accommodations the person will need. After the point of hire, if the disability is not obvious to the employer, the burden is on the employee to tell the employer about the disability and the need for accommodation. Once alerted of a disability, the employer should begin an interactive process with the employee to learn what accommodation, if any, the employee needs. With this information, the employer can decide if and how the accommodation can be provided.

Reasonable accommodation becomes unreasonable if it would cause the employer an undue hardship. An undue hardship is an action that is significantly difficult or expensive in relation to the size of the employer, the resources available, and the nature of the business.

Medical examinations and inquiries; job applicants. It is a violation of ORS 659A.133 *for an employer to conduct a medical examination of a job applicant, to ask w*hether the applicant is a disabled person, or to make inquiries as to the nature or severity of any disability of the applicant. Some exceptions are noted in the rule.

Medical examinations and inquiries; employees. Except as provided in ORS 659A.136, an employer cannot require an employee to submit to a medical examination, cannot ask if the employee is a disabled person, and cannot make inquiries of an employee as to the nature or severity of any disability, unless the examination or inquiry is shown to be job-related and consistent with business necessity.

An employer may conduct voluntary medical examinations, including voluntary medical histories that are part of an employee health program available to employees at the job site. An employer may make inquiries into the ability of an employee to perform job-related functions.

Prohibitions Against Retaliation or Discrimination for Opposing Practices

An employee who opposes employment practices that he or she believes, in good faith, are unlawful and who is subsequently terminated or suffers an adverse employment action, such as a reduction in pay or a transfer to a less desirable job, may successfully sue his or her employer for retaliation or discrimination under state or federal law or file an administrative complaint with BOLI or the EEOC. Employers should know what the laws are and should seek legal advice in avoiding liability and preventing retaliatory action or discrimination.

Example

Peter, an employee of Acme construction, complains to Joe, the supervisor of the project, that Bill, an Acme foreman, is sexually harassing Sue, a female co-worker. One week after Peter's complaint, Joe terminates Peter because he believes Peter should mind his own business and because he believes Peter may encourage Sue to file a lawsuit for sexual harassment against Acme. In this scenario, Peter has cause of action against Acme for retaliatory discharge under both state and federal law.

Federal Law
Several federal laws prohibit retaliation against a person who has, in good faith, made a Title VII complaint or assists another's complaint.

The Age Discrimination in Employment Act prohibits retaliation against an applicant or employee who makes an ADEA complaint or who assists another's complaint.

The Americans with Disabilities Act also prohibits retaliation for asserting one's rights, opposing unlawful conduct, or assisting another complaint.

Oregon Law
It is against Oregon law to discriminate against an individual who has:
- Opposed any discriminatory practice, assisted another's complaint, or attempted to do so
- Opposed a practice prohibited by the Oregon Safe Employment Act or assisted another's complaint
- Exercised his or her individual rights or inquired about his or her rights under the workers' compensation system, the disability laws, OR-OSHA, family leave laws, and/or other laws prohibiting discrimination
- Used, invoked, or assisted a complaint under the workers' compensation system
- Testified before the Legislative Assembly
- Testified at an unemployment hearing
- Made a wage claim or discussed a wage claim with anyone
- Reported, in good faith, what that person believes to be criminal activity, caused a criminal complaint to be filed, cooperated with law enforcement, brought a civil proceeding against an employer, or testified at a civil proceeding or criminal trial

Miscellaneous Discrimination Laws
Miscellaneous discrimination laws cover the following areas:
- It is unlawful to discriminate because of an expunged juvenile record
- It is unlawful to discriminate against an individual solely because another member of that individual's family works for the employer
- It is unlawful to require as a condition of employment that an individual refrain from lawful tobacco use during nonworking hours
- It is unlawful to discharge or commit certain acts against an employee due to his or her jury service
- It is unlawful to deny accrued paid leave to an employee donating bone marrow
- It is unlawful to discharge a person because his or her wages are garnished.

- It is unlawful to discriminate against an employee for reporting a violation of health or residential facilities laws
- It is unlawful to refuse to grant leave to a member of the National Guard called into service

Additional Statutory Rights of Employees

Under certain circumstances, employees are entitled to rights related to family obligations, medical leave for themselves or certain family members, worksite injuries, or disabilities. Employers must comply by allowing employees to exercise their rights under those laws and by not retaliating against the employees for doing so or for inquiring about their rights.

Family and Medical Leave Laws

This section describes family medical leave under both federal and state laws. If there are greater rights under Oregon law, those laws will apply. In practical terms, that means, in most instances, Oregon Family Medical Leave laws will apply for Oregon employees since coverage is broader under the state law than under federal law. Additional information on the Oregon Family Medical Leave law can be found at the BOLI website: www.Oregon.gov/BOLI.

Federal: Family and Medical Leave Act (FMLA)

The Family and Medical Leave Act (FMLA) allows eligible employees of an employer to take up to 12 work weeks of unpaid leave in any 12-month period. This is commonly referred to as "protected" leave because taking family medical leave cannot be counted against a job applicant or an employee in assessing his or her work record. Family medical leave also "protects" an employee's job by allowing him or her to return to his or her job once the leave is over (except in some limited situations). The FMLA also allows that an employee's medical benefits remain at the same level while the employee is on leave and that the employee must generally be allowed to return to the same or an equivalent position upon return from leave. Under the FMLA, both male and female employees are eligible for family leave for the birth, adoption, or foster care placement of a child.

FMLA leave is available, as well, to care for a spouse, child, or parent with a serious health condition. The FMLA defines a "serious health condition" as an illness, injury, impairment, or physical or mental condition that involves inpatient care in a hospital, hospice, or residential medical care facility; or continuing treatment by a health care provider.

An employer may require medical certification from a health care provider to verify that an employee or the employee's family member has a serious health condition. In the case of an unanticipated emergency, an employer must allow at least 15 days for the employee to obtain the medical certification form from his or her physician. In general, no direct contact by the employer with the employee's health care provider is permitted.

Employers who have reason to doubt the validity of the initial medical certification may require a second opinion at the employers' expense; however, the ability to obtain a second or third medical opinion is limited by law. It is a good idea to attach the employee's job description to the medical certification form so the health care provider may refer to it when filling out the medical certification form and any subsequent Fitness for Duty Reports.

State: Oregon Family and Medical Leave Act (OFLA)

The Oregon Family and Medical Leave Act (OFLA) provides unpaid leave of absence for up to 12 weeks to eligible employees of Oregon employers for certain family and medical reasons. Eligible employees may request OFLA leave for any of the following qualifying purposes:

- Parental leave for the addition of a child to the family through birth, adoption, or placement by foster care
- Serious health condition leave to care for a family member with a serious health condition or the employee's own serious condition
- Pregnancy disability leave for pregnancy disability or prenatal care
- Sick child leave to care for a sick child who does not have a serious health condition but requires home care

Employees must give written notice to the employer 30 days in advance of the leave unless the leave is taken for an emergency. Employees who fail to give written notice may be subject to discipline by the employer.

There is no requirement that family leave be paid. However, employees must be allowed to use any existing accrued sick leave or vacation leave. When employees return to work from leave, they are entitled to their former job, or to an available equivalent job if the former job has been eliminated. Employers covered under both OFLA and FMLA must allow the employee on leave to return to the former job, if that job still exists.

"Overlapping" of FMLA and OFLA with Workers' Compensation and the ADA and Oregon Disability Laws

The overlapping of these laws can become complicated. In some situations, employers may want to seek legal advice.

When covered by more than one employment law, the employer must follow the one most beneficial to the employee. Larger companies will be covered by both OFLA and FMLA. The OFLA applies to employers with 25 or more employees whereas FMLA applies to employers with 50 or more employees.

In an absence due to a workers' compensation claim, the absence cannot be counted as family leave under OFLA. However, if the injured worker refuses a valid offer of suitable light duty before becoming medically stationary, OFLA leave commences immediately upon the refusal. During the time when a claim is pending, an OFLA covered employee may be entitled to use OFLA. If the claim is accepted, any OFLA leave counted against the employee must be restored to him or her. If the claim is ultimately denied, any OFLA leave will be deducted from the employee's entitlement. Injured worker leave is counted against FMLA.

When an employer grants a family leave for a condition that is also a disability under the ADA, the employer must reasonably accommodate an employee's disability if it does not create undue hardship. If an employee's family leave entitlement has been exhausted for a serious health condition that is also a disability, the reasonable accommodation obligation remains.

An example would be an employee who suffered permanent injuries to his or her back, and although able to return to work, needs special office furniture or equipment to allow him or her to perform the job after the 12-week family leave period.

The National Labor Relations Act (NLRA)

The National Labor Relations Act (NLRA) protects the rights of both union and nonunion employees to: engage in self-organization; form, join, or assist labor organizations; bargain collectively through representatives of their own choosing; and engage in other collective bargaining activities.

Enforcement of Laws Protecting Employee Rights

Federal Laws

BOLI takes complaints of violations of Title VII of the Civil Rights Act of 1964, through a work share agreement with the U.S. Equal Employment Opportunity Commission. Title VII also provides for actions in court; however, an employee must first have exhausted all administrative remedies, including filing with BOLI or with the EEOC, prior to going to court. Refer to the specific federal law to determine administrative or judicial rights of action under that law.

Oregon Law

BOLI investigates and pursues complaints of violations of most state civil rights laws. Many such state laws also provide for filing actions in court. Consult an attorney who practices employment law to determine rights.

Sexual Harassment

Sexual harassment is defined as unwelcome sexual advances, requests for sexual favors, or conduct of a sexual nature (verbal, physical, or visual), that is directed toward an individual because of gender. It can also include conduct that is not sexual in nature but is gender related. Sexual harassment includes the harassment of the same or opposite sex.

Sexual harassment can take many forms, including repeated sexual flirtations, advances or propositions, continued or repeated language of a sexual nature, graphic or degrading comments about an individual or his or her appearance, the display of sexually suggestive objects or pictures, or any unwelcome or abusive physical contact of a sexual nature. Sexual harassment also includes situations in which employment benefits are conditioned upon sexual favors.

An employer is automatically liable for sexual harassment when a "tangible employment action" occurs in connection with the harassment. A tangible employment action is very broadly defined and need not be negative. Examples include termination, failure to promote, and changes in work assignment or schedule.

The employer is also liable if the employer knew or should have known about the harassment and failed to take immediate and appropriate corrective action. The Civil Rights Division will find that the employer should have known of the harassment unless the employer can show both that:
- The employer exercised reasonable care to prevent harassment
- The complaining employee unreasonably failed to take advantage of preventative opportunities, such as the employer's complaint process

An employer should have a written policy that defines and prohibits sexual harassment and that emphatically states that it is not tolerated. All supervisors or managers should be trained on the sexual harassment policy. The policy should be distributed to employees, discussed with employees, and posted at all job sites. Records should be kept of training, distribution, and posting of the policy.

Employers should allow verbal or written complaints, and should provide a complaint procedure that allows the employee to bypass his or her immediate supervisor. The policy should describe the disciplinary actions that may be taken, up to and including termination. The policy must also clearly state that an employee, who in good faith reports harassment, will not face retaliation.

If an employer learns of possible sexual harassment, the employer must make a prompt, thorough investigation to determine whether harassment has occurred. All steps of the investigation should be thoroughly documented. Employers may wish to consult an attorney for assistance with harassment investigations and developing an anti-harassment policy.

Other Harassment

Harassment violates Title VII of the Civil Rights Act if it involves discriminatory treatment based on race, color, sex (with or without sexual conduct), religion, national origin, age, or disability. In addition, an employee may be harassed as retaliation because he or she opposed the discrimination or participated in an investigation or complaint. Conduct like simple teasing, offhand comments, or isolated incidents that are not extremely serious are not considered harassment. The conduct must be sufficiently frequent or severe to create a hostile work environment or result in a tangible employment action, such as hiring, firing, promotion or demotion, or undesirable reassignment. Decisions can also be tangible employment actions when they result in significant changes in benefits, compensation decisions, or work assignments.

An employer is responsible for discrimination by one of his or her supervisors, and liable for discrimination by co-workers, only when the employer fails to make reasonable efforts to stop the harassment.

If harassment occurs, the employer must exercise reasonable care to prevent and promptly correct any harassment, and prove that the employee unreasonably failed to complain to management or avoid harm. Employers should establish, distribute, and enforce a harassment policy that sets out procedures for making complaints. For small businesses, the owner can tell employees that harassment is prohibited.

If the business conducts a prompt, thorough, and impartial investigation of any complaint, and undertakes a swift and corrective action, it will have fulfilled its responsibility to effectively prevent and correct harassment.

Hiring Practices

Questions that Can and Cannot be Asked During the Hiring Process

An employer may not ask if an applicant is disabled or inquire about the nature or severity of a disability. Employers may be liable if they ask questions that would elicit information about a disability; for example, "How many times have you been sick in the last year?" Employers should focus inquiries on an applicant's ability to perform job-related functions.

An employer cannot require a medical examination until after a job offer has been made. However, an employer may condition a job offer on the results of a post-offer medical examination if the employer requires all entering employees in the same job category to take the examination.

Upon receiving a request for reasonable accommodation, an employer may request additional information, including medical verification of the condition requiring accommodation.

Federal and state law prohibits employers from advertising or making any inquiry expressing a preference based on protected class status. Therefore, all pre-employment questions should be designed to obtain information relating only to qualifications for successful job performance. Questions that should be avoided include those asking for:

- Direct information about an individual's race, sex, age, marital status or other protected class status.
- Information typically evaluated differently for men and women, such as questions regarding childcare arrangements.
- Information that could be used to screen out members of protected classes, such as questions about religious practices or medical conditions.

Employers can ask questions about an individual's ability to perform essential tasks, but the ADA prohibits questions relating to physical impairments or disabilities. Questions about an applicant's medical condition should also be avoided.

Below are some examples of illegal questions that could violate an applicant's protected class status:

- **Do you have a physical or mental condition that would interfere with your ability to perform the job?**
  Instead, ask, "Can you perform the essential functions of the job with or without a reasonable accommodation?"

- **Marital status: Are you married? Divorced? Separated? Who do you live with? How many children do you plan to have? What does your spouse do for a living?**
  Since it is illegal to discriminate on the basis of marital status, such inquiries are inappropriate.

- **Age: Birth date? How old are you?**
  If you need to know if an applicant is over a certain age for legal reasons, ask, "Are you 21 or over?" or "Are you 18 or older?"

- **Race, Gender: What is your race? Gender? Furnish a photograph. Hair and eye color.**
  If it is necessary to ask for this information for affirmative action purposes, a statement indicating that the information is needed for affirmative action reporting purposes only and will not be used to discriminate should accompany such inquiries. A photograph should not be required unless physical appearance is a bona fide occupational requirement for the job.

- **Sex: Are you pregnant? Do you plan to start a family?**
  Oregon law clearly states that discrimination on the basis of pregnancy is sex discrimination. According to the law, pregnant employees must receive the same benefits as other employees in similar job classifications.

- **Injured Worker: Have you ever applied for workers' compensation?**
  This question is unlawful under the ADA. In addition, Oregon employers with six or more employees cannot refuse to hire an applicant because of that person's prior workers' compensation claims.

- **Religion: What is your religious affiliation? Are you able to work Saturdays and Sundays?**
  Since it is unlawful to refuse to hire an applicant because of a religious affiliation, such questions could be perceived as discriminatory.

- **National Origin: Were you born in the U.S.? Are you a citizen of the U.S.?**
  It is better to state that if hired, it will be necessary to present identification in accordance with Immigration Reform Control Act (IRCA) requirements.

- **Family Relationship: Do you have any relatives currently employed in this company?**
  An employer cannot refuse to hire because the applicant has a relative working for the same business, unless one family member would work in a supervisory capacity over the other, or unless the employer could prove the existence of some other bona fide occupational disqualification.

- **Convictions/Arrests?**
  An employer may ask about relevant convictions but not about arrests. An employer should not have a blanket rule of rejecting all ex-convict applicants. Employers should instead consider the relationship between the crime and the job. Employers should state on the job application that a conviction will not necessarily bar employment. In assessing a conviction, the employer should consider how old or recent the conviction is, the age of the applicant when the crime occurred, the seriousness and nature of the crime, and any rehabilitation the applicant has undergone. Applicants should only be excluded from employment based on job-related convictions.

- **Driver's License/Insurance/Reliable Vehicle?**
  An employer can inquire about these issues if driving is an essential function of the job (but not for purposes of determining whether the person can get to work).

Giving and Getting References

The main risk in giving references is that the employer may end up defending a claim that adversely reflects on an employee's abilities or character. Under Oregon law, employers are protected if the statements:

- Relate to job performance
- Are made with a good-faith belief that they are true
- Serve a business interest or purpose
- Are limited to that specific business interest or purpose
- Are made on a proper occasion
- Are communicated to proper parties

Employers are not required to give references. However, a consistent policy should be adopted that one person or department will handle all requests for references. If the policy is to decline requests for references, prospective employers should be informed of the policy so no negative or positive reflection on the employee is imparted.

It is a good idea to require that all requests be in writing on company letterhead and to require a written release signed by the employee or former employee. Also, it is recommended that you keep a note of what was said.

When answering questions, avoid opinions and limit comments to documented observations. Do not discuss an employee's disability (if any), physical or mental limitations, medical, or claims history.

There is no law that requires reference checks. However, employers must exercise reasonable care to ensure that employees, customers, clients, and visitors are free from harm inflicted by unfit employees if the employer either knew or should have known of the employee's dangerous actions. Employers who fail to exercise reasonable care to screen out unfit employees may be sued for negligent hiring or negligent retention of unfit employees.

Some suggestions for getting references include the following:
- Write a letter requesting references from each employer listed
- Obtain a written release from the applicant and send this with the letter requesting references from each employer
- Verify educational degrees
- Look for gaps in employment history, obtain explanations for the gaps, and verify the explanation

Age Discrimination

Oregon law prohibits employment discrimination because a person is 18 years of age or older. This contrasts with the federal Age Discrimination in Employment Act, which protects employees 40 years of age or older. The Oregon statute applies to all Oregon employers.

Blacklisting

Blacklisting is the intentional prevention of the future employment of an employee by the former employer. Blacklisting usually occurs when the former employer makes representations to prospective employer(s) that the individual should not be hired. It should be distinguished from a reference, which is essentially a request for information about job performance. Blacklisting is an unlawful employment practice in Oregon.

Verifying Employee Eligibility

The Department of Homeland Security, Citizenship and Immigration Services, implements the law that requires employers to hire only American citizens and aliens who are authorized to work in the U.S. As a contractor with employees, you must verify the employment eligibility of anyone hired after November 6, 1986. The employee completes Section 1 and the employer completes Section 2 of Form I-9.

The law also prohibits discrimination in hiring and firing on the basis of citizenship status or national origin.

Form I-9 Requirements
As an employer, to comply with the Form I-9 requirements, you must:
- Complete Form I-9 and keep it on file for at least three years from the date of employment or for one year after the employee leaves the job, whichever is later.
- Verify on Form I-9 that you have seen documents establishing identity and work authorization. This must be done for both U.S. citizens and non-citizens.
- Accept any valid documents provided by your employees. You may not ask for more documents than those required, and you may not demand to see specific documents, such as a "green card," because that is considered an act of discrimination.
- Be aware that work authorization documents must be renewed on or before their expiration date. Form I-9 must be updated at the same time.

Avoiding Discrimination
To comply with the Immigration and Naturalization Act (INA) antidiscrimination provisions, an employer should:

- Let employees choose which documents to present as long as they prove identity and work authorization.
- Accept documents that appear to be genuine and related to the individual.
- Treat all people equally when you announce the job, take applications, interview, offer the job, and verify employment eligibility, hire, and fire.
- Avoid "citizens only" hiring policies.
- Give out the same job information over the phone and use the same form for all job applicants.
- Base all decisions about hiring and firing on job performance and on-the-job behavior rather than on appearance, accent, name, or citizenship status of employees.

Employers would be wise to develop training on Form I-9 procedures, implement a compliance program, and develop a tickler file as a reminder of when all Form I-9s need to be re-verified or when they can be destroyed.

Employers who do not comply with the Form I-9 requirements may face fines and penalties. Employers who discriminate may be required to pay fines and penalties, to hire or rehire the employee, and to pay back wages.

Hiring Procedures

Employment Application

When you hire new employees, make sure to use a written employment application. Make sure the application contains questions about any safety training a prospective employee may have received in the past. This will provide a point of reference so you will know what minimum training the employee has already received and what training you must provide.

Skills at Trades by Verifying References

Trade skills may be verified by checking with references listed on the employment application. In some cases, prospective employees may have certificates verifying that they have completed certain trade courses.

Train Employees on Safe Procedures for Trades

Training employees consists of two activities:

Education

Provide information so the employee learns the process and why it works, and develops attitudes and behaviors about the process.

Training

Explain how the process works and teach the employee the knowledge and skills needed to perform the process. In training, the emphasis is on performance.

Appendix A

Contact Information

U.S. DEPARTMENT OF LABOR FOR OREGON
Portland District Office U.S. Dept. of Labor, ESA Wage & Hour Division 1515 SW Fifth Avenue, Suite 1040 Portland, OR 97201-5445 503-326-3057
FEDERAL OSHA OFFICE - REGION 10
1111 Third Avenue, Suite 715 Seattle, WA 98101-3212 206-553-5930 www.osha.gov
OR-OSHA OFFICE
Oregon OSHA 350 Winter Street NE, Room 430 Salem, OR 97301-3879 503-378-3272 or 800-922-2689 (in Oregon) www.orosha.org
WORKERS' COMPENSATION DIVISION
Oregon State Workers' Compensation Division Employer Compliance 350 Winter Street NE Salem, OR 97309-0405 503-947-7815 email: wcd.employerinfo@state.or.us www.oregonwcd.org

National Council on Compensation Insurance (NCCI)
800-622-4123 and ask for the Oregon desk.
Insurance Agents
Ask your insurance agent if his or her agency provides workers' compensation coverage.
Insurance Companies
For a list of insurance companies providing workers' compensation insurance, contact: DCBS Small Business Ombudsman PO Box 14480 Salem, OR 97309-0405 503-378-4209

Appendix B

Bureau of Labor and Industries Office Locations

PORTLAND OFFICE
Portland 800 NE Oregon Street, Suite 1045 Portland, OR 97232 971-673-0761 971-673-0824 (Technical Assistance for Employers) Fax: 971-673-0762 www.oregon.gov/boli

FIELD OFFICES
Bend (Apprenticeship Division ONLY) 1645 NE Forbes Road, Suite 106 Bend, OR 97701 541-322-2435
Eugene 1400 Executive Parkway, Suite 200 Eugene, OR 97401 541-686-7623
Medford 119 N Oakdale Avenue Medford, OR 97501-2629 541-776-6270
Salem 3865 Wolverine Ave NE, Building E, Suite 1 Salem, OR 97305-1268 503-378-3292

Appendix C

Reference Materials

Order Bureau of Labor and Industries handbooks and posters here:
http://www.oregon.gov/boli/TA/Pages/T_Tabooks.aspx

Download required posting documents here:
http://www.oregon.gov/boli/TA/Pages/Req_Post.aspx

The following reference materials may be obtained from Oregon Bureau of Labor and Industries (BOLI).

Handbooks

Wage and Hour Laws	$40
Civil Rights Laws	$40
Family Leave Laws in Oregon	$40
Policy Writing Guidelines	$40
Employee Classification & Wage and Hour Exemptions	$30
Child Labor Laws	$15

Posters

Commonly Required Postings in Oregon (8-in-1) poster - English	$10
Commonly Required Postings in Oregon (8-in-1) poster - Spanish	$10
Guide to Employee Leave Laws in Oregon poster - English	$15
Commonly Required Postings in Oregon (6-in-1) poster - English *(for private employers with 24 or fewer employees in Oregon)*	$10
Commonly Required Postings in Oregon (6-in-1) poster – Spanish *(for private employers with 24 or fewer employees in Oregon)*	$10
Postings for Employers in Agriculture (11-in-1) poster – bilingual	$15

Chapter 2

Oregon Minimum Wage Poster   Free

Oregon Family Leave Act Poster   Free

"Why Do I Need Workers' Compensation Insurance?" - pamphlet may be obtained from the Workers' Compensation Division or viewed at www.cbs.state.or.us/wcd/communications/publications/2852.pdf.

Oregon Business Guides may be obtained from:

Business Information Center Public Service Building, Suite 151 255 Capitol Street NE
Salem, OR 97310-1327
503-986-2200
www.filinginoregon.com

Employment Division Central Office 875 Union Street NE
Salem, OR 97311
503-947-1488 (Oregon Business Information Center)

Sample Questions

CHAPTER 2

1. **Which is true about the employment of minors?**

   ❑ 1. Minors under 16 years of age are allowed to work in the construction field.

   ❑ 2. Minors are not required to have a Social Security card.

   ❑ 3. An employer must get an annual employment certification for each minor at the time the minor is employed.

   ❑ 4. Minors must be paid the Oregon minimum wage rate.

2. **Which is NOT true about the Prevailing Wage Rate law?**

   ❑ 1. It is also known as the "Little Davis-Bacon Act."

   ❑ 2. Employees on public improvement projects are paid prevailing wage rates for the entire project when the initial contract price is less than $50,000 and later increases to exceed $50,000.

   ❑ 3. The law applies to public improvements like major renovations, remodeling, or alteration of existing structures or roads that cost less than $50,000.

   ❑ 4. Contractors on a public improvement project where prevailing wage rates apply must post the rates in a conspicuous and accessible place on the project.

3. **Which of the following criteria is used as part of the "economics realities" test to determine whether an independent contractor status or an employee relationship exists?**

   ❑ 1. Degree of control by the employer.

   ❑ 2. Accommodation of special requests by the employee.

   ❑ 3. Number of hours worked in a week.

   ❑ 4. Level of experience of the employee.

Answers: 1. [4]
         2. [3]
         3. [1]

CHAPTER 3
CONTRACT LAW

Objectives

At the end of this chapter, you will be able to:

1. Identify and explain elements of contract law.
2. Understand the purpose of the following elements in a construction contract: the parties, scope of work to be performed, contract price and payment schedule, time for performance, substantial completion, retainage and responsibility for changes and delays.
3. Explain why it is important to have a clear, concise contract.
4. Recognize when a written contract is required by law.
5. Identify the advantages of written contracts and potential problems of oral contracts.
6. Identify the benefits of written change orders and potential problems of verbal changes.
7. State a contractor's responsibilities for his or her work and the work of others.
8. Describe the consequences to contractors and others for not carrying out their responsibilities.
9. Describe the difference between material and non-material breach of contract.
10. Identify and explain remedies for breach of contract, such as calculation of damages, cost of repair and delay damages, or liquidated damages.
11. Describe the types of dispute prevention and resolution including partnering, negotiation, mediation, arbitration, and litigation.
12. Describe the purpose of the "Buyer's Three Day Right to Cancel and Buyer's One Day Right to Cancel."

Overview

Contract law describes and controls the relationships between individuals when they agree to exchanges of items with value (for example, work for payment of money). A contract creates obligations or duties for certain individuals or "parties" to do or not to do a particular action. When the contract is in writing, it serves as proof of the individuals' or parties' obligations.

Elements of Contract Law

The four basic elements of contract law are: **formation, performance, breach**, and **remedies**.

Formation

To form a legally enforceable contract, the following basic elements are necessary:
- Parties with legal capacity
- An offer to provide a product or perform work
- An acceptance of the exact terms of the offer
- A valid (legal) purpose
- Consideration

Performance

- Contractor does the work
- Owner pays

Breach of Contract

- Contractor fails to do all the work, fails to do it on time, or fails to do it properly
- Owner fails all sums due or fails to pay on time

Remedies

- Monetary damages or specific performance can be ordered by a court to compensate for loss or injury caused by a breach of contract

When an offer is made and accepted on its exact terms, both the party making the offer and the party accepting the offer will be bound by the stated terms, and a contract is formed. Any "acceptance" that attempts to change or alter the terms of the original offer is not a true acceptance and does not lead to formation of a contract. Instead, it is a new offer, the prior offer is rejected, and a contract can only be formed if the other party accepts the new offer on its exact terms. A contract is formed only when the parties are in mutual agreement on all essential terms.

After the contract is formed, the parties to the contract are deemed to be in *privity of contract* and the performance of duties and responsibilities by the parties is based upon the terms of the contract. If one party does not perform as required, the party that did not satisfactorily perform has breached the contract. The other party may demand a remedy for damages.

Basic Definitions in Contract Law

To understand the law of contracts, it is necessary to become familiar with some terms that sound like "legal jargon" but have special meanings used in written laws and by the courts. The following definitions are general summaries. More detailed definitions are available in the Glossary.

Acceptance occurs when a party agrees to the exact terms of another party's offer. Offer and acceptance are the two basic elements in formation of a contract.

Breach of Contract occurs when a party does not do what the contract requires.

Changes are any new or different items that are not covered in the original contract. If a change is substantial, the parties should sign a change order.

Consideration is what a party offers to do if the other party performs contract obligations. Under the law, consideration can be actual performance (for example, a contactor building a house), or it can be a *promise* to perform or not perform some act. Whether a *promise* or *actual performance* is adequate consideration depends on what the offer asks for. In most construction contracts, the contractor's consideration is a promise to perform services or provide materials, and the owner's consideration is a promise to pay a specified amount for those services or materials.

Construction Contract means a written or oral construction agreement, including all plans, specifications, and addenda relating to activities including:
- Excavating, demolishing, and detaching existing structures and other preparation of land for making and placement of a building or structure.
- Creation or making of a building or structure.
- Alterations, partial construction, and repairs done in and upon a building or structure.

Contract is a mutually understood agreement that has a legal purpose and is made by two or more parties, each party having legal capacity.

Covenant is a term of a contract, either expressly stated by the parties or implied by law. Implied-by-law covenants are discussed later in this chapter.

Damages are financial losses that occur when there is a breach of contract. Examples of damages are money or profits lost by the contractor when the owner doesn't pay, or the cost to an owner to have a contractor's defective or incomplete work finished by another contractor. Awarding monetary damages is a remedy that a court may provide when there has been a breach of contract.

Developer means a contractor who owns property or an interest in property and arranges for construction.

General Contractor means a contractor whose business operations require the use of more than two unrelated building trades that the contractor supervises or performs. General contractor does not include contractors who perform work in CCB categories of specialty contractors or limited contractors. The general contractor is often referred to as the "prime" or "original" contractor - i.e., a contractor who has a direct contract with the property owner.

Legal Capacity means that a party to a contract has the right and ability to enter into a contract. In most cases, this means that the party is 18 years old and has the mental ability to understand the terms of the contract.

Material Supplier means any person or entity that provides materials or products under a construction contract by any contractual means including oral authorization, written contract, purchase order, price agreement, or rental agreement.

Mitigation of Damages is action taken by a non-breaching party to lessen or reduce the harm caused by a breach of contract.

Offer is what starts the process of forming a contract. In construction, an offer is generally in the form of a proposal, bid, or binding estimate to perform work or provide products or materials in return for payment.

Offeree is the person or business entity receiving an offer.

Offeror is the person or business entity making an offer.

Performance is doing what is required of a party by a contract.

Privity of Contract is the direct relationship that exists between parties to the same contract. *Privity of contract* is an important concept as it affects and limits the remedies of a party to a contract. In the most common construction situation, a general contractor and the property owner are parties to one contract, while the general contractor and subcontractors are parties to one or more separate contracts (in which the owner is not a party). The owner and general contractor, as parties to the same contract, are in *privity of contract* with each other and can sue each other for breach; the general contractor and subcontractor, as parties to another contract, are in *privity of contract* with each other and can sue each other for breach. Because the owner and subcontractor are not parties to the same contract, they are not in *privity of contract* and cannot directly sue each other for breach.

Remedies are the lawful actions that can be taken by a party who has been damaged by a breach of contract to enforce a right or recover damages.

Retainage is the holdback by a property owner or general contractor of a part of the price to be paid for work until conditions specified in a contract are satisfied.

Substantial Performance occurs when a party has made a good faith effort to perform his or her obligations under a contract and has completely performed all *essential* obligations. A contract may be substantially performed even if minor, nonessential obligations have not been fully performed.

Basic Requirements of a Contract (Formation)

In addition to understanding the requirements of a contract, it is important to note that the CCB regulates construction contracts and what must be contained in residential construction contracts. The CCB requires that contracts with residential property owners for over $2,000 must be in writing. In addition, if a contractor is required by the CCB to have a written contract, the CCB has a rule that specifies the minimum requirements of a written contract. The CCB's website, under the Contractor Forms section, includes the following forms to assist contractors with the CCB's written contract requirements: Residential Construction Contract Checklist and CCB Recommended Contract Addendum to Satisfy Contract Terms. See Appendix A for an example of a residential construction contract that includes the terms required by the CCB. Please note, however, that the example is for informational use only.

Parties with Legal Capacity
One party must offer to enter into a legal agreement and another party must accept the terms of the offer.

Legal capacity
Both parties entering into the contract must have legal capacity.
- Individuals must be 18 years of age or older.
- Individuals must not be operating under a legal disability, such as a court order depriving the individual of the ability to make contracts and appointing a legal representative to manage his or her financial affairs.

Business entities (such as corporations, limited liability companies, and limited liability partnerships) must be in compliance with state requirements by filing annual statements and required documents with the Secretary of State (except general partnerships and sole proprietorships), and complying with assumed business name requirements.

Licensed contractors

For construction contracts, contractors must be licensed with the CCB. Unlicensed contractors lack the legal capacity to perform work requiring a license, and courts generally will not permit unlicensed contractors to enforce contracts.

Offer

An offer is a promise made by one party to do, or not to do, a specific act or acts. The construction contractor usually makes the offer in the form of a proposal, bid, or binding estimate. A valid offer requires three things:

1. **Intent.** The parties must each intend to enter into a contract, and their spoken or written words must communicate that intention. Joking or offhand comments or discussion that may incidentally contain both an offer and acceptance are not sufficient to form a contract. The intent of the parties to be legally bound must be clear from their words and conduct.
2. **Legal capacity to enter contract.** In addition to age and other elements of legal capacity previously discussed, a contractor must be licensed and display his or her CCB license number on estimates, bid forms, business cards, and contracts.
3. **Definite statement of required terms:**
   - Identification of parties
   - Scope of work
   - Price

Besides the three requirements of a valid offer, it is recommended that the following terms also be included in the offer:
   - Time for performance of work
   - Schedule or project duration
   - Number of days of work
   - Special conditions that may affect the work like time, materials, or cost
   - How changes to the work will be requested and agreed upon (change orders)
   - Provisions for dispute resolution (may include mediation and/or arbitration).
   - Any other terms and conditions that may affect performance by the contractor or payment by the property owner or general contractor.

Acceptance

Acceptance of an offer occurs when a person to whom the offer has been directed makes an appropriate statement of agreement with the terms of the offer. For an acceptance to be valid, it must be voluntary (not the result of threats or made under duress), and the party accepting must have legal capacity to accept the definite and explicit terms of the offer. To form a contract, the acceptance must be of the *exact* terms of the offer. Any attempt to change terms is legally a rejection of the offer, and the changed terms become a counteroffer, which can then be accepted or rejected by the other party.

Example

A contractor's offer includes installation of 20 can lights at a given price. The owner responds by requesting only 10 can lights and specifying a lesser price. The owner's response is a rejection of the first offer and a counteroffer that the contractor can accept or reject. If the contractor decides to reject the counteroffer, he or she can make a new counteroffer (for example, only 10 can lights but at a higher price than the owner offered). The process continues until the parties are in full agreement on all terms, or until negotiations break off without formation of a contract.

Valid Legal Purpose

A contract must have a legal purpose in order to be enforceable. The courts will not enforce a contract that does not have a legal purpose. A legal purpose means:

- That the performance of the contract is not in and of itself unlawful, and
- That performance of the contract will not violate law.

Example 1

A contractor cannot enforce a contract to extort money from the homeowner. ("Pay me $1,000 extra for the work or I will steal your car.")

Example 2

A homeowner cannot force a contractor to perform a contract that requires the contractor to violate the building code. ("Use my architect's plans that call for less reinforcement because it's cheaper.")

Consideration

Consideration is required from all parties in order to form a contract. Consideration can be something actual, like money or property, or can be a promise to do or not to do some action. The terms of the offer determine what kind of consideration is needed to form a contract.

Example

A contractor's offer contains a promise to perform construction work and the owner promises to pay a specified amount for that work. The *promises* of the parties are sufficient legal consideration for a contract to be formed.

Contractor's Consideration

A contractor usually provides consideration by promising to perform specified work either directly or through a subcontractor. Once the contract is formed, the contractor then has the duty to do what was promised. The standard construction contract specifies the contractor's responsibilities and rights.

The contractor's primary contractual right is to be paid for the work. A well-drafted contract specifies when and how payment will be made, including when progress payments and final payment are due. The contract should define procedures for allowing and paying for added project costs. The contract should specify exact start and completion dates and discuss when time extensions or accelerations of time will be allowed. The contract establishes schedules for bonuses and for withholding pay because of incomplete or inadequate work, as well as establishing consequences for late work.

An owner's contract with a general contractor will ordinarily allow the general contractor to hire subcontractors, order materials, and implement whatever construction methods, processes, and coordination of activities the contractor thinks are appropriate. The contract may contain an escalation clause or describe how the contractor will be reimbursed for unexpected increases in the cost of labor, equipment, or materials.

The following are a number of basic responsibilities for contractors that are either implied or specifically stated in contracts:
- Give sufficient attention to the project to fully perform the required work in a timely manner
- Complete the project as specified
- Follow project designs, drawings, and specifications
- Obey all laws and regulations, including those dealing with employment, environmental protection, and safety
- Provide all relevant insurance coverage.
- Inform owners of any changes, delays, problems, or errors
- Act in good faith and deal fairly
- Warrant good workmanship

The general contractor is responsible for work performed by the subcontractors. He or she is obligated to provide adequate overall supervision. Inadequate supervision is the basis for many claims against general contractors.

Owner Consideration

The owner, in return, provides consideration by promising to pay, and then performs by paying the agreed amount as specified. In addition, the owner has the following obligations that are usually specifically stated or implied in the contract:
- Provide plans and specifications that are complete, accurate, drafted according to code, and suitable for the intended purpose of the contract.
- Make timely payments to the contractor and provide access to the job site. Even if the contract is silent on the matter, the owner has an implied duty to provide the contractor with access to the job site.

- Provide permits, fees, and licenses required before proceeding with the project. Under building codes, the property owner is responsible for obtaining construction permits. However, the contractor can offer to obtain the needed permits as a service. Under Oregon law, before the contractor performs any work, the required construction permits must have been obtained.

Owners are not allowed to interfere with the contractor's work, direction, work methods, or control. A contractor is considered by law to be an independent contractor and not the owner's employee. Owners who do not allow a contractor to proceed independently may be in breach of contract.

Among the owner's rights that may be found in a construction contract are the rights to:
- Make modifications, additions, or deletions to the project.
- Offer other contracts related to the project.
- Inspect project work without interfering with progress.
- Perform any work on which a contractor defaults.
- Use substantially complete portions of the work, so long as that use does not interfere with the progress of remaining work.
- Require a performance or payment bond from the contractor in addition to the surety bond each licensed contractor posts with the CCB.
- Accelerate or extend completion times under specified conditions.
- Retain a portion of progress payments until the contractor's work is complete.
- Withhold or deduct from payments due to pay for work that is incomplete or has not passed inspection.

Special Contract Relationships in Construction: *Privity of Contract*
If there is a general contractor, the general contractor (but not the subcontractors) is a party to a contract with the owner of the property. Since they are parties to the same contract, the general contractor and the owner are in *privity of contract* with each other.

Subcontractors are parties to contracts with the general contractor but not the property owner. The subcontractors and the general contractor are in *privity of contract* with each other.

Subcontractors are not in *privity of contract* with the property owner.

Example
An owner contracts with a general contractor to build an addition to a house, including installation of electrical wiring. Instead of performing this work directly, the general contractor contracts with a subcontractor to perform the electrical work. The electrician is a subcontractor of the general contractor.

The owner and the general contractor have signed one contract, and are in *privity of contract*. The electrician and general contractor are parties to a separate contract for the electrical work and are in privity of contract with each other. Since the owner and the electrician have not signed the same contract, the electrician is *not* in *privity of contract* with the property owner.

Performance

General Contractor, Subcontractor, and Supplier Duties

Contractors and subcontractors are obligated to perform their contractual duties unless those duties have been excused by a material breach of contract by the other party to the contract. Who has the right to enforce performance of those duties will vary depending on the parties to the contract.

General Contractor

The general contractor on a major project is usually the only contractor in a direct contract relationship with the owner. The responsibilities of the general contractor to the owner are to provide for completion of the entire project. The general contractor typically does not need to directly perform the work. Instead, the general contractor can, and often does, subcontract portions of the work.

Regardless of whether the general contractor has subcontracted for the performance of any part of the work, the general contractor is directly responsible to the owner for all performance. If a subcontractor or supplier fails to perform, the owner can hold the general contractor fully responsible.

The general contractor's responsibilities include the scheduling and coordination of trades, purchasing materials, and all construction work. Slow performance or delivery by a subcontractor or supplier will not usually serve as an excuse in the general contractor's dealings with the owner.

The general contractor also has the duty to provide for overall workplace safety. While both original contracts and subcontracts frequently address this issue, the general contractor has control over the job site and must maintain safe working conditions.

Subcontractors

Subcontracts are between the general contractor and other independent contractors, and the owner is generally not a party. Therefore, the subcontractor must look only to the general contractor in the event of a breach (subject, however, to the subcontractor's lien rights).

Suppliers
Suppliers furnish materials and equipment, in contrast to labor and services. Suppliers may have a contract with a subcontractor, the general contractor, and in some cases, with the owner of the project.

Performance
In the performance of their duties, general contractors, subcontractors, and suppliers are held to a standard of performance equivalent to the generally accepted standards and practices of the industry in the geographic area where the work is being performed. The owner is entitled to insist on compliance with the plans and specifications. The contractor must fully perform the essential elements of the work to achieve substantial completion. This is what the owner bargained for and this is what the owner is entitled to receive for his or her payments.

Substantial Completion
Unless otherwise specified, a contractor has fulfilled a contract when the project is substantially complete. However, although the performance of the contract may be substantially complete, the owner of a project may be allowed to set aside funds from the final payment sufficient to cover the cost of completing or correcting minor items necessary to achieve final occupancy.

The CCB defines "Substantial Completion" as follows:
- "Substantial Completion may occur at the time of but not be limited to the first occurring of any of the following events: final inspection is completed, certificate of occupancy is issued, the structure or portion of structure is in a habitable or usable condition, most or all of payment is made."
- Work under a contract warranty provision or repair to already completed work does not extend the date of substantial completion, except that removal and replacement of completed work may extend the date of substantial completion to the date the replacement work was substantially complete.

In determining substantial completion, the owner and the contractor frequently have different interpretations of when the project is adequate for the owner's beneficial use. For this reason, many contracts clearly state and define when the project will be deemed substantially complete. It is usually better for the contractor and owner to reach consensus on this issue before signing the contract then to wait until the project is nearing completion. A well-written contract can prevent delays in payment and the possible need for court action or other dispute-resolution activity.

Most construction contracts include both present and future duties that must be performed by a contractor. Present duties include performance of the work needed to reach substantial completion.

Future duties can include:
- Performance needed to comply with the warranty of good workmanship that is implied by law in every construction contract
- Performance needed to comply with explicit written warranties
- Performance of any contract duties of maintenance or continued service

Conditions – Acts or Events that Must Occur Before Performance is Due

Condition precedent is a legal term that describes an act or event that must occur before performance under a contract is required. If the act or event doesn't occur, the performance is excused.

Example
The contract states that the general contractor is not required to begin performance until the property owner provides a permit. If the owner does not obtain the permit, the contractor's duty to perform is excused.

If the owner does obtain a permit, the law says that the condition precedent has been *satisfied* and the general contractor must now perform.

Subcontractor Contracts
General Contractor Responsibilities for Work of Subcontractors
The general contractor is responsible to the property owner for performance of their contract. It is the general contractor's responsibility to determine who will perform the work. The general contractor may take a role in performing some activities, or may assign responsibilities to employees or subcontractors.

When work is subcontracted, the general contractor must verify that the subcontractor is a licensed independent contractor with active surety bond and liability insurance. If the subcontractor will perform electrical, plumbing, or HVAC activities, the general contractor must confirm with the Building Codes Division that the subcontractor is a registered business and licensed to perform the scope of work in the subcontract. In addition, the general contractor must maintain a list of subcontractors performing work on each project.

The list includes the subcontractor's name, address, and license numbers. This list must be delivered to the CCB within 72 hours after the CCB requests it from the general contractor.

Subcontract

Elements of a subcontract include the basic elements of a contract:
- Offer and acceptance
- Consideration
- Parties with legal capacity
- Legal purpose

Duties and Conditions

A subcontract is an agreement between the general contractor and a subcontractor. The role of the subcontractor is to perform certain aspects of construction work according to the original contract between the owner and the general contractor, and the subcontract with the general contractor. The subcontractor does not have a direct relationship (is not in *privity of contract*) with the owner but only with the general contractor.

Typically, subcontracts are awarded for work in specialty trades within the construction industry such as plumbing, heating, ventilation and air conditioning (HVAC), earthwork, and foundation. A subcontractor, unless prohibited by the terms of the subcontract, may contract with other contractors to perform parts of the subcontractor's work. In such a situation, just as the general contractor is responsible for the work of his or her subcontractors, the subcontractor is responsible for the sufficiency of the other's work.

Most subcontracts specify that subcontractors must comply with all the conditions of the general contract and the project documents. While verbal subcontracts may be valid for small jobs, a detailed written subcontract will help avoid many potential disputes. In some cases, the approval of the owner is required for each subcontract.

Consistent with the general or original contract, subcontractor payments can be negotiated and paid in a variety of ways. Virtually all subcontracts require the general contractor to pay subcontractors promptly following owner payments to the general contractor. See page 3-30 for more information relating to prompt payment regulations for public and private projects in Oregon. As with general contracts, subcontracts often contain terms describing progress payments, retainage, and bonding.

Mutual Concerns of Contracting Parties

A mutual concern of contracting parties is communication flow within performance. Once the general contractor begins work or assigns activities, it is important to establish a communication flow for monitoring and reporting progress of work. The owner is part of this communication flow through understanding progress billings and paying for work performed.

The following contract provisions have a bearing on communication flow:
- Making changes by means of approved change orders
- Coordinating payment schedule with progress of work
- Distributing revised project schedule

Suggested Checklist for Subcontractor's Construction Contracts
Subcontracts contain nearly all of the content found in a general construction contract. The provisions need to be consistent with the terms and conditions in the general contractor's contract with the owner.

A subcontractor can use the following in preparing a subcontract:
- The contractor's name, address, and license number
- The subcontractor's name, address, and license number
- The nature, general description, and scope of the project
- The exact description of the work to be subcontracted
- The address and general description of the property
- The starting and completion dates of the subcontracted work
- The identification of relevant drawings and specifications
- The subcontract amount and payment arrangements
- Proof of active surety bond and general liability insurance
- Workers' compensation coverage if nonexempt status
- Job-safety plan (recommended, not required)
- Attorneys' fees recovery provision
- Provisions for timely distribution of revised project schedules
- Process for making changes to the scope of subcontracted work by approved change orders
- Indemnity provision and appropriate coverage with property damage and liability insurance

Breach of Contract

A breach is an unexcused failure by a party to a contract to do what the contract requires. A party is in breach of a contract when, without a legally sufficient excuse, there is a failure to fully and properly perform a duty.

Material or Immaterial Breach
When a *material* breach occurs, it creates a right in the other party to enforce contract remedies. An *immaterial* breach may not create enforcement remedies.

Determining Whether a Breach is Material or Immaterial

The following factors determine whether a breach is *material* or *immaterial* (in other words, the seriousness of a breach).

- The importance of the breach.

Example

Walking off the job before it is half finished would be material; failing to completely clean the job site each day would ordinarily be immaterial.

- Whether the breach was caused as a result of negligence, or if the breaching party acted deliberately with knowledge that harm to the other party would occur.
- The amount of harm suffered by the non-breaching party.
- What is required to cure the harm suffered by the other party.
- Whether or not the non-breaching party could lessen the harm suffered and what it would take to do so. Measures taken by the non-breaching party to lessen harm are called "mitigation of damages."

Example

The owner could have prevented damage by reattaching a piece of plastic that came loose over an opened window while the owner was on-site and tools were handy (immaterial), or

Example

It was necessary for the owner to re-bid the entire project when the original contractor walked off the job (material).

Consequences of Material or Immaterial Breach

Material Breach

A material breach is one that will cause great harm or substantially lessen the value of the contract for the non-breaching party.

Example

Failure to use a specified type of product described in the contract and important for the structural integrity of the project would be a material breach.

A material breach can have several consequences, among them:

- Canceling the non-breaching party's duty to perform contract obligations.
- Giving the non-breaching party an immediate right to pursue enforcement remedies.

Immaterial Breach

An immaterial breach is one that does not significantly lessen the value of the contract for the other party or does not result in significant harm to that party.

Example

A delay of one day past the scheduled date for completion would not generally be considered material, unless the contract specified that *time is of the essence* or had a liquidated damages clause for late completion.

Depending on the type of breach and the amount of harm suffered by the non-breaching party, damages may be awarded, but an immaterial breach will not allow the non-breaching party to terminate the contract.

Remedies for Breach of Contract

When a breach of contract occurs, the non-breaching party must decide what type of remedy to seek. The choice will depend on whether the non-breaching party wants to void the contract or seek damages for the breach. The choice of what type of remedy to seek is called "election of remedies."

Legal and Equitable Remedies

Courts have the power to grant two types of remedies: legal and equitable. Legal remedies for breach of contract include actions for damages, which is the remedy most often applied to construction contract disputes. Equitable remedies include rescission, reformation, and injunctions and are only granted if there is no adequate legal remedy available. In most construction contract cases, equitable remedies are not available because the legal remedy of damages will be sufficient to cure harm suffered by the non-breaching party.

Rescission is a remedy that is intended to restore the parties to their original positions before the contract existed

Rescission and restitution are not usually awarded in construction contract cases. There are two types of rescission. Legal rescission occurs when the parties to a contract mutually agree to cancel their respective obligations and return to their pre-contract positions. Equitable rescission is available only through the courts.

Note: Buyer's Three-Day Right to Cancel

Oregon law (ORS 83.710-83.750) contains a mandatory, three-day right of a buyer to cancel a home solicitation contract when the contract is solicited at any place that is not the seller's permanent place of business. A construction contract is subject to this law if there is a personal solicitation made by the contractor or the contractor's agent and the contractor's offer is accepted anywhere other than the contractor's permanent place of business. Regardless of who initiates the contact, in every such situation, the property owner must be given notice of his or her right to rescind the contract.

When the property owner cancels the contract within the specified time, the contractor must deliver to the owner all payments or other evidence of money owed by the owner (such as promissory notes or contracts calling for installment payments) within 10 business days, and the owner must make available any goods or materials delivered to the property by the contractor within 20 calendar days.

In the case of any contract fitting the definition of a home solicitation sale, the contractor is taking a great risk in performing any services or delivering any goods before the owner's right of cancellation expires.

If the contractor provides services of a non-emergency nature and the contract is then cancelled in a timely manner, the contractor is not entitled to compensation for the work performed.

Example
A contractor is distributing flyers advertising his or her services and meets with a homeowner who opens the door. The two parties sign a contract during their meeting. This is a home solicitation contract as described above.

Note: Buyer's One-Day Right to Cancel.
Oregon law (ORS 701.310) permits a property owner to cancel any initial contract for construction, improvement, or repair of a residential structure by giving the contractor a written notice of cancellation prior to midnight of the next business day. Some exceptions apply such as work already substantially begun.

The buyer is required to provide the contractor a written notice of cancellation. The contractor does not have any notice requirements.

The form of notice specified by ORS 83.710-83.750 (i.e., Buyer's Three-Day Right to Cancel) is as follows:

NOTICE OF BUYER'S RIGHT TO CANCEL

(1) (Date) You, the buyer, may cancel this agreement without any penalty, cancellation fee or other financial obligation by mailing or delivering a notice to the seller within THREE BUSINESS DAYS from the above date.

(2) If you cancel:

    (a) Any property you traded in, any payments you made under the sales contract and any checks or notes you signed will be returned within 10 business days following receipt by the seller of your notice of cancellation. Any security interest that arises from the transaction will be canceled.

    (b) You may either make available to the seller at your residence, in substantially as good condition as when received, any goods delivered to you under the sales contract or you may comply with the seller's instructions regarding the return shipment of the goods at the seller's expense and risk.

    (c) If you make the goods available to the seller at your residence and the seller does not pick up the goods within 20 days of the date of your notice of cancellation you may keep or discard the goods without further obligation,

    (d) If you do not make the goods available to the seller, or if you agree to return the goods to the seller and you do not return the goods, you must perform all of your obligations under the sales contract.

(3) To cancel this transaction, mail or deliver a signed and dated copy of this notice or other written expression of your intention to cancel, or send a telegram, to (name of seller) at (address of seller's place of business) not later than 12 midnight on (date), the third business day after you signed the written agreement or offer to purchase.

I HEREBY CANCEL THIS TRANSACTION

_____

(Signature of Buyer)   (Date)

Damages

Damages compensate the non-breaching party for economic losses arising from a breach of contract. Such losses can occur as a result of **reliance** on the contract, or because the non-breaching party's **expectation of gain** (usually called the "benefit of the bargain") has been lost.

Enforcement Through Damages

A lawsuit or other action (such as arbitration) seeking damages is the usual way to enforce a construction contract.

Before a party has a right to seek enforcement of a contract, two things must occur:
- There must have been a breach of the contract by the other party; and
- The party seeking enforcement must have suffered economic or other loss as a result of the breach.

The usual remedy for breach of contract is monetary damages. Monetary damages awarded in a breach of contract action will be calculated to include:
- Actual losses suffered by the non-breaching party.
- The benefits that would have been received from performance of the contract by the non-breaching party (called the "benefit of the bargain" by lawyers and judges). For the contractor, benefit of the bargain will include the profit the contractor would have made from the job. For the owner, benefit of the bargain is usually the difference between the original contract price and the amount the owner actually had to pay to have the work completed by a different contractor after a breach by the original contractor.

Expectation (Benefit of the Bargain) Damages

In a simplified example of a construction contract, if the property owner breaches by not paying, the contractor's expectation damages will equal the net profit that would have been received if payment in full had been made. If it is the contractor who breaches, the property owner's expectation damages will be the difference between what the owner agreed to pay the breaching contractor, and the amount the owner must pay to complete the work after the breach occurs. The purpose of awarding expectation damages to the non-breaching party is to provide the benefits that would have been received if the contract were fully performed by both sides (the benefit of the bargain).

Reliance Damages

The purpose of reliance damages is to return the non-breaching party to the position he or she would have been in if the contract had not been made. Reliance damages are usually an alternative to expectation damages. They are used when it is not possible to show with any reasonable certainty the amount of the expectation damages, and in cases where a breach occurs very early in the course of the contract. Reliance damages will ordinarily be measured by the costs expended by the non-breaching party in performing (or getting ready to perform) the contract up to the breach date.

Example

An owner and contractor enter into a written contract for the construction of a wooden deck. In preparation for performance, the contractor purchases the necessary materials and is preparing to have them delivered to the job site when the owner tells the contractor that the owner is canceling the contract. Reliance damages for the contractor would equal the contractor's actual cost of purchasing the materials, assuming that the contractor cannot return them without charge or use them within a very short time on another job. (See the discussion of the duty to mitigate elsewhere in this chapter.)

Liquidated Damages

Liquidated damages consist of an amount of money agreed upon by the parties as being fair compensation to the innocent party if a breach of contract occurs. The amount is included in a special provision of the contract that must be carefully worded to be enforceable by the courts. The amount of liquidated damages must reasonably estimate the actual damages that would be suffered in the event of a breach. If the amount stated in the contract is so large it is out of proportion to the harm that may be suffered, a court may refuse to award the amount stated in the contract.

Special

Special damages arise due to the special nature or circumstances of the non-breaching party or the project, and may be awarded by a court to cover losses not included in "benefit of the bargain" damages.

Example

An owner dependent on a wheelchair is moving into a new home and hires a contractor to build ramps and other accessibility devices. The contractor fails to perform the work properly and the owner suffers additional injuries when a ramp collapses. Benefit of the bargain damages would compensate the owner for the extra cost of having the work done properly by another contractor. The court may also award special damages to cover the cost of the owner's physical injuries and loss of use of his or her new home.

Consequential

Consequential damages are indirect losses to the injured party. These damages are recoverable if the injured party can prove that the damages were foreseeable at the time the contract was made.

Example

An individual inherits a piece of property, but his or her ownership is conditioned upon constructing a residence on the property within a specified period of time. The individual then contracts with a builder, including a provision that the residence must be constructed within the required time and explaining the reason for the time requirement. The builder defaults and breaches the contract. The individual contracts with another builder to finish the construction, but completion comes too late and ownership of the property passes to another.

In this situation, the individual would have two claims for damages from the breaching builder:

- General damages in the amount of the difference between the total amount paid to construct the residence and the amount of the original contract.
- Consequential damages equal to the value of the property the individual lost as a result of builder's breach.

Measurement of Damages

Certainty

All damages, whatever their nature, must be proved with reasonable certainty to be recoverable. A claim for damages based on speculation or guesswork is not sufficient. Generally, there must be clear and objective evidence of the amount of damages actually sustained to allow recovery. A property owner's damages for a contractor's breach may be determined with certainty by the difference in cost necessary to bring in another contractor to perform the work. A contractor's lost profit in a job may be calculated by subtracting the cost of labor and materials (and related overhead expenses) from the total contract price.

Other ways to prove damages with certainty are testimony from expert witnesses or the records of other businesses to show that a contractor's calculation of damages is in line with actual industry standards. The more objective the basis for calculation, the more certain the proof of damages.

Mitigation

The non-breaching party has a duty to minimize the damage it suffers as a result of the breach. Both expectation and reliance damages will be reduced by the amount that could have been avoided if the non-breaching party had taken reasonable measures to reduce the harm.

Foreseeability

Damages will be limited to those suffered as a predictable result of the breach. Courts and attorneys refer to such predictable damages as being "foreseeable." Whether certain damages claimed are foreseeable is a factual determination made on a case-by-case basis.

Example

A property owner can easily predict that a contractor will lose both expenses and profit if the owner refuses to pay for work performed. Those damages would be foreseeable. However, it would not be foreseeable that the owner's failure to pay would cause the contractor to drink heavily and cause the complete failure of the contractor's business. Accordingly, the owner would be responsible for damages to compensate the contractor for the expenses and lost profit from this one job, but would not be liable for damages for the failure of the contractor's business.

Specific Performance as an Equitable Remedy

Specific performance is an equitable remedy that is rarely available in construction contract law. In a breach of contract action, the doctrine of specific performance requires the breaching party to perform a specific act, usually what they had agreed to perform under the terms of the contract. A court may grant specific performance when money damages would provide inadequate compensation for the breach.

Types of Contracts: Verbal and Written

Verbal Contracts

Also referred to as "oral" or "spoken" contracts, this contract category refers to contracts that are not in writing. Unless prohibited by law, verbal contracts are valid. However, even in those instances where a verbal contract is valid, enforcing the contract terms may be difficult or impossible.

Example

An owner and contractor enter into a verbal contract to build a deck. The owner says the deck was to be 16 feet wide, the contractor says the agreed width was 14 feet. The parties take their dispute to court, and each side testifies as to their understanding on the deck width. The court hears directly contradictory testimony, and has no written contract it can use to settle the matter. Under the circumstances, the court believes the owner is the more truthful witness. The contractor loses.

Although verbal contracts may be legally permitted for construction jobs of $2,000 or less, the CCB recommends using a written contract for every job.

Written Contracts

A written contract is a negotiated document, signed by and identifying all parties, explaining the consideration given by each party, and stating the rights and duties of each party. Written contracts are required for all residential construction jobs between the property owner and the contractor where the consideration to be paid is more than $2,000. In addition, as mentioned above, the CCB has regulations that require specific terms to be placed in written contracts in the situations where the CCB requires a written contract. The CCB can penalize a contractor for failing to abide with the written contract requirements.

When the contract is put in writing, it describes the agreement of the parties, with terms and conditions, and serves as proof of the parties' obligations. Contractors may work with an attorney in drafting a contract appropriate for the contractor's business and typical projects, or contractors can use standard forms with general terms and conditions that are common to construction contracts. Form contracts are available from trade associations and office supply vendors. Some of the trade associations are listed in Appendix B, and contractors can adapt these general contract forms to specific projects when creating contractual relationships.

In addition, written contracts are required for a variety of other business transactions, including all real estate transactions and various commercial transactions. The Statute of Frauds requires a written contract for the sale of goods having a value of $500 or more and in all circumstances where performance of contract duties may take longer than a year.

Explanation and Example
There are exceptions to this rule that apply to direct purchases of goods with immediate payment. Frequently, contractors make contracts with suppliers without realizing it, such as opening an account with a lumber company. This is a contract – the lumber company promises to deliver lumber and the contractor agrees to pay when billed.

Advantages of Written Contracts
Some of the advantages of using written contracts follow:
- Written contracts provide a much higher level of certainty than verbal contracts so there is less potential for disagreement regarding the rights and duties of the parties.
- By including a provision allowing for recovery of attorneys' fees, a written contract can permit recovery of legal fees in the event of a dispute.
- A written contract can precisely state warranty terms (rather than relying on implied warranties).
- A written contract can provide for alternative dispute resolution (for example, partnering, mediation, or arbitration).
- Less ambiguity can lead to easier enforcement. Because of the certainty of terms, a written contract is usually easier to enforce.

Change Orders
When a change in the work is necessary or desired by the parties, a change order needs to be processed. While verbal change orders can alter a valid verbal contract for work having a total value of less than $2,000, for the reasons noted above, all contracts and all change orders should be in writing.

The advantages of written change orders are similar to those of written contracts. A written and approved change order:

- Describes and serves as proof the parties agreed to the change
- Sets payment for performance of the change
- Brings the change within the scope of work to be performed under the contract and its general terms and conditions

Elements of Change Orders

It is common for an owner to verbally request a change in the project, but it is important that the contractor obtain a written, signed, and approved change order. All change orders should include the following matters:

- Description of the change(s).
- Descriptions of any increase or decrease in compensation to be paid to the contractor.
- Date of change order.
- If the change order will materially affect the project completion date, a new date must be agreed upon and included in the written change order.
- Signatures of the parties to the original contract or subcontract. A valid, written change order needs to be signed by both the owner and the contractor, or for a subcontract, by the general contractor and the subcontractor.

Situations Calling for Change Orders

Time Extensions

Unavoidable conditions may arise that delay the construction project. Some delays are justifiable; others are not. A contract often addresses justifiable conditions that merit a time extension. When these conditions lead to a delay, the parties should sign a written change order providing for an extension to the completion date. In such cases, the contractor does not breach the contract or face payment of damages.

Examples of justifiable delays that may lead to time extensions are:

- Owner/architect project changes
- Owner/architect start date changes
- Owner/architect project design errors
- Owner/architect project additions
- Legal delays (not caused by the contractor)
- Public agency/utility delays (not caused by the contractor)
- Environmental delays
- Extreme weather delays (extreme rain, etc.)
- Labor strike, civil uprising, or war
- Acts of God

Contracts frequently contain a provision that provides for a project time extension for owner-caused delays. Some contracts designate that the owner pays a contractor's expenses arising from an owner-caused delay. Other contracts specify that owners are not liable for damages or expenses stemming from owner-caused delays.

Time extensions are usually not authorized for conditions that a reasonable contractor should have anticipated or for conditions that existed when the contractor signed the contract. For example, in parts of Oregon an extension would be given because of a flood, but would probably not be given because of excessive rain.

Whenever a contractor determines that a significant construction delay is possible, the contractor should immediately notify the owner in writing regarding the exact nature of the delay. Failure to do so may result in denial of a time extension.

A cautious contractor must plan for delays, develop contingency plans to help avoid delays, and deal promptly and truthfully with the owner when delays arise. A display of good planning and adoption of contingency plans to avoid delays may lead the owner to be flexible and grant time extensions not required by the contract if unavoidable delays occur.

However, it is foolish to rely on the good will of the owner, who may be facing substantial time pressures of his or her own. Appropriate contract time schedules for performance and good planning are the best defenses against potentially damaging delays. (See also the Scheduling and Project Management sections in Chapter 6.)

Time Accelerations

An owner may include an option in the contract to direct the contractor to complete the project before the established completion date. In such cases, the contract should specifically state that the owner would pay any additional expenses of the contractor that are a result of accelerating the project.

If a project has been delayed through the fault of the contractor, an owner may require acceleration of performance of the balance of the contract work to meet the original completion date. In such cases, the contractor may be liable for any added acceleration expenses.

Concealed or Differing Site Conditions

Concealed or unusual and unforeseen site conditions, or site conditions different from those the parties expected at the time of the contract formation often lead to construction delays. Examples of such conditions are the discovery of dry rot during a bathroom remodel or the discovery of rock formations requiring blasting during an excavation project.

A well-drafted construction contract will include a description of the steps to be taken to complete the project when unexpected conditions occur. Such steps may include:

- negotiation by the parties of adjustments in the scope of work, time of completion, and price through signing a written change order; and
- providing for a method (such as mediation and/or arbitration) to resolve matters that the parties cannot negotiate.

During the bidding process, the owner is obligated to fully disclose all available information pertaining to the site. At the same time, the contractor is obligated to assess the information provided and compare it to other known information and the findings of any pre-bid site inspection. Contracts frequently contain disclaimers that say the owners and architect are not liable for variances in the subsurface data they supply, and that contractors must themselves investigate the actual conditions.

If project documents contain mistaken or misleading information about the site, the owner may be liable for added construction costs. Otherwise, the contractor can only collect additional costs arising from site conditions to the extent the contract permits.

Dealing with Verbal Requests for Changes

Frequently, a party to a contract will verbally request changes in the work. When there is a written contract between the parties, the contractor has the legal right to insist on a written change order for every requested change and should do so as good business practice. Failure to insist on a written change order could result in performance of additional work without the ability to legally enforce the right to receive payment for that work. Even in the rare situation when a valid verbal contract for construction work is permitted and has been formed by the parties, a written change order will help avoid conflicts and misunderstandings. Remember, the first rule of construction contracts should be "get it in writing." Verbal contracts and verbal change orders should be avoided.

Other Forms of Contracts

Implied (Unjust Enrichment)

An implied contract is one that is not formed by an explicit agreement of the parties. Instead, it is inferred in law from acts or conduct of the parties that show the existence of an agreement between them. In certain situations, a court will examine the conduct of parties and the circumstances surrounding their transaction, and will determine that a contract can be implied from the conduct and circumstances to prevent one party from unjustly benefiting at the expense of the other party.

[Note: Oregon law also adds to every contract (written, oral, or implied), certain "implied covenants," including a covenant that each party will act in good faith and deal fairly. For construction contracts, this means an implied warranty of good workmanship by the contractor. These implied covenants are different from the concept of implied contract, but it is important to remember that they will exist in every construction contract, whether or not they are stated in the terms agreed to by the parties.]

Quasi Contract

A quasi contract is neither a verbal nor written contract; in fact, it is not a contract at all, because there was never an actual agreement between the parties as to all essential terms. Rather, a quasi contract is an obligation created by law in circumstances where one party receives a benefit from the actions of another, and it would *unjustly enrich* the party receiving the benefit if no compensation was paid.

Example

A contractor agrees with a property owner that he or she will construct a retaining wall on a specified parcel of property. Through a simple mistake, the contractor builds the wall on an adjacent parcel of property also owned by the same owner. No contract for that work was ever formed by the parties, because their discussions dealt entirely with construction on the other property, but it turns out the owner intended to build a retaining wall on the other property at a later date. Nonetheless, if a court were to find that construction of the retaining wall on the other property did confer an actual benefit on the owner, then to prevent the owner from being unjustly enriched at the expense of the contractor, a court may find that a quasi contract exists and require the owner to pay the contractor the value of the services rendered.

Special Categories of Construction Contracts

Construction contracts are often categorized by the way compensation is measured or paid, or by the type of work to be performed. The following describe common types of construction contracts.

Cost-Plus-Fee

The contractor will be paid all costs of materials, supplies, subcontractors, services and overhead, plus an agreed-upon fee in a specific dollar amount or percentage of the total expenditures.

Unit Price

This form of contract is used in situations where specific tasks, each of which can be separately priced, are to be performed. A price is fixed for each task or unit of the work, and the total cost is the number of units times the price per unit.

Time and Materials

The contractor will be paid the actual (or marked up) costs of all materials, supplies, subcontractors, and services used plus an hourly fee for time spent on the project.

Guaranteed Maximum Price

The contractor will be paid for time and materials, supplies, subcontractors, and services up to a maximum amount that is agreed upon by the parties. Progress payments are frequently provided for in this form of contract. Sometimes, such a contract will also specify the minimum price that will be paid to the contractor.

Lump Sum

The contractor will be paid a set price for the work to be performed, usually due at completion of the work.

Principles of Contract Interpretation

For the most part, parties are free to establish the terms of their own contracts. When a dispute occurs, a court or arbitrator will enforce the contract according to its meaning and the intent of the parties. For this reason, it is important that contractors carefully read contract language. If there is any doubt as to the meaning of contract terms, contractors should seek legal advice. Legal advice obtained during the process of forming the contract can help to prevent problems or disputes from occurring.

There are commonly used terms that appear over and over again in written contracts. These provisions require special attention while negotiating the contract. Such terms can affect the scope of work, time, and price provisions of a contract, and can have a substantial impact on contractor and owner rights and duties. The following are general descriptions of how these terms have been interpreted by courts over the years, but a contractor who sees these terms in a written contract may want the advice of legal counsel before signing.

"Time is of the Essence"

Construction contracts frequently contain conditions relating to time, in particular the project starting and completion dates. If a contract is silent on the time for performance of work, the courts will infer a reasonable time for performance. When the contract states that "time is of the essence," the completion date or time is critical and time itself has a high value. When a contract provides that "time is of the essence," failure to meet a performance deadline can be a breach of contract. In addition to being grounds for a breach of contract, "time is of the essence" provisions can affect compensation under a contract. Contracts often stipulate rewards for early completion and impose damages for late completion. When "time is of the essence," the dates for performance, bonuses, and penalties are strictly enforced.

Liquidated Damages

Liquidated damages provisions set a dollar amount that will be forfeited, or paid, if a certain type of breach of contract occurs. Special contract drafting rules apply to liquidated damages provisions and an attorney should be consulted before including them in a contract.

Contract Price and Payment Schedule

A written contract will state the contract price and may indicate a payment schedule.

Example

In a contract that will last several months, the payment schedule may provide for monthly payments and may also specify dates for submission of invoices. The payment schedule may provide for retainage by the owner of part of each invoice amount. Retainage is a portion of the agreed upon contract price deliberately withheld until the work is substantially complete, or upon the occurrence of some other event as per the terms of the contract, to assure that the contractor or subcontractor will satisfy its obligations and complete their work according to the terms of the contract. Retainage does not exceed 5 percent on Oregon public improvement projects. However, the percentage of retainage in private projects can be set at any amount the parties agree upon. Retainage in a contract between an owner and general contractor is usually reflected in the contracts between the general contractor and the subcontractors.

A construction contract may also provide for retainage by the owner of part of each invoice amount until the contractor's performance is complete.

It is important for the contractor to negotiate the payment schedule with an eye toward the cash-flow needs of the business. This includes the financial obligations incurred from performance of the project like paying direct job costs, business overhead, and profit. The contractor's project schedule can be used in planning approximate dates for progress billings and negotiating a payment schedule.

Different types of construction contracts will involve different calculations of progress payment due amounts.

Lump-Sum Contract

Payment requests are typically prepared by estimating the percentage of work completed and in place, including the percentage of work completed by subcontractors based on their submitted invoices.

Unit-Price Contract
Requests for payments are typically based on actual quantities of each bid item completed to date. The contract generally states how the parties will determine the completed quantities.

Cost-Plus-Fee Contract
Payments to the contractor under a cost-plus-fee contract are generally based on reimbursement of expenses incurred by the contractor during the preceding performance period, plus an agreed-upon fee for the contractor's services. Maintenance by the contractor of complete and accurate cost records is essential for preparation and support of payment requests.

Within each type of construction contract, Oregon law requires provisions that call for timely payments to contractors.

Oregon Private Owner Prompt Payment Requirements
By laws adopted in 2003, (see ORS 701.620-701.640), construction contracts in which the owner is a private party (rather than a government or public agency) *may* provide for progress payments if performance of the contract is expected to take less than 60 days, but *must* contain provisions for progress payments if the work is expected to take longer. An owner is generally required to make payments within 14 days of billings by the contractor, and the contract must provide for 30-day billing cycles unless the contractor agrees to a different cycle and that agreement is spelled out on each page of the plans and specifications. The law does have provisions for handling disputes and specifications for appropriate billings by the contractor. Upon completion of work, final payment must be made within seven days.

Oregon Public Owner Prompt Payment Requirements
Contracts between a public agency, as the property owner, and a contractor have special requirements in Oregon law to assure prompt payment (See ORS 279C.550-279C.570). All such contracts must include provisions for progress payments and must provide for payment within the earlier of 30 days after submission of an invoice or 15 days after approval of that invoice by the public agency. The law also contains provisions for interest on late payments, and handling disputes.

Scope of Work
To avoid uncertainty and help prevent disputes, the scope of work to be performed should be detailed in the construction contract. If there is insufficient detail, a dispute could lead to an attempt by a court or arbitrator to determine the intent of the parties at the time the contract was formed. In defining the scope of work, the contractor may reference plans and specifications used in preparing the contract price, or identify such plans and specifications as an exhibit to the contract.

Enforceability of a Contract
Elements of a Valid Contract
Only contracts that are properly formed and contain all required elements will be valid. The elements necessary for a valid contract are:
- Parties with legal capacity
- An offer
- An acceptance of the exact terms of the offer
- Legal purpose
- Consideration

In addition to the foregoing elements, a contract's terms must be sufficiently clear and definite so that the parties understand them at the time of entry into the contract. The more clear, precise, and well defined the terms of the contract, the more likely it will be enforceable. As mentioned above, the CCB has requirements relating to contract terms that must be placed in contracts with residential property owners for over $2,000.

Unenforceable Contracts
Verbal or written contracts may be unenforceable because of a failure to comply with all the elements of contract formation. Sometimes even a contract that is validly formed will be unenforceable because of practical considerations.

Types of Legally Unenforceable Contracts
Void Contracts
A void contract has no legal force or binding effect generally because the purpose of the contract is illegal or against public policy.

Example
A contract that requires performance of a crime.

Voidable Contracts
Even if a contract is made for a legal purpose, some contracts may be subject to cancellation:

- **Mutual Mistake:** Both parties are mutually mistaken with regard to a material fact.

  ##### Example
  Both the owner and contractor believe at the time of forming the contract that permits can be obtained for the work to be performed, but in reality permits cannot be obtained because of zoning issues.

- **Lack of Legal Capacity of One or Both Parties:**

    Example

    A contract made by a 15-year-old child will be subject to cancellation if it is not for a necessity of life such as food, clothing, shelter, or medical treatment.

    Example

    A contract made by an unlicensed contractor for work requiring a license is unenforceable by the unlicensed contractor. Even if he or she performs the work, the owner may not be legally required to pay.

Contracts Unenforceable as a Practical Matter

Sometimes, contracts are unenforceable even if they appear to be legally valid. This can occur when:

- Contract terms are too vague and uncertain to interpret.
- The defaulting party is "judgment proof." In other words, available assets are insufficient to pay damages awarded in litigation.

Defenses to Claims of Breach of Contract

Defenses to breach of contract apply to situations where a breach of contract claim is alleged. The law recognizes a number of defenses that can protect a party from liability arising from a failure to fully perform or from incorrect performance. These defenses may lessen, or completely prevent, liability for payment of damages.

Impracticability/Impossibility

It is a defense to a claimed breach that performance is physically impossible because of circumstances beyond the control of the obligated party.

Example

If a contract calls for steel support beams, but wartime conditions have diverted all steel to military uses, then performance is impossible.

Naturally, a party must exercise all reasonable measures to attempt to complete performance, but if it is truly impossible, then the party is relieved of the duty.

Illegality

An act or obligation that is illegal and contrary to legal principles may not be the subject of a contract. A contract is not enforceable when it is formed around an illegal purpose, such as performance that is criminal or against public policy.

Coercion or Duress

A contract is not enforceable when an individual is threatened or forced to agree or perform against his or her free will.

Mistake

Mistake as to a material fact can be a defense to breach of contract claims, but a mistake made by only one party is not a defense. Only mistakes made by both parties as to the same material fact will serve as a defense.

Unilateral Mistake

A unilateral mistake is defined as a mistake or misunderstanding as to the terms or effect of a contract by one of the parties but not by the other. A unilateral mistake is usually not a defense to breach of contract claims.

Mutual Mistake

A mutual mistake of a material fact is a defense to an alleged breach of contract. If it can be established that both parties were in error regarding a major fact leading to the contract formation, the contract may be determined to be null and void, or the contract may be reformed (this means that the court rewrites the contract to agree with the actual intent of the parties at the time of formation). Use of this defense is extremely limited, and a mistake by one party will not usually void the contract unless the other party knew or should have known about the mistake and tried to take advantage of the situation.

Fraud

Fraud is deliberately giving false information, or deliberately withholding information known to be important. If a party enters into a contract as a result of fraud by the other party regarding a material matter, the contract may be void. It is a principle of the law that contracts should be maintained as valid if at all possible. If the fraud is only with regard to an immaterial matter, a court might decide not to invalidate the whole contract. This defense is difficult to use, as it requires proof of the falsity of the information, as well as proof that the party making the false statement knew it was false and had the intent to deceive.

Repudiation of the Contract by the Other Party

Letting the other party know, by word or action, that the first party no longer intends to be bound by a contract is called "repudiation." When the second party receives notice of this intent, that second party's duty of performance is terminated. If the party who repudiated the contract later sues for breach, the other party can use the repudiation as a defense. Use of this defense is always tricky, and the party relying on the defense must present evidence that will convince the court that repudiation occurred.

If a contractor intends to use this defense, it is good practice to provide notices to the other party of that party's repudiation and to state in the notice that the contractor will consider the contract repudiated if the other party does not perform all outstanding obligations within a specified period of time.

Performance Excused – Failure of Condition Precedent

A party can defend against a breach of contract claim by showing that a condition precedent (i.e., an event which must occur before performance under a contract becomes due) did not occur.

Example

An electrical specialty subcontract may provide that the subcontractor is not required to begin performance until special materials ordered by the general contractor arrive at the site. Arrival at the site of those special materials is a condition precedent to the subcontractor's duty to perform. If the materials never arrive, then the electrician's duty to perform is excused. If the general contractor brings a breach of contract claim against the electrician, the electrician can defend on the ground that his or her performance is excused due to failure of a condition precedent.

Dispute Prevention and Resolution

"An ounce of prevention is worth a pound of cure." Most of us have heard this old saying, and its truth is established almost every day in construction contracting. When entering into a contract, look for ways to stop disputes from arising, minimize disputes that do occur, and provide a mechanism for quick and relatively inexpensive resolution.

Dispute Prevention
Partnering

Partnering is a technique in which the property owner, general contractor, architect, and principal subcontractors establish ongoing and open lines of communication through all stages of the project. Each party contributes to all significant decisions, and the group attempts to anticipate problem areas of the project and work out plans to deal with unforeseen problems. The cornerstone of the system is prompt and full disclosure of problems that arise.

Dealing with problems early reduces the likelihood of serious disputes. An important part of the partnering process is to make certain that changes in the work or other duties and responsibilities are fully documented in writing. Partnering concepts are being increasingly incorporated into substantial project contracts.

Negotiation

In situations where partnering mechanisms are not being used, prompt disclosure and negotiation are the preferred methods of dealing with potential and actual disputes. As soon as a contractor sees that a problem might arise, or discovers an unforeseen problem, the contractor should start immediate negotiations with the property owner, architect, and/or subcontractor(s) to resolve the problem with minimal cost and disruption of the project. If an agreement is worked out, it should be in writing and signed by all the parties.

Alternative Dispute Resolution

When a contract is formed, parties can agree to terms and conditions for alternative dispute resolution. The cost and time involved in court litigation of disputes, and the desire to keep disputed projects as much on track as possible, have led to the use of a variety of alternative (to courts) dispute resolution methods.

[Note: The parties must agree to all alternative dispute mechanisms (except for court-ordered arbitration) either in the original contract or a subsequent written agreement. In addition, the CCB's regulations require that contracts with residential property owners for over $2,000 include an explanation of the property owner's rights under the contract, including but not limited to, the ability to file a complaint with the CCB and the existence of any mediation or arbitration provision in the contract.]

Owner's and Contractor's Duties in a Residential Construction Dispute

The Owner's Duty to Contractor law (ORS 701.560 – 701.600) promotes early resolution of construction defect-related disputes. The law requires residential property owners and contractors to follow some specific steps before pursuing court action or arbitration.

Contractors must, as part of this law, notify every residential owner for whom they work about the owner's responsibility to comply with the law. Contractors should deliver the *Notice of Procedure* to residential owners along with a *Consumer Protection Notice*. The notices are given at the time a written contract is required. Contractors may make the notices part of their contracts or provide them to the residential owner directly. The *Notice of Procedure* is available on the CCB website, www.oregon.gov/CCB, and in the Appendix of Chapter 1.

The law obligates a residential property owner to notify a contractor of an alleged construction defect and give the contractor an opportunity to mitigate the defect before beginning court action or arbitration. Written notice must be sent to the contractor by registered or certified mail, return receipt requested, giving the name and mailing address of the owner, a statement that the owner may seek arbitration or court action, the address and location of the residence having the defect, and a description of each defect, the necessary remediation, any incidental damage not curable by remediation, and any reports or proof of the defect and incidental damage. Within 14 days of receipt of this notice, the contractor must give written notice to any known contractor, subcontractor, or material supplier who may be responsible for some or all of the alleged defects.

Within 14 days of receiving such a notice, a contractor or supplier may send a notice to the owner requesting an inspection of the property. This notice must state the nature and scope of the inspection, any testing to be performed, and an estimate of the time necessary to make the inspection. Upon receipt of such a request, the owner must make the property available for inspection within 20 days.

Within 90 days after the owner's original notice of defects, each notified contractor, subcontractor, or supplier must deliver to the owner a written response including one or more of the following for each defect described in the notice or discovered during inspection of the property:

- Acknowledgment of the existence, nature, and extent of the defect without regard to responsibility for the defect.
- A statement describing the existence of a defect different in nature or extent from the defect described in the notice or secondary notice, without regard to responsibility for the defect.
- Denial of existence of the defect.
- A copy of any written report or other proof of the results of the inspection relating to the existence or nonexistence of the defects described in the notice or discovered during inspection.
- One or more of the following:
  - An offer to perform some or all of the remediation, with a specified date for completion;
  - An offer to pay a stated amount of monetary compensation to the owner for some or all of the acknowledged defects, including any incidental damage, with a specified date for payment.
  - Denial of responsibility for some or all of the acknowledged defects or incidental damage.

Within 30 days after receiving the written response, any owner may accept or reject an offer by delivering notice in writing to the contractor, subcontractor, or material supplier. Failure to deliver notice within 30 days is a rejection of any offers made.

If an owner accepts an offer, completion of the remediation work or payment of the amount offered satisfies the claim for the defect.

If an owner does not send the required notice, he or she may not begin arbitration or litigation regarding alleged defects. An owner that does send the required notice may start arbitration or court action against a contractor, subcontractor, or material supplier if:

- The contractor, subcontractor, or material supplier does not send a timely written response
- The written response of the contractor, subcontractor, or material supplier does not offer remediation or monetary compensation
- The owner rejects a written offer, or any part thereof
- The contractor, subcontractor, or material supplier fails to perform to the terms of the accepted offer

The notice and written response are admissible in arbitration or court action only for the purpose of establishing that the owner is authorized to begin arbitration or court action.

Mediation

Mediation is a facilitated negotiation presided over and guided by an experienced legal or construction practitioner. An effective mediator has received special training and has a strong working knowledge of construction law and practices. The mediator will hear the claims and factual presentations of the various sides to the dispute and will call upon his or her experience to help work out an agreement satisfactory to the parties. Mediation is not binding, but if the parties are open to a negotiated resolution, the process can be extremely effective. Typically, the parties agree on a mediator and each side pays one-half of the mediator's fees. If the mediation is successful, the mediator will help prepare a written settlement agreement that will be signed by the parties to resolve the dispute. The CCB provides mediation for timely filed complaints that are within the jurisdiction of the CCB.

Arbitration

A contract can provide for the parties to arbitrate disputes. However, parties can voluntarily agree to arbitrate even if the contract does not have terms for arbitration or resolving disputes. A court can order arbitration in matters having relatively low economic damage claims. Binding arbitration is much more common in the construction industry. When efforts to negotiate and/or mediate a matter have failed, an appointed arbitrator will conduct what is for all intents and purposes a trial of the matter. The arbitrator will issue a ruling that is binding on the parties and can be enforced through court processes. The arbitration process is usually as costly as litigation in terms of attorneys' and arbitrators' fees. The advantage over litigation is that the matter can usually be arbitrated much more quickly than conducting a court trial.

Court Litigation

In the absence of agreed-upon or mandatory alternative dispute mechanisms, court litigation is the last resort for the resolution of disputes. Little need be said about this method of dispute resolution, except to emphasize the importance of including in every written contract a comprehensive attorneys' fees recovery provision. In the absence of such a written provision or a statute that provides for prevailing party attorney fees, the winning party cannot recover their attorneys' fees from the other side.

This is an example of a residential construction contract.
It is intended for informational use only.

Appendix A

Sample Construction Agreement for Residential Construction Work

This is a contract for construction work to be performed by **ABC Construction, LLC** ("ABC") for _____ ("HOMEOWNER") made this _____ day of _____ .

Information

1. ABC is located at 1234 SE Milken St., Portland, Oregon 97999. ABD's phone is (503) 123-999.

   HOMEOWNER's name and address are:

   [Insert name, address and phone number.]

   The worksite is located at:

   [Insert address or location of job site.]

Scope of Work

ABC shall perform the following work for HOMEOWNER:

[Insert description of the work to be performed, who is paying for materials, material specifications if any, who is responsible to obtain permits, a reference to contract drawings if any and any other terms that define the scope of work.]

Payment Terms

HOMEOWNER shall pay for the work on the following schedule:

[Insert the payment schedule.]

Explanation of HOMEOWNERS's Rights

1. Consumers have the right to receive the products and services agreed to in the contract.
2. Consumers have the right to resolve disputes through means outlined in the contract.
3. Consumers have the right to file a complaint with the CCB. Any arbitration or mediation clauses in the contract may need to be complied with during the resolution of the CCB complaint.

Explanation of Mediation or Arbitration Clause

An "arbitration or mediation clause" is a written portion of a contract designed to settle how the parties will solve disputes that may arise during, or after the construction project. Arbitration clauses are very important. They may limit a consumer's ability to have their dispute resolved by the Oregon court system or the Oregon Construction Contractors Board.

☐ This contract contains an arbitration or mediation clause.
☐ This contract DOES NOT contain an arbitration or mediation clause.

The Oregon Construction Contractors Board urges consumers to read and understand the entire contract – including any arbitration clause before signing a construction contract. Consumers are not obligated to accept contract terms proposed by the contractor, including arbitration provisions. These may be negotiated to the satisfaction of both parties.

_____   _____   _____   _____

Homeowner   Date   John Smith, Manager   Date

                                                   ABC Construction, LLC

Appendix B
Resources

Contractors who do not have an attorney and need legal advice may contact the Oregon State Bar Lawyer Referral and Information Service. Ask for an attorney who practices business and construction law.

> **Oregon State Bar Lawyer Referral Service**
> **5200 SW Meadows Road**
> **Lake Oswego, OR 97035**
> **Telephone: 503-684-3763**
> **Toll-free in Oregon: 800-452-7636**
> **Fax: 503-684-1366**
> **http://www.osbar.org/public/ris/ris.html**

Following is a list of resources for obtaining standard language from contracts that are appropriate and adhere to Oregon law: AGC, AIA, ORA.

> **The American Institute of Architects (AIA)**
> **Portland Chapter**
> **403 NW 11th Avenue**
> **Portland, OR 97209**
> **Telephone: 503-223-8757**
> **Fax: 503-220-0254**
> **www.aiaportland.org/**
>
> **AIA Knowledge Center**
> **Washington, D.C.**
> **800-242-3837**
>
> **The Associated General Contractors of America, Inc.**
> **Oregon Columbia Chapter**
> **9450 SW Commerce Circle**
> **Wilsonville, OR 97070**
> **Telephone: 503-682-3363**
> **Fax: 503-682-1696**
> **www.agc-oregon.org/**
>
> **Publications - AGC National Office**
> **Washington, D.C.**
> **800-242-1767**
> **www.agc.org/**
>
> **Oregon Remodelers Association**
> **147 SE 102nd Ave.**
> **Portland, OR 97216**
> **Telephone: 503-788-2274**
> **Fax: 503-788-2277**
> **www.oregonremodelers.com/**

Chapter 3

Sample Questions

CHAPTER 3

1. When is a written contract required in Oregon?

☐ 1. When the total price of a subcontract exceeds $1,000.

☐ 2. When the total contract price between the property owner and contractor for a residential project exceeds $2,000.

☐ 3. When the contract includes warranty language, completion dates, or a progress payment schedule.

☐ 4. When the parties agree to arbitration or mediation as a method to resolve disputes.

2. Which of the following is NOT one of the four elements of contract law?

☐ 1. Formation.

☐ 2. Performance.

☐ 3. Remedies.

☐ 4. Builder's Risk Insurance.

3. Which of the following is an example of a contractor's material breach?

☐ 1. Completing a job several days before the scheduled completion date.

☐ 2. His or her tools were stolen from the job site.

☐ 3. Failure to appear for arbitration in resolving a dispute with a customer.

☐ 4. Failure to install the specified air-conditioning system.

Answers: 1. [2]

2. [4]

3. [4]

CHAPTER 4
OREGON CONSTRUCTION LIEN LAW

Objectives

At the end of this chapter you will be able to:

1. Explain how lien laws protect contractors, suppliers, and property owners.
2. Identify the differences between an *Information Notice To Owner About Construction Liens* and a *Notice of Right to a Lien*.
3. Explain how the notices protect owners and contractors.
4. Explain what can happen to a contractor who contracts directly with a homeowner and fails to follow lien law procedures.
5. Explain when and how to record a valid Oregon construction lien.
6. Identify the steps and notices to be given, to whom they should be given, and the timelines for both pre-lien notices, which are delivered before a lien is recorded, and post-lien notices, which are delivered after the construction lien is recorded.
7. Recognize that differences exist between Oregon's lien laws and those of other states.

What is a Construction Lien?

Definition

In general terms, a construction lien is nothing more than a security interest in real property. A construction lien is intended to secure payment of a debt due to someone who worked on a construction project or provided materials or services for the project. This law gives contractors the right to secure a debt owed to them for work on real property by recording a construction lien.

The right to get paid for the work is not automatically secured. Suppliers and contractors must follow certain steps to properly exercise their lien rights.

If a contractor waits until work is completed before evaluating the construction lien rights, it may be too late for some of the steps required to perfect a lien claim. A contractor should evaluate the construction lien rights **before the bid is submitted or work is begun on a project.**

Example

If a bank loans money to a consumer for a car, the bank's name is put on the title to the car. That way, if the bank is not paid by the consumer, the bank can repossess the car and sell it to recover the loan. Similarly, construction liens can give contractors the ability to force the sale of the property on which they worked to receive payment if necessary. When the recorded lien is foreclosed through a lawsuit, it may provide funds from the sale of the improvement to satisfy the lien.

Some contracts are written to require a contractor to waive (release) his or her lien rights at the outset of the project even if he or she does not get paid. Contractors usually do not want to waive their lien rights unless they have been paid in advance – thus, you should carefully examine all contracts. Also, it is good practice to insist on payment in the form of a cashier's check or wait until a regular check clears before waiving a right to lien.

What Is the Purpose of Oregon's Construction Lien Law?

Oregon's Construction Lien Law intends to balance the owner's interest in the improvement with the contractor's right to secure a debt. This law:

- Allows a contractor to work with owners to improve real property with less concern about not getting paid for the work
- Provides that if a contractor furnishes labor, materials, or equipment that will increase the value of the owner's property, the debt due to the contractor is secured by the property

- Has safeguards intended to protect the rights of lenders, subcontractors, and suppliers who are not parties to the contract between the original contractor and property owner
- Informs an owner of contractors and suppliers who may have lien rights against the owner's property
- Helps an owner avoid paying contractors and suppliers twice for the same work by knowing who has lien rights

Language in Oregon Construction Lien Law

Oregon's Construction Lien Law uses many terms that have special definitions. To gain a basic understanding of Oregon's Construction Lien Law, contractors need to become familiar with these terms and their definitions. These terms are defined in the Oregon Revised Statutes (the Glossary includes the statutory definitions).

The following are only **general** summaries of these definitions.

Commencement of the improvement when the first contractor actually begins work on the site or the materials are first delivered.

Commercial improvement for *construction lien* purposes means a structure that is not used or intended for use as a residential building (see definition of residential building below). This term is referred to by the law governing the *Notice of Right to a Lien.*

Construction is creating an improvement or performing work on an improvement (see definition of improvement below).

Contractor is a person who enters into a contract to perform construction work.

Improvement includes any building or structure and can include related work necessary for construction of the building or structure.

Interest holder is someone who has a legal interest in land or the improvements to the land. A lender (or mortgagee) is an example of an interest holder.

Mortgagee is a lender (it could be a bank or a person) who has a financial interest in the land or improvements as evidenced by a mortgage or trust deed, which is filed with the recorder's office in the county where the land is located.

Original contractor is a contractor who contracts directly with the property owner.

Owner is anyone who claims or has an ownership interest in land or the improvements. Ownership can include those who own the land, those who lease the land or those who are buying the land on a long-term sale contract.

Preparation means preparing the land for construction.

Residential building means a building or structure that will be occupied by the owner as a residence and that contains not more than four units. This term is referred to by the law governing the *Notice of Right to a Lien.*

Residential construction or improvement means the original construction of residential property and the repair, replacement, remodeling, alteration or improvement of residential property. (See definition of residential property below). This term is referred to by the law governing *Information Notice to Owner About Construction Liens.*

Residential construction or improvement contract is a written agreement (oral or written) between an original contractor and an owner to perform home improvement work. This term is referred to by the law governing the *Information Notice To Owner About Construction Liens.*

Residential property includes, but is not limited to, a residential dwelling and the driveways, swimming pools, terraces, patios, fences, porches, garages, basements, other structures and land that are adjacent or appurtenant to a residential dwelling. This term is referred to by the law governing the *Information Notice to Owner About Construction Liens.*

Site is the land where the construction work is performed.

Subcontractor is a contractor who does not have a contract directly with the property owner(s).

Working days are days when work may be performed, but do not include Saturdays, Sundays, or holidays.

Who is Entitled to a Construction Lien?

A contractor who does work directly for an owner of a residential structure where the contract price exceeds $2,000 must have a **written** contract or the contractor will not have a right to assert a lien claim. The specific terms that are required in the written contract are available at CCB website. Subject to this requirement, the following persons are entitled to assert a construction lien:

- Licensed contractors who properly and substantially perform their work with the consent of the property owner or the owner's agent.

- Persons who perform work or provide materials or equipment as described by the construction lien law, including:
  - Performing labor, transportation, or furnishing any materials or rental equipment used in the construction of the improvement.
  - Preparing a lot or parcel of land, improving an adjoining road, or leasing or renting equipment for land preparation or improvements.
- Trustees of employee benefit plans that have contributions allocated by labor performed on an improvement.
- Certain persons performing work related to construction activity such as: architects, landscape architects, land surveyors, and registered engineers who prepare plans, drawings, or specifications for construction of an improvement, or who supervise the construction.
  - Landscape architects, land surveyors, or other persons who prepare plans, drawings, surveys or specifications for landscaping, or preparation of a lot or parcel, or who supervise the landscaping or preparation.

Construction Liens Secure Payment to the Contractor

The construction contract describes terms of payment to the contractor for the work to be performed by the contractor. If the contractor performs according to the contract, a debt is due and the contractor becomes a creditor when not paid.

A valid construction lien secures the contractor's right as a creditor to receive payment. The lien is recorded (filed) in the county recorder's office of the county where the project is located. The recording, also known as "perfecting the lien," is required for the lien to be effective.

> **Example**
> A bank requires a mortgage from a borrower to secure the bank's right to be repaid the money the bank has loaned to the borrower. Similarly, the mortgage is recorded in the county where the property is located and becomes a lien against the property.

Contractors must have general knowledge about construction liens to comply with the current law. The legislature has the ability to change Oregon's Construction Lien Law, so it is important to consult with an attorney in properly exercising lien rights.

Lien Laws Vary Among States

Each state has a different lien law for construction contractors. Each state also has jurisdiction to decide if a contractor has lien rights, and the statutory procedures for creating and enforcing them. Consequently, contractors need to know the lien law of the state where the job site is located before proceeding with work. Oregon contractors who work in other states need to know the construction lien laws in those states, such as what notices should be given, when the notices should be delivered, and to whom the notices should be delivered.

No Construction Lien on Public Improvements

Collection procedures in contracting public improvements are a complicated area of law regulated by different Oregon Revised Statutes rather than the Oregon Construction Lien Law. On public improvements, a contractor cannot record construction liens against a public works project or "public improvement" that is constructed on public property and owned by a local, state, or federal government. Instead, a contractor may have rights under the Federal Miller Act or Oregon's Little Miller Act. Generally, a successful bidder must execute and provide a bond on a public improvement project. Rights under the "Miller Act" are against the bond.

However, if the local, state, or federal government has given up an interest in its property to a private person or entity (by a lease or otherwise), a contractor may be able to claim a construction lien against that interest. For more information, contact an attorney.

Pre-Claim Notices Required before Filing a Claim of Lien

There are two types of pre-claim construction notices in Oregon. They are the *Information Notice To Owner About Construction Liens* (Appendix A) and the *Notice of Right to a Lien* (Appendix B).

These notices are necessary to preserve the contractor's lien rights. The notices inform owners of legal rights in protecting their real property interests.

Determining the Need for Pre-Claim Notices

For purposes of pre-claim notices, an "original contractor" is the contractor who has a contract directly with the owner. For lien law purposes, the term "general contractor" is not used. If a contractor does not have a contract with the owner, he or she is a subcontractor.

Information Notice To Owner About Construction Liens

Original contractors must give the property owner an *Information Notice To Owner About Construction Liens*. This notice defines lien law in non-technical terms and describes the rights and responsibilities of the owner and original contractor. Contractors can get a copy of the form from the CCB website. It is required by original contractors when the contract price exceeds $2,000 and the project involves residential construction or improvement on residential property. "Residential property" is broadly defined to include not only the dwelling but nearly all of the structures associated with the dwelling (see definition above).

The original contractor must give this notice even if the contractor does not intend to record a construction lien. If the *Information Notice To Owner About Construction Liens* is not given when required, the original contractor cannot claim a lien.

In addition, CCB may ask the original contractor for written proof of delivery of this notice. Proof normally means the *Information Notice To Owner About Construction Liens* signed by the property owner. The contractor may deliver the *Notice* in person or by registered or certified mail. It is recommended that the property owner sign and date the *Notice* and that the contractor retain a copy as proof of proper delivery.

Each original contractor gives an *Information Notice To Owner About Construction Liens* to:
- The first purchaser of residential property constructed by the contractor and sold within 75 days following the completion of construction
- The owner at the time a contract is signed
- The owner within five working days after the contractor determines, or should reasonably be able to determine, that the contract price will exceed $2,000

An *Information Notice To Owner About Construction Liens* need not be given when:
- The property owner is a contractor licensed with the CCB
- The aggregate (total) contract price is $2,000 or less

Original contractors should keep proof that the required *Information Notice To Owner About Construction Liens* was given. One way to do this is to make the notice part of the contract, or request that the owner sign a copy that is kept with other records of the project. If the contractor cannot prove the notice was given, and the owner denies receiving the notice, the contractor may lose his or her lien rights and may be subject to a CCB fine of up to $5,000 or license suspension.

Notice of Right to a Lien

The *Notice of Right to a Lien* is given by subcontractors and material suppliers. It is usually mailed by certified mail, return receipt requested, to the owner of the project. There are lien services that will send this notice. Subcontractors or material suppliers do not always have to give the *Notice of Right to a Lien*. However, if the subcontractor or supplier chooses not to give the notice, they may give up the right to claim a lien.

This notice:
- Gives the owner the name of the person who requested the subcontractor or supplier to provide services or materials
- Identifies the subcontractor or supplier
- Describes the work to be performed

If the notice is delivered during the progress of work and no later than eight working days from the date the subcontractor or supplier began to provide labor, material, equipment or services (not including Saturdays, Sundays, and holidays), the notice will allow the subcontractor or supplier to file a lien for all of its labor or materials.

Example
Sam Electric is a subcontractor to Oscar Original on a residential project. Sam delivers a *Notice of Right to a Lien* by certified mail, return receipt requested, to the property owner, Jane Doe. The notice inform Ms. Doe that the original contractor, Oscar Original, ordered Sam Electric to provide labor or materials for electrical activities required for the improvement. Appendix B illustrates a completed sample *Notice of Right to a Lien.*

If no holidays are involved and Sam Electric begins to work on Monday, he must deliver the *Notice of Right to a Lien* to Jane Doe by Wednesday of the following week in order to preserve his lien rights in full.

Subcontractors and material suppliers for residential buildings must provide this notice. For purposes of this law, a residential building means a dwelling that will be occupied by the owner and contains no more than four units (see definitions above). This term is more limited than the term "residential property" that applies to the *Information Notice To Owner About Construction Liens.*

Subcontractors on commercial improvements may not have to provide this notice to preserve their lien rights. Commercial improvement means any structure or building not used or intended for use as a residential building (see definitions above). Since commercial improvements are more complex than improvements to residential buildings, it is advisable for contractors to seek legal advice in preserving and perfecting their lien rights involving commercial improvements.

A business that performs labor upon a commercial improvement, provides labor and material for a commercial improvement, or rents equipment used in a commercial improvement, does not need to give the *Notice of Right to a Lien* in order to perfect a lien. However, a *Notice of Right to a Lien* must be delivered to mortgagees (lenders with recorded interests) when materials are provided. This delivery of the *Notice* preserves potential priority of the materials portion of a lien claim over the mortgagee's recorded interest.

The following chart outlines under what circumstances the notice is required.

AM I REQUIRED TO GIVE A *NOTICE OF RIGHT TO A LIEN*?						
	I Provide Material		I Provide Labor & Material		I Provide Labor	
	Owner	Mortgagee	Owner	Mortgagee	Owner	Mortgagee
I am the Commercial Original Contractor	No	Yes**	No	Yes**	No	No
I am the Commercial Subcontractor	Yes	Yes**	No	Yes**	No	No
I am the Residential Original Contractor*	No	Yes**	No	Yes**	No	No
I am the Residential Subcontractor	Yes	Yes**	Yes	Yes**	Yes	No
*The original contractor for a residential structure must also provide an owner or agent of the owner with an Information Notice to Owner at the time a written contract is signed.						
**A Notice of Right to a Lien must be delivered to mortgagees or lenders in order to preserve priority of the material portion of a potential lien claim over the lender's interest.						

After receiving the *Notice of Right to a Lien*, the owner may make a written demand for:
- A list of materials and supplies with the amount of costs incurred to date
- A description of the labor or services supplied or
- A statement of the contractual basis for supplying the materials, services or labor, including the percentage of the contract completed, and the costs incurred to the date of the demand

The responsive information must be delivered by certified mail, return receipt requested, to the owner within 15 working days of receiving the owner's demand. If the information is not delivered within 15 working days from the date of the demand, the lien claimant's ability to recover attorney's fees and costs will be lost.

Recording a Claim of Lien

Contractors that have given the required pre-claim notices and have not been paid may file a *Claim of Lien*. A *Claim of Lien* is a legal document filed in the county where the job site is located. After filing, the county official "records" the document in the county records.

A *Claim of Lien* must contain the following information:
- A statement of demand for amounts owed, after deducting all credits and offsets
- The name of the owner (or reputed owner) of the project – if known

- The name of the person that employed the lien claimant or purchased materials or rented equipment from the lien claimant
- A description of the property – including the address

The information in the lien must be sworn, under oath, to be true. If it is not true, the contractor may be subject to criminal penalties for a reckless or frivolous claim, and may owe the owner damages and attorney fees. The person who signs the lien must know that all the information in the lien is correct and accurate. As the signor, he or she will be a witness if the lien is foreclosed.

Using an Attorney

Consult an attorney to review the *Claim of Lien* to ensure it is proper and capable of being enforced. An attorney can assist the contractor in exercising and enforcing lien rights. The contractor should consider the following when deciding to use the services of an attorney:

- Are there unusual circumstances involved, such as multiple properties or interest holders?
- Is the claim based on items subject to a lien?
- What are the potential pitfalls of recording a reckless claim?
- What rights does a contractor have to recover attorney fees, costs, and disbursements?

In some cases, a lien manager and filing service may be able to assist a contractor in preparing and filing a *Claim of Lien*.

Recording Requirements for the Claim of Lien

The *Claim of Lien* must be recorded within 75 calendar days after the last substantial performance of labor, delivery of materials, or rental of equipment, or 75 calendar days after the completion of construction, <u>whichever is earlier</u>.

A small amount of work or repairs on incorrectly performed work may not count as valid "last days." The requirements for the 75-day time period are the same for commercial and residential projects and are the same for original contractors and subcontractors. If the 75-day time period concludes on a day that the county recorder is closed, such as a weekend or a holiday, the *Claim of Lien* must be recorded before the weekend or holiday and before the time period expires.

Consequently, contractors must track progress of their work, so they know when the 75-day period is expiring. Others, like trustees of employee benefit plans, architects, engineers, and design professionals, must also file their liens within 75 days of when construction is substantially complete.

After a Lien is Recorded, Post-Claim Notices Must be Given

Types of Post-Claim Notices

There are two types of post-claim notices in Oregon: *Notice of Filing a Claim of Lien* and *Notice of Intent to Foreclose*. Everyone who records a *Claim of Lien* must give these notices. The notices are typically given to the property owner, as well as any lender who may have a legal interest in the property (such as a mortgage). The requirements are the same, whether the project is a commercial or residential, and whether the lien claimant is an original contractor or subcontractor.

Generally, claimants can combine the *Notice of Filing a Claim of Lien* and *Notice of Intent to Foreclose* into one written notice. If the contractor does not deliver these notices, the lien may be valid but other rights will be lost, such as the right to recover attorney fees, costs, or disbursements.

Notice of Filing a Claim of Lien
A person filing a *Claim of Lien* must mail a written notice that the claim has been filed, no later than 20 days after the date of recording, to the owner as well as to the mortgagee (bank or an individual who lends money). A copy of the *Claim of Lien* must be attached to the notice. A notice should be mailed to the owner who received the *Notice of Right to a Lien* unless the person giving notice knows that ownership of the property has changed. Likewise, a notice should be mailed to the mortgagee who received the *Notice of Right to a Lien,* unless the person giving the notice knows that the mortgagee for the property has changed.

Notice of Intent to Foreclose
A person intending to foreclose a lien must send a notice in writing, no later than 10 days before beginning the foreclosure action, to the owner of the property upon which the lien is claimed. The notice must state the intention to begin foreclosure of the lien. Notice must also be delivered to the mortgagees of record.

Providing Requested Information to Owner when Demanded
After the *Notice of Intent to Foreclose* is sent, the owner may demand a list of materials and supplies with the costs incurred to date, or a statement of the contractual basis for the owner's obligation, for which a claim will be made by the contractor in foreclosure. If that list or statement is not delivered within five calendar days from the date the owner demands it, the contractor may lose his or her lien rights to recover attorney fees and costs.

Liens Must be Foreclosed Within a Short Time Period

Construction liens do not last forever. If the lien is not paid, the contractor will need to begin foreclosure. A lien is foreclosed by filing a lawsuit. The lawsuit to foreclose a lien must be filed within 120 days after the lien is recorded. Attorneys need some time to evaluate all the pertinent information and prepare the lawsuit. Thus, contractors who are not paid within 70 to 80 days of when their lien was recorded should seek legal advice to ensure they do not miss the deadline for filing the lawsuit to foreclose the lien.

Foreclosure must occur within the time period, and typically cannot be changed or extended even if the owner and lien claimant agree to do so.

Consequences of Failing to Follow Lien Law Procedures

Contractors that do not follow Oregon's lien law procedures:
- May lose their rights to pursue a lien claim
- Could pay an opposing party's attorney fees in a foreclosure lawsuit
- Might have their license suspended by the CCB for a discretionary period of time
- Could be assessed a civil penalty by the CCB

CCB Complaints by Owners against Contractors for Recording Liens Against their Property

Owners may file a complaint with the CCB against an original contractor whose subcontractors or material suppliers have filed a lien against the owner's property if:
- The owner has paid the original contractor for work performed
- The original contractor has not paid obligations, including money owed to subcontractors laborers, or material suppliers.

APPENDIX A

For educational purposes. This form may be revised.

Information Notice To Owner About

Construction Liens

(ORS 87.093)

This is not a lien. Your contractor is required by law to provide this notice to inform you about construction lien laws. This notice explains the construction lien law, and gives steps you can take to protect your property from a valid lien. As an owner, you should read this *information notice* carefully. This information notice is required to be given if you contract for residential construction or remodeling, if you are buying a new home, or at any time the contract price exceeds $2,000.

- Under Oregon law, your contractor and others who provide labor, materials, equipment, or services to your project may be able to claim payment from your property if they have not been paid. That claim is called a Construction Lien.

- If your contractor does not pay subcontractors, employees, rental equipment dealers, materials suppliers, or does not make other legally required payments, those who are owed money may place a lien against your property for payment. It is in your best interest to verify that all bills related to your contract are paid, even if you have paid your contractor in full.

- If you occupy or will occupy your home, persons who supply materials, labor, equipment, or services ordered by your contractor are permitted by law to file a lien against your property only if they have sent you a timely Notice of Right to Lien (which is different from this Information Notice), before or during construction. If you enter into a contract to buy a newly-built, partially-built, or newly-remodeled home, a lien may be claimed even though you have not received a Notice of Right to a Lien. If you do not occupy the building, a Notice of Right to Lien is not required prior to filing a lien.

This notice is not intended to be a complete analysis of the law. You should consult an attorney for more information.

Common Questions and Answers About Construction Liens

Can someone record a construction lien even if I pay my contractor? Yes. Anyone who has not been paid for labor, material, equipment, or services on your project and has provided you with a valid Notice of Right to Lien has the right to record a construction lien.

What is a Notice of Right to Lien? A Notice of Right to Lien is sent to you by persons who have provided labor, materials, or equipment to your construction project. It protects their construction lien rights against your property.

What should I do when I receive a Notice of Right to Lien? Don't ignore it. Find out what arrangements your contractor has made to pay the sender of the Notice of Right to Lien.

When do construction liens need to be recorded? In Oregon, construction liens generally need to be recorded within 75 days from the date the project was substantially completed, or 75 days from the date that the lien claimant stopped providing labor, material, equipment, or services, whichever happened first. To enforce a lien, the lien holder must file a lawsuit in a proper court within 120 days of the date the lien was filed.

Note to Contractor: This notice must be delivered personally, or mailed by registered mail, certified mail, or by first-class mail with a certificate of mailing. Ask the signing parties to provide you with an original or copy to retain in your files. You should retain proof of delivery of this notice for at least two years. **(Over)**

Steps That Consumers Can Take to Protect Themselves

- **Contact the Construction Contractors Board (CCB) and confirm that your contractor is licensed.** The law requires all construction contractors to be licensed with the CCB. Check a contractor's license online at the CCB consumer website: www.oregon.gov/ccb, or you can call 503-378-4621.

- **Review the Consumer Protection Notice (ORS 701.330(1)),** which your contractor must provide to you at the time of contract on a residential structure.

- Consider using the services of an escrow agent to protect your interests. Consult your attorney to find out whether your escrow agent will protect you against liens when making payments.

- Contact a title company about obtaining a title policy that will protect you from construction lien claims.

- Find out what precautions, if any, will be taken by your contractor, lending institution, and architect to protect your project from construction liens.

- **Ask the contractor to get lien waivers or lien releases** from every subcontractor, materials provider, equipment provider, and anyone else the contractor is responsible for paying. Do this before you give your contractor a progress payment.

- Have a written contract with your contractor. A written contract is **required** for projects greater than $2,000. An original contractor that fails to provide a written contract as required by law may not place a construction lien against the owner's property.

- If you receive a Notice of Right to Lien, ask for a statement of the reasonable value of the materials, labor, equipment, or services provided to your project from everyone who sends you a Notice of Right to Lien. If the information is not provided in a timely manner, the sender of the Notice of Right to Lien may still be able to file a construction lien, but will not be entitled to attorney fees.

- When you pay your contractor, write checks made jointly payable to the contractor, subcontractors, materials, equipment, or services providers. The checks can only be cashed if **both** the contractor and the subcontractor, materials or equipment provider endorses it. This ensures that the subcontractor and other providers will be paid by your contractor, and can eliminate the risk of a lien on your property.

- Should you have a dispute with your contractor, you may be able to file a complaint with the CCB and be reimbursed in whole or in part from the contractor's bond. For more details about help available through the agency, write to the CCB at PO Box 14140, Salem, OR 97309-5052 or call 503-378-4621.

- **Consult an attorney.** If you do not have an attorney, consider contacting the Oregon State Bar Referral Service at 503-684-3763 or 1-800-452-7636.

Signing this Information Notice verifies only that you have received it. Your signature does not give your contractor or those who provide material, labor, equipment, or services, any additional rights to place a lien on your property.

Job Site Address: _____

CONTRACTOR: CCB#: _____   PROPERTY OWNER:

_____   _____
Print Name (as it appears on contract)   Print Name (as it appears on contract)

_____   _____   _____   _____
Signature   Date   Signature   Date

F:information_notice_liens.adopted 1-01-10.

APPENDIX B
Completed Sample

NOTICE OF RIGHT TO A LIEN
(ORS 87.021)

Warning: Read this notice.
Protect yourself from paying any contractor or supplier
twice for the same service.

To: __Jane Doe__   Date of mailing: __December 10, 2010__
  (Owner)   *(registered or certified mail)*

__123 NE 60th Avenue__

__Anytown, OR 97210__
  (Owner's address)

This is to inform you that __Sam Electric__ (name of contractor) has begun to

provide __labor, materials and rental equipment__

_____ (description of

materials, equipment, labor or services) ordered by __Oscar Original__ for

improvements to property you own. The property is located at __246 NE Taylor__.

A lien may be claimed for all materials, equipment, labor and services furnished after a date that is eight days, not including Saturdays, Sundays, and holidays, as defined in ORS 187.010, before this notice was mailed to you. Even if you or your mortgage lender has made full payment to the contractor who ordered these materials or services, your property may still be subject to a lien unless the supplier providing this notice is paid.

THIS IS NOT A LIEN. It is a notice sent to you for your protection in compliance with the construction lien laws of the state of Oregon.

This notice has been sent to you by:

Name: __Sam Electric__

Address: __3402 SE 50th Street, Anytown, OR 97209__

Phone: __(123) 456-7890   CCB NO. 012345__

If you have questions about this notice, feel free to call us.

See reverse side for more important information.

Under Oregon's laws, those who work on your property or provide labor, equipment, services or materials and are not paid have a right to enforce their claim for payment against your property. This claim is known as a construction lien.

If your contractor fails to pay subcontractors, materials suppliers, rental equipment suppliers, service providers or laborers, or neglects to make other legally required payments, the people who are owed money can look to your property for payment, *even if you have paid your contractor in full.*

The law states that all people hired by a contractor to provide you with materials, equipment, labor or services must give you a *Notice of Right to a Lien* to let you know what they have provided.

WAYS TO PROTECT YOURSELF ARE:

- RECOGNIZE that this *Notice of Right to a Lien* may result in a lien against your property unless all those supplying a *Notice of Right to a Lien* have been paid.

- LEARN more about the lien laws and the meaning of this notice by contacting the Construction Contractors Board, an attorney or the firm sending this notice.

- ASK for a statement of the labor, equipment, services or materials provided to your property from each party that sends you a notice of right to a lien.

- WHEN PAYING your contractor for materials, equipment, labor or services, you may make checks payable jointly to the contractor and the firm furnishing materials, equipment, labor or services for which you have received a notice of right to a lien.

- OR use one of the methods suggested by the "Information Notice to Owners." If you have not received such a notice, contact the Construction Contractors Board.

- GET EVIDENCE that all firms from whom you have received a notice of right to a lien have been paid or have waived the right to claim a lien against your property.

- CONSULT an attorney, a professional escrow company or your mortgage lender.

Learn more about the lien law by requesting a booklet from the Construction Contractors Board called *Construction Liens* (503-378-4621 or www.oregon.gov/CCB). It contains an explanation of construction liens, how consumers can protect themselves and contractor responsibilities.

f/ntcrtlien/10-08

Appendix C
Required Pre-Claim Notices

	Notice of Right to a Lien – Commercial Projects	*Information Notice To Owner About Construction Liens – Residential Projects*	*Notice of Right to a Lien – Residential Projects*
Who gives it?	Persons or entities who do not have a contract with the owner must give notice to all owners, mortgagees, and lenders. Those who provide on-site labor and material **and** who do not have a contract with the owner should give notice to mortgagees or lenders.	Original contractors who contract directly with the owner or sell to first purchaser of a **residential** construction or improvement. Original contractors need not provide this notice to an owner who is also a licensed contractor.	Persons or entities who provide materials only, on-site labor and material, on-site labor only or rental equipment **and** who do not have a contract directly with the owner must provide this notice.
Who gets it?	All owners of the improvement. In addition, those persons or entities providing materials only or on-site labor and materials must give the notice to all mortgagees or lenders to maintain priority of the material portion of their claim.	The owner or first purchaser of the residential construction or improvement constructed by the contractor and sold before or within 75 days following the completion of construction.	All owners of the structure that contains not more than four units capable of being used or occupied by the owner as a residence. Those who supply materials only or on-site labor and materials must give the notice to all mortgagees in order to maintain priority of the material portion of their claim.
When is it given?	This notice may be given at any time during progress of the improvement but only preserves the right to perfect a lien for those materials provided within a date that is not more than eight working days prior to providing the notice.	At the time the written contract is signed for more than $2,000 to perform residential construction or improvements, including all labor, services, and materials furnished under the contract. If the price of the work was initially less than $2,000, but during performance exceeds $2,000, the notice must be given within five days of when the contractor knows or reasonably should know that the contract price will exceed $2,000.	This notice may be given at any time during progress of the building or structure, but only preserves the right to perfect a lien for work that was provided within a date that is not more than eight working days prior to providing the notice.
How is it given?	Registered or certified mail, return receipt requested, as proof that the notice was properly delivered. Also, this notice can be delivered in person.	The notice may be hand-delivered or mailed, registered or, certified with return receipt requested. With either, the contractor must maintain proof of delivery for a period of two years.	Registered or certified mail, return receipt requested, as proof that the notice was properly delivered. Also, this notice can be delivered in person.
Consequences for not giving the notice?	Materials-only providers may lose their lien rights, even on commercial projects.	If not given when required, contractor will lose lien rights. Also, CCB may suspend the original contractor's license or impose a civil penalty.	Persons or entities lose their lien rights for work on the residential building or structure.

Appendix D

| \multicolumn{3}{c}{**Summary of Oregon Construction Lien Claims**} |||
DOCUMENTS	NOTES	DEADLINE
Information Notice to Owner (ORS 87.093)	Must be given by original contractor to residential property owner. *Exception:* Not required if residential property owner is a licensed contractor.	The first purchaser of residential property constructed by the contractor and sold within 75 days following the completion of construction. The owner at the time a contract is signed. The owner within five working days after the contractor determines, or should reasonably be able to determine, that the contract price will exceed $2,000.
Notice of Right to a Lien (ORS 87.021)	**Use for:** On-site labor and materials if residential. Materials on all projects unless hired directly by owner. Rental Equipment on residential projects unless hired by owner. Send to lender to maintain potential priority for materials portion. (ORS 87.025)	There is an eight business day "reach back" period.
Claim of Lien (ORS 87.035)	Record construction lien claim with recorder in county where project is located. No lien rights if residential over $2,000 and no written contract. (ORS 87.037) No lien rights if residential and contractor not properly licensed with CCB. (ORS 87.036)	Within 75 days from the earlier of substantial completion of the project, or the lien claimant's last substantial day of work on the project. Use substantial completion date for architects, engineers, and union trust funds.
Notice of Filing Claim of Lien (ORS 87.039)	May combine with Notice of Intent to Foreclose.	Within 20 days of lien recording.
Notice of Intent to Foreclose (ORS 87.057)	May combine with Notice of Filing Claim of Lien.	At least 10 days before filing lawsuit. May be required to furnish information within five days upon demand of notice recipient.
Lawsuit to Foreclose Lien Claim (ORS 87.055; 87.060)	Must name and serve all necessary parties including all parties with legal interest in the property plus parties in privity. Attorney fee provisions in ORS 87.060 and ORS 20.082 (for actions under $10,000).	Within 120 days from the date of recording the construction lien claim.

Appendix E

Construction Liens

- **Explanation of construction liens**

- **Notices required**

- **How consumers can protect themselves**

- **Contractor responsibilities**

f:constructionlienspamphlet/3-11print 11-12

**Oregon Construction Contractors
Board
PO Box 14140
Salem, OR 97309-5052
700 Summer St. NE, Suite 300
503-378-4621, Fax: 503-373-2007**

This pamphlet explains Oregon lien laws but should not be considered legal advice.

Contractors needing assistance providing notices, filing liens, or obtaining lien priority, should consult an attorney. Some attorneys specialize in construction law and may offer classes or publications relating to liens.

To find a construction law attorney, contact construction industry associations, or the Oregon State Bar Attorney Referral Service at 1-800-452-7636 or www.osbar.org/ *public.*

Explanation of construction liens

What is a construction lien?

Construction liens have been a part of Oregon's law for over 100 years. Under this law, anyone who constructs improvements on property, supplies materials, rents equipment, or provides services for improvements has a right to collect payment from the property if they are not paid. If the general contractor is not paid or does not pay the subcontractors, laborers, material suppliers, or equipment rental companies, those persons may claim a lien against the property.

What is the purpose of the construction lien law?

The purpose of the law is to ensure that people are paid for value that they add to someone's property. A bank can reclaim a car if payments are not made. Work done to real estate, however, is permanent and cannot be reclaimed. The lien laws protect those persons working on the property who do not have a contract directly with the property owner (who contracted only with the general contractor).

For purposes of the lien law, what is the difference between a general contractor and a subcontractor?

Usually, the property owner has a contract with a general contractor. The general contractor then contracts with subcontractors to provide services such as roofing, drywall, plumbing, electrical, painting, or window installation. The property owner does not usually hire the subcontractors.

Who can claim a lien?

General contractors, subcontractors, employees, material suppliers, and equipment rental companies that do not receive payment can claim liens. Even if the property owner pays the general contractor in full, the subcontractors, employees, material suppliers, and equipment rental companies may not be paid. These persons and companies may then claim a lien against the owner's property.

What are the property owner's responsibilities to a lien holder?

Property owners can be forced to pay the lien holder (the person claiming the lien) or face a potential court order to sell the property for payment.

> Property owners can be liable if the general contractor does not pay subcontractors, employees, materials suppliers, and equipment rental companies.

Chapter 4

Notices Required

What information or warnings must be given to the property owner by the general contractor?

Any contractor who contracts directly with a residential property owner or sells a new residence directly to the owner must provide an Information Notice To Owner about Construction Liens. Contractors can obtain the form online at www.oregon.gov/ccb under Contractor Forms.

What is the purpose of an Information Notice To Owner about Construction Liens?

The Information Notice To Owner about Construction Liens explains Oregon lien law and gives steps that property owners can take to protect themselves. It describes the rights and responsibilities of property owners and general contractors. If a contractor fails to deliver the notice as required under the law, the contractor loses the right to claim a lien against the property.

Who must provide and receive an Information Notice To Owner about Construction Liens?

A contractor who contracts to construct or improve residential property, or who constructs and sells a new residence, must give the owner or buyer the notice. The notice must be given if the construction contract is for more than $2,000, or if the sale of a new residence occurs within 75 days of the completion of construction. If the property owner who contracts for construction work is a licensed contractor, the notice does not have to be given. Note: "residential property" may include property not occupied by the owner.

What if the contract price is less than $2,000 but goes over $2,000 during the job?

If the contract goes over $2,000 during construction, the Information Notice to Owner about Construction Liens must be mailed or delivered no later than five days after the contractor knows that the contract exceeds $2,000.

> The Information Notice to Owner about Construction Liens explains Oregon lien law and gives steps that property owners can take to protect themselves.

When, and how does the Information Notice to Owner about Construction Liens need to be given?

If there is a written contract for construction, the notice must be given on or before the date that the contract is signed. Oregon law requires a written contract for jobs that exceed $2,000. The notice contains signature lines for both the contractor and the property owner. Delivery must be made personally, by registered or certified mail, or by first class mail with a certificate of mailing.

If the general contractor is the builder-owner and sells the residence within 75 days of the completion of construction, the notice must be delivered to the **new** owner. It must be given at the time the builder-owner agrees to sell the property.

Is there other information that owner-builders must provide when they sell a house?

While not a notice requirement, under the 2003 Homebuyer Protection Act, a builder-owner must provide protection for the buyer against lien claims. The CCB provides a form that the builder-owner should complete to show how the builder-owner has complied with the law. The form, Notice of Compliance with the Homebuyer Protection Act (HPA), is available from the CCB at www.oregon.gov/ccb.

What information or warnings must be given to the property owner by persons other than general contractors who may claim a lien?

Subcontractors, employees, material suppliers, and equipment rental companies usually must provide a Notice of Right to a Lien to property owners in order to claim a valid lien if they are not paid. The Notice of Right to a Lien is available online at www.oregon.gov/ccb under Contractor Forms.

> Subcontractors, employees, material suppliers, and equipment rental companies usually must provide a Notice of Right to a Lien to property owners.

Chapter 4

What is the purpose of a Notice of Right to a Lien?

A Notice of Right to a Lien lets the property owner know of the possibility that a lien could be placed on their property by subcontractors, employees, material suppliers, and equipment rental companies who are not paid. A Notice of Right to a Lien gives the property owner the name of the person who ordered the services or materials. It also gives the name of the subcontractor, employee, material, equipment, or service provider and describes the materials, equipment, or services ordered.

Who must provide and receive a Notice of Right to a Lien?

Unless the material, equipment, services, or labor were requested by the property owner, the subcontractors, employees, material suppliers, and equipment rental companies must provide a Notice of Right to a Lien to the property owner. If a person provides labor or labor and materials for a commercial improvement, a Notice of Right to a Lien does not need to be given. A "commercial improvement" is a structure or building that is not intended for occupancy as a residence.

When and how does the Notice of Right to a Lien need to be given?

The Notice of Right to a Lien may be given at any time during the construction, but **it should be given within eight working days of the start date of the work or the delivery date of the materials or equipment**. If the notice was delivered to the property owner on day nine, then the subcontractor or materials provider would not be entitled to payment for anything that occurred on the first day of the job. The Notice of Right to a Lien is considered given when it is personally delivered or mailed.

What is the difference between a Notice of Right to a Lien and a filed lien?

Sending a Notice of Right to a Lien is not the same as filing a lien claim. The notice protects the right of the person sending the notice to later file the lien. A construction lien should be filed with the recording officer in the county or counties where the construction occurred. A lien holder has 75 days after completing the construction, or ceasing work on the construction, in which to file the lien. Only liens that have been properly filed can be enforced by a lawsuit in court.

Sending a Notice of Right to a Lien is not the same as filing a lien claim.

How consumers can protect themselves

What can I do after receiving an Information Notice to Owner About Construction Liens or a Notice of Right to a Lien?

These notices list several ways to protect yourself from having a lien filed on your property:

- **One way is to issue joint checks**. A check can be written jointly payable to the contractor and to the subcontractor, material supplier, or any other party who gave the property owner a Notice of Right to a Lien.
- **Another way is to use lien waivers or releases**. Before you make any payments to your contractor, ask every person who gave you a Notice of Right to a Lien to provide you with a signed lien waiver or release. Contact an attorney for more information on using lien waivers or releases.

Do I have any additional rights when I receive a Notice of Right to a Lien?

Yes. A property owner who receives a Notice of Right to a Lien may send a letter to the person who delivered the notice demanding:

- a list of materials or equipment, or
- a description of labor or services supplied, or
- a statement of the contractual basis for the material, equipment or labor, including a percentage of the contract completed and the charges incurred.

The person who delivered the notice must respond within 15 days of receiving the letter (not including Saturdays, Sundays, or holidays). Failure to respond does not invalidate the lien, but will result in a loss of any claim for attorney fees or costs in a lawsuit to foreclose the lien.

Can someone file a lien if they have not provided an Information Notice To Owner About Construction Liens or a Notice of Right to a Lien?

Usually, a lien is not enforceable against your property unless you were given the proper notices. If you are buying a new or partly-built home, you may not receive lien notices because the work was done when the builder-seller still owned the property. It is the builder-seller who would have received the lien

The Information Notice to Owner About Construction Liens and the Notice of Right to a Lien, list ways for property owners to protect themselves.

Chapter 4

notices. In this case, a lien may be claimed against the property even though you did not receive any lien notices. The Homebuyer Protection Act passed in 2003 may provide protection in this type of situation (see next question).

Is there a law that protects new home buyers from liens?

Yes. In 2003, the Oregon legislature enacted a law, called the Homebuyer Protection Act, to protect new home buyers from liens filed related to construction work performed before the sale.

The law applies to the sale of a new single family home (or duplex, triplex, or condominium unit) or to an existing single family home (or duplex, triplex, or condominium unit) that was remodeled at a cost of $50,000 or more.

To protect the buyer and comply with the law, the builder-seller must complete the Notice of Compliance with the Homebuyer Protection Act (HPA) of 2003 (a form available from the CCB website). Both seller and buyer must sign the form and retain copies for their records. As stated on the form:

The builder-seller must provide protection for the buyer against claims of lien by:
- Purchasing title insurance;
- Retaining at least 25% of the sales price in escrow;
- Obtaining lien waivers or releases;
- Obtaining a bond or letter of credit; or
- Waiting to complete the sale after the deadline for properly filing liens (usually 75 days).

Who is likely to file a lien against my property?

Liens are usually filed by one of your general contractor's subcontractors, employees, material suppliers, or equipment rental companies, because the general contractor did not pay for the work performed, materials supplied, or equipment rented. Your general contractor may file a lien if you have not paid him or her.

The Homebuyer Protection Act protects new home buyers from liens related to construction performed before the sale.

Chapter 4

Is having a lien against my property a serious matter?

Yes, if the lien is valid and you do not pay the person filing the lien, you could be legally forced to sell your property to pay the lien holder.

But I already paid my general contractor. Does this mean that I will have to pay twice?

Yes, it could mean exactly that. Even though you paid your general contractor in full, the construction lien law says that you can still be responsible for bills for services, labor, material, and equipment rentals.

What should I do if a lien is filed against my property?

Consult an attorney. Lien laws are complicated and your attorney is your best source of advice.

Can a lien be invalid, and, if so, under what circumstances?

It is possible that a filed lien is invalid. The contractor filing the lien may not have been licensed with the CCB when the work was done. The person filing the lien may have failed to provide you with the proper notices, or may not have provided the notices at the required time. These are just a few examples. Again, your attorney is your best source of advice.

If I find that a lien is valid, what do I do?

You may be able to file a complaint against your contractor for liens filed by subcontractors, employees, material suppliers, and equipment rental companies. Contact the CCB at www.oregon.gov/ccb or 503-378-4621 to obtain a form entitled Breach of Contract Complaint Form for Owners and Prime Contractors. Read and follow the instructions carefully. You must give the contractor written notice that you plan to file a complaint with the CCB. When you complete the form, be sure, on item number 4 (Nature of Complaint) to mark the box "Complaint by Owner – Construction Lien Filed." You will send the complaint form and other required documents to the CCB office. If the CCB determines it can process the complaint, it will request that you pay a fee of $50.

The CCB may be able to help you obtain money from the general contractor to pay all or part of the money owed. Filing the complaint form is the first step in getting help from the CCB.

If a valid lien is filed against your property, you should contact an attorney and also seek relief through the CCB complaint process.

Chapter 4

What else does the CCB need besides a completed complaint form?

You should attach the following documents to your completed complaint form:

1. A copy of your contract
2. Records of payments made to your primary contractor
3. A copy of the Information Notice provided by your primary contractor
4. A copy of the Notice of Right to a Lien, if you received one from the subcontractor or others
5. A copy of the lien with the county recorder's seal
6. A copy of any foreclosure documents that you may have received, and
7. Copies of invoices from the company that filed the lien (the subcontractor, material supplier, or equipment rental company)

What happens after I send this information to the CCB?

The CCB will schedule an on-site meeting to mediate the dispute between you and your contractor. If your contractor elects not to participate, or is unwilling to resolve the dispute, you need to pursue a court action. If you prevail, you may provide the judgment in your favor to the CCB. The CCB will notify the contractor's bonding company to pay you.

Will the CCB automatically process my complaint?

The CCB cannot process your complaint if:

- Your general contractor was not licensed when the work was done.
- If the contractor's bond has already been paid out to others who filed complaints before you.

The CCB complaint process, if successful, can obtain money from the general contractor's surety bond to pay all or part of, the money owed.

A contractor filed a lien on my home a year ago and is refusing to take it off. How can I get the lien removed?

Liens are invalid after 120 days if no lawsuit to foreclose on the lien has been filed and no extension of time has been awarded. Contact your attorney for further information.

My primary contractor did not pay the subcontractor because the subcontractor's work was of poor quality. Now, the subcontractor has filed a lien on my property. What can be done to get me out of the dispute? Can I file a complaint against the subcontractor?

You can request that the general contractor and subcontractor settle their differences in court or that they file CCB complaints against each other and let the CCB help resolve their dispute.

You can also file a complaint against your general contractor if the lien is not immediately released. You cannot file a complaint against the subcontractor because you must have a contract with someone in order to file a complaint against them. Your general contractor can file a complaint against the subcontractor.

Property owners cannot file complaints against subcontractors because there must be a contract between the two parties in order for one party to file a complaint against the other.

Chapter 4

Contractor responsibilities

Who sends what notice to property owners?

- If you contract directly with an owner of residential property, you must provide the Information Notice To Owner about Construction Liens.
- If you have no direct contract with an owner of property, and you wish to have a right to file a lien, you must send a Notice of Right to a Lien to the property owner.

There are some exceptions. Refer to pages 27 -30 for the exceptions that may apply.

Are there any specific requirements for contractors that have built a house on their own property, or have rehabilitated an existing house that they own, and are now selling the house?

Yes. Under the Homebuyer Protection Act, if the sale involves:

- A new single family home, duplex, triplex, condominium unit, or
- Remodeling an existing single family home, duplex, triplex, condominium unit for a cost of at least $50,000 within three months prior to the sale

If so, the builder-seller must provide protection for the buyer against claims of lien by:

- Purchasing title insurance;
- Retaining at least 25% of the sales price in escrow;
- Obtaining lien waivers or releases;
- Obtaining a bond or letter of credit; or
- Waiting to complete the sale after the deadline for perfecting liens (usually 75 days)

The builder-seller must complete the Notice of Compliance with the Homebuyer Protection Act (HPA) of 2003 (a form available from the CCB website). Both seller and buyer must sign the form and retain copies for their records.

> Contractors who have contracts with the property owner must give the Information Notice to Owner About Construction Liens.

Failure to provide the Notice of Compliance with the Homebuyer Protection Act (HPA) not later than the date of sale of residential property, is a Class "A" violation under Oregon law. In addition, if the builder-seller fails to provide the buyer with the protections required, and the buyer is damaged as a result, the buyer may seek recovery from the builder-seller for an amount up to twice the actual damages, plus attorney fees, costs, and disbursements.

Are there any residential property owners for whom general contractors do not need to provide an Information Notice To Owner About Construction Liens?

Yes. If the owner of the residential property is a licensed contractor, the notice is not required. This is also the case, for example, when a general contractor is constructing a house for a property owner who is also a licensed contractor. The general contractor does have lien rights against the property, but is not required to deliver an Information Notice To Owner About Construction Liens to the property owner.

Do I need to provide an Information Notice To Owner About Construction Liens when I bid a commercial job?

No. The notice is for residential construction only.

How important is the Information Notice To Owner About Construction Liens and what happens if a general contractor does not provide one to a residential property owner?

The notice is very important! If the general contractor fails to provide it to the property owner, the contractor loses lien rights, faces possible suspension of his or her license, and a civil penalty of up to $5,000.

The notice has signature spaces for the general contractor's signature and the property owner's signature. The general contractor should either provide duplicate originals that are each signed, or provide a copy of the signed original to the property owner. The general contractor must keep an original or a copy as proof that the notice was provided to the property owner. CCB's rules require that you maintain proof of delivery of this notice for a period of two years after entering into the contract.

The general contractor must keep proof of delivery of the Information Notice to Owner About Construction Liens for two years after entering into a contract.

Where can I get copies of the Information Notice To Owner About Construction Liens?

The current notice was last revised on January 1, 2010 (always make sure you are using the latest form available). Licensed contractors may download and print copies from the CCB website, or call the CCB and request a copy.

Suppose the general contractor fails to provide an Information Notice To Owner About Construction Liens to the residential property owner. Can a subcontractor, employee, material supplier, or equipment rental company still file a lien against the property owner?

Yes, as long as the subcontractor, employee, material supplier, or equipment rental company has given the property owner a Notice of Right to a Lien and has met all deadlines for sending the notice.

If I am a subcontractor, is it true that I cannot file a lien against a residential property owner unless I have previously sent a Notice of Right to a Lien?

That is correct. Since your contract is with the general contractor, you must provide a Notice of Right to a Lien to the property owner (with whom you have no contract). The notice must be given within a required time period (see below).

When should a subcontractor or supplier send a Notice of Right to a Lien?

The Notice of Right to a Lien should be given within eight working days of the start date of the work provided, or the delivery date of materials or equipment. For example, if a subcontractor began work on December 12, 2007 (a Wednesday) the subcontractor would need to provide the Notice of Right to a Lien no later than December 24, 2007 (a Monday following two weekend days) in order to have a right to a lien on all work performed beginning the day the subcontractor started work. The Notice of Right to a Lien is considered given when it is personally delivered or mailed. (Also see explanation below.)

Subcontractors, employees, material suppliers, and equipment rental companies must give the property owner a Notice of Right to a Lien if they want to protect their lien rights.

Are there any other persons that I need to notify about the possibility that I may file a lien?

In order to obtain priority (preference) over a previously filed mortgage or trust deed on the property, persons providing materials or supplies must also provide the Notice of Right to a Lien to the holder of a recorded mortgage or trust deed. The notice should be given within eight working days of the delivery date of the materials or supplies. If the notice was delivered to the mortgage or trust deed holder on the ninth day after delivery of the materials or supplies, then the supplier would not be entitled to payment for the materials or supplies provided on the first day of the job. You may wish to contact an attorney for more specifics on this notice requirement.

What happens if I sent the Notice of Right to a Lien too late or to the wrong address, or if I had some other problem with its delivery?

You lose your lien rights. You may want to contact an attorney.

Where can I get Notice of Right to a Lien forms?

The form is available from the CCB website www.oregon.gov/ccb.

How do I go about filing a lien?

Consult an attorney. A lien involves a notary, legal description, recording fee, several deadlines, and extensive paperwork. If anything in the process is not done correctly, the lien may be invalid, or you could lose your right to collect attorney fees should you have to foreclose on the lien.

What is the deadline for filing a lien? What if I file the lien after that deadline?

You have 75 days to file a lien from:

1. The date you last worked or delivered materials to the property or
2. The date of substantial completion of the construction,

whichever date came first.

The lien will be invalid and cannot be enforced if it is filed more than 75 days after the applicable date.

If you intend to file a lien, you should consult an attorney. If anything in the process is done incorrectly, the lien may be invalid.

Chapter 4

The requirements for pursuing a lien are so strict. Why?

Foreclosure of a lien is a serious matter – someone can lose his or her property. The strict requirements are also intended to prevent abuses which may result in homeowners having to pay twice for the same materials, equipment, services, or labor.

What do I need to do after I file a lien and it is recorded?

Within 20 days after the lien is filed, the lien claimant must mail a written notice to the owner and any mortgage or trust deed holder, stating that the lien claim has been filed. A copy of the lien must be attached to the written notice. Failure to deliver this notice does not invalidate the lien, but you will be unable to recover costs, disbursements or attorney fees upon foreclosure of the lien.

What happens after a lien is filed and recorded?

Either the property owner pays the amount you are owed, or you may file a lawsuit to foreclose the lien. Within 120 days of the date you recorded the lien, you must bring a lawsuit to foreclose on the lien. The lien will become invalid after 120 days if a court action is not filed.

How do I initiate a foreclosure action?

The CCB cannot help you file a foreclosure action, which is a type of lawsuit filed in court. You will need to talk to an attorney.

As the general contractor, I just want to get the money that the property owner owes me. Is there an easier way for a general contractor to get paid?

If you are the general contractor and you improved property at the owner's request, you must file a lien to rightfully claim an interest in the property, to obtain your payment. However, if you prefer, you may file a claim in state small claims court (for amounts of $10,000 or less), or in state circuit court (for larger amounts). The CCB has no authority to resolve contractor disputes against property owners. The CCB may get involved if the property owner requests the dispute resolution assistance.

If a general contractor has not been paid by the property owner, he or she can file a claim in state small claims court, or in state circuit court.

Can a subcontractor, laborer, material supplier, or equipment rental company file a lien against a licensed general contractor who did not pay them in full?

Usually, the answer is no. The only time that a lien can be filed against the general contractor is if the general contractor owns the property. In that case, subcontractors do have lien rights – without providing an Information Notice to Owner About Construction Liens.

Are there other ways that subcontractors, laborers, material suppliers, and equipment rental companies can get the money that they are owed by a general contractor?

Yes. A subcontractor, material supplier, or equipment rental company can file a complaint with the CCB or file a lawsuit in court. If the process is successful, payment may be made from the contractor's bond. Bond payments to non-owner complainants are limited to $3,000.

How does a subcontractor, employee, material supplier, or equipment rental company file a complaint with the CCB against the general contractor?

You should obtain the appropriate complaint form from the CCB website, or contact the CCB at 503-378-4621 and ask for a form. There are three forms that you may obtain online at www.oregon.gov/ccb:

- Breach of Contract Complaint Form for Subcontractors
- Breach of Contract Complaint Form for Employees
- Breach of Contract Complaint Form for Material/Equipment

You must file the complaint within one year of the date of the debt.

Suppose a property owner, who has had a valid lien filed against his or her property, files a complaint with the CCB. What does this mean?

If the general contractor was paid in full, a property owner may file a complaint with the CCB against the general contractor to obtain an award to pay all or part of the money owed to a subcontractor, material supplier, or equipment rental company.

If a general contractor has not paid subcontractors or other suppliers, those persons may file a complaint with the CCB.

Chapter 4

If the contractor is unable or unwilling to pay, the property owner prevails and obtains a judgment, CCB may require that payment be made from the contractor's bond. The CCB will process the complaint if:

1. It is filed within the one-year filing period, and
2. If the general contractor was licensed when the work was done.

This process can take several months.

What if the subcontractor, material supplier, or equipment rental company begins the process to foreclose their lien while the property owner's complaint is pending?

The property owner has the right to request that the court issue a stay. This will delay the foreclosure proceedings until the CCB finishes processing the complaint.

In summary, what are the most important things for a general contractor to do in order to file a valid residential lien?

1. The general contractor must be licensed with the CCB, and
2. The general contractor must give the property owner an Information Notice to Owner About Construction Liens if it is required, and
3. The lien must be filed within 75 days of the last day labor was provided or materials furnished.

In summary, what is important for a subcontractor, material supplier, or equipment rental company to do in order to file a valid residential lien claim?

Send the Notice of Right to a Lien by registered or certified mail, or deliver it in person within eight working days of starting the work or providing the materials or equipment.

Where can I get more information about Oregon's lien laws?

You may wish to contact an attorney or review Oregon's Lien Law, found in ORS Chapter 87.

> To protect their lien rights, contractors should be licensed, and should provide the required notices to property owners.

Construction Contractors Board
PO Box 14140
Salem, OR 97309-5052

Sample Questions

CHAPTER 4

1. **Which of the following is NOT true about an *Information Notice to Owner*?**

   ❏ 1. It protects an original contractor's lien rights.

   ❏ 2. It explains the rights and responsibilities of the owner and original contractor.

   ❏ 3. It may be given any time before construction is completed but only covers work done eight days before the notice is delivered and all work after the notice was delivered.

   ❏ 4. It must be given to the owner, or first purchaser, on a residential project over $2,000 even if the original contractor will not record a lien claim.

2. **A claim of lien must be recorded within 75 days of:**

   ❏ 1. The date the contractor's payment was due.

   ❏ 2. Receipt of the owner's demand for list of materials, supplies, and labor provided.

   ❏ 3. When the project is substantially completed.

   ❏ 4. Delivery of the *Notice of Right to a Lien* to the owner.

3. **Which of the following is true about the *Notice of Right to a Lien*?**

   ❏ 1. It must be given at the time of bidding a project.

   ❏ 2. It must be given to an owner when you have a contract directly with that owner.

   ❏ 3. It need not be given if you provide only labor and materials on a commercial project.

   ❏ 4. It need not be given if you provide only materials on a commercial project.

Answers: 1. [3]

          2. [3]

          3. [3]

CHAPTER 5

TAXES, RECORDKEEPING, AND BUSINESS PRACTICES

Objectives

At the end of this chapter, you will be able to:

1. Identify the types of business entities available to construction contractors
2. Explain requirements for conducting business in Oregon, such as identification numbers and where to obtain them.
3. Identify tax issues related to different forms of business ownership.
4. Understand the basics of financing a small business.
5. Recognize the importance of recordkeeping and the need for record retention.
6. Explain the basic concepts of accounting systems, including internal controls and financial statements.
7. Identify required taxes, tax forms, and appropriate filing dates.
8. Understand payroll tax calculations, reporting and payment.
9. Explain profit, cash flow, and other basic financial terms, concepts, and methods.
10. Understand the basics of cash flow management.
11. Identify tools used to analyze financial information, including calculating break-even points, employer labor costs and working capital.
12. Identify the benefits of using an accounting practitioner and/or attorney.
13. Realize the basic issues surrounding the cause and effects of bankruptcy.

Introduction

When starting a business in Oregon, individuals need to understand the financial responsibilities involved. The information in this chapter is organized for a start-up business. It discusses the following topics:

- Business start-up issues, including choosing a business entity (form of business), and financing a business.
- Keeping records and reasons for retaining them.
- The basics of accounting systems, including financial statements.
- How to use information from an accounting system.
- Regulatory requirements, including payroll tax responsibilities.
- Being aware of the issues involved when a business files bankruptcy.
- Understanding the benefits of working with professionals.

Business Start-Up

Business owners must manage the financial health of their business just as they manage the work performed by their employees at the job site. Business failures are more often due to time and financial problems than construction problems. Problems can be avoided and a business can be successful by following good finance and business management principles. This chapter introduces income tax issues related to forming a business. Because this is a complicated subject, with many more issues than can be discussed here, individuals starting a business are encouraged to seek out other resources should they have more in-depth questions.

Choosing a Business Entity

The CCB recognizes sole proprietorships, partnerships, joint ventures (JV), limited partnerships (LP), limited liability partnerships (LLP), corporations, limited liability companies (LLC), and business trusts as business entities for the construction industry. The form of business chosen will affect the amount of income taxes paid, the tax forms required, and the accounting reporting methods used.

Each entity has advantages and disadvantages. There is no one right way to form your business. A sole proprietorship might be right for one business, while a corporation is best for another. The owner's willingness to accept personal liability, the owner's management experience, tax considerations, and the financial condition of the business affect the choice of entity.

The following table shows the types of business entities that may be chosen.

Business Entity Types

	Single Owner	Multiple Owner
Sole Proprietorship	X	N/A
Partnership, Limited Partnership (LP), or Limited Liability Partnership (LLP)	N/A	X
Corporation	X	X
S-Corporation	X	X
Limited Liability Company	(1)	(2)

(1) If the entity has a single owner, the entity may elect to be taxed as a sole proprietor or as a corporation.

(2) If the entity has two or more owners, the entity may elect to be taxed as a partnership or as a corporation.

N/A indicates not applicable.

Use the business ownership information in the CCB application (see Chapter 1) and, if needed, the advice of an accountant and an attorney to help determine which entity to choose.

Sole Proprietorship

Structure

A sole proprietorship is the simplest and least expensive business entity to set up. No legal steps are required to organize a sole proprietorship. In a sole proprietorship, one person owns, operates, and supervises the business. One owner (*proprietor*) has sole control and sole responsibility for all the business decisions and actions. Sole proprietors may be personally liable, however, for all debts and obligations of the sole proprietorship.

Tax Considerations

In a sole proprietorship, the business does not pay income taxes. Instead, the owner pays income taxes on the net profit generated from the business at the owner's individual tax rate.

A sole proprietor is not an employee of the business. There is no paycheck and, thus, no taxes are withheld and forwarded to the government by the business. However, a sole proprietor may need to estimate his or her income tax and make an estimated tax payment to the IRS on a quarterly basis.

As discussed later in this chapter, Social Security and Medicare taxes are withheld from employee paychecks and matched by equal employer contributions. Since a sole proprietor does not receive a paycheck, no such withholding or matching occurs. But payments for Social Security and Medicare still must be made—this is called the self-employment tax. In

2014, the self- employment tax is 15.3percent of net self-employment earnings. In addition to the self-employment tax, the income may be subject to an additional 0.9 percent Medicare surtax, depending upon income and filing status. The tax is generally paid quarterly.

Partnership or Joint Venture (JV)

Structure

A partnership or JV is made up of two or more individuals, business entities, or a mixture of both. Unlike a general partnership, a JV is normally established for a single, large project. If a partner or joint venturer leaves the business, the contractor must obtain a new license before continuing to conduct a contracting business because it becomes a new legal entity.

To form a partnership or JV, it is advisable to consult an attorney and obtain a written partnership or JV agreement. The purpose of the agreement is to define the rights and obligations of the partners or joint venturers. Individual partners or joint venturers are generally liable for the debts of the partnership or the JV.

Tax Considerations

Partnerships do not pay income taxes. Instead, partners are taxed individually on their share of profits at their own individual tax rates. Partners may need to estimate their income and make tax payments quarterly. In general, partnership profits are subject to the self-employment tax.

Limited Liability Partnership (LLP)

Structure

An LLP is an association of two or more licensed individuals doing business. In this form of organization, the liability of all of the partners is limited. Generally, the partners are not responsible for the debts, obligations, or liabilities of the partnership resulting from the actions or negligence of another partner, employee, or agent of the partnership. The partners may be liable for their own acts or omissions, or those of employees or agents under their direct supervision.

Tax Considerations

LLP's do not pay federal or state income taxes though they may be subject to state filing fees and some local income taxes. Instead, partners are taxed individually on their share of profits at their own individual tax rates. Partners may need to estimate their income and make tax payments quarterly. In general, partnership profits are subject to the self-employment tax and possibly the Medicare surtax.

Corporation
Structure
A corporation is a legal entity created under law by *articles of incorporation*. To form a corporation in Oregon, an entity must file its articles of incorporation with the Oregon Corporation Division, Business Registry, together with a required fee. A corporation is owned by *shareholders* who have no liability for corporate debts and obligations. A corporation exists separately from its owners and continues to exist even though the shareholders may change.

Corporations are managed by a *board of directors*. The directors must elect a president and secretary, who are called *officers* (the directors may elect or appoint other officers). The directors must also adopt *bylaws*. A corporation must have a *registered agent* in Oregon, who must have a physical street address.

A corporation formed in Oregon is a *"domestic"* corporation. A corporation formed in another state is a *"foreign"* corporation. If a foreign corporation wishes to perform construction in Oregon, it must register to transact business in Oregon and provide the name and address of an Oregon registered agent.

A corporation may also elect a federal tax designation as a "Subchapter S corporation" (small business corporation), which, under certain conditions, allows it to have its undistributed tax income taxed to its shareholders.

Tax Considerations
Unlike sole proprietorships and partnerships, a corporation does pay income tax on profits made. Often, the corporate tax rate is lower than individual taxpayer rates. Shareholders pay taxes on salaries and dividends received from the corporation. Corporations may need to estimate income and make quarterly tax payments.

S-Corporation
An S-Corporation is like other corporations in all aspects except income taxation. Generally, there is no federal income tax for an S-Corporation at the corporate level. There may be state filing fees and some states tax S-Corporations.

Tax Considerations
Shareholders are taxed personally on their share of profits, in addition to any salary paid to them by the S-Corporation. Distributions of profits are generally not subject to self-employment taxes.

Limited Liability Company (LLC)

Structure

An LLC is an unincorporated association having one or more members. It is formed under *articles of organization.* To form an LLC in Oregon, an entity must file its articles of organization with the Oregon Corporation Division, Business Registry, together with a required fee. An LLC can be managed by its members or by a manager. An LLC has the flexibility and tax advantages of a general partnership but its liability is limited like that of a corporation.

Managers of an LLC can be compared to corporation directors and *members* can be compared to corporation shareholders. The internal affairs of an LLC are governed by *operating agreements*, which can be compared to corporation bylaws. An LLC must have a *registered agent* in Oregon who must have a physical street address.

Tax Considerations

Depending on how an LLC is organized, it can have the tax attributes of a sole proprietorship, partnership, or a corporation. In other words, the income taxes might be paid by the business at a corporate tax rate, or by the owners at their individual tax rates. An election is made with the filing of the first income tax return. This flexibility has made the LLC a popular choice of business entity. An LLC is formed under state law. For federal purposes it may be taxed as a Sole Proprietor, a Partnership, an S-Corp, or C-Corp. Some states tax LLC's differently than other states.

Owner(s) Compensation

No matter which type of business entity is chosen, the business is considered a separate legal entity from the owner. How an owner wants to be paid is a factor in determining the business entity that is chosen. Owner compensation for different business types is handled in the following ways:

- Sole proprietors are not paid a salary but may take money from the business as a draw.
- Partners generally are not paid a salary but may make withdrawals from the business (a distributive share).
- Corporation shareholders may be paid a salary and/or dividends.
- S-Corporation shareholders may be paid a salary and also may take a distribution.
- LLC members may be paid a salary in certain circumstances. The manner of compensation depends on how the entity elects to be taxed and/or take a distribution.

Consult with an accountant for suggestions and advice.

The following illustration summarizes the types of businesses and corresponding requirements.

	DESCRIPTION	WORKERS' COMPENSATION	BUSINESS NAME AND REGISTRATION REQUIREMENT WITH THE OREGON CORPORATION DIVISION	TAXES
SOLE PROPRIETORSHIP	Exists when a single individual owns and operates his or her own business. In effect, the owner is the business. The funds for the business come from the owner's personal funds, or loans or gifts to the owner. The owner's personal assets can be used to satisfy debts and taxes owed by the sole proprietor. Personal assets may also be attached to pay any legal damages resulting from lawsuits filed against the business. A sole proprietor reports income (or losses) in the owner's tax return. If a sole proprietor dies, the business ceases to exist.	Required if the sole proprietor is a commercial contractor. Otherwise, not required unless the sole proprietor has employees.	Does not have to be registered with the Oregon Corporation Division Business Registry *unless* it uses an assumed business name. If the name of the business does not include the full legal name of the business owner, the business name must be registered as an assumed business name with Business Registry.	The business does not pay income taxes; the owner pays income taxes on the net profit generated from the business at the owner's individual tax rate.
GENERAL PARTNERSHIP or JOINT VENTURE	A voluntary association of two or more persons for the purpose of owning and operating a business. In a general partnership, the partners contribute assets to the partnership and share the management, profits and losses. All partners are personally liable for the obligations of the partnership. Property acquired by a partnership is property of the partnership and not of the partners individually. Upon death or withdrawal of one of the partners, the partnership may be subject to dissolution. Must file an informational tax report. Individual partners must report, and pay, taxes on their share of the partnership income, even if the partnership income is reinvested in the business. A *joint venture* is a partnership that is formed solely for the purpose of a single business undertaking.	Required if the partnership is a commercial contractor. Otherwise, not required unless the general partnership has employees or if there are more than two partners that are not all members of the same family.	Does not have to be registered with the Oregon Corporation Division Business Registry unless it uses an assumed business name. If the name of each general partner is not conspicuously disclosed in the business name, then the business name must be registered as an assumed business name with Business Registry.	Partnerships do not pay income taxes. Instead, partners are taxed individually on their share of profits at their own individual tax rates.
LIMITED LIABILITY PARTNERSHIP (LLP)	An association of two or more licensed, professional individuals (including licensed contractors) doing business as a partnership. The concepts of a general partnership are generally applicable, except that partners in a registered LLP are directly liable for their own negligent or wrongful acts (or those committed by persons under their direct supervision and control), but not vicariously liable for other partnership obligations. A qualifying general partnership may convert to an LLP without making a conversion from one form (partnership) to another (corporation) and thus avoid a potentially taxable conversion.	Required if the LLP is a commercial contractor. Otherwise, not required unless the LLP has employees or if there are more than two partners that are not all members of the same family.	The name of the limited liability partnership must contain the words "Limited Liability Partnership" or the abbreviation "L.L.P." or "LLP" as the last words or letters of its name. The name must be registered with the Oregon Corporation Business Registry. If the limited liability partnership will be using a name other than its registered name to conduct business, it must also register that name as an assumed business name.	

	DESCRIPTION	WORKERS' COMPENSATION	BUSINESS NAME AND REGISTRATION REQUIREMENT WITH THE OREGON CORPORATION DIVISION	TAXES
LIMITED PARTNERSHIP	A partnership formed by two or more persons having one or more al partners and one or more limited partners. (The associating "persons" may include individuals, partnerships, limited partnerships, trusts or corporations – but not limited liability companies). The general partners control the business and are liable for the debts and obligations of the partnership. *See* "General Partnership." The limited partners take no active role in the management of the business. Limited partners are similar to shareholders in a corporation because their liability for debts and obligations of the limited partnership is limited to the amount of their contribution to the business. Profits or losses are typically allocated to limited partners on the basis of their percentage of ownership. Death or withdrawal of a general partner ordinarily dissolves the limited partnership (unless the partnership agreement provides otherwise). Death or withdrawal of a limited partner has no effect on the partnership.	Required if the LP is a commercial contractor. Otherwise, not required unless the LP has employees or if there are more than two partners that are not all members of the same family.	The name of the limited partnership must contain the words "limited partnership." The name must be registered with the Oregon Corporation Division Business Registry. If the limited partnership will be using a name other than its registered name to conduct business, it must also register that name as an assumed business name.	
CORPORATIONS	A legal entity separate from its owners, who are called shareholders. Corporations are created by filing articles of incorporation with the state in which the corporation is formed. Acts as a single entity. It exists separately from its owners (shareholders) and continues to exist even though the shareholders may change. A corporation may own property, sue and be sued. Has board of directors and officers and observes certain legal formalities such as annual shareholder meetings and the creation of meeting minutes. Corporations have limited liability – meaning that while the corporation is fully liable for all of its business obligations, individual shareholders are liable only to the extent of their investment. For income tax purposes, for-profit corporations file either as a C Corporation or as an S Corporation. A C Corporation pays taxes on its income and the corporation's shareholders pay taxes only on income distributed to them, as by dividends. A corporation with 75 or fewer employees may elect to be an S Corporation. An S Corporation's income is allocated to the shareholders and is taxed at their personal rate, similar to a partnership.	Required if the corporation is a commercial contractor. Otherwise, not required unless the corporation has employees or if there are more than two corporate officers that are not all members of the same family.	The name of the corporation must contain either "corporation," "incorporated," "company," or "limited," or an abbreviation of one of those words. A corporation's name must be registered with the Oregon Corporation Division Business Registry. If the corporation will be using a name other than its registered name to conduct business, it must also register that name as an assumed business name.	A corporation pays income taxes on profits made. Often, the corporate tax rate is lower than individual taxpayer rates. Shareholders pay taxes on salaries and dividends received from the corporation. Note: Generally, there is no income tax for an S Corporation at the corporate level. Instead, shareholders are taxed personally on their share of profits.

	DESCRIPTION	WORKERS' COMPENSATION	BUSINESS NAME AND REGISTRATION REQUIREMENT WITH THE OREGON CORPORATION DIVISION	TAXES
LIMITED LIABILITY COMP. (LLC)	An unincorporated association having one or more members. The LLC can be managed either by its members or by one or more managers. Managers can, but are not required to, be members. LLC managers are similar to directors of corporations. Members are like corporate shareholders. To become a member of an LLC, a person ordinarily contributes cash, assets or services. LLCs provide the limited liability protection and operational flexibility of a corporation, together with pass-through taxation ordinarily found in S Corporations (without the restrictions of an S Corporation).	Required if the LLC is a commercial contractor. Otherwise, not required unless the LLC has employees or if there are more than two members that are not all members of the same family.	The name of the limited liability company must contain the words "limited liability company" or one of the abbreviations, "L.L.C." or "LLC". If the LLC will be using a name other than its registered name to conduct business, it must also register that name as an assumed business name.	Depending on how it is organized, an LLC can have the tax attributes of a sole proprietorship, partnership, or a corporation. An election is made with the filing of the first income tax return.
BUSINESS TRUST	Any association engaged in or operating a business under a written trust agreement or declaration of trust, the beneficial interest under which is divided into transferable certificates of participation or shares. Generally, business trusts are subject to the laws governing corporations. The trustees, shareholders or beneficiaries of a business trust are not personally liable for obligations of the business trust.	Required if the trust is a commercial contractor. Otherwise, not required unless the trust has employees or if there are more than two trustees that are not all members of the same family.	A trust's name must be registered with the Oregon Corporation Division Business Registry. If the corporation will be using a name other than its registered name to conduct business, it must also register that name as an assumed business name.	

Financing a Business

It takes money to start and operate a business. Most small business owners use their own funds to start their business, or they may borrow from family and friends. If additional capital is required for the business, how will it be obtained?

Business Plan

The first step is to write a business plan. A written business plan showing where the owner wants to go and how he or she plans to get there is extremely important. Be aware that a business plan is an ever-changing document; as the business grows and expands, the plan should be updated. Use it to evaluate problems and find solutions. Then, update it to set revised goals.

Financing Alternatives

Businesses have two basic choices when raising money: equity or debt. Equity means cash is received in exchange for a share of the business (the business takes on another owner). For debt, the business makes interest payments and repays principal, but the business' creditors are not owners of the business.

Small construction businesses typically borrow money in one of the following ways:

- Traditional commercial loan—obtained from a bank and used to buy equipment or an inventory of specific items.
- Line of credit—obtained from a bank or credit union. These funds may be used to cover operating expenses as well as special purchases. The line of credit has a preapproved limit, which may be borrowed against up to the limit without getting additional approvals. The credit is paid down when funds are available.
- Intermediate loans—for one year or longer and usually secured by specific assets. These may have installment payments due monthly.
- Second mortgage— based on equity the owner has in a home.

Before financial institutions lend money, they have to be convinced it is in their best interest. Remember, banks and credit unions invest other people's money, so they will be cautious. That means it can be very difficult to get a bank loan. It helps to understand the banker's concerns.

In evaluating the loan application, the banker will consider the business owner's credit history, credit score, and the Five C's of Credit:

- **Capital**. How much money and equipment has the owner invested in the business? Most bankers want to see that the owner has plenty at stake.
- **Capacity**. Will the net cash flow of the business enable the owner to meet financial obligations?
- **Collateral**. What assets can be pledged as security for the loan? For small business loans, bankers often ask for personal guarantees.
- **Character**. Is the borrower trustworthy, determined, and hard working? Does he or she have what it takes to make this business work?
- **Conditions**. Is the business in an expanding or shrinking trade? Do market conditions support claims of income potential?

Additional Start-up Issues
Choice of Accounting Period

An accounting period is generally a period of 12 consecutive months used by a business for accounting and reporting of income and expenses. A business can choose an accounting period that is a calendar year or a fiscal year. Choosing an accounting period, which is also used for tax reporting purposes, must be an informed decision, usually best made with the help of an accounting practitioner. This decision is made before the business files for its federal Employer Identification Number (EIN) and Oregon Business Identification Number (BIN). Choice of entity will also be a determining factor.

Calendar Year

A calendar year is 12 months beginning on Jan. 1 and ending on Dec. 31. Generally, sole proprietors, partnerships, and S-corporations choose to use a calendar year, although any business entity may adopt the calendar year.

Fiscal Year

Some businesses use a natural business year, ending at the annual low point in business activity, at the end of a season, or perhaps a model year. A fiscal year is 12 consecutive months ending on the last day of any month except December.

Employer Identification Number (EIN)

Just as individuals use Social Security numbers for identification, businesses use Employer Identification Numbers (EIN). All businesses with employees are required to obtain a federal EIN. Also, any business entity that is not a sole proprietorship or single member LLC is required to obtain an EIN. A sole proprietorship without employees may use the owner's Social Security number for identification but may wish to use an EIN instead for confidentiality reasons. The bank may require an EIN for your business account.

To obtain an EIN, access the online application at www.irs.gov. The owner will need to answer a series of questions about himself or herself and the business and will receive an EIN upon verification of the information. Reviewing Form SS-4 before applying will allow one to review the questions first to determine the answers before trying to apply.

Business Identification Number (BIN)

Employers are required to obtain a Business Identification Number (BIN) from the Oregon Department of Revenue to register the business entity for reporting taxes and related activity.

To register for a BIN, use the Combined Employer's Registration Report (Form 150-211-055) available from the Department of Revenue (800-356-4222), or apply online at the Central Business Registry at https://secure.sos.state.or.us/ABNWeb. The BIN is used to report, pay, or make inquiries about:

- Oregon withholding taxes
- Oregon unemployment insurance

- Transit taxes
- Workers' Benefit Fund (WBF) assessments

The business owner may wish to work with an accountant to help make sure reports and deposits are filed on time.

Recordkeeping Systems

A recordkeeping system is an important step in the accounting process. Recordkeeping organizes information that supports the financial statements, tax returns, and analysis of business operations.

Reasons for Recordkeeping

It is important to keep records of all business transactions. Besides meeting regulatory requirements for business operations, accurate records are needed to:
- Obtain financing
- Prepare estimates for bids
- Prepare payroll
- Control inventory
- Invoice customers
- Calculate taxes and withholdings
- Prepare tax returns
- Assist in business decisions and planning

In addition to the usual taxation issues, other legal reasons include:
- Contract disputes
- Lien claims
- Subcontractor or supplier claims
- Payroll disputes

Mechanics and Frequency of Recordkeeping

Business records and reports are generally prepared in cycles. The common bookkeeping cycle occurs monthly. Each month, a business will: record incoming monies; record outgoing payments; invoice customers for work performed; record payroll; and make payroll deposits. After these transactions are recorded, monthly bank statements are reconciled, accounts receivables and payables are reviewed, and monthly financial statements and reports are prepared. By following this monthly cycle, an owner will have the necessary information to effectively manage his or her business.

Keep the following business practices in mind when recording transactions:
- Always keep business and personal finances separate.
- Identify source of receipts. When cash is received, record the source.

- Record all deposits and expenses as they occur.
- Do not write checks payable to *cash*. Why the check was written is easily forgotten and difficult to substantiate. There is also no proof of how the money was spent. If a check must be written to *cash*, follow up with a receipt showing the paid expense.
- When making a personal draw out of the business, the owner should make the check payable to him or herself, not payable to *cash*. The draw should then be deposited into the owner's personal bank account.
- Record business expenses when they occur. To account for expenses, write a check when paying them. In writing checks, be sure to record in the checkbook register the amount, date, purpose, and to whom each check was written.
- Substantiate items on income tax returns. This allows the business to verify the items reported if the IRS examines the business' income tax return. A business must be able to support income and expense items on the return by sales slips, invoices, receipts, bank deposit slips, canceled checks, and other documents. These documents are necessary for adequate and complete records.

Good recordkeeping practices provide adequate records or sufficient proof of deductions. Receipts, canceled checks, or a petty cash log will provide such proof.

Ways to Organize Records
There are several methods for organizing records. A small business may be able to use envelopes or folders to organize receipts, using one for each type of expense. Filing records chronologically and alphabetically by each vendor with which the business has transactions should make them easy to locate.

Filing Systems
A filing system is a necessity for quickly finding records. One process is to divide the filing system into major divisions, which might include:
- Accounts payable
- Accounts receivable
- Bank statements and canceled checks
- Contracts
- Copies of all tax returns
- Correspondence
- Credit card receipts
- Employee records
- Financial statements
- Insurance
- Inventory
- Job files

- Month-end reconciliations and support for journal entries
- Proposals and bids
- Vendors

Generally, businesses file alphabetically within each division. Names of businesses or individuals within these broad categories should be filed by full business name or last name of individual. Ignore the initial words "the" and "a" when filing. An example of alphabetical filing is shown below.

File all papers promptly. If the paper volume is small, filing can occur weekly; otherwise, filing is a daily business practice. Do not let filing build up as it makes it difficult to quickly find information.

A Filing System

AMCO Windows	Use title
Building Supply Company, A	Ignore the initial "A"
Forrest Products	
Jerry Meyer Electrical	Jerry Meyer is part of the business name
Merrill, Richard	Individual names are placed last name first
Tiffany Tile Company, The	Ignore the initial "The"
Western Door, Inc.	

Typical Records

The records that are kept are essential to maintaining a successful business. Deciding what records need to be kept and how long to retain them depends on the nature of the business' work and record-retention requirements. Certain projects or contracts may require that some records be kept longer than others. Documents typically required in a construction business are explained below.

Permanent Documents

Any permanent business documents must be kept indefinitely. Examples are:

- Articles of Incorporation
- Articles of Organization
- Partnership agreements
- Insurance policies
- Loan documents
- Lease agreements
- Credit applications
- Contracts
- Annual financial statements
- Copies of filed income tax returns
- Other official documents

All businesses should have copies of their contracts for informational purposes as well as for protection in the case of lawsuits.

Time Cards
A business is required to keep accurate records on wages and hours worked by its employees. Time cards report the hours of labor for each worker and the work categories of labor performance as well as by project. An employer would generally maintain this information anyway, but in the case of a business subject to the Fair Labor Standards Act, these records are required.

Customer/Job Files
Keep a file on all jobs performed. This should include the name, address, and other pertinent information of all customers. Before closing a job file, make sure all payments have been recorded and the customer has paid in full. After a project is completed and closed out, records should be kept in a secure place. They do not need to be maintained in the active file system but need to be attainable if questions arise about the project at a later date.

Contractors are required to deliver certain lien notices on projects and a copy of these lien notices must be kept to prove the notices were delivered in a timely fashion. Keep all of these records in a safe, fireproof place if possible.

Supplier or Vendor Files
Keep a file on all suppliers or vendors with which the company does business. When making a final payment to a supplier, check the records to make sure all payments have been made and recorded. Files can be put into storage after the tax returns have been prepared. These records can also give helpful information for ordering supplies in the future.

Bank Statements and Canceled Checks
These give proof of money spent or bills paid, and are corroborative with invoices and receipts to verify a transaction.

Customer Billing
These are critical for tax calculations and to prepare cash flow reports.

Administrative Expense Records
Also critical for tax calculations. They help determine the costs of running the business.

Job Cost Receipts
Valuable when you prepare your next estimate and to determine if your job is profitable. They are also critical for tax purposes.

Record Retention Guidelines
The length of time a document should be kept depends on the action, expense, or event, the document records. For general business practice, records should be retained for up to seven years.

Records on assets like vehicles, equipment, buildings, or land, must be kept for as long as the assets are owned. Keep records relating to property until the period of limitations expires for the year in which the property was disposed in a taxable disposition. Records must be kept so the owner can figure any depreciation, amortization, or depletion deduction, and to figure the basis for computing gain or loss when the property is sold or otherwise disposed.

Records that support an item of income or deductions on a tax return should be kept until the period of limitations for that return runs out. The period of limitations is the period of time in which a tax return can be amended to claim a credit or refund, or the IRS can assess additional tax. The following table contains the periods of limitations that apply to income tax returns. Unless otherwise noted, the years refer to the period after the return was filed. Returns filed before the due date are treated as filed on the due date.

IF you...	THEN the period is...
1. Owe additional tax and situations (2), (3), and (4), below, do not apply to you	3 years
2. Do not report income that you should report and it is more than 25% of the gross income shown on the return	6 years
3. File a fraudulent return	Not limited
4. Do not file a return	Not limited
5. File a claim for credit or refund after you filed your return	Later of: 3 years or 2 years after tax was paid
6. File a claim for a loss from worthless securities or a bad debt deduction	7 years

NOTE: If you have employees, you must keep all employment tax records for at least four years after the date the tax becomes due or is paid, whichever is later.

Different agencies have different rules for how long records need to be retained:

- Oregon's Department of Revenue requires timecards and payroll records be retained for at least six years after filing the required report.
- Other tax authorities may also have specific requirements.

An accounting practitioner can answer questions and advise the business owner on how long to keep the documents.

Accounting Systems

An accounting system is a set of procedures to collect, record, and summarize business transactions.

Methods of Accounting

An accounting method is a set of rules that dictates **when** to record business income and expenses. There are two basic methods: the cash method and the accrual method.

The Cash Method

This method records income when cash is received and records expenses when paid. In this system, a sale on credit is not recorded until the payment is received, and invoices from suppliers are not recorded until the bills are paid. Although the cash method is simple to use, it generally does not give an accurate picture of the business's real financial position as noncash transactions are not included. In addition, this method is not always acceptable for tax and generally accepted accounting principles (GAAP) reporting purposes.

The Accrual Method

This method records income at the time the income is earned, even though payment may not be received until later. Expenses are recorded at the time incurred, even though payment may not be made until later. A disadvantage of using the accrual method is the additional required recordkeeping. An advantage is that financial statements show more thorough and useful information. The accrual method is the generally accepted method of accounting for the construction industry.

Revenue Recognition

Contractors can choose how they are going to recognize or measure the amount of revenue and profit or loss. Revenue results from providing services and materials to customers. This revenue results in a profit or loss after expenses are deducted. In order to measure the revenues in a given accounting period, the contractor needs to select the method of accounting that most accurately reflects his or her business activity.

For construction contractors, revenue can be recognized using two methods:

Percentage-of-Completion Method (PCM)

Under the PCM method, revenue, costs, and profits or losses are recognized in each accounting period as construction progresses to completion. This method typically is used for high-dollar and long-term contracts. The contractor's accounting system must provide reasonable estimates for completion rates and reliable recordkeeping for job cost control during progress of work. This system will support the contractor's progress billings.

Completed-Contract Method (CCM)

Under this method, revenue, costs, and profits or losses are deferred until the project is complete. It is most often used for smaller or short-term contracts.

Accounting System Mechanics

Accounting systems range from simple checkbook registers to comprehensive computer programs. The best system for each business depends on the business' complexity, need for information, and ability to use the information generated. Either a single-entry or double-entry system of accounting may be used.

Single Entry

The single-entry system is a simple listing of transactions, like keeping a checkbook register. The single-entry system is the simplest to keep. A number of single- entry systems are available at office supply stores.

Double Entry

A double-entry system records each transaction separately using credits and debits that must balance or equal each other. The double-entry system has built-in checks and balances that provide accuracy and control. It can be complicated to learn, although computerized accounting systems perform the double entries automatically and simplify the process significantly.

Journals and ledgers are used as components of an accounting system. Transactions are entered in the appropriate journal, probably on a daily basis. At the end of the month, the journal entries are added up and posted to a general ledger which is summarized and used to prepare the financial statements.

Journals are found in both handwritten and computerized accounting systems. Typical journals include:

- **Payroll journal.** This contains employee wage information. This system is set up to gather and monitor labor cost data broken down by specific job types. The data may be used for future contract estimates.
- **Cash disbursements journal.** In this journal, all checks written are recorded, including the amount paid and the purpose of the payment.
- **Cash receipts journal.** This shows all cash received and the source of the receipts.
- **General journal.** This is used to record transactions that are not captured in the other journals or to make corrections.

Internal Controls

Internal controls are systems established to safeguard a business' assets, minimize errors, and assure information received about the business is reliable. The following are examples of internal control procedures:

Accounts Payable

All bills should be paid from the business bank account. No check should be signed by the owner or authorized officer without first reviewing and reconciling related documents such as the vendor invoice and packing slip. The invoice should be marked paid to reduce the potential for double payment.

Accounts Receivable

All receipts from customers should be compared to the original invoice sent to verify the payment amount. Receipts should be deposited in the business bank account as soon as possible.

Compare to Budget

The authorized officer or owner should compare actual cash receipts and disbursements with budgeted amounts and follow up if there are significant variances.

Monthly Bank Statements

The authorized officer or owner should receive monthly bank statements unopened. He/she opens and reviews the statement and canceled checks, then delivers them to the bookkeeper for reconciliation.

Payment by Check

Except for small expenditures out of petty cash (see below), all business expenses should be paid by check, electronic transfer, or credit card in order to leave a traceable trail of the transaction. Checks should be pre-numbered and should be approved by the authorized corporate officer or business owner before payment is made.

Petty Cash Fund

Petty cash is a small amount of money kept on hand for payment of incidental expenses. One person should be in charge of the petty cash and must keep records of amounts spent. These records should be reviewed by the business owner or bookkeeper before the petty cash fund is replenished.

Separation of Duties

A good system of checks and balances can be achieved by separating duties so no one individual handles an entire transaction from start to finish. Separating duties may be difficult in small businesses with few employees. In those cases, additional oversight responsibility falls on the business owner.

Signature Plates and Check Stock

Signature plates, mechanical check signers, and check stock should be kept under the custodial control of the authorized officer or owner.

As the business grows, consult with an accounting practitioner to modify internal controls to fit the volume of revenue and size of operations. It is important that the benefits achieved from these controls are worth the time and cost of applying them.

Financial Statements

Financial statements are very useful tools for making business decisions. If the accounting entries properly record business transactions and operations, the financial statements will accurately represent the financial condition of the business. This is crucial if the owner is asked to provide financial statements to lenders, bankers, vendors, or regulating agencies to verify the financial condition of the business.

The duration of time reported on the statement is referred to as an accounting period. The needs of the business dictate how often financial statements are prepared. At a minimum, financial statements are prepared annually. However, quarterly or monthly statements are recommended because project activities can change in short periods of time and affect the amounts on the financial statements.

The basic financial statements are:
- Balance sheet
- Income statement
- Cash flow statement

Income Statement

The income statement is sometimes referred to as the statement of operations, or profit and loss statement. It reports the revenue and expenses that occurred over a given time period with the resulting profit or loss.

The income statement contains the following categories:
- **Revenues** are the operating income from the normal business activity.
- **Direct costs** include items that can be charged directly to a specific project. Materials, subcontracts, labor, equipment rentals, permits, and bonds are examples of direct costs. Included in labor are payroll taxes, insurance, and other employee benefits operating revenues are shown as other income.
- **Indirect costs** are costs that cannot be traced to a single project, but apply to a number of different jobs. An example is a business vehicle and its fuel.
- **Gross profit** is a subtotal. It is the excess of revenues over direct and indirect costs. In Appendix A, Sample Construction Company reports a gross profit of $325,503 after subtracting direct job costs of $1,036,153 and indirect job costs of $46,590 from total revenue of $1,408,246.
- **General and administrative expenses** include general business expenses such as office rent, office insurance, heat, electricity, office supplies, telephone, accounting expenses, advertising, and the payroll of office employees.
- **Other income/expenses** (non-operating revenues or expenses) are items not directly related to the business's primary activity. For example, gains or losses resulting from the sale of assets are part of other income/expenses.

Net income or net profit is the bottom line after all costs, expenses, and income taxes have been deducted from the revenue.

The income statement can be summarized as follows:

> **Revenue - Direct Job Costs - Indirect Job Costs = Gross Profit**
> and
> **Gross Profit - General and Administrative Expenses - Income Taxes = Net Income**

Although this information offers insight into the historical performance of the business, the income statement specifically shows operating conditions only for the accounting period for which the overall financial statement is generated.

An example of an income statement is shown in Appendix A.

Balance Sheet

The balance sheet shows the financial condition of the business by summarizing business assets, liabilities, and owners' equity at a particular point in time. Think of the balance sheet as a snapshot of financial condition, while the income statement is more like a video showing activity over a period of time.

Assets show the cost of items the business owns such as cash, receivables, equipment, land, and supplies. These are balanced against liabilities such as accounts payable, bank loans, mortgages, and any other financial obligations owed by the business. Finally, the balance sheet shows the owners' equity, which reports owner investment into the business plus profits not yet distributed to the owners.

The basic equation for the balance sheet is as follows.

> **Assets = Liabilities + Owners' Equity**

An example of a balance sheet is shown in Appendix A.

Cash Flow Statement

Cash flow refers to the money received by the contractor for work performed and money disbursed for expenses like office rent, or materials or payments to subcontractors. A cash flow statement summarizes the cash inflows and outflows from operating, investing, and financing activities during the accounting period.

An example of a cash flow statement is shown in Appendix A.

Using Financial Information

Once financial statements have been prepared, this information should be thoroughly reviewed and analyzed for evaluating the financial condition of the business and for preparing future estimates and bids.

Estimating Worksheets

Estimating worksheets are used in preparing a proposal or bid, and this process is discussed in more detail in Chapter 6, Project Management. Generally, expenses from the income statement are used for estimating company overhead and an appropriate markup in pricing work.

In addition, estimating worksheets help in analyzing and comparing estimates from prior jobs. This will show how closely the estimate compares to actual time, revenue, and expenses. Analyzing financial statements for the same time period can reveal how project activity affected the financial condition of the business. If the estimate was effective, it covers job costs, project and company overhead, and results in a profitable project. If the estimate was not effective, the estimator will know where to adjust pricing in future proposals.

Cash Flow

Cash flow is the inflow of available funds to a business and the outflow of cash for paying obligations. A positive cash flow means cash received was greater than cash disbursements. Conversely, a negative cash flow means receipts were less than disbursements.

Inadequate cash flow is one of the major causes of failure for small construction businesses. A business must maintain enough cash to meet payroll, pay material suppliers, make equipment payments, and satisfy other financial obligations as they come due. This can be tricky because expenditures often must be made before cash is received from customers.

The following are some keys to effective cash flow management:
- Send out accurate invoices. If prices or quantities do not match what the customer expects, it could take time to straighten out the problems and for the business to get paid.
- Send invoices on a timely basis. Customers need to receive a bill before they will pay.
- Build progress payments or upfront payments into the construction contracts.
- Age receivables. An aging is a list of all amounts owed to the business and how long they have been outstanding. This list can help the owner focus on slow-paying customers.
- Follow up with slow-paying customers on a regular basis.
- Check invoices from suppliers for accuracy.
- Monitor expenditures. Timely information should be provided through the business' accounting system.
- Pay bills on time and take advantage of early payment discounts.
- If bills cannot be paid on time, contact suppliers to work out a payment plan.
- If funds are limited, consider leasing or renting rather than buying equipment.
- Keep an accounts payable tickler file showing what bills are due and when. This can be a computerized report; a white board hung where it cannot be ignored, or a series of colored file folders.
- Prepare careful estimates for bids and proposals (more on this in Chapter 6), including sufficient amounts to cover overhead and provide a profit.

It is important to note that net cash flow is not the same as net income on the income statement. A business might have a positive net income, yet no money in the bank. There are some very complicated accounting reasons this may occur, but some simple reasons include:
- Customers owe money on jobs for which revenue has already been recorded.
- Supplies or materials were paid for in advance.
- Cash was used to pay for equipment or tools.
- Cash was withdrawn for personal use.
- Cash was used to repay a loan.

Working Capital

Working capital is a measure of the business' ability to meet short-term obligations. It measures cash plus other assets that will soon result in cash (like receivables) compared to short-term debts. Bankers and other creditors look for a positive working capital amount as an indication of the business' likelihood to meet current obligations.

A company's working capital is calculated by subtracting current liabilities from current assets (see the *Common Balance Sheet Ratios and Formulas* table later in this chapter).

Current is defined as within the next 12 months. The difference between the liabilities and assets gives an amount of money left over, as if the business were to suddenly pay off all current debts by liquidating current assets. For example, in Appendix A, Balance Sheet, Sample Construction has working capital of $39,524 ($1,374,012 - $1,344,488) as of Dec. 31.

Calculating working capital helps determine how well the business will survive in the short term. Successful contractors maintain enough working capital to meet all business requirements. Bankers often want to see a good cushion of working capital before loaning money to a business.

In addition to working capital, contractors need to think about the future cash position of their construction business. There may be periods of time when collection of accounts receivable is slow and working capital is insufficient to pay obligations due during that period. A contractor can prepare for such times by maintaining cash reserves and a credit line. Also, opening and maintaining good credit allows the business to draw operating funds from that credit line. Remember, though, that when using a credit line the business is borrowing working capital (and paying interest on it). It is recommended that the draw not exceed the amount the business requires. If it is anticipated that the business will need to borrow money, identify this need early so loan arrangements can be made in a timely manner.

Financial Ratio and Trend Analysis

Though numbers on the financial statements can be difficult to understand, financial statements provide valuable information on the business' financial trends, so learning about them is time well spent. Current financial statements can be compared to ones from earlier months or years to see trends, and thus more effectively manage cash flow and monitor financial objectives. This provides valuable insight on effective business operations.

Financial ratios and formulas applied to information from financial statements further help evaluate the business. Financial ratios show relationships between figures on the financial statements. Generally, ratios show percentages or fractions such as, 2 to 1, 2:1 or 2/1. Ratios will provide answers to questions like:

- Does my business have too much debt?
- Is the business carrying too much inventory?
- How timely are customers in paying the business?
- Are overhead expenses excessive?

Ratios give information about a company's financial strengths and weaknesses.

Three common financial ratios are computed from balance sheets. These are: quick ratio, current ratio, and debt-to-equity. They are explained in the table below, along with the term working capital.

Common Balance Sheet Ratios and Formulas

Financial Ratio	Application
Quick Ratio or "Acid Test": Cash + Accounts Receivable Current Liabilities	Measures immediate financial "liquidity" of a business to pay current liabilities with current assets such as cash and accounts receivable, without selling inventory.
Current Ratio: Total Current Assets Total Current Liabilities	Measures a company's financial strength to pay current liabilities by only using current assets, including inventory. The higher the current ratio, the greater difference between current liabilities and a company's ability to pay them (the company is at less risk of default).
Working Capital: Total Current Assets – Total Current Liabilities	Measures available funds to finance current business activities. Generally, it is the amount of money left over when all current liabilities are paid by liquidating current assets.
Debt-to-Equity: Total Liabilities (or Debt) Total Owners' Equity	Measures the relationship between capital contributed and invested by the owners and the funds provided by creditors. It indicates the extent of protection provided by the owners for creditors. The higher the ratio, the greater the risk to a current or future creditor. A lower ratio means the company is more financially stable and is probably in a better position to borrow.

Bankers often determine credit worthiness of a business by applying ratios to financial statements and comparing them to other businesses in the industry or in the Pacific Northwest.

An accounting practitioner can help analyze financial statements by:

- Providing industry or regional averages, standards, measures, and percentages
- Applying other financial ratios to help a business owner understand and improve his or her business
- Looking at financial trends to better position a business

Operating Budgets

Successful construction companies have budgets and operate their businesses within those budgets. An operating budget is created annually based on information gathered from previous years showing how much it cost to operate the business for a year. Generally, these costs are categorized under general and administrative expenses on the income statement.

There are four parts to the budgeting process:

- Identify the budget items and estimate expenditures for the coming year.
- Monitor and record the actual expenditures when they occur.
- Compare and analyze the difference between the budgeted and actual amounts.
- Take corrective action and make adjustments, as necessary.

Operating budgets help determine how much company overhead to include when bidding projects. Chapter 6 discusses pricing and shows examples of markup for company overhead and profit that is added to estimated costs.

Actual expenses need to be compared to budgeted expenses. To do this, accurate records and detailed cost information must be maintained. By comparing budgeted and actual amounts for the same period from previous years, a business can improve budget analysis, see trends, and collect important historical information.

Job Costing

It is important to price profit into a project and monitor job costs to gain that profit. Generally, profit from a project is the amount remaining after job costs and allocated overhead are subtracted from the project's contract price. Chapter 6 discusses project pricing, job costing and job-cost reports in more detail. By analyzing job-costing records, a business will be able to prepare better estimates and take corrective action before a job ends.

A job-cost system should be tailored to each particular business and developed to define production units as well as dollars. A production unit for a paving contractor, for example, might be certain number of square feet of paving completed or tons of asphalt mix used. Production standards are created based on these units and can be useful in job estimates and proposals.

Also, an effective job-cost system provides a way for project management to monitor work in progress, make adjustments, and take corrective action to complete a profitable project.

Break-Even Analysis

Break-even analysis helps the contractor figure out how a change in sales volume will affect the financial results of the business. The break-even point is the volume at which total revenue equals total costs. The break-even point is calculated by the following formula:

Overhead Expenses

Break Even = Gross Profit Margin (GPM) %

GPM % is calculated as:
Revenue - Direct Job Costs – Indirect Job Costs
Revenues

Break-even analysis emphasizes the importance of a well-prepared operating budget in addition to accurate job cost data. The analysis can be used in selecting, pricing, and budgeting projects for profit. It also helps determine the gross profit needed on jobs to cover overhead.

Regulatory Requirements

Forms for Reporting Business Income Taxes

Each type of business entity has different forms for reporting financial activity and business taxes. These forms have different filing deadlines. Forms required for reporting business taxes are identified in the following table:

Income Tax Reporting Forms

Business Entity	Federal	State and Local*
Sole Proprietorship	Form 1040 Schedule C Schedule SE	Form 40
Partnership	Form 1065 Schedule K-1 (Partners may have to pay self-employment tax on flow-through income.)	Form 65
Subchapter S Corporation	Form 1120-S Schedule K-1	Form 20-S
C-Corporation	Form 1120	Form 20/20-I
Limited Liability Company	Can elect or choose to be taxed as sole proprietorship, partnership or corporation.	

* Consult an accounting practitioner to determine the forms and reporting deadlines for local taxes in areas such as Portland, Multnomah County, Tri-Met, Lane Transit, etc.

Oregon State Corporate Excise Tax

An excise tax is a tax on corporations for the privilege of doing business in Oregon. The federal and Oregon corporate excise taxes are based on Oregon taxable income.

For tax years beginning on or after Jan. 1, 2013, the tax rate is:

Oregon Taxable Income	Tax Rate
$1,000,000 or less	6.6%
$1,000,001 or more	$66,000 plus 7.6% of the amount over $1,000,000

There is a minimum excise tax amount on corporations, ranging from $150 to $100,000 depending on the business' Oregon sales amount.

To pay excise tax, corporations file Form 20 (Excise). S corporations use Form 20-S. Returns are due on the 15th day of the month following the due date of the federal return for the tax year. Quarterly estimated payments are required if the business expects to owe more than $500 of tax.

1099 Information Reporting

Generally, Form 1099-MISC must be filed for each independent contractor or business entity that is not a corporation and to which an amount of at least $600 has been paid for services rendered in a calendar year. The amount includes parts and materials provided with those services. The Form 1099-MISC identifies the business and reports the amount paid to the unincorporated entity that received payment. These unincorporated entities may be subcontractors, vendors, or suppliers.

In filing Form 1099-MISC, furnish two copies of the form to the unincorporated entity no later than Jan. 31.

Also, send a copy to the IRS by Feb. 28 with the accompanying Form 1096, Annual Summary and Transmittal of U.S. Information Returns. If filing electronically using the IRS FIRE system, the due date is extended to March 31. The following procedures outline 1099 Information Reporting for Independent Contractors:

1099 Information Reporting for Independent Contractors
▪ When you first engage in receiving services, obtain completed Form W-9 from each business entity. This provides the information necessary to file, or proves that the company is incorporated and filing is not required
▪ By January 31, furnish two copies of completed Form 1099-MISC to each unincorporated entity that has been paid at least $600 during the previous calendar year.
▪ By February 28, file Forms 1099-MISC on each unincorporated entity, together with the transmittal Form 1096.

Payroll Tax Responsibilities

Recordkeeping for Employers

Time cards are accounting records for both payroll tax and job-cost reporting.
In addition to time cards, employers should keep the following employee
records and information:

- Form W-4 indicating withholding exemptions claimed
- Hours worked
- Wage rates
- Accumulated overtime
- Amounts and dates of all wage payments including withholding, vacation or sick pay, and fringe benefits
- Written authorizations from employees for deductions other than taxes
- Any employee copies of Form W-2 that were returned as undeliverable

Employers must also keep records of employee withholdings and payroll taxes
paid to the government. The records must contain dates and amounts of tax
deposits made.

Regardless of how many employees a business has, the business may prefer to
use a payroll service to handle some or all aspects of its payroll accounting.
Employers must ensure that tax returns are filed and deposits and payments are
made, even if the employer contracts with a third party for these services.

Labor Costs

Payroll records help determine labor costs and are useful in developing
estimates for a bid or proposal. Labor costs include more than just the wages
paid. For each employee, the total labor cost can be calculated by adding:

- Gross wage rate
- Payroll tax responsibilities of the employer
- Benefits (such as medical coverage) paid by the employer
- Workers' compensation insurance coverage

For more information, refer to wage and hour requirements in Chapter 2 for
deductions from wages and the discussion of labor costs in Chapter 6.

Payroll Taxes

There are several federal, state and local taxes imposed on wages earned by employees. Some of these taxes are paid by the employer and some are paid by the employee. Here is a summary:

	Paid by employer	Paid by employee
Federal income tax		X
State and local income tax		X
FICA (Social Security)	X	X
Medicare	X	X
Federal unemployment tax	X	
State unemployment tax	X	
Workers' benefit fund	X	X

Note: Employers pay workers' compensation insurance premiums in addition to the taxes listed in the table above. Local jurisdictions may also impose taxes, such as the Lane County or TriMet Transit taxes.

Federal and State Income Tax Withholding

Employers must withhold federal and state income taxes from employee paychecks and then forward this money to the appropriate government agency. The amount to withhold is determined as follows:

Calculate gross pay

Gross pay includes regular hours worked, overtime hours worked and reported vacation or sick pay hours, each multiplied by the applicable hourly wage rate.

Check an employee's W-4

When hired, every employee must provide a Form W-4 showing how many allowances he or she is claiming.

Consult *Circular E, Publication 15*

Annually, the IRS publishes Circular E, Employer's Tax Guide (also known as Publication 15). It defines payroll tax terms and lists pertinent rules and regulations. It also contains tax withholding tables. The tables show the amount of federal income tax that should be withheld based on the following:
- Payroll period - whether weekly, biweekly, monthly, etc.
- Employee's marital status - single or married
- The number of withholding allowances the employee claimed on the W-4
- Gross wages

You also must withhold state income taxes. The procedure is the same as for federal income tax withholding, but using the Oregon withholding tax tables.

Social Security and Medicare Withholding

Social Security and Medicare taxes are paid equally by the employer and the employee. For every dollar withheld from an employee's paycheck, the employer contributes an equal amount. The amount is determined as follows:

- FICA (Federal Insurance Contributions Act, more commonly known as Social Security): The Social Security Tax Withholding Rate for an employee is 6.2 percent to a maximum wage base of $117,000 for 2014. Note: This maximum changes often. Circular E, also known as Publication 15 Employers Tax Guide, will contain any revisions to this rate.
- Medicare: The employee portion of the Medicare Tax to deduct from wages is 1.45 percent. You must withhold 0.9 percent additional Medicare Tax from wages you pay to an employee in excess of $200,000 in a calendar year. You are required to begin the withholding of Additional Medicare Tax in the pay period in which you pay wages in excess of $200,000 to an employee and continue to withhold it each pay period until the end of the calendar year. Note: Additional Medicare Tax is only imposed on the employee. There is no employer share of Additional Medicare Tax.

Remember, the employer must match dollar-for-dollar any amounts withheld from employees for Social Security and Medicare.

Local Taxes

Some Oregon cities and counties impose local taxes, such as the Tri-Met transit tax or Lane Transit District (LTD) tax. These taxes are usually imposed on the employer. Businesses should check with their jurisdiction to see if any such taxes apply.

Federal and State Unemployment Taxes

Employers pay both the Federal Unemployment Tax (FUTA) and the State Unemployment Tax (SUTA). These taxes are not withheld from employee paychecks.

In 2014, FUTA is currently 6.0 percent of the first $7,000 earned per employee. Once an employee has earned $7,000 during the year, the employer stops paying unemployment taxes based on that employee's wages until the next year. A 5.4 percent credit is given if all state unemployment taxes are paid.

The SUTA tax rate varies based on the history of unemployment claims against the employer. The top rate is 5.4 percent with many new businesses paying less. In 2014, the tax is paid on the first $35, 000 of wages per employee.

Workers' Benefit Fund (WBF)

The Worker's Benefit Fund (WBF) is managed by the Workers' Compensation Division as a retroactive program to provide benefits to claimants or beneficiaries who are eligible for compensation under workers' compensation insurance. These benefits are lower than compensation to injured workers.

The workers' compensation payroll assessment is paid into the WBF. In 2014, this assessment is 3.3 cents per hour. Employers contribute one-half and deduct one-half from employees' wages.

Payroll Reporting Responsibilities for Employers

Federal 941 taxes and reporting

Employers must file Form 941, Employer's Quarterly Federal Tax Return, to report federal income tax withholding, Social Security tax, and Medicare tax.

Federal 940 taxes and reporting

Employers must file Form 940 annually to report Federal Unemployment Tax and deposit the balance of FUTA due by January 31.

Oregon forms and tax reporting

Oregon employers must file Form OQ and Form 132 for quarterly reports on Oregon state income tax withholdings. This also reports the employer's part of Oregon payroll taxes.

When quarterly filings or deposits are required, they must be made by the dates shown in the following table:

Required Dates for Tax Responsibilities

Quarter	Period Ending	Quarterly Filing Date
Jan-Feb-Mar	Mar 31	Apr 30
Apr-May-Jun	Jun 30	Jul 31
Jul-Aug-Sep	Sep 30	Oct 31
Oct-Nov-Dec	Dec 31	Jan 31

In Oregon, corporate officers, partners, or responsible employees may be personally liable for any withholding tax the business fails to pay.

Individual circumstances for each employer can vary greatly. Responsibilities for withholding, depositing, and reporting employment taxes can differ. An accounting practitioner can help determine these responsibilities. The following table provides a brief summary of an employer's basic responsibilities.

Employer Reporting Responsibilities

New Employees:	Quarterly (By April 30, July 31, Oct. 31, and Jan. 31):
<ul><li>Verify work eligibility of employees (Form I-9)</li><li>Copy employees' names and SSNs from Social Security cards (Form W-9)</li><li>Furnish and obtain completed Form W-4</li></ul> **Each Payday:** <ul><li>Withhold federal and state income taxes based on each employee's Form W-4</li><li>Withhold employee's share of Social Security and Medicare taxes</li><li>Deposit monthly or semiweekly:<ul><li>Withheld federal and state income tax</li><li>Withheld and employer Social Security taxes</li><li>Withheld and employer Medicare taxes</li></ul></li></ul>	<ul><li>Deposit FUTA tax to the Electronic Federal Tax Payment System (EFTPS) if liability exceeds $100</li><li>File Form 941</li><li>File Oregon Quarterly Report (Form OQ)</li></ul> **Annually (by Jan. 31):** <ul><li>Remind employees to submit a new Form W-4 if they need to change their withholding exemptions</li><li>Ask for a new Form W-4 from employees claiming exempt from income tax withholding</li><li>Furnish each employee a Form W-2</li><li>File Copy A of Forms W-2 and the transmittal Form W-3 with the Social Security Administration by February 28</li><li>File Oregon Annual Withholding Tax Reconciliation Report (Form WR)</li><li>File Form 940 or 940-EZ</li></ul>

Payroll Tax Deposits

Withheld taxes are considered to be trust funds that do not belong to the business and cannot be used for any other purpose. Funds withheld must be available when tax deposits are due.

There are monthly or semiweekly deposit schedules for determining when to deposit Social Security, Medicare, and withheld income taxes. Generally, all new employers are monthly depositors for the first calendar year of their business. This means that payroll taxes need to be deposited by the 15th day of the month following the end of the payroll period.

A payroll service may be helpful in meeting these requirements. However, if an employer does not use a payroll service, required tax deposits can be made as shown in the above table.

All required Federal Tax Deposits must be made electronically using The Electronic Federal Payment System (EFTPS) except in certain cases when the deposits may be paid when filing Form 941 or Form 944 or paid by credit or debit card.

To enroll in EFTPS, call 1-800-555-4477. Additional information on EFTPS requirements can be obtained by accessing Publication 966, Electronic Federal Tax Payment System; or by registering online using the EFTPS website at www.eftps.gov.

Mail your Oregon Quarterly Reports (Form OQ) to the Oregon Department of Revenue with a check payable to the Oregon Department of Revenue in the amount of the tax.

If payroll taxes exceed $50,000 annually, the employer is a semiweekly schedule depositor for a calendar year. Generally, the IRS notifies applicable businesses. This means that Form 941 payroll taxes on payments made on Wednesday, Thursday, and/or Friday need to be deposited by the following Wednesday. By the following Friday, deposit amounts accumulated on payments made on Saturday, Sunday, Monday, and/or Tuesday. Refer to *Circular E, Publication 15* for more information about how to determine when to deposit employment taxes. Oregon follows the federal schedule.

Out-of-State Business Issues

A company planning to do business in another state should contact agencies in that state for business and tax reporting requirements. Since Washington and California are neighboring states to Oregon, the following information is provided.

Washington	
Department of Revenue	800-647-7706 or www.dor.wa.gov
Department of Labor & Industries	800-647-0982 or www.lni.wa.gov
Secretary of State	360-725-0377 or www.sos.wa.gov/corps
California	
Board of Equalization Department of Consumer Affairs Contractors State Licensing Board	800-400-7115 or www.boe.ca.gov 800-321-CSLB or www.cslb.ca.gov
Secretary of State	916-653-6814 or www.sos.ca.gov

Business Licensing

Some municipalities require a business license (for example, the city of Portland) based on business profits.

Businesses working in Washington, Clackamas, or Multnomah counties have the option of obtaining a Metro License rather than individual city licenses. Note that the city of Portland does not participate in the Metro License program. For information on this license, visit www.oregonmetro.gov.

General Guide to Taxes

The IRS website has information and publications about the various types of taxes and federal tax forms. Go online to www.irs.gov.

To obtain information about Oregon tax requirements, contact:
Oregon Department of Revenue
955 Center Street NE
Salem, OR 97310-2555
503-378-4988
www.oregon.gov/DOR/

Bankruptcy Overview

The following information is provided as an overview of bankruptcy and should not be relied upon as legal advice. Businesses should consider consulting a knowledgeable attorney about their particular situation before filing a bankruptcy petition.

Bankruptcy is a legal process in which a person or business (the debtor) declares an inability to pay debts. Any available assets are liquidated and the proceeds are distributed to the people or companies (creditors) to which the debtor owes money.

Bankruptcy proceedings take place in federal court. A person or business may be declared bankrupt under one of several chapters of the federal bankruptcy code: Chapter 7; Chapter 11; or Chapter 13. These three are outlined below.

- **Chapter 7** allows a business to liquidate its assets upon deciding that it is not capable of paying the debt it has accrued. Once the business assets have been sold and the funds have been distributed to creditors, the business is free from liability. A corporation or partnership ceases to exist if it files Chapter 7. Chapter 7 may be the best choice when the business has: no future; no substantial assets; debts that are so overwhelming that restructuring them is not feasible.
- **Chapter 11** is best described as a reorganization or rehabilitation of the business. The goal of Chapter 11 is to restructure the business and debt payments in such a way as to allow the business to meet its obligations from future earnings. Chapter 11 reorganizations are supervised by a court-appointed trustee. Chapter 11 is very costly, complicated, and time consuming.
- **Chapter 13** allows individuals to undergo a financial reorganization supervised by a federal bankruptcy court. Chapter 13 involves a very specific repayment plan of how debtors will settle their debts over three to five years while allowing the debtor to protect him or herself from debt collection by creditors and preserve assets, such as a home or business equipment.

Advantages of Bankruptcy

Depending on which form of bankruptcy is chosen, bankruptcy may:

- Provide relief and a fresh financial start for someone with serious financial problems
- Temporarily stop all creditors from seeking to collect debts until the debts are sorted out according to the law
- For chapters 11 and 13, stop foreclosure on property, including a residence or business equipment, while allowing the debtor an opportunity to catch up on missed payments
- Restore or prevent termination of utility services

- Stop creditors from garnishing wages and taking other debt-collection actions.
- Allow a debtor to challenge the claims of creditors who are trying to collect more than they are owed
- Restructure debts so that they are more manageable over time

Disadvantages of Bankruptcy

Although bankruptcy may seem very attractive to people with large debts, the disadvantages to bankruptcy are:

- It can affect individual debtors' credit for 10 years. The debtor may not be able to get credit cards or loans or may have to pay higher interest rates.
- It does not necessarily mean all debts are avoided. The most common debts that are not discharged are child and spousal support, criminal restitution, student loans, and, in Chapters 7 and 11, certain taxes, penalties, and fines.
- If a debtor receives an inheritance, property settlement, or life insurance benefits within 180 days after filing for bankruptcy, that money or property becomes property of the estate to be paid to creditors.
- It requires a debtor to reveal all details about business and personal finances. Because bankruptcy filings are public records, the debtor's information will be fully available to the public.
- It is a temporary solution. If the debtor does not improve financial management practices, the same problems may recur and seeking bankruptcy protection again may not be an option or may be much more difficult.

Alternatives to Bankruptcy

Because filing bankruptcy is such a serious step, a business should explore its alternatives before filing. In some situations, a non-bankruptcy course of action may be your best remedy. If the main concern is pesky creditors, use federal and state debt collection laws to stop the abusive and harassing debt collector conduct. Free help may be available from nonprofit debt or credit counseling services such as Consumer Credit Counseling. Some services will also help with restructuring debt through a payment plan, which may help avoid a bankruptcy filing.

Information on the Oregon State Bar Web Law/Tel-Law website at www.osbar.org may also be useful.

Benefits of Working With Professionals

An accounting practitioner is one professional in a team that a business owner can develop as a resource for making business decisions. The type of accounting practitioner and advice needed is determined by the business' accounting requirements. A contractor should seek the services of a competent accounting practitioner, perhaps a Certified Public Accountant (CPA), Public Accountant (PA), Licensed Tax Consultant (LTC), or Enrolled Agent (EA).

Generally, an accounting practitioner advises and prepares income tax statements and business tax reports as well as other accounting services. In addition, they offer valuable and useful services that include:

- Developing financial plans
- Tax planning
- Preparing financial statements, reports, budgets, and income tax returns.
- Advising on cash flow
- Explaining complex transactions to help with decision-making
- Reviewing costs that need to be covered in pricing jobs for a profit

An accounting practitioner can refer a business owner to other professionals, like an insurance and bonding agent, bank officer, and an attorney. Be sure to find professionals who have an established practice or client base of construction contractors, for example an attorney who practices business and construction law.

Be prepared to call on these professionals for resources and guidance in making business decisions. An accounting practitioner can help assess a business' financial position and an attorney can advise on legal consequences or actions. An insurance agent may contribute information on risk management. Over time, professionals who develop relationships with a business are able to offer valuable insight and advice that might not otherwise be available to a business owner working without professionals.

Ask for Details

An accountant should be able to explain any financial statements a business owner does not understand or assist in analyzing ratios or financial trends. An accountant can explain how the financial statements relate, report, and reconcile with a business' accounting records.

Make Comparisons

Financial statements should be compared to some standard, like statements from prior years, budgets, cash flow projections, or all three. Comparison will cause unusual amounts to stand out and show activities that need to be improved. Just as experience will help a business owner plan and review project performance, timely, consistent financial statements produced and reviewed each month will help detect errors to better manage a business.

Summary

A proper financial accounting system is not limited to maintaining and producing financial records. The contractor's accounting system must provide the types and amount of financial information that are needed to both control and grow the business toward its greatest potential profit.

Proper accounting is the basis for job costing, estimating, and project cost control. Additionally, a quality financial system keeps the contractor informed of cash flow and the financial condition of the business. Finally, it provides important support data for legal issues that might come up.

Appendix B provides a listing of systems, schedules, and forms that are needed for conducting the financial part of a business. Where possible, web addresses have been provided to help with acquiring forms and other information.

Income Statement

SAMPLE CONSTRUCTION COMPANY
FOR THE PERIOD ENDED DECEMBER 31, 20XX

Revenue

Sales – Construction Contracts	$ 1,408,246	
Total Revenue		**$ 1,408,246**

Direct Job Costs

Materials	168,950	
Labor	261,430	
Subcontractors	350,090	
Truck Supplies	63,190	
Permits	4,550	
Equipment Rental	80,640	
Payroll Taxes and Insurance	45,750	
Other Direct Costs	61,553	
Total Direct Job Costs		**1,036,153**

Indirect Job Costs

Vehicle Expense- Shop	4,670	
Extended Warranties on Equipment	26,940	
Tools and Supplies	8,590	
Repairs	6,390	
Total Indirect Job Costs		**46,590**
GROSS PROFIT		**325,503**

General and Administrative Expenses

Marketing and Advertising	15,830	
Travel and Entertainment	4,470	
Salaries	59,860	
Payroll Taxes and Insurance	10,475	
Office Expense	2,127	
Rent	9,000	
Storage	600	
Bank Fees	570	
Dues and Subscriptions	337	
Insurance	2,517	
Business Licenses	2,760	
Professional Fees	4,825	
Utilities	1,330	
Telephone	4,600	
Vehicle Expense – Office	7,369	
Depreciation	23,201	
Total General and Administrative Expenses		**149,871**
Net Income before Tax		**175,632**
Income Taxes		(43,182)
Net Income		**$ 132,450**

BALANCE SHEET

SAMPLE CONSTRUCTION, INC.

FOR THE PERIOD ENDED DECEMBER 31, 20XX

Assets

Cash	
Accounts Receivable	375,964
Inventory	349,643
Prepaid Expenses	18,180
Total Current Assets	1,374,012
Equipment	172,105
Leasehold Improvements	183,760
Vehicles	93,070
Total Fixed Assets	448,935
Accumulated Depreciation	(135,609)
Total Fixed Assets, Net of Accumulated Depreciation	313,326
Total Assets	**$1,687,338**

Liabilities & Equity

Accounts Payable	1,002,747
Payroll Taxes Payable	33,345
Credit Line	275,677
Income Taxes Payable	1,654
Employees Payable	21,065
Total Current Liabilities	1,334,488
Notes Payable	250,000
Total Liabilities	1,584,488
Common Stock	1,000
Retained Earnings- Prior Years	101,850
Retained Earnings- Current Year	.
Total Owners' Equity	102,850
Total Liabilities & Equity	**$1,687,338**

STATEMENT OF CASH FLOWS

SAMPLE CONSTRUCTION, INC.

FOR THE PERIOD ENDED DECEMBER 31, 20XX

Cash Flow Provided from Operating Activities:

Net Income	$ 132,450	
Adjustments to reconcile Net Income to Net Cash- Non-cash adjustments for Depreciation	23,201	

Changes in Balance Sheet accounts which affect Operating Activities:

(Increase) Decrease in Accounts Receivable	(92,946)	
(Increase) Decrease in Inventory	14,183	
(Increase) Decrease in Prepaid Expenses	(1,200)	
Increase (Decrease) in Accounts Payable	28,708	
Increase (Decrease) in Payroll Taxes Payable	(2,395)	
Increase (Decrease) in Income Taxes Payable	236	
Increase (Decrease) in Employees Payable	2,005	
Net Cash (Used) Provided by Operating Activities		**104,242**

Cash Flow (Used) Provided by Investing Activities

Purchases of Fixed Assets	(28,245)	
Net Cash (Used) Provided by Investing Activities		**(28,245)**

Cash Flow (Used) Provided by Financing Activities

Net Borrowing (Payment) on Notes Payable	(122,590)	
Net Cash (Used) Provided by Financing Activities		**(116,532)**
Net Increase (Decrease) in Cash		**(40,535)**
Cash, Beginning of Period		630,225
Cash, End of Period		**$589,690**

Chapter 5

List of Tax Forms and Documents
With Websites for Obtaining Them

Federal Tax Forms

- www.irs.gov/businesses/small/index.html

- Form SS-4: Application for Employer Identification Number
  www.irs.gov/pub/irs-pdf/fss4.pdf

- Forms 940/940-EZ: Employer's Annual Federal Unemployment (FUTA) Tax Return
  www.irs.gov/pub/irs-pdf/f940.pdf
  www.irs.gov/pub/irs-pdf/f940ez.pdf

- Form 941: Employer's Quarterly Federal Tax Return
  www.irs.gov/pub/irs-pdf/f941.pdf

- Form W-2: Wage and Tax Statement
  www.irs.gov/pub/irs-pdf/fw2.pdf

- Form W-3: Transmittal of WAGE and Tax Statements
  www.irs.gov/pub/irs-pdf/fw3.pdf

- Form 1099/1096 Information Reports
  www.irs.gov/formspubs/index.html

- Form 1040-ES: Estimated Tax for Individuals
  www.irs.gov/pub/irs-pdf/f1040es.pdf

Federal Tax Publications

- www.irs.gov/formspubs/index.html

- Tax Guide for Small Business: IRS Publication 334
  www.irs.gov/pub/irs-pdf/p334.pdf

- Circular E, Employer's Tax Guide: IRS Publication 15
  www.irs.gov/pub/irs-pdf/p15.pdf

- Tax Calendars: IRS Publication 509
  www.irs.gov/pub/irs-pdf/p509.pdf

Oregon Tax Information

- www.dor.state.or.us/forms.html

- Combined Employer's Registration Form and Business Identification Number (BIN)
  www.dor.state.or.us/withhold/211-055.pdf

- Form OQ: Oregon Quarterly Tax Report; Form 132: Wage Detail Report; and Form OTC: Personalized Oregon Tax Coupons
  http://findit.emp.state.or.us/tax/forms.cfm

- Withholding tax questions: 503-945-8091 (registrations, order forms, change address, etc.)
  www.dor.state.or.us/withhold/withhold.html

- Oregon Form WR: Annual Withholding Reconciliation
  www.dor.state.or.us/withhold/WR-03.pdf

For other Oregon documents, forms, or to obtain information about Oregon tax requirements, contact:

Oregon Department of Revenue
955 Center Street NE Salem,
OR 97301-2555
503-378-4988 (General questions) 800-356-4222
(Toll-free in Oregon) 503-947-2017 (Electronic Funds
Transfer [EFT]) www.dor.state.or.us

Internal Revenue Service

The IRS has many assistance programs and tax information materials (paper, video, and electronic formats) for you. The IRS local office is located at:
1220 SW Third Avenue
Portland, OR 97204
503-265-3501
www.irs.gov

- **Automated Tax Assistance** – 800-829-1040

- **Tax Publications and Forms** – 800-TAX-FORM

TTY/TDD – Access to teletypewriter/telecommunications device for the deaf. Call the IRS at 800-829-4059 for information and to order IRS forms and publications.

Chapter 5

Websites of Interest to Businesses

These sites will be of interest to Oregon businesses. Many contain links to other equally valuable sources of business information.

Business in Oregon www.oregon.gov
  (go to drop-down menu at top left of page)

Electronic Federal Tax Payroll System EFTPS – Online
  www.EFTPS.gov

Insurance Pool Governing Board
  www.ipgb.state.or.us

Multnomah County Library
  www.multcolib.org

OR Assn. of Minority Entrepreneurs
  www.oame.org

OR Construction Contractors Board
  www.oregon.gov/ccb

OR Department of Consumer & Business Services
  ww.cbs.state.or.us

OR Department of Revenue
  www.dor.state.or.us

OR Employment Department
  http://findit.emp.state.or.us/tax/

OR Secretary of State's Office
  www.sos.state.or.us

OR Secretary of State Corporation Division
  www.filinginoregon.com.

OR Workers' Compensation Division
  www.cbs.state.or.us/external/wcd/

Portland Development Commission
  www.businessinportland.org

Portland Bureau of Licenses
  www.portlandonline.com/licenses/

SCORE Business Counselors
  www.score.org

Small Business Administration
  www.sba.gov

Small Business Development Centers
  www.bizcenter.org

Wall Street Journal for Entrepreneurs
  www.startup.wsj.com

WA Department of Revenue
  www.dor.wa.gov

WA Small Business Fair
  www.bizfair.org

Gives information on starting a business, confirming an owner of a business, obtaining a certificate of good standing, obtaining a Registry for ABN, Corp., and other new business information, including the Oregon Business Guide. Business Information Center: 503-986-2200.

Order a free copy of *The Small Business Resource Guide, CD-ROM 2004* from the IRS at www.irs.gov/businesses/small/page/0,,id=7128,00.html or by calling 800-TAX-FORM (800-829-3676).

An Overview of Greater Portland Area Local Taxes and Business License Requirements

City	Phone	Comments (fees are subject to change*)
Banks	503-324-5112	Annual fee
Beaverton	503-526-2255	$50 plus additional annual fee based on # of employees/rental units. www.ci.beaverton.or.us
Clackamas Co.	503-650-3079	Requires home occupation permit and various licenses for specific types of businesses. www.co.clackamas.or.us
Cornelius	503-357-9112	$80 initial application fee plus annual fee. www.ci.cornelius.or.us
Durham	503-639-6851	Annual fee based on # of employees.
Fairview	503-665-7929	Annual fee; requires home occupation permit and vending machine license. www.fairvieworegon.gov
Forest Grove	503-992-3227	$72 covers 10 years; also requires home occupancy permit. www.ci.forest-grove.or.us
Gaston	503-985-3340	Annual fee.
Gladstone	503-656-5225	$25-$35 plus $3 per employee/year; also requires home occupation permit. www.ci.gladstone.or.us
Gresham	503-618-2370	Annual fee; requires various licenses for specific types of businesses and may require home occupation permit. www.ci.gresham.or.us
Happy Valley	503-783-3800	Annual fee; also requires home occupation permit.
Hillsboro	503-681-6100	$80 initial application fee, annual fee thereafter; also requires home occupation permit and various regulatory licenses for specific type of businesses. www.ci.hillsboro.or.us
King City	503-639-4082	$100 initial application fee, annual fee thereafter.
Lake Oswego	503-635-0390	Annual fee; must comply with home occupation provisions.
Maywood Park	503-255-9805	No business license requirements.
Metro	503-797-1710	Contractor's Business License is optional; annual fee that licenses construction and landscape contractors in 19 cities in the Portland area, but not including Portland. www.metro-region.org
Milwaukie	503-786-7555	Annual fee plus $3 per employee each year; also requires home occupation permit. www.cityofmilwaukie.org
Multnomah Co.	503-823-5148	Business income tax; fees also required for transient lodging and vehicle rentals (503) 988-3440). www.co.multnomah.or.us

* Annual fees and fees per employee are subject to change. Contact the appropriate jurisdiction to get the current fee.

Chapter 5

City	Phone	Comments (fees are subject to change*)
North Plains	503-647-5555	$70 initial application fee with annual fee thereafter; also requires home occupation permit. www.northplains.org
Oregon City	503-657-0891	Annual fee; also requires license for certain coin-operated machines. www.ci.oregon-city.or.us
Portland	503-823-5157	Annual fee based on income ($100 minimum/year); also requires various regulatory licenses for specific types of businesses and home occupation permit. www.portlandonline.com/licenses
Rivergrove	503-639-6919	No business license requirements (home occupation restrictions apply).
Sherwood	503-625-5522	Annual fee plus $5 per employee annually; also requires home occupation permit. www.ci.sherwood.or.us
Tigard	503-639-4171	Annual fee; also requires home occupation and temporary use permit. www.ci.tigard.or.us
Tri-Met	503-378-4988	Payroll/income based on wages/self-employment income administered by the Oregon Dept. of Revenue. www.dor.state.or.us
Troutdale	503-665-5175	Annual fee; also requires separate amusement device license. www.ci.troutdale.or.us
Tualatin	503-691-3058	Annual fee based on # of employees. www.ci.tualatin.or.us
Vancouver, WA**	360-487-8600	Annual fee; also requires various regulatory licenses for specific types of businesses. www.ci.vancouver.wa.us
West Linn	503-656-4261	Annual fee; also requires home occupation permit. www.ci.west-linn.or.us
Wilsonville	503-570-1586	Annual fee plus $3 per employee working within the city. www.ci.wilsonville.or.us
Wood Village	503-667-6211	Registration with the city is required; home occupation permit is required. www.ci.wood-village.or.us

Door-to-door or home solicitation regulations and requirements for each jurisdiction need to be researched before doing this type of business.

* Annual fees and fees per employee are subject to change. Contact the appropriate jurisdiction to get the current fee.

** Those planning to do business in the state of Washington should contact the Washington Department of Revenue at 800-647-7706 or www.dor.wa.gov.

Sample Questions

CHAPTER 5

1. **Which is NOT true about cash flow?**

   ❑ 1. Inadequate cash flow is a major reason why many construction businesses fail.

   ❑ 2. Positive cash flow can increase the amount of working capital.

   ❑ 3. Cash flow is important for having enough money to pay bills when they are due.

   ❑ 4. Cash flow is the same as profit.

2. **Accounting records should be retained for:**

   ❑ 1. Three years.

   ❑ 2. Five years.

   ❑ 3. Up to seven years.

   ❑ 4. Ten years.

3. **Which is true about Income Statements?**

   ❑ 1. Insurance, office furniture, and vehicle repairs are examples of direct costs.

   ❑ 2. Subcontracts, equipment rentals, and performance bonds are examples of direct costs.

   ❑ 3. Labor, materials, and permits are examples of indirect costs.

   ❑ 4. Office rent, office supplies, and utilities are examples of direct costs.

Answers: 1. [4]
           2. [3]
           3. [2]

CHAPTER 6
PROJECT MANAGEMENT

Objectives

At the end of this chapter, you will be able to:

1. Explain the importance of project management.
2. Develop an estimate for a bid or proposal.
3. Determine project costs, company overhead, and profit.
4. Develop a project budget and understand its importance.
5. Explain the purpose and benefits of project scheduling.
6. Implement procedures for proper project documentation.
7. State two benefits of good project closeout procedures.

Introduction: What is Project Management?

Project management has been described as the wise or careful allocation and efficient use of resources for timely completion of a project within the estimated construction budget. The resources required are money, workers, equipment, materials, and time. The project management practices introduced in this chapter are common among successful firms in the Oregon construction industry. They do not replace a company's need for professional advice; instead, they serve as general guidelines for planning, organizing, and managing a successful project.

Why Project Management is Important

Every project is unique, presenting new challenges for a project manager. A skilled project manager needs to carefully organize, schedule, and control all phases of project operations. Effective management skills can save projects from failing and provide the company with reliable cash flow and profitable performance. They create satisfied customers who bring other projects and refer potential customers. Effective project management leads to successful projects tomorrow.

A company needs a business plan and an annual operating budget, and must have the financial resources to meet the plan. The business plan allows project managers to understand the company's purpose and how the project helps fulfill that purpose.

Purpose of Project Management

Project management involves coordinating all necessary resources to satisfy the client and produce a profit for the company. This includes meeting contract requirements and completing projects on time and on budget. This applies to all construction companies regardless of size or type of projects. Every project needs a plan that includes a budget and a schedule, and achieves the desired goals whether it takes only a few hours or takes an entire year or longer. The shortest construction time possible results in a satisfied client and a successful project.

Develop an Estimate and Construction Budget

The project budget begins with the estimate. The estimate is designed around how the owner will pay the contractor. The payment method also determines the type of construction contract that the parties sign when the bid or proposal is accepted. Categories of construction contracts are discussed in Chapter 3.

The contractor needs a detailed and accurate project estimate, regardless of project size or complexity. If the owner pays by unit price, or by time and materials, the estimate and budget will be developed by unit price. If the owner makes progress payments, the estimate and budget are based on the detailed survey method of estimating. These estimating methods are explained in the following pages.

Schedule Construction

A conspicuously posted schedule helps everyone on the project know when to do their jobs, both labor (subcontractors and employees at the job site), and delivery of materials or equipment.

Manage the Project

Project planning and budget management pay huge dividends when done correctly. The project needs to be broken down into major tasks, and each task needs to be thoroughly understood with its costs for performance. When this is done, a contractor can effectively plan how the total project will be performed.

Develop an Estimate for a Bid or Proposal

What is an Estimate?

Construction estimating is the process of listing all costs involved in a building project, then arriving at a close guess of the total cost of a project to prepare a bid or proposal. It will always be a guess, but careful estimating will bring the contractor's guess much closer to actual job cost.

When starting a business, the owner will probably do the estimating, but eventually the company may employ someone to estimate work. This person needs to be familiar with building codes and regulations applicable to each job and know requirements for submittals, quality control, and material testing. Estimate questions must be directed to the project architect or engineer. The estimator may also consult with an accountant, bonding company, insurance agent, or attorney to gain specific information about a project's legal and financial obligations.

Construction estimating is a valuable service that provides important information for owners, and/or design professionals, and may be performed for compensation. Owners may need a detailed appraisal of a project to determine design, scope, and viability. An owner may need to consider the cost of a proposed project before making a real estate transaction. A proposed project may need a budget evaluation to determine if the design and scope will meet the owner's financial goal(s) for improvement and/or development. If an owner has a proposed project, but does not have complete construction drawings and specifications, and wants input from qualified contractors about methods, materials, and costs - that owner will likely be asked to pay for such input. These are just a few examples of compensatory construction estimating.

After the total costs of a project are established, a markup percentage is added to the project costs. The markup percentage covers annual company overhead of the business, plus a desired profit before taxes. *A bid or proposal should never be submitted until this procedure has been completed!*

The ultimate goal of any estimate is to accurately predict all project costs, giving the business the desired gross profit. Many business failures result from excessive errors in estimating. This results in either loss of profit (estimate too low) or loss of jobs (estimate too high).

Purpose of Estimating

Estimating is the first step in winning a contract to perform a project. Contractors base their bid or proposal on the estimate. A bid must be accurate and allow for completion of the project on time with a reasonable profit. Accurate estimating considers these factors and more:

- Labor
- Experience
- Work Attitude
- Materials
- Subcontractors
- Equipment and tools
- Rentals
- Contingencies
- Weather
- Construction site complications
- Project overhead or "soft costs"
- Company operating overhead

Types of Estimates

There are several methods used to estimate a construction job. Two primary methods are the detailed survey, or lump sum method, and the unit price estimate.

Detailed Survey Method

The detailed survey estimate is an accurate method that lists all project items needed and the materials and labor required for each item. A specific price is assigned to each item or task. This type of estimate requires that a quantity survey (take off) be made.

A take-off is a complete listing of materials and items of work needed in the project. A contractor cannot assume that bidding documents are accurate or complete. Contractors need to complete their own surveys based on drawings and specifications. The results are then categorized and transferred to a summary sheet. The summary sheet guides the contractor in estimating materials, labor, equipment, and overhead costs. The estimated overall cost plus profit is the price for a lump sum bid or proposal.

The following steps are needed for the detailed survey method:

- Assume a bid on the installation of 200 feet of underground piping. Costs included in the estimate are material, labor, equipment rental, permits, supervision, project overhead, and general overhead.
- The contractor prepares a material quantity survey from the project drawings and specifications. Vendor quotes are obtained for the materials to be used.
- Rental quotes are obtained from equipment vendors for additional equipment needed.
- The contractor does a detailed labor study and estimates labor costs.
- Project overhead requirements, including supervisor's salaries, are estimated and costs are added in.
- The contractor determines the percentage of annual company overhead that applies to this project. This amount is added to the estimate.
- A decision is made about what the profit should be. This figure is added to the estimate.
- The resulting amount constitutes the bid price.

Unit Price Estimate

Some construction projects do not work well with a detailed survey bid. They may require a unit price bid, a bid broken down into several segments or units. Estimates are assigned to each unit of construction. A quantity survey is performed, but all units are kept separate. Using the previous bid created for the detailed survey method, if the resulting bid price were $15,000, the unit price would be $75 per linear foot - $15,000 divided by 200 feet of underground piping = $75 lf.

Example

For a civil project, separate prices are estimated for excavating units, utility units, paving units, and so forth. Each unit price includes material, labor, subcontractor activity, overhead and profit. The bid shows costs for each unit of the project.

Unit pricing particularly helps on jobs where specific quantities are difficult to determine. Also, sometimes project requirements in a contract require jobs to be bid per unit price.

Example

An excavation project requires the removal and hauling of an undetermined amount of fill material. Since the amount of work is not defined, the contractor quotes a certain amount per cubic yard on the bid form. This amount includes equipment rental and maintenance costs, labor costs, fixed overhead costs, and profit.

Specialized Computer Estimating Programs

Accurate estimating is difficult in the variable domain of construction. Job sites are not the same. Materials, labor, delivery, weather, and other factors make estimating a challenge. Specialized computer programs can help increase the accuracy. The creation of national and regional cost indexes can help as well. The American Society of Professional Estimators (ASPE) and the American Association of Cost Engineers (AACE) are currently working on uniform estimating standards and guidelines.

Parts of an Estimate

Material Costs

Materials are defined as anything supplied that becomes part of the final project, such as concrete, fasteners, lumber, steel, and drywall. Delivery, material inspection, and storage costs are considered part of material costs. Material costs do not include installation, service, or progress inspections.

Sometimes contractors pre-purchase and stock materials, however, most contractors purchase materials and have them delivered just before they are needed, which preserves working capital. Contractors should obtain written price quotations for all materials to ensure that:

- All needed materials were included in the suppliers' quotes.
- The materials will be available once the project is started.

Labor Costs

Labor cost is one of the most difficult aspects of estimating. Direct labor and indirect labor are two terms that all estimators should understand.

Direct Labor Costs are basic hourly wages paid for actually installing, building, or modifying a task item. Labor market research can help a contractor learn typical wages in the area and determine whether union or federal pay scales are required.

Indirect Labor Costs or Labor Burden are labor costs related to wages or required payroll deductions. Examples are federal and state withholding, unemployment insurance, Federal Insurance Contribution Act (FICA), and workers' compensation insurance. An employee trust benefit in place for the employees can also be an indirect labor cost.

Indirect labor costs can range from 25 to 70 percent of the base wage rate. Once the percentage is determined, it can be added to direct labor costs. Some estimators combine direct and indirect costs on a task for a single hourly or "shop" rate. Others estimate these costs separately or as a task item.

Be aware that for public improvements, there are required prevailing wage rates as well as required deductions for figuring a base wage rate.

Overtime

Employees working more than 10 hours a day or 40 hours in any one week may be paid an overtime rate. If the project is a prevailing wage project, overtime pay is required after 8 hours a day unless there is a special agreement. Refer to ORS 279.316 for specific requirements on public contracts and OAR 839.020-0030 on private projects.

For estimating purposes, an overtime rate may be calculated by:
- Direct labor cost plus the extra for time and a half or double time.
- Then determine which portion, if any, of indirect labor costs apply to the overtime rate, and add these. Workers' compensation, for example, would not apply.

Labor estimates are developed in one of two ways:
- Dollars per unit of work, for example, dollars per block laid, or dollars per electrical box installed.
- Completed work units in units-per-work-hour.

The benefit of the second is that the units per work hour are constant and can be applied to future estimates at labor rates adjusted for inflation and other relevant factors. The following table gives equations that illustrate the two ways:

Masonry labor
1. Cost/unit is $3/block. So $3 each x Number of Blocks = labor cost of total job.
If there are 240 blocks, then $3 x 240 = $750 or
2. Let's say the average worker can lay 12 blocks/hr. So total number of blocks ÷ 12 blocks/labor hr. = total labor hours. Labor hours x Labor cost/hr. = labor cost of total job.
So, if there are 240 total blocks, and the average worker can lay 12 blocks per hour, then 240 / 12 = 20 units of work. If the average block layer cost is $36/hr., then 20 units of work x $36/hr. = $270.

Of course, due to possible job conditions or other variables, a mason may or may not be able to average 12 blocks per hour. If overtime is needed because weather, or other factors slow the work, the estimate may be low. These variables emphasize the need to thoroughly understand the specifications, job site conditions, and abilities of the company's labor force.

Equipment Costs

Equipment is generally understood to be all tools, large and small, that are purchased or rented by the contractor to complete a project. Hand tools, cords, hoses, forklifts, graders, and cranes should all be considered equipment. Equipment costs also includes all operating expenses such as fuel, oil, filters, tires, equipment repair, storage, delivery, finance costs, insurance, and taxes.

Accurately estimating equipment costs relies on understanding the project requirements and schedule. Equipment is rented or costed on a time measure. If the life span of a piece of equipment is expected to be the same length as the project, then the cost of the entire piece can be used in the estimate. Some equipment is rented or leased for use in several projects. For such projects, the equipment cost is estimated by applying the rental or lease rates according to the time the equipment is used in the project.

Equipment cost guides have been established by the federal government, major equipment suppliers, and the Associated General Contractors of America (AGC).

As with labor costs, equipment cost is typically assigned on a monthly, weekly, daily, or hourly basis. These costs can also be included in production rates.

Example

If a loader moves an average of 40 cubic yards per hour, and the total number of cubic yards to be loaded is known, the loader cost for the project can be estimated. So if total material to be loaded is 4,000 cubic yards, then 4,000 divided by 40 cubic yards per hour will equal total equipment hours required (100). Then if cost per equipment hour is $100, the estimated equipment cost is $100 times 100 equipment hours, or $10,000.

This calculation presumes that the loader will maintain continuous productivity. Keep in mind that equipment breakdowns, scheduling problems, inclement weather, and any number of unexpected problems can affect actual productivity per hour.

Subcontractors

Subcontract Work

If the scope of work requires subcontracting, the independent contractors need to have the ability and qualifications to perform the work. Although general contractors may prefer a particular subcontractor, competitive bids help ensure a good price. To bid fairly, all subcontractors should receive the same general information and detailed specifications for the project. Also, subcontractors should be given enough time to submit a carefully prepared bid.

Risks to Avoid

Make certain subcontractors are licensed by the CCB. When licensed, they are required by the CCB to provide a bond and carry proper insurance. Verify and keep proof of insurance, licensing, and worker's compensation insurance before the subcontractor starts work on the project. In addition, specialty contractors like plumbers, electricians, and asbestos abatement contractors must be licensed and register their businesses according to the Building Codes Division or Department of Environmental Quality (DEQ). During a project, maintain a list of all subcontractors and contractors performing work on the project. The list should include subcontractor names, addresses, and license numbers, which can be requested by the CCB. If the CCB requests a contractor's subcontractor list, it must be delivered within 72 hours of the request.

Overhead

Overhead includes two types: **annual company overhead and project overhead or "soft costs."** Contractors planning for success will have at least a one-year business plan including a company overhead budget of general and administrative expenses. This is used for calculating overhead in pricing work.

Project Overhead or "Soft Costs"

Project (or job) overhead includes expenses that directly relate to the project but are not included as construction labor or materials. These are costs for work typically described in Division 1 or General Conditions of the project specifications.

The following are examples of project overhead:
- Permanent company owned materials or equipment.
- Required project bonds and insurance.
- Fees for surveying, building layout, or testing.
- Site supervision.
- Schedules, reports, and shop drawers.
- Electricity, telephone, water, and sanitary facilities for the project.
- Project security, flaggers, and safety expenses such as hand rails or fall projection.

- Survey project horizontal or vertical control.
- Temporary lighting, heating, barricades, signs, and fences.
- Mobilization, garbage removal, and site cleanup.
- Incidental tools, or small tools and equipment.
- Construction cleanup.
- Final cleanup.
- Legal fees related to the bid and contract.

Estimating project overhead differs from company overhead. Rather than using a predetermined percentage added to each bid, which is commonly used for company overhead and explained in the next section, a more accurate method is to list and include costs for each item when developing the estimate summary.

Annual Company Overhead

Every construction company has annual overhead, whether the business is located in a home office or in a stand-alone building. To calculate overhead percentage, the following formula applies:

Anticipated Annual G&A Expense ÷ Annual Anticipated Revenue

Typically, the amount of company overhead is the same as general and administrative expenses found on the company's income statement (see Figure 5-4, Income Statement). Examples of these business expenses are:

- Advertising
- CCB license fee
- General liability insurance
- Non-project equipment, such as the owner's truck
- Office rent or mortgage payments
- Office furniture and equipment (computers, telephone, fax machines)
- Office utilities and maintenance
- Office supplies
- Office employee salaries
- Other rent, such as equipment rent
- Owner's salary
- Professional fees

While these expenses are not directly related to a particular project, every project must help pay a percentage of the company's annual overhead.

Profit or Fee

Usually an estimate will include reasonable profit. This does not mean a desired profit will always be achieved. In order to win the bid, the bidder must walk the fine line between offering the lowest bid and making a reasonable profit.

Profit markup factors to consider are:
- Value of estimated labor (very risky).
- Value of supervision. Work can only be produced efficiently with qualified supervision. The availability of qualified supervision directly affects company growth, and the profit for each project should reflect this.
- Return that is needed on capital invested in the company.

Prepare for the Estimate

Review Project Documents

Before preparing an estimate, the owner or estimator should review the project documents, which include the contract documents, to decide if the company can meet the requirements of the project and wants to perform the work.

If proceeding, carefully read and interpret all information, all contractual requirements and all other specific requirements for the estimate. Include all bidding instructions, proposal forms, alternates, and similar documents. This is important since the estimate becomes the basis for a bid or proposal and establishes a budget for actual job costs.

Architects, engineers, and attorneys often prepare project documents for the owners. On larger projects, these documents are usually available at Plan Centers. Project documents include:
- Insurance
- Surety bond forms
- General conditions
- Supplemental conditions
- Drawings or plans
- Specifications
- Allowances
- Supplements
- Addenda

Bonds and Insurance

Insurance

Some projects may require insurance coverage and limits that are greater than a contractor or subcontractor carries. Verify the company's insurance agent can provide the required insurance before preparing the estimate.

Bonds

Some projects require labor and material or performance bonds in addition to the surety bond required for an active license with the CCB. A company's bonding surety and accounting practitioner can help verify that the business can provide the required bonds for a project.

Bid Bonds

A bid bond, or a proposal bond, is a guarantee backed by an insurance company that the successful bidder will enter into the project contract for the agreed-upon price. Instead of a bond, owners may require a certified check as bid security. Many contractors use bonds to avoid tying up capital in bid securities. Bid bonds are returned to unsuccessful bidders shortly after bid opening. Though not required on all projects, bid bonds are usually required on public works projects.

Allowances

Allowances are funds that must be allotted directly to a special item in the project. For example, a lighting allowance would establish that all light fixtures for the project be purchased from a certain fund amount. If owners wanted more expensive fixtures, they would have to be purchased by the owner above and beyond the contract price. Allowances eliminate the need for contractors to produce exact estimates on those items of work.

Supplements

Supplements provide additional information on the project. Supplements can include soil reports, project studies, land surveys, or other documents.

They are marked or stamped "For Informational Purposes" and are used as design criteria by the architect or engineer.

Addenda

Sometimes design or writing errors in specifications slip through and need to be corrected or modified. Addenda are additions or clarifications made to the project after it has been released for bidding, but before bids or proposals are returned to the owner. Addenda are often responses to bidders' questions.

Drawings or Plans

Drawings are documents describing the design of a project, while plans are technically drawings that show the total project. Drawings must give all needed details for estimating and construction. Architects, designers, and engineers usually prepare plans and drawings that can be warranted as accurate to existing site conditions, complete, suitable, and unambiguous for their intended purpose. Drawings consist of plans, elevations, sectional drawings, and details. Details clarify by showing a small, more complex portion of the structure in greater detail and larger scale than that shown on the plans.

Specifications

Specifications spell out materials, work methods, and quality requirements for the project. They must be studied thoroughly for information that is not on the drawings. Generally, specifications on complex projects follow the CSI format (see Appendix B). (Note: This format was changed with the 2004 edition from 16 Divisions to the current 49 Division format.)

On smaller projects, specifications are described by notes on the drawings. Consult material suppliers or engineers if technical specifications call for unfamiliar work methods or applications not readily available to the contractor.

General Conditions

These are generally the duties and obligations required in the contract for performing work and are included as project overhead or soft costs in the contract price. On larger projects, General Conditions are in Division 1 of the specifications when the project follows the CSI format.

Preparing shop drawings or submittals is an example of costs that must be estimated from General Conditions. Another example might be maintaining as-built drawings concurrent with progress of work. As-built drawings show changes after change orders are approved and how the structure was constructed. The contract may require that one or more sets of as-built drawings be provided to the owner when the project is completed.

Supplementary Conditions

Supplementary Conditions modify the General Conditions and must be estimated accordingly. Review Supplementary Conditions for prevailing wage rates and other possible important modifications to the General Conditions.

Job Site Visit

Before preparing the estimate, the contractor must become familiar with job site conditions. Environmental conditions will invariably affect project costs. The following types of information should be determined from the site visit:

- Probable weather conditions.
- Site access and security restrictions.
- Space and staging limitations.
- Condition of existing buildings and/or other nearby structures.
- Availability of electricity, water, telephone, and other utility services.
- Natural vegetation and type of foliage or shrubs, including such things as nettles or poison oak for health and safety measures.
- Surface topography, trees, and drainage.
- Subsurface soil, water, and rock.
- History of site or Environmental Impact Statement.
- Special safety or traffic-control requirements.

If the contractor is adding onto existing structures, the condition of those structures must be considered. Special care must be taken when tying to existing structural components. Electrical lines, sewage, water, and mechanical connections may need to be maintained to the structure and to nearby buildings. Shoring and protecting finished surfaces may be necessary to preserve existing buildings and other nearby structures.

The person inspecting the job site should be experienced in estimating and all aspects of construction. It is often helpful to record the visit with a camcorder or camera, write down tape and sight measurements, and make notes or sketches. A written job site report is a vital reference in preparing the estimate, contract, and insurance coverage.

Project Location and Environmental Conditions

Environmental issues can seriously impact the project cost and schedule. A careful environmental assessment must be part of the contractor's site visit.

The following are common environmental conditions that a contractor may see and document while visiting a job site.

- Environmentally sensitive areas, such as bodies of water, wetlands, protected trees and wildlife. These may require permits or restrictions that must be factored into the estimate.
- Subsurface investigation, searching for signs of old dumping sites, buried fuel or storage tanks, or any other contamination requiring extra cleanup and

disposal costs. Even archeological or significant historical remains can disrupt a project schedule and budget.

- Utility locations.
- Asbestos or lead-based paint.
- Local tree ordinances that affect site clearing. Trees may need to be removed before construction. Or they may need to be protected during construction and removed trees may need to be replaced after construction. Both involve costs and may require permits.
- Earthwork and excavation will likely need to follow erosion control laws (review of local jurisdictions is required). Erosion control measures have initial costs and permit fees, and must be maintained during the project.
- Permits, approvals, and inspections by environmental agencies during preparation and progress of work must be factored into the estimate and schedule. These may involve land use and environmental controls, and may require specialized equipment or the final acceptance of an erosion control plan. Be aware that environmental requirements are covered by different agencies than building requirements.

Even if a contractor has no direct responsibility for an environmental condition, it must be considered in the pre-bid investigation and estimate. Chapter 9 describes environmental requirements. See Chapter 9, Appendix A for resources and contacts regarding environmental site conditions.

Attend Prebid or Proposal Meetings

Prebid or proposal meetings are held with the owner to clarify any items, procedures, or specifications that are ambiguous or uncertain. These items are then amended or modified in Addenda. On larger projects or public improvements, a meeting may require mandatory attendance by the owner to explain the project to all interested contractors.

Process of Estimating

A thorough estimate follows many steps. Figure 6-1, Estimating Flow Chart, shows a general sequence of steps in estimating.

Figure 6-1. Estimating Flowchart

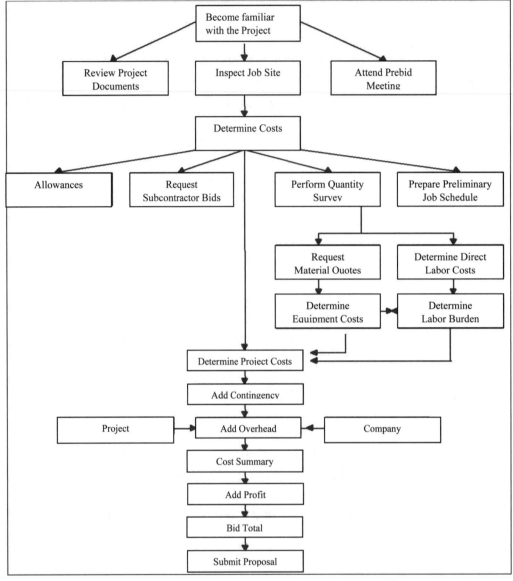

Itemized Summary

The itemized summary is the basis for a complete and accurate estimate of project costs and lists all major items of work in the order they are to be performed.

After the quantity survey (take off) is complete, each item is classified and totaled onto a summary sheet. The summary sheet lists the total material and labor needed for each task item and is a basis to estimate overall costs. Missing any task items results in estimating mistakes and bids that are too low or high. Such bids lead to unprofitable jobs or loss of prospective jobs.

Residential Template

Figure 6-2, Sample Template for Cost Estimate Breakdown in Residential Construction, is an example of an itemized summary for new home construction.

CSI MasterFormat

The Construction Specifications Institute (CSI) is an international organization that has developed a coding system used to describe material and activities that go into a project. Many architects use CSI as a method for organizing the specification booklet that accompanies project plans. For additional information, refer to Appendix C for a listing of the CSI Format. [Note: MasterFormat was expanded in the 2004 edition.]

Developing Costs

Allowances

Allowances do not need to be estimated, and can be set aside for later inclusion in the bid. Common allowance items are lighting fixtures, plumbing fixtures, appliances, and floor coverings. Allowances are made for items that have not been specified at the time the project estimate is prepared. Therefore, in the project contract, allowances are noted and clearly explained. Allowance amounts are typically provided to the bidders, but not always.

Subcontract Work

Subcontractors must be contacted early in the process to provide the general contractor with competitive bids. The general contractor determines a scope of work and invites licensed independent contractors and suppliers to offer bids on subcontract work, equipment and materials. The bids must be timely, accurate, and provide the general contractor with enough information to prepare and submit the bid or proposal before the owner's deadline. The subcontractor should reference plans and specifications used, as well as any addenda used to prepare the bid. He or she should also address the duration of time the bid will be honored by the subcontractor. Multiple subcontract bids help assure the subcontract bid is competitive, and that a low subcontractor is not "buying the work."

Figure 6-2. Sample Template for Cost Estimate Breakdown in Residential Construction

Owner _____   **Site** _____

	HRS LAB	HRS CARP	Labor	Material	Sub	Total
1. Plan cost and drafting labor						
2. Permit fees						
3. Construction preparation and layout						
4. Drop boxes for dirt and debris						
5. Excavation						
6. Trucking						
7. Demolition						
8. Foundation						
9. Concrete flatwork						
10. Steel and mesh work						
11. Rain drain or drywell						
12. Waterproofing and dust protection						
13. Fill material or back fill						
14. Framing material						
15. Framing labor						
16. Trusses and/or structural beam						
17. Rough hardware – nails, staples, hangers						
18. Windows / Patio doors / Skylight						
19. Siding, material and labor						
20. Finish carpentry exterior						
21. Roofing						
22. Gutters and downspouts / Sheet metal						
23. Electrical						
24. Heating / Air conditioning						
25. Plumbing						
26. Attic ventilation and/or exhaust venting						
27. Insulation						
28. Underlayment and kraft paper						
29. Sheet rocking / Drywall / Plaster						
30. Doors / Interior						
31. Finish carpentry / Closet poles / Shelving						
32. Paneling / Wallpaper						
33. Special ceilings						
34. Finish hardware – door knobs, hinges, etc.						
35. Mirrors / Shower doors / Bathroom hardware						
36. Door weather stripping						
37. Garage doors						
38. Fireplace and/or wood stoves						
39. Masonry						
40. Vinyl flooring (allowance)						
41. Special floors (allowance)						
42. Carpeting (allowance)						
43. Ceramic tile						
44. Plastic laminate						
45. Cultured marble						
46. Kitchen cabinets						
47. Bathroom vanity						
48. Kitchen appliances (allowance)						
49. Light fixtures (allowance)						
50. Cleanup						
51. Painting and staining						
52.						

Self-Performed Work

Quantity Survey (Take Off)

The contractor should prepare a complete and accurate quantity survey. The take off is a listing of all the required materials and task items.

Plans and drawings should be used, as well as a quantity survey take off worksheet. The labor and equipment required for each task item or unit of material can then be estimated.

Remember, each item should be listed in appropriate pricing units on the quantity survey worksheet and calculations should be double checked. Being systematic and grouping similar items reduces the chance of missing an item. Most contractors have references to aid them, and computer programs are available to assist in this effort. On large projects, a number of quantity survey specialists may use the CSI format and work just in their areas of expertise.

Job-Costing Data

When estimating, cost information is gathered from previous similar projects to form the basis of the new estimate. This data is used to establish labor, material, equipment, and overhead costs for a new project. Costs are adjusted to reflect current wage rates, location, and special conditions of each project. Keeping accurate job-cost records gives a company very helpful information for estimating future projects. Also, it is often helpful if the people who will actually be doing the work confirm the costs and quantities estimates.

Start-up contractors may want to consider using a regional cost index.. An index provides time standards on most construction tasks and duration estimates for both labor and equipment hours. Remember, though, the index does not address individual project complexities that affect how long a project might take, and thus how much the project may cost.

Compute Labor Costs

Labor hours are computed by breaking the job down into individual tasks and assigning labor hours to each task. The more detailed a task list, the greater its accuracy for estimating. Remember to include tasks like on-the-job tool maintenance, scaffold erection and take-down, clean-up, breaks, safety, and coordination meetings. Also, it is often helpful to include time for occasional mistakes or rework, and time providing customer service.

Once labor hours are assigned to tasks, labor costs can be applied to the tasks. Trade practice rates and prevailing wage rate laws need to be considered.

Compute Material Costs

Every piece of material that will be used on the job, including waste, should be included. In estimating lumber, there is always some loss for bending or twisting out of shape (warpage), water damage, and other waste.

Compute Equipment Costs

Rental equipment needs to be verified for daily, weekly, and monthly rates. For a large project, an outright purchase of required equipment may be more cost-effective than leasing or renting.

Prepare a Preliminary Project Schedule

Resources (money, workers, equipment, materials and time) are assets used to produce a profitable project. Time (scheduling) needs to be considered carefully in project costs.

Although detailed scheduling is usually done after the cost estimate is complete, a preliminary schedule is needed to estimate labor, equipment, and project overhead costs. These are the cost categories most affected by construction scheduling.

Estimated labor unit costs are projections of how many hours it takes workers to complete the project at a specific cost per hour. Equipment costs and many job site overhead items are measured in units of time (hours, days, weeks, or months). Any difference between the budgeted time and the time actually spent results in a cost overrun or under run.

Again, records from previous similar projects are a great resource for estimating time. For example, suppose a contractor knows that a particular house was framed by certain employees in three weeks (15 work days). He can safely estimate a similar house can be framed by the same employees in approximately 15 work days. Adjusting for any wage change, the contractor can easily compute the cost of this portion of the work.

The order of tasks is important in the schedule. An efficient sequence cuts job time and reduces special costs such as temporary facilities, use of staging areas, and equipment costs. Whenever tasks can be scheduled at the same time, overhead costs are usually reduced, making the bid more competitive.

Overtime pay affects actual costs and should be included in the cost estimate.

If overtime is needed to meet project deadlines, labor costs are increased. On the other hand, job site overhead is usually based on calendar days, so overtime labor will get the job done more quickly and thus reduce job site overhead.

Summarizing Project Costs and Add-Ons

To determine project costs, a contractor starts with material and equipment costs from the quantity survey. He or she then adds direct labor costs and labor burden. Project overhead or soft costs are listed as line-item costs and added in. Project allowances and subcontractor bids are added into the itemized summary. Finally the cost of performance and payment bonds as well as builder's risk insurance and any other requirements of the project should be included.

Add Company Overhead

In exercising good business management practices, Sample Construction Inc. has a budget for annual company overhead that itemizes general and administration (G & A) expenses. The example used in Figure 6-3, Operating Budget for Sample Construction, Inc., shows annual company overhead of $120,000. This is not generated by only one project. A company incurs these expenses whether or not it is working on a project, and company overhead must be figured into project pricing.

So once project costs and overhead have been determined, the next step is to add an appropriate percentage for company overhead costs. Company overhead will vary from 3 percent to 40 percent of annual revenue, depending on the type of work performed by the company.

Example

Based on anticipated gross sales of $600,000, a company has an annual company overhead budget of $120,000. This budget was developed from the company's general and administrative expenses and constitutes 20 percent or .20 of the company revenue.

$120,000 ÷ $600,000. = .20

If a particular project is estimated at $48,000, when overhead is added, it will be 10 percent of the company's annual sales. Therefore, 10 percent of the G & A expenses, or $12,000 would have to be added to the project, bringing the total estimate to $60,000. (To simplify this calculation, "profit," the next topic, is not included here.)

$48,000 / .8 = $60,000 $60,000 / $600,000 = .10

Figure 6-3. Operating Budget

SAMPLE CONSTRUCTION, INC.
BUDGET

REVENUE	**$600,000**

COST OF GOODS SOLD

Materials	93,000
Field Labor	75,000
Subcontracts	228,000
Other Direct Costs	54,000
TOTAL	**450,000**
GROSS PROFIT	**$150,000**

GENERAL AND ADMINISTRATIVE EXPENSES:

Advertising	9,000
Auto and Truck Expense	3,565
Bad Debt	500
Contributions	300
Depreciation	3,400
Dues and Subscriptions	850
Equipment Leasing	2,700
Gas, Oil and Maintenance	3,750
Insurance General	5,800
Interest and Bank Charges	4,200
Legal and Accounting	3,200
Licenses and Taxes	1,000
Office Employment Benefits	4,200
Office Expenses	1,800
Office Rent	6,200
Operating Supplies and Tools	5,400
Salaries – Clerical	18,500
Salaries – Officer	30,000
Taxes – Payroll	8,785
Travel and Education	2,200
Utilities and Telephone	3,100
Warranty Work	1,000
Miscellaneous	550
TOTAL	**120,000**
NET PROFIT BEFORE TAXES	**$ 30,000**

Add Profit

A company must make a profit to survive and grow. A contract bid must include a certain percentage of markup for profit. The profit range may be 5 to 30 percent of the costs or more, depending on the type of project and the nature of the market. The amount of profit markup can be affected by a number of variables:

- Size and complexity of the project
- Duration of the Contract
- Location of the project
- The economic climate of the area
- The amount of expertise the project will require and whether this expertise is available in-house
- The contractor's level of interest in taking the job

Profit and overhead are usually determined as a percentage of the contract amount, which is added to the estimate. The first example below shows an easy mistake to make when adding overhead and profit margin.

Example 1

Sample Construction, Inc. estimates a $20,000 project cost and desires a 25 percent margin for overhead and profit **(20 percent for overhead and 5 percent for profit).**

> 1. Contract amount = cost + percent for overhead + profit
>
> $20,000 x .25 = $5,000 to add for overhead and profit
>
> $20,000 + $5,000 = $25,000 Contract Amount
>
> *However,* $5,000 $25,000 (Contract Amount) = 20 percent not 25 percent

As a result, this becomes a break-even project; not a profitable one. Overhead is 20 percent, with no bankable profit.

For a profitable project, Sample Construction needs to use an inverse mathematical calculation of the percentage of overhead and profit.

Example 2

Using the same construction estimate of $20,000 to establish a contract amount:

> 2. Contract amount = project costs 1 – the percent for overhead and profit
> $20,000 .75 = $26,667 (Contract Amount)
>
> $26,667 - $20,000 = $6,667 for overhead and profit
> $6,667: $26,667 = 25 percent

This would be a profitable job for Sample Construction with overhead covered at 20 percent and profit at 5 percent.

Add for Bonds and Insurance

Some projects/owners require the contractor to supply or "put up" certain bonds to protect the owner; performance and payment bonds are the most typical. It may also be incumbent or prudent for the contractor to carry builder's risk insurance. The cost of any bond(s) and/or insurance necessary on a project is included into the overall price the owner pays for that project.

Add Contingency

Because of the many variables and risks in a project, contractors often include a contingency value. Contingency may be added to several items in an estimate depending on the nature of the item, or to the total estimate. The value depends on the company's confidence in estimating, scheduling, and managing the project. It also depends on outside factors that affect the project like weather, project complexity, labor, and political unrest.

Bid or Client Proposal

Bid Format

Some owners require contractors to present bids in a certain format. If so, the format is described in their Invitation to Bid documents. These instructions need to be followed carefully and completely. When the owner is a public agency, deviations, modifications, or amendments to this form may cause a contractor's bid to be considered "non-responsive," meaning it is rejected.

These rejected bids will not be considered for award. Bids for public improvement work are required to be submitted in writing before a specified date and time. A bid submitted after the deadline will generally be considered "non-responsive."

Bidders must disclose first-tier subcontractors within two hours after submitting a bid to a public agency for a public improvement when the contract value is more than $100,000. Contract documents, especially the Invitation to Bid, usually require substantial subcontractor information. Failure to submit this information on the correct form by the deadline will result in a "non-responsive bid".

Proposals Presented to Clients

A proposal contains a price to perform certain work and includes a concise "scope of work," "statement of price," "qualifications," and "marketing material." Proposals should be neat, organized, and contain the following:

Clear and concise scope of work. The following task item in a proposal for Sam Jones' kitchen specifies the quantity, quality, type, and finish or style of the cabinets: *Remove existing cabinets and replace with 18LF (Linear Feet) of base cabinets, raised colonial panel, cherry, light, or natural finish.*

- **Statement of the price with** payment items. A contractor may require a certain percentage be paid as a down payment, prior to the start of a four-week project. The balance would be due upon completion or progressive payment with final payment at completion of the work. It is also wise to include a qualifying statement such as, "Prices good for 30 days from date of proposal." This protects the contractor if, six months later, the customer decides to accept the proposal and meanwhile cabinet, labor, or other prices have risen unexpectedly.
- **Qualifications.** Provide company experience [annual volume, years in business, etc.], office and workforce experience, resumes of project team, financial stability, and insurance coverage.
- **Marketing material** showing previous project experience, photos, awards, and references from satisfied customers

The goal is to provide a topnotch proposal. Award of the project often goes not to the lowest bidder, but to the bidder with the best overall proposal.

Prepare a Written Budget

When the contract is awarded from a successful bid or proposal, a contractor begins a project budget. This lists each item of work from the estimate and the amount allocated for it. When the contract is a long-term, the project budget also provides a basis for calculating progress payments that are due. Figure 6-4 is an example of a budget and progress payment schedule for a typical project.

Construction Scheduling

When estimating a construction project, a preliminary schedule is prepared and becomes part of the project plan. In an ideal world, scheduling is simple, but construction projects have unique owners, details, and site conditions. Consequently, a detailed project plan and schedule should be prepared immediately after the contract is signed. This schedule coordinates individuals, activities, and events for the project.

Scheduling the project helps the contractor look for cost and time savings throughout the project. The contractor organizes the work and becomes familiar with the site. As he becomes familiar with the project, he can identify ways to save time and money, and other ways to make the project successful. Such things as coordinating work with the owner's schedule and lifestyle, knowing community restrictions and working around subcontractors' availabilities goes a long way to smooth a project's path.

Figure 6-4. Budget for a Typical Project

SAMPLE CONSTRUCTION, INC.
1234 MAIN
Your Town, Oregon. 00000

Project: Executive Office Building   Location: Your Town, Oregon
Periodic Estimate No.: 3   For Period: End of third month

ITEM NO.	ITEM DESCRIPTION	Total Cost (1)	Completed To Date (2)	Cost to Complete (3)	Percent Complete (4)
1	Award of Contract (A)	10,000	10,000	0	100
2	Permits - General Requirement (Y)	36,000	20,000	16,000	55
3	Site Work and Grubbing (EE)	22,000	22,000	0	100
4	Site - Building Layout (FF)	3,000	3,000	0	100
5	Materials – Stored on Site (T)	9,000	4,500	4,500	50
6	Pile Driving (Z)	30,000	30,000	0	100
7	Excavation (K)	26,000	26,000	0	100
8	Site Utilities (KK)	25,000	20,000	5,000	80
9	Concrete – Foundation & Pit (H)	56,000	56,000	0	100
10	Backfill (J)	14,000	14,000	0	100
11	Site Survey, Ext. Imp.(GG)	3,000	3,000	0	100
12	Structural Steel – decking (II)	100,000	75,000	25,000	75
13	Electrical Rough-in (M)	28,000	7,000	21,000	25
14	Roofing (DD)	52,000	52,000	0	100
15	Plumbing Rough-in (CC)	18,000	3,800	14,200	21
16	Concrete – Floor Slabs (G)	18,000	0	18,000	0
17	Concrete – Pre-cast Panels.(I)	65,000	0	65,000	0
18	Block Masonry (C)	30,000	0	30,000	0
19	HVAC (Q)	37,000	0	37,000	0
20	Stairway (HH)	20,000	0	20,000	0
21	Mechanical Elevator & Sprinkler (U)	64,000	0	64,000	0
22	Partition & Drywall Installation (W)	36,000	0	36,000	0
23	Windows Hollow Metal Doors (LL)	40,000	0	40,000	0
24	Insulation (R)	11,000	0	11,000	0
25	Painting and Decorating (V)	14,000	0	14,000	0
26	Ceiling Installation (D)	13,000	0	13,000	0
27	Finish Flooring & Molding (O)	15,000	0	15,000	0
28	Finish Electrical (L)	34,000	0	34,000	0
29	Finish Plumbing (BB)	22,000	0	22,000	0
30	Carpentry - Trim and Mill (JJ)	26,500	0	26,500	0
31	Hardware and Fixtures (P)	4,800	0	4,800	0
32	Planter Construction (AA)	2,200	1,000	1,200	45
33	Sub-grading and Base Course (X)	30,000	5,500	24,500	18
34	Concrete – Curb and Walks (F)	22,000	0	22,000	0
35	Asphalt Paving (B)	35,000	0	35,000	0
36	Landscaping & Irrigation (S)	20,000	0	20,000	0
37	Cleanup (E)	6,500	750	5,750	12
38	Final Inspection and Services (N)	2,000	0	2,000	0
	Column Totals	$1Million	$353,550	$646,450	
	Change Order No.	$0	$0	$0	
	Total Contract Amount	$1Million			35.3%
A	Cost of Work Performed to Date		$353,550		
B	Less 10% Retention		$35,350		
C	Net Work Performed and Materials		$318,200		
D	Less Amount of Previous Payment		$118,200		
E	Balance Due This Payment		$200,000		

What is a Schedule?

A schedule is arranging a group of events in a given order to complete a project in a specific time period. Scheduling assigns tasks a specific time duration that fits well into the sequence of construction activities. Time duration can be expressed in hours or shifts but most often it is expressed in working days. A schedule should be flexible, but not so much that it is ineffective.

Prepare a Schedule

A written and posted schedule helps everyone associated with the project know when their work is required. A schedule in someone's head is more difficult for others to work with. Scheduling needs flexibility and revision throughout the project. Many factors can cause project activities to change. The schedule needs to adjust to actual conditions, in order to control the project efficiently. Each task involves coordination of time, materials, labor, and equipment.

Benefits of Proper Scheduling

When a job is properly scheduled, a contractor will have productive employees worth their wages. Approved materials will arrive at the job site as they are needed. Rental equipment will be active and used during the rental period. Work activities will follow a logical sequence at the job site, for example, rough-in electrical will be complete, inspected, signed off, and approved before hanging of sheetrock or drywall begins.

Proper and thorough scheduling has a number of benefits:
- Reduces overtime and idle time.
- Provides increased control over materials.
- Increases employee and management awareness of time required for various tasks.
- Reduces total job time.
- Minimizes peaks and valleys in resource usage.

Consequences of not properly scheduling a job

When daily schedules are not reviewed or monitored, it will be difficult to know when subcontractors or laborers fall behind. Once a job is behind schedule, working overtime or hiring extra laborers creates job-cost overruns. If the contract completion date is not met, the contractor risks breaching the contract. Subcontractors may have disputes from poor coordination of construction activities, interference, or work delays. Poor scheduling results in inefficient use of resources, labor, subcontractors, rental equipment and materials, and the costs of performance increase.

Other examples of inefficiencies are:

- Paid employees standing around, unsure of what work to do.
- Supplies and materials delivered to the job site before they are needed, requiring the contractor to find safe storage and earlier payment to the supplier.
- Costly rental equipment not being used at the time it was scheduled.
- Subcontractors who are scheduled at another project and cannot meet the revised schedule and must either schedule additional time at additional cost; or, they may be committed to other work and unable to return.

A Schedule Assures Quality Control

A quality-control program includes approval of materials, inspections, and testing or review of workmanship. If these requirements are in the contract, the contractor must ensure that they are scheduled and carried out.

Example

Before the project begins, the contractor generally needs the owner or design team to approve materials before they are ordered. Most often, this is accomplished through the submittal process. When the materials are approved, the contractor sets a delivery date so that materials are ready for the scheduled task. Any needed quality control checks and tests must be scheduled so the project is not delayed until a quality control representative is available.

Preparing and Using a Schedule

A preliminary schedule coordinates time with money in estimating the project and is a good starting point in scheduling.

List of Activities

The itemized summary of the estimate already details major items of work. Now it's time to list **all** activities. This exercise will help the estimator organize and plan the project as well as prepare the schedule. To do this, determine:

- What type of crew will be needed to complete the activity?
- What materials will be required for the activity?
- What subcontractors will be needed?
- What equipment will be needed?
- Who needs to do each task?
- Where will each task be done?
- When will materials or equipment be needed?
- How long will equipment be used?
- When can each task start?
- How long will each task take to complete?
- What are the relationships and dependencies among the tasks?

Sequence of Activities

Next, place the tasks in proper sequence. Preparing a bar chart may help in this. Figure 6-5 House Construction Schedule, details the sequence and duration of work activities for a project and is an excellent example of this type of bar chart or Gantt chart. It is easy to follow, and is the most common schedule-tracking tool seen on job sites. However, it does not show how tasks relate to each other, so should not be used alone for planning large projects.

When placing the tasks in proper sequence, group the tasks into fundamental operations and analyze each operation to determine the:

- Sequence of work, called "Job Logic" (concrete forming, concrete pouring, and concrete finishing).
- Duration of tasks (including curing times).
- Relative independence of tasks (roofing, landscaping).
- Location of tasks (second floor dry walling, main floor kitchen cabinetry).

Duration of Activities

After the project tasks have been grouped and sequenced with duration times, the next step is to schedule contingency times. Ideally, projects progress without delays. In the real world, delays are inevitable. Material deliveries, unforeseen job site difficulties, inclement weather, work order changes, or the owner not sure of a style or color choice may cause delays.

When developing a schedule, the sum of the duration of "critical path tasks" determines the total duration of the project. Tasks not on the critical path can be completed later than initially scheduled. The term "float" is the amount of time a task can go beyond its earliest expected completion without delaying the entire project.

Noncritical float tasks can occur concurrently with critical tasks. But if noncritical tasks are not completed within the float, they become critical.

For example, roofing may be noncritical to electrical and plumbing rough-ins, which are critical tasks. But if roofing is not complete by the time rough-ins are complete, it then becomes critical for interior insulation and drywall since roofing is required for protection of interior work.

Contingency time is a buffer, reducing the negative impact unexpected delays have on the remaining schedule. The amount of contingency time needed depends on how likely a delay is to occur. For example, more contingency time would be allowed for exterior work than interior work, and more for specialized work than general work. Experience can be invaluable in this area.

Figure 6-5. House Construction Schedule

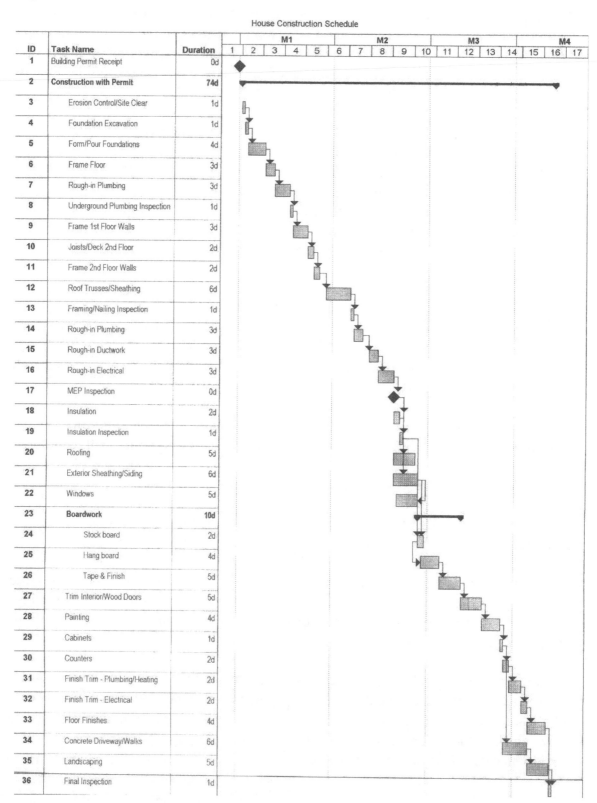

House Construction Schedule

ID	Task Name	Duration
1	Building Permit Receipt	0d
2	**Construction with Permit**	**74d**
3	Erosion Control/Site Clear	1d
4	Foundation Excavation	1d
5	Form/Pour Foundations	4d
6	Frame Floor	3d
7	Rough-in Plumbing	3d
8	Underground Plumbing Inspection	1d
9	Frame 1st Floor Walls	3d
10	Joists/Deck 2nd Floor	2d
11	Frame 2nd Floor Walls	2d
12	Roof Trusses/Sheathing	6d
13	Framing/Nailing Inspection	1d
14	Rough-in Plumbing	3d
15	Rough-in Ductwork	3d
16	Rough-in Electrical	3d
17	MEP Inspection	0d
18	Insulation	2d
19	Insulation Inspection	1d
20	Roofing	5d
21	Exterior Sheathing/Siding	6d
22	Windows	5d
23	**Boardwork**	**10d**
24	Stock board	2d
25	Hang board	4d
26	Tape & Finish	5d
27	Trim Interior/Wood Doors	5d
28	Painting	4d
29	Cabinets	1d
30	Counters	2d
31	Finish Trim - Plumbing/Heating	2d
32	Finish Trim - Electrical	2d
33	Floor Finishes	4d
34	Concrete Driveway/Walks	6d
35	Landscaping	5d
36	Final Inspection	1d

Advanced Scheduling Programs

Several computerized scheduling programs are available that are very effective for construction projects. Most of these programs use an adaptation of the critical path method (CPM) of project analysis. They graphically show the longest continuous sequence of activities in a project (the critical path), showing the overall time required to complete the project. A delay in any task on the critical path will cause a corresponding delay in the final completion of the project.

Monitoring the Schedule

From the first day of the project to the day of completion, the project schedule must be constantly monitored. By doing this, project managers can identify delays and find solutions early, with the least possible disruption to the job.

Management of the Project

After the solid foundation of estimating, planning, and scheduling, the actual project work can begin. But planning and scheduling cannot guarantee good weather, accident-free work, breakdown-proof equipment, or timely material delivery. Problems will arise, and the "artistry" of good management is needed to overcome obstacles as they arise.

Importance of Experience

Experience is vital to successful completion of any project. Also, following the old adage, "Do what you do best," can pay handsome dividends in the business of construction.

Project managers must be highly proficient in a variety of skills. To produce a profit and keep a satisfied client, a project manager must be able to organize, schedule, and control all phases of construction. Along with technical skills required to visualize the finished product, the successful project manager must have skills in problem solving, decision making, recordkeeping, documentation, computer, and above all, strong people skills.

Responsibilities of Managing a Project

The company has a responsibility for managing its projects. Too many projects at one time or projects in remote locations can seriously stress a manager's efficiency and ability to produce profitable results. A good company selects projects that fit the experience and abilities of its project managers, and wisely allocates company resources. The project manager's responsibilities may cover one project or extend over several projects in different phases of construction. Successful project management drives the company to success.

Project managers are responsible for developing a project plan to meet client requirements and provide company profitability. Project responsibilities are described in the project documents, including the contract documents. The project plan can be one of the most time-consuming activities for a contractor or project manager; however, it can pay huge dividends when done correctly.

The project manager is also responsible for managing the budget, which includes project costs and soft costs. The company office can help coordinate these requirements and tasks with the project manager. For example, the office may take on most of the project paperwork, such as keeping records, maintaining job files on subcontractors, suppliers or vendors, purchase orders, and making entries for job-cost reports.

Contract Documents

While preparing the estimate, the contractor reviews project documents that define the project and provided legal information. On further review of those documents, the contractor identifies performance requirements and assigns responsibilities to comply with the contract documents. Also, the project documents describe requirements such as reports, schedules, as-built drawings, and project records that are required during progress of work or at completion.

Job site Safety

General contractors and subcontractors are jointly responsible for job site safety and Oregon Occupational Safety and Health Administration (OR-OSHA) safety practices. They are also subject to OR-OSHA enforcement provisions. A contractor should know that subcontracting work does not relieve the general contractor of overall responsibility for safety requirements. Chapter 8 contains more information on subcontractor and job site safety practices.

Quality Control

Quality control programs can vary greatly depending on the type, size, location, and special conditions of a project. The owner, architect and owner's representative, or general contractor may carry out a quality control plan.

A designated quality control representative usually has no authority to change work, manage, or relieve the contractor from any obligations. The representative's job is simply observing the work to see if it does or does not conform to contract requirements or industry standards.

The owner may require the contractor to actively inspect the work process and make available quality control records. A particular project may require reporting to the owner on a daily or weekly basis about project progress, problems, and corrective measures that were taken.

Managing Project Documents

From the beginning, it is important to maintain necessary project documentation. The project manager must have a copy of the contract and be completely familiar with its content. Once permits have been obtained, keep them in a safe place at the job site as required by the issuing agency or jurisdiction. Keep records of any inspections that are conducted. If the project involves a wetlands area or any other environmental issues, such as lead or asbestos, get the proper permits and follow required guidelines and record keeping.

Benefits of Proper Project Documentation

Project documents generally describe requirements for performance, record progress of work, and support the contractor's performance in resolving disagreements. Without schedules, records, or reports, there is little proof of what, when, or how construction tasks were performed.

For resolving disagreements, it is good business practice for contractors to maintain the following project documents on every project:

- Written contract and related subcontracts signed by the owner
- General conditions documents
- Specifications, drawings or plans, and related documents
- Daily job reports, or a diary and a telephone log
- Job log and any meeting minutes
- Progress reports
- Project checklist
- Cost controls or a system for tracking actual job costs
- All project correspondence
- Accident report forms
- Safety meeting minutes (must be kept for three years)
- Change orders
- Course of construction photos
- Submittals or customer selection list
- Lien waiver forms
- Production package checklist
- Project schedule
- Notice to Proceed
- Purchase order system
- Time cards

After project completion, proper project documents must be retained as business records. These documents (and others) may support the contractor in resolving disagreements with a homeowner, through the CCB's dispute resolution process or for use in court or arbitration.

These records give the contractor historical data on how the work progressed and cost information for estimating future work.

Daily Job Report

Whatever the size of a project, daily job reports, or work logs, are good management practices. These are a written record describing any special incidents that took place during the day, including activities that may have caused delays to the project. A job report may also be a good place to record any out-of-pocket expenses that occurred. Contractors should keep a separate report or log for each construction project.

Items documented in the log should include:
- Work performed, both type and amount
- Equipment used
- Any problems and how they were resolve.
- Any conditions or events that differ from plan or schedule.
- Subcontractors on-site
- Employees or laborers on-site
- Visitors on-site (including the owner, inspectors, union, utility, Oregon-OSHA officials, or government agents)
- Accidents
- Weather conditions
- Deliveries of rental equipment, materials, or supplies (including any damages, shortages, or unloading problems)
- Deliveries that failed to arrive
- Photographs or videotapes

The daily report, including any visual images, establishes facts and work performed to support a contractor when resolving disagreements. A sample job report is shown in Figure 6-6.

Notices

The project manager is responsible for giving notices, as required in the contract, and for preparing work activities. For instance, utility companies need to know when and what type of work will be done on a residence or facility. They need notice to mark locations of buried lines before excavations or to provide temporary power to the site. The Department of Environmental Quality (DEQ) offers a Web site at http://deq12.deq.state.or.us/fp20 as a "Facility Profiler" with instructions for searching databases on permits, underground storage tanks, and environmental cleanup. Environmental site conditions may require notices and permits.

Figure 6-6. Example of Daily Job Report

Sample Construction Company
Daily Job Report

PROJECT NAME/NUMBER			NO. OF WORKERS	
Hindrance to Normal Progress of Work:		Trade		
		Project Manager		
		Project Engineer		
		Other Engineers		
		Project Superintendent		
		Ass't Superintendent		
		Office Personnel		
Accidents:		Foreman		
		Carpenters		
		Laborers		
		Cement Masons		
Work Progress – Subs:		Teamsters		
		Oper. Engnrs./Oilers		
		Subcontractors		
		(List Names)		
Work Progress				
		TOTAL		
		WEATHER: High Temp.	Low Temp.	
		Fine _____ Rain _____ Snow _____		
		Shift: Start Time:	End Time:	
		Changes		
		Tests		
		Pictures		
VISITORS:				
REPORT NO.		SIGNED:		
DATE:				

Manage the Budget

Job cost control begins the moment the contract is signed. Before beginning work, the estimator must exchange information with the project manager (unless the estimator is managing the budget).

Constant monitoring of costs does the following:
- Improves control over cash flow
- Improves job site performance
- Provides comparison for future estimates
- Provides comparison for profit margins between different types of work
- Assists the contractor in calculating amounts due for in-progress payments
- Provides individual project profit and loss performance data.

To achieve success on a project, continuous comparisons must be made between the budget and actual costs for labor, materials, and subcontractors. Information that is unreliable, too general, or delayed will hinder a manager's cost-control decisions. Careful procedures for cost information will justify the expense.

With a system in place for collecting and assigning cost data, it is possible to monitor in-progress costs. Those costs are often analyzed both on a separate item-by-item report for details, and on a summary report for the big picture. This dual analysis may show, for example, that higher than budgeted labor costs may result in lower overall concrete costs. Or perhaps additional labor will speed the overall project completion. In either case, when the summary report shows a cost savings, a higher cost item can be traded for an overall project savings. Also, keeping an eye on details in item-by-item reports can result in significant savings.

Job-cost reports generally focus more on labor and equipment costs. Material, subcontractor, project and company overhead costs, are usually more fixed and therefore, more certain. While general cost reports may be produced monthly, specific labor and equipment reports are often produced weekly, daily, or even hourly – depending on the scope of the project, the interest of the contractor, and the requirements of the project contract.

Labor Cost Control

Generally, labor receives hourly wages. Each employee uses a time card showing hours worked, and allocates those hours to a given project and task item. Also, the project manager reports daily the amount of work performed by workers. Work amounts can be measured in a variety of ways (i.e. number of bricks laid, square footage of bricks laid, linear feet of bricks laid). The method of measurement is usually consistent with the estimated method.

Weekly time cards and weekly production reports can be used to determine the production rate of each worker.

Example
If a crew of 10 masons worked 40 hours a week and cost $20 per labor hour, they would work a total of 400 hours ($8,000) in one week, and they would average 500 blocks per day (2,500 blocks). The productivity and unit cost would be 6.25 blocks per labor hour or $3.20 per block.

If this labor cost is higher than estimated, the contractor may explore ways to reduce or justify it.

If information collected is not accurate, it may lead the contractor to take action when none is required, or to not take action when something should be done to lower costs. If information is not provided in a timely manner, it may be too late to make a cost-control correction. For this reason, information about highly variable costs such as labor should be collected daily.

Material Control
Good material control requires timely purchase of materials, on schedule delivery to the job site, and careful storage and handling. Using a purchase order system with a limited number of authorized users provides effective material control. By carefully controlling materials, several benefits are realized:

- Increased net working capital
- Reduced time and expenses in handling materials
- Simplified job costing
- Reduced exposure to theft or loss
- Reduced inventory

For effective material handling, the contractor should consider the following:

- Is there adequate on-site material storage?
- How far must materials be moved?
- Will landscaping be damaged in construction or transporting materials?
- What are the most accessible and practical material storage locations?

The proper material inventory depends on several factors, such as type of work, volume of work, and distance from suppliers. Excess materials tie up work space and working capital.

A contractor may consider ordering all of the materials and products necessary to complete some jobs, such as a kitchen remodel, and stockpile it in the owner's garage. If the owner can get by without use of the garage during construction, this action may shorten the overall construction period and minimize inconvenience to the owner.

Manage the Schedule

Tasks must be sequenced carefully to prevent activities from interfering with each other. For example, paint and floor covering installed in a room at the same time would reduce productivity and probably lower quality.

Typical scheduling and logistic problems are:
- What will the owner do without a kitchen or bathroom once demolition has begun?
- How will inclement weather affect working or living conditions of the homeowner once a roof, or perhaps an exterior wall, has been removed?

Manage the Project Plan

Project planning involves analyzing a project's tasks and finding the most effective construction method. In each project, the manager develops the construction schedule and budget, determines quality standards and procedures, and follows through with daily job reports, written logs, and time cards.

Manage Activities

While controlling the schedule and budget, these tasks need to be kept in mind:
- Schedule material ordering, delivery, and any special handling requirements for material.
- Determine how much on-site supervision is needed.
- Locate all utilities and ensure they are not disturbed. Before doing any digging or excavating, call **"Call Before You Dig" at 800-332-2344.**
- Determine how to get temporary power to the project.
- Conduct weekly job meetings with the production manager, and perhaps occasionally, with all the subcontractors and employees. This will keep management and employees up to date on the project, and can help create good will with employees.
- When conducting job site meetings with owners, subcontractors, or building inspection officials, be sure to keep minutes of the meeting.
- Keep a log of all project-related phone calls. Record who was called or who called the company, topic of call, date, time, and outcome or action to be taken.
- Conduct employee safety meetings. Remember, in addition to not wanting any employees to get hurt, a company has a responsibility under OR-OSHA to create and maintain a safe working environment for all employees.

Employment issues need to be managed when they occur. These range from workers' compensation claims to employees' concerns about wages. When unsure, if possible, consult with legal counsel or seek professional advice before taking action.

Purpose of Coordination

Coordinating a project with everyone involved ensures it will run smoothly. Usually this includes subcontractors, suppliers, architects, engineers, equipment dealers, and, when working with government agencies, a contract administrator. In a home remodeling project, the homeowner must be aware of how the project will proceed and what he or she needs to do. It is a good idea to give the owner two schedules:

1. The general project production schedule that shows when work activities will occur and their completion dates.
2. The owner's timeline, showing what the owner is to do, and when.

This instructs the owner when to:
- Move personal items, valuables, furniture, or pictures from walls.
- Prepare site access or a place for material storage.
- Select items like cabinet style and color or floor covering.

The project manager has the responsibility of coordinating all these activities. If the project manager is someone other than the contractor, the project manager must have the same broad authority as the contractor.

Subcontractors

Subcontractors can fail to perform their work, and the general contractor assumes the risk. Consequently, contractors should verify the financial soundness of subcontractors and pay them on time. Project managers can encourage good performance from subcontractors by coordinating work well so they are allowed sufficient time to do their work.

When subcontractors have cash flow problems, they may miss payments to suppliers. Using 2 checks, one to the subcontractor and another to the material supplier can make sure the supplier gets paid. This precaution protects the owner from liens on the property if the general contractor does not require the subcontractors or suppliers to sign lien waivers.

Oregon does not have standardized construction lien waivers. Office supply stores sell these forms, or the person requesting the release can draft a form and his or her attorney may review the form before it is used. Contractors can send the lien waiver forms to subcontractors and their suppliers to sign and return with their application or invoice for payment. In signing the lien waiver, subcontractors and suppliers release construction lien rights against the property, either for a specific amount of payment, or for a specific scope of performance. What releases are made depends on the exact language of the release form. Waivers can be conditional or unconditional.

While a contractor does not provide workers' compensation insurance coverage for subcontractors, the contractor must make sure that subcontractors have workers' compensation coverage for their employees before the subcontractor arrives on site. Otherwise, the contractor is responsible for providing coverage for all subject workers. Also verify and keep proof of licensing and insurance for the duration of the subcontractor's contract.

Time and performance details show a contractor whether he or she wants to use that subcontractor again. Records on subcontractor work help evaluate their performance and effectiveness, both in working with others and with a schedule. If a subcontractor works effectively, the contractor will want to use them on future projects, particularly if they work well with others.

Project Closeout

Project closeout includes all parties involved with the project, including subcontractors, material vendors, and manufacturers' representatives. It is always wise to plan for closeout during the estimate and construction phases so costs and responsibilities are fully covered in the budget and project plan. Project closeout occurs when the project, or a specified part of it, is complete enough that the owner can use it for its intended purpose.

The project closeout process is as follows:

1. The contractor submits formal notice to the architect and the owner that the construction project is substantially complete.
2. Based on his observations and on discussions with the contractor, the architect documents substantial completion with the owner and contractor. Substantial completion may activate certain warranties, depending on provisions of the contract.
3. During phased projects, the architect and the owner may recognize some but not all of the building systems as being substantially complete. This should be clearly documented, since start dates for warranty and guarantee periods for various building systems may vary.
4. The architect and owner make an on-site walk-through punch list noting needed corrections. The contractor corrects all work noted on the punch list. The architect and owner may then make a final observation of the corrected work. When the owner accepts the work, the architect issues a certificate of completion to the contractor with a copy to the owner. The certificate documents that the contractor has completed the work specified in the contract documents.
5. The contractor documents and delivers to the owner a complete keying schedule, with master, sub-master, room, and specialty keys.

6. The contractor submits all record drawings, as-built drawings or plans, testing and balancing reports, and other documents required by the contract.
7. The contractor submits all guarantees, warranties, certificates, and bonds required by the contract documents or technical specifications.
8. All required operation and maintenance manuals (O & M's) are forwarded to the owner.
9. The contractor submits the final consolidated payment request, including approved and signed change orders, as final accounting of the project.
10. In the final accounting documents, the contractor submits final lien waivers and any affidavits, as required by the contract. Generally, the contractor needs to show the owner that all invoices, including those from any subcontractors or suppliers, have been paid with the exception of amounts due on the final payment request. The contractor submits these documents with the final payment request.
11. The architect sends a final certificate of payment to the owner, with a copy to the contractor.
12. The contractor provides any required certificate of occupancy, indicating that the building authorities who have jurisdiction over the project approve occupancy of the space for the intended use.
13. The owner makes final payment to the contractor and notifies the architect.

The extent to which this process applies to a project depends on the scope of work and the type of project. However, to avoid problems, it is just as important or perhaps more important to formally close out smaller projects or segments of projects with as much thoroughness as larger projects. Often in remodeling projects, the homeowner begins using some parts of a project before the total project is complete. A contractor can be forced to install a new shower, for example, if a homeowner damages a shower and it was not inspected by both the owner and the contractor and shown to be free of damage before it was turned over to the owner for use.

The closeout is an important part of the project, and a closeout form or checklist helps do this efficiently. Such a form or checklist needs to be flexible to allow for the needs and requirements of each project. For complex work or projects where several trades are coordinated, a closeout form for each trade may be useful.

As the project is closed out, and the contract requirements are completed, the contractor transfers responsibility and risk to the owner. Figure 6-7 is an example of a Project Completion Final Punch List for Remodeling Projects.

In summary, everyone wins when the contractor plans ahead, manages efficiently, and covers tasks thoroughly, doing it right from start to finish.

Figure 6-7. Project Completion Final Punch List for Remodeling Projects

**** Project Completion Final Punch List ****		
Tasks To Be Performed Upon Completion	Date:	
	Yes	No
1. Completion form has been filled out and signed. Comments:		
2. All change orders have been accounted for and billed. Comments:		
3. Final bill has been delivered and paid. Comments:		
4. Final building inspections have been completed. Comments:		
5. Copies of all building inspections have been placed in file. Comments:		

6. All warranties, product information, keys, etc. have been delivered
     to owner.
     Comments:		

7. Job site sign and lockbox have been returned to the office. Comments		

8. Project has been checked for any tools, ladders, or material that may
     have been left behind.
     Comment:		

9.		
10.		
11.		
12. Project folder, along with all pertinent information, has been turned in to the front office.		

Notes: _____

_____

_____

Signed: _____
                        Project Superintendent

Date: _____

Appendix A. Construction Bid Outline
(Estimating Checklist, for Educational Purposes Only)

Work Summary	Contractor	Start	End	Est.	Bid	Cost	Total	Total Paid
a. Pre-Construction:								
Plans, engineering								
Building permit								
Sewer permit								
Water meter service								
b. Site Work:								
Erosion control								
Grading, excavation, and fill								
Driveway concrete cutting and removal								
Removal and disposal of contaminated soils								
Rain drains and other drainage								
Sewer labor and materials								
Street cut/patch and city fee								
Landscaping and grading								
Hazardous material removal								
Asbestos								
Lead								
c. Concrete:								
Concrete foundations (labor and materials)								
Concrete floors, walkways, driveways, (labor and materials)								
Retaining walls								
d. Metals:								
Deck and railings								
Exterior steel railing								
e. Woods and Plastics:								
Lumber material (miscellaneous)								
Siding (labor and material)								
Finish lumber								
Finish labor								
Underlayment (labor and materials)								
Windows								
Doors (interior and exterior with hardware)								
Trim, door & window								
Garage doors with opener								
Cabinets								

Chapter 6

Work Summary	Contractor	Start	End	Est.	Bid	Cost	Total	Total Paid
f. Thermal and Moisture Protection:								
Foundation dampproofing								
Moisture barrier, siding								
Insulation, ceiling								
Insulation, walls								
Roofing (labor and materials)								
Flat roof waterproofing								
Gutters, downspouts, flashing								
g. Finishes:								
Sheetrock (labor and materials)								
Hardwood flooring								
Vinyl flooring								
Carpet								
Tile								
Countertops								
Hardware (bolts, connectors, etc.)								
Finish hardware (mirror, towel bars, and shower doors)								
Painting and wallpaper								
h. Specialties:								
Fireplaces								
Appliances								
i. Mechanical:								
Plumbing (complete with fixtures)								
Heating and air-conditioning								
j. Electrical:								
Electrical wiring complete								
Electrical fixtures								
Miscellaneous costs (wiring for television, intercom, computer, security system, hot tub)								
SUBTOTAL								
Office/General Overhead								
Project Overhead (soft costs)								
Cost of Bond (if required)								
Fee								
Contingency								
TOTAL PROJECT COST:								

Appendix B

MasterFormat™ 2004 Edition – Numbers & Titles
November 2004

Division Numbers & Titles

Division Numbers and Titles

PROCUREMENT AND CONTRACTING REQUIREMENTS GROUP

Division 00   Procurement and Contracting Requirements

SPECIFICATIONS GROUP

GENERAL REQUIREMENTS SUBGROUP
Division 01   General Requirements

FACILITY CONSTRUCTION SUBGROUP
Division 02   Existing Conditions
Division 03   Concrete
Division 04   Masonry
Division 05   Metals
Division 06   Wood, Plastics, and Composites
Division 07   Thermal and Moisture Protection
Division 08   Openings
Division 09   Finishes
Division 10   Specialties
Division 11   Equipment
Division 12   Furnishings
Division 13   Special Construction
Division 14   Conveying Equipment
Division 15   Reserved
Division 16   Reserved
Division 17   Reserved
Division 18   Reserved
Division 19   Reserved

FACILITY SERVICES SUBGROUP
Division 20   Reserved
Division 21   Fire Suppression
Division 22   Plumbing
Division 23   Heating, Ventilating, and Air Conditioning
Division 24   Reserved
Division 25   Integrated Automation
Division 26   Electrical
Division 27   Communications
Division 28   Electronic Safety and Security
Division 29   Reserved

SITE AND INFRASTRUCTURE SUBGROUP
Division 30   Reserved
Division 31   Earthwork
Division 32   Exterior Improvements
Division 33   Utilities
Division 34   Transportation
Division 35   Waterway and Marine Construction
Division 36   Reserved
Division 37   Reserved
Division 38   Reserved
Division 39   Reserved

PROCESS EQUIPMENT SUBGROUP
Division 40   Process Integration
Division 41   Material Processing and Handling Equipment
Division 42   Process Heating, Cooling, and Drying Equipment
Division 43   Process Gas and Liquid Handling, Purification, and Storage Equipment
Division 44   Pollution Control Equipment
Division 45   Industry-Specific Manufacturing Equipment
Division 46   Reserved
Division 47   Reserved
Division 48   Electrical Power Generation
Division 49   Reserved

Div Numbers – 1

Chapter 6

Appendix C

Additional Suggested Resources

Construction Products Resources

Sweets Catalog Reference Manuals

Construction Management Resources

Books

Construction Methods and Management, S. W. Nunnally *Construction Project Scheduling*, Michael T. Callahan *Construction Management*, Daniel W. Halpin *Fundamentals of Construction Estimating*, David Pratt *Construction Scheduling*, David A. Carchman *Construction Project Management*, Henry Naylor *Construction Job Site Management*, William R. Mincks

Book Resource

www.buildingtechbooks.com
Toll-free: 1-800-ASK-Book

Sample Questions

CHAPTER 6

1. Which is NOT true about project documentation?

☐   1. Project documentation can be used to support a contractor's case in a court of law or a CCB claims hearing.

☐   2. Good project documentation will show the history of the specific project. 3. Daily job logs are written, when needed, on complex projects over $2,500.

☐   3. It is important to plan what documents will be needed before starting a project.

2. Which is NOT true about project scheduling?

☐   1. A bad project schedule can result in contractors not knowing when to do their work.

☐   2. Improper scheduling may increase total job time.

☐   3. Project schedules are only required on major projects.

☐   4. If a project schedule is too general or too detailed, it can be unusable.

3. Which is true about overhead?

☐   1. Project overhead is a percentage of direct job costs.

☐   2. There are two types of overhead: company and "soft" costs.

☐   3. A proportional percentage of company overhead should not be included in each bid.

☐   4. Company overhead includes expenses like surveying fees, site barricades, and permits.

Answers:

1. [3]
2. [3]
3. [2]

CHAPTER 7
BUILDING CODES

Objectives

At the end of this chapter, you will be able to:

1. Know where to find building codes and code books that apply to your trade.
2. Understand the process for code amendments.
3. Identify when a permit is required.
4. Know the type of information needed to obtain a permit.
5. Identify penalties for failure to obtain a permit, for permit violations, or for working without a license.
6. Identify when an inspection is required.
7. Identify when a specialty license and/or a specialty inspection is required.
8. Explain the consequences of a stop work order.
9. Understand the purpose of a final inspection.

Introduction

The Building Codes Division (BCD) of the Department of Consumer and Business Services, in conjunction with its seven advisory boards, develops the statewide building code. BCD also administers exams for specialty trade licenses and some inspector certifications. Most permit and inspection services are provided by local city or county building departments. These services are essential in building safe and effective structures in Oregon.

BCD Activities
The BCD enforces and administers the state building code. The BCD provides the following services:

- **Code Development and Interpretation**. BCD develops and maintains Oregon's construction codes and rules for use by state and local jurisdictions. BCD helps local building officials, contractors, and those who need authoritative interpretation of various specialty codes.
- **Compliance.** Services are provided to local jurisdictions, contractors, and the public to ensure compliance with the appropriate laws, including licensing, permitting and code requirements.
- **Licensing and Certification.** BCD administers exams and issues licenses required for plumbing; electrical; elevator installation and repairs; boiler installation, maintenance and repair; and manufactured dwelling installation. BCD also processes and issues inspector certifications. BCD records continuing education credits for licensed professionals.
- **Permits and Inspections.** The BCD issues permits and administers the building code in a few smaller jurisdictions and for the elevator and boiler programs. The permit process includes the review of plans for construction. State inspection services are provided to manufacturers and dealers of prefabricated structures and components.
- **Training.** BCD offers training opportunities for license holders, inspectors, and others. The training encompasses the state building code and the division's policies and procedures related to permits and inspections. Information can be found at www.bcd.oregon.gov.

BCD Boards for Code Development and Interpretation
Seven advisory boards help the Building Codes Division adopt and amend the specialty codes. These boards also have varying levels of responsibility for specialty trade licensing, enforcement and code appeals. The following boards are comprised of industry and public representatives:

- Building Codes Structures Board.
- Electrical and Elevator Board.
- Oregon State Plumbing Board.
- Mechanical Board.

- Residential and Manufactured Structures Board.
- Board of Boiler Rules
- Construction Industry Energy Board.

Provisions for the construction of low-rise multi multiple-family dwellings are now covered under the *Oregon Structural Specialty Code.*

Modern-Day Codes

New codes and standards have been developed since the early 20th Century to ensure consistency in workmanship and increased safety in construction. Oregon has been in the forefront of code adoption.

Currently, the BCD adopts national model codes that are modified with Oregon amendments. There are a variety of national code bodies that adopt model codes including, International Code Council, American Society of Mechanical Engineers, National Fire Protection Association, and the International Association of Plumbing and Mechanical Officials.

Process for Code Adoption and Revisions in Oregon

The BCD adopts uniform building codes in Oregon. The national model codes are amended and adopted in the state as Oregon specialty codes. Any individual can submit a code amendment proposal during the code adoption process. Codes are generally adopted every three years with many codes moving to a six-year cycle with minor updates occurring at the three-year mark. Between national code adoptions, the Oregon specialty codes can be amended as allowed by the appropriate statutes.

Since codes can change, contractors should consult with the building jurisdiction that governs the site where the project is located. In preparing an estimate, it is recommended that the contractor verify project code requirements, plan review requirements, the process for obtaining permits, and when to call for inspections.

Codes Used in Oregon

The following is a list of the codes used in Oregon. Refer to www.bcd.oregon.gov for information and recent changes.

2014 Oregon Residential Specialty Code

Oregon adopted the 2014 *Oregon Residential Specialty Code with an* effective date of Oct. 1, 2014. It is based on the 2009 edition of the ICC *International Residential Code* with enhancements added in 2014. The plumbing and electrical chapters of the International Code are not used in Oregon. The *Oregon State Plumbing Code* and the *Oregon State Electrical Code* apply in Oregon. The scope of the *Oregon Residential Specialty Code* includes one- and two-family dwellings, townhouses, and their accessory structures.

2014 Oregon Structural Specialty Code (OSSC)

The OSSC consists of the 2011 edition of the *International Building Code with Oregon amendments*, which was effective July 1, 2014 with a grace period extending to Oct. 1, 2014. This code applies to all structures not regulated under the *Oregon Residential Specialty Code*, including:

- Commercial structures
- Transient lodging, such as hotels and motels
- Certain residential structures subject to licensure by the Oregon Department of Human Services
- Low-rise multiple family dwellings

The OSSC also includes the construction provisions located in the fire code.

2014 OSSC - Oregon Energy Efficiency Provisions

The energy provisions of the 2014 OSSC are published in a separate document known as the *2014 Oregon Energy Efficiency Specialty Code (OEESC)*. The 2014 OSSC Energy provisions were adopted effective July 1, 2014 with a grace period extending to Oct.1, 2014. This is the last code cycle where the energy provisions will be published as a separate publication.

2014 Oregon Mechanical Specialty Code (OMSC)

Oregon adopted the *2014 Oregon Mechanical Specialty Code (OMSC)*, which is based on the 2012 *International Mechanical Code*, Oregon amendments and the *2012 International Fuel Gas Code,* as an appendix, effective July 1, 2014 with a grace period extending to Oct. 1, 2014.

The OMSC applies to all structures not covered under the *Oregon Residential Specialty Code.*

2014 Oregon Plumbing Specialty Code (OPSC)

Oregon adopted the *2014 Oregon Plumbing Specialty Code* with an effective date of Oct. 1, 2014. It is based on the 2009 edition of the *Uniform Plumbing Code* with enhancements added in 2014

2014 Oregon Electrical Specialty Code (OESC)

Oregon adopted the *2011 Oregon Electrical Specialty Code* with an effective date of Oct. 1, 2014, which is based on the 2014 edition of the *NFPA 70, National Electrical Code*. This code contains requirements for electrical installations.

2010 Oregon Manufactured Dwelling Installation Specialty Code

Effective April 1, 2010, Oregon adopted the *Manufactured Dwelling Installation Specialty Code (MDISC)* to replace the *2002 Manufactured Dwelling and Park Specialty Code (MD&P)*. The new *MDISC* code is based on the 2002 *MD&P*, U.S. Department of Housing and Urban Development (HUD) installation standards, and national recognized manufactured dwelling installation standards.

The *2010 MDISC* does not contain all the information previously covered under the scope of the *MD&P*. This includes, but is not limited to, alternate uses, certificate of occupancy, change of occupancy, warranty work, alterations, and the regulation of manufactured dwelling parks. Because these items do not relate to installation requirements of manufactured dwellings, they have been adopted into BCD's administrative rules in Chapter 918 of the Oregon Administrative Rules.

2011 Oregon Elevator Specialty Code

The 2011 Oregon Elevator Specialty Code was effective Jan. 1, 2012. It is comprised of the *Oregon Specialty Lift Code,* 2005 edition, the 2010 edition of *American Society of Mechanical Engineers (ASME) Standard A 17.1, Safety Code for Elevators and Escalators,* the 2010 edition of *ASME Standard 17.2, Guide for Inspection of Elevators, Escalators, and Moving Walkways,* the 2010 edition of *ASME 17.6, the Standard for Elevator Suspension, Compensation, and Governor Systems,* the 2008 edition of *ASME 18.1, Safety Standard for Platform Lifts and Stairway Chairlifts,* and the 2009 edition of *ASME A90.1, Safety Standard for Belt Manlifts.* Oregon amendments to this code were effective Jan. 1, 2012.

2014 Oregon Boiler Specialty Code

Effective Jan. 1, 2015, Oregon's Boiler and Pressure Vessel Specialty Code (which regulates operating and inspection parameters of the vessels/boilers), consists of the:
- 2013 ASME Boiler and Pressure Vessel Code
- 2012 edition of ANSI/ASME B31.1 Power Piping Code
- 2012 edition of ANSI/ASME B31.3 Process Piping Code
- 2013 edition of ANSI/ASME B31.5 Refrigeration Piping Code
- 2011 edition of ANSI/ASME B31.9 Building Service Piping Code
- 2013 edition of National Board Inspection Code ANSI/NB2
- 2011 edition of NFPA 85, Boiler and Combustion Systems Hazards Code
- 2012 edition of ASME CSD-1, Controls and Safety Devices for Automatically Fired Boilers

2014 Oregon Fire Code

The *2014 Oregon Fire Code* is based on the *2014 ICC International Fire Code* with Oregon amendments.

2010 Oregon Solar Installation Specialty Code

Effective Oct. 1, 2010, the division adopted the *2010 Oregon Solar Installation Specialty Code (OSISC)*, which is the first solar code for Oregon and the first statewide solar code in the nation. The code is part of the division's overall goal to facilitate green building technologies. The OSISC standards are for the installation of the structural components for installation, alteration, replacement, or repair of solar photovoltaic systems. The electrical requirements are contained in the *Oregon Electrical Specialty Code* and reproduced in the OSISC's Appendix A.

2011 Reach Code

The *2011 Oregon Reach Code* is a voluntary set of construction standards intended to expedite high performance homes and commercial structures. It also introduces builders and building officials to new methods and technology. The Reach Code offers a chance to use new standards and technology without having to go through a site-specific approval process. The Reach Code was drafted to be more energy efficient than the statewide mandatory codes. It includes alternate methodologies for vegetative roofs, residential straw clay construction, and residential composting toilets.

How to Use Appropriate Code Books

Although all the codes differ somewhat in their specific requirements, each code is arranged in a similar manner.

It is quite easy to use a code book. First, determine the term or subject area for which information is needed. This is called the key word. Then look up that item in the index.

Statutes and Rules

The statewide building code covers the technical requirements of construction projects, while statutes and rules dictate licensing, permitting, and other administrative processes. The statutes and rules that govern BCD's activities can be found on its Website at www.bcd.oregon.gov.

Permits

Permits are required for most new construction and alterations or additions to existing buildings, including structural, plumbing, mechanical, and electrical work. Individual jurisdictions, whether city or county, may have additional requirements based on local geographic, seismic, and climatic conditions.

There may be property owners who do not want a contractor to obtain a building permit even though they want the contractor to perform work. If a licensed contractor works without a required permit, the CCB may revoke or suspend the contractor's license and assess a penalty.

In addition, BCD Compliance will take action against the contractor, who must comply with permit and building code requirements.

Contractors must apply for a permit at the building department that has jurisdiction in the area where the construction work will be performed. To find the appropriate building department, call the nearest city hall, give the address of the construction project or installation, and ask for contact information of the building jurisdiction that issues the permit. Contractors will need to provide their address and the type of work they are planning to perform. Contractors should contact the local jurisdiction building official with any code or permit questions. Appendix A provides a list of local jurisdictions. A list of local building departments is also on the BCD's website at www.bcd.oregon.gov.

Permit Application

To apply for a permit, information about the project must be prepared before a plan review. If the jurisdiction does not require a plan review, the information needs to be presented when the permit application is submitted.

Generally, the following project information is prepared and submitted in applying for a permit:
- Address or directions to the job site where inspections will be conducted.
- Local government or jurisdictional approvals, if needed, such as:
  - Land-use actions completed
  - Zoning approvals
  - Sanitation verification and approval
  - Fire district approval
  - Septic system or sewer permit
  - Water district approval
  - Soils report
  - Erosion control plan and required permit

- Complete sets of legible plans, which include:
  - Site or plot plan drawn to scale
  - Foundation plan
  - Basement and retaining walls
  - Floor plans
  - Cross section(s) and details
  - Elevation views
  - Wall bracing or lateral analysis plans
  - Floor and roof framing assemblies
  - Beam calculations
  - Manufactured floor and roof truss design details
- Energy Code Compliance
- Engineer's calculations, if required

Forms

To obtain a structural permit, the contractor must complete an Application for Structural Permit and attach the plans for review along with the appropriate payment for the permit. An example of an Application for Structural Permit is shown in Appendix B.

Plumbing, mechanical, and electrical specialties also require permits.

Fees

Fee schedules and valuation tables are available to help contractors determine permit fees. The fee tables vary from jurisdiction to jurisdiction. Contact the jurisdiction (listed in Appendix A) where work will be performed.

Drawings

Refer to applicable state and local building codes and to other local ordinances to find requirements for submitting drawings for a permit.

Generally, a licensed architect or engineer must prepare drawings if the floor area is 4,000 square feet or more, or the height of the structure is more than 20 feet. This does not apply to single family dwellings and their accessory uses nor to certain other exempt structures.

Online Permit Services

With the support and cooperation of local government and the construction industry, the BCD established and continues to expand, online permit services.

Basic Services

This program is now used by 47 jurisdictions and counting. Basic Services allows contractors to apply and pay for multiple non-plan review permits from multiple building departments from a single online location at buildingpermits.oregon.gov.

Full Service Permits

Currently, 27 jurisdictions offer a full range of building department services online and eight more jurisdictions are expected to come online with the full-service system by the end of 2014. This system provides online building department services for contractors and participating locations in the state through a one-stop website. Services include:

- Application, payment, and receipt of trade and building permits
- Intake, electronic document review, and tracking of plans
- Scheduling, tracking, and reporting of inspections
- Tracking of construction and permit activity from plan intake and review through final sign-off

Specialty Licenses

Generally, any person who installs, alters, or repairs another person's property involving selected specialty trade practices is required to be licensed with the BCD. Contractors or businesses with two or more specialty licenses in electrical, elevator, boilermaker, or plumbing trades may combine licenses and renew them at the same time.

Specialty Trade Licensing

Certain specialty trades must be licensed with the BCD, including:

- Boiler or pressure vessel licensees Classes 1-6
- Electricians in various classifications
- Elevator journeymen and limited elevator mechanics
- Manufactured dwelling installers
- Plumbing journeymen in various classifications

Refer to www.bcd.oregon.gov for a complete list of specialty trades that must be licensed.

Compliance with the Building Codes Division

Besides having a boiler, electrical, elevator, and/or plumbing license, businesses must also be licensed as contractors with the CCB.

In addition to any other sanction or penalty, the appropriate board may suspend or revoke a license if the contractor:

- Does not comply with the requirements of that license
- Engages in an act that causes the CCB to impose a sanction

Inspections

Inspection Requirements

The permit holder requests inspections when each phase of the construction is ready. Usually, inspections are made within 48 hours of the request. If, however, the inspection is not made, the portion of construction requiring inspection must remain open until the inspector gives approval.

Footing or Foundation Inspection

Footing or foundation inspections are made after forms are set and steel is in place, but before concrete is placed.

Concrete Slab or Under-Floor Inspection

Concrete slab or under-floor inspections are to be made after all in-slab or under-floor building services are installed, and plumbing and mechanical systems are installed, but before the concrete is poured or the deck or subfloor is installed.

Plumbing, Mechanical, and Electrical Systems Rough Inspections

Rough installations are required to be inspected and approved prior to the framing inspection. Some jurisdictions have multi-certified inspectors who can inspect these systems at the same time the framing inspection is done.

Framing and Masonry Inspection

Framing and masonry inspections are made after all mechanical, plumbing, and electrical systems are inspected, framing is completed, and fire-stopping is installed, but before the insulation is installed.

Insulation and Vapor Barrier Inspections

Insulation and vapor barrier inspections are made after all insulation, required vapor barriers are installed, and before wall coverings are installed. Exception: attic and under-floor insulation that is visible at the time of the final inspection can be inspected at that time.

Final Inspection and the Certificate of Occupancy

Final inspection shall be made after the successful completion of all the required inspections and before the structure is ready for occupancy. The purpose of final inspection is to assure that there is no fire, life, safety, or health issues, and that the structure is code compliant for occupancy. All new residential dwellings and townhouses must now have a certificate of occupancy if the structural permit was applied for on or after April 1, 2008. This is a change, as these structures could previously be occupied after successful completion of final inspection. Other structures are issued a Certificate of Occupancy before occupancy is allowed. The contractor must contact the local jurisdiction in preparing for final inspection.

How to Help Inspections go Smoothly

If a contractor has questions about code or compliance for a project, he or she should call the local building jurisdiction before beginning work. This shows the contractor's intent to do proper work that passes inspections the first time. Here are several steps a contractor can take to make sure the inspection goes smoothly:

- Make sure the project is ready for inspection.
- Put the Inspection Record Card in a weatherproof cover and post in an accessible and conspicuous place to allow the building official to make required entries, if required.
- Know the code and make sure the project is compliant with it.
- Relate to inspectors in a businesslike manner.

The local building official would prefer to help before the project is finished than see incorrect work and have to re-inspect the project.

Local Building Official's Authority and Code Interpretation

The local building official has authority to interpret the code in applying it to a project. These interpretations must conform to, or be consistent with, the intent and purpose of the code.

The local building official is permitted to enter, at reasonable times, any building, structure, or premises to perform duties authorized by the code. This authority includes entry for cause of a possible violation, or for unsafe, dangerous, or hazardous conditions.

In addition, applicants for permits may appeal the final decision of a building official to the Oregon Building Codes Division. Please see www.bcd.oregon.gov for more information

Contractor's Rights and Responsibilities

The contractor is responsible for knowing when work must be inspected, making timely requests for inspections, providing information for job-site inspections, and code compliance.

Contractors have the right to appeal the decision of any inspector or local building official when they disagree with the application of the code. They can also propose code changes through the code adoption process.

Special Inspections

In addition to code-stimulated inspections, building officials in the job site jurisdiction may require other inspections to ensure compliance with special code requirements. Check with the local jurisdiction, listed in Appendix A, for additional inspection requirements in the following categories: Mechanical, Plumbing, Electrical, and Manufactured Dwellings. Boilers and pressure vessels and elevators are inspected by the state.

Certified Master Builder Program

The Certified Master Builder (CMB) program is administered statewide by the BCD. In addition to qualifying for an application and training, an individual must pass a written examination covering appropriate aspects of the state building code. If a local government has a master builder program, it can waive certain plan review and building inspection requirements for those contractors holding a master builder certificate.

An individual may apply to the BCD to be tested and certified as a master builder. An individual must meet the minimum certification criteria established by the department, which include the following:

- The individual must be an owner or regular employee of a qualified construction company and be authorized by the company to provide assurance that all state and local code requirements are met.
- In each of the five preceding calendar years, the individual must either have performed or supervised a dwelling construction or whole dwelling remodel. In at least two of the years, the work must have occurred in a geographic area with a CMB program.
- The individual must have completed a program sponsored by a local building trade committee or other program approved by the department that provided training relating to the *2014 Oregon Residential Specialty Code.*
- The individual must have scored at least 75 percent on a written examination approved and administered by the DCBS, covering the *2014 Oregon Residential Specialty Code.*
- The individual must not be the subject of an adverse final order issued by the CCB or the BCD based on acts committed within the last 36 months.

Stop Work Orders

What is a Stop Work Order?

A stop work order notice is issued by a building official. It requires the work listed in the order to stop immediately.

How to Avoid Getting a Stop Work Order:

- Make sure the project has a valid permit.
- Inform the inspector about any corrections or violation notices.
- Execute the work in compliance with code provisions, approved plans or drawings, and other applicable laws.

What to do if a Stop Work Order is Posted on the Job Site

If a stop work order is posted on a job site, it is essential that the contractor communicate with the person who posted it. The stop work order states what work must be stopped and lists the conditions under which work may be resumed. The building official is not required to give notice before stopping the work.

Failure to Comply with a Stop Work Order

Not complying with a stop work order can have very serious consequences. Non-compliance could lead to civil penalties, to permit or license revocation, or to court action.

Enforcement of Codes and Specialty License Requirements

CCB Penalties for Working Without a License

The CCB may revoke, suspend, or refuse to issue or reissue a license, and the CCB may assess a civil penalty if it is found that the licensee has violated the licensing law. The maximum civil penalty shall be $5,000 for each offense.

CCB investigators are obligated to check for licenses of individuals suspected of performing work without the proper license. They will require proof of compliance.

BCD Penalties

In addition to possible penalties from the CCB, penalties for working without a specialty license are established by the appropriate boards of the BCD.

The BCD can charge a penalty for failure to obtain a permit, for working without the proper license, or for allowing others to work without the proper license. These penalties can range up to $5,000 for a single occurrence or $1,000 a day for a continuing violation.

Sources of Building Codes

To purchase code books, go to the BCD Website at www.cbs.state.or.us/external/bcd/codestandards.html where a list of sources for purchasing code books can be found. There may be other businesses and organizations that offer code books, so check online.

The following is a list of places to check to view code books without purchasing:
- Most public libraries
- University libraries
- City building departments (see contact information in Appendix A).
- County building departments (see contact information in Appendix A).
- Building Codes Division www.bcd.oregon.gov. (ICC codes are available for viewing on the BCD's website.)

Appendix A

Local Jurisdictions

The most recently updated information can be found on the BCD website at www.cbs.state.or.us/external/bcd/jurisdictions.html and clicking on the Local Building Department Directory (LBDD).

City	Phone Number	City	Phone Number
Albany	541-917-7552	Hillsboro	503-681-6144
Ashland	541-488-5309	Hood River	541-387-5202
Astoria	503-325-1004	Independence	503-838-1212
Aurora	503-588-5147	Irrigon	541-481-9252
Baker City	541-524-2054	Junction City	541-998-2153
Beaverton	503-526-2403	King City	503-639-4082
Bend	541-388-5528	La Grande	541-962-1317
Boardman	541-481-9252	Lake Oswego	503-635-0290
Brookings	541-469-2163 x206	Lakeside	541-759-3981
Canby	503-266-9404	Lebanon	541-258-4906
Cannon Beach	503-436-2045	Lincoln City	541-996-2153
Central Point	541-664-6325, x250	Lowell	541-937-2157
Coburg	541-682-7852	Manzanita	503-368-5343
Columbia City	503-397-4010	McMinnville	503-434-7314
Coos Bay	541-269-8918	Medford	541-774-2380
Coquille	541-396-2115	Metolius	541-475-4462
Cornelius	503-357-3011	Milwaukie	503-786-7613
Corvallis	541-766-6929	Monmouth	503-751-0139
Cottage Grove	541-942-5501	Newberg	503-537-1240
Creswell	541-895-2531	Newport	541-574-0629
Culver	541-546-6494	North Bend	541-756-8525
Dallas	503-831-3571	Oakridge	541-782-2258
Dayton	503-864-2221	Ontario	541-881-3220
Dunes City	541-997-3338	Oregon City	503-722-3789
Durham	503-639-6851	Pendleton	541-966-0239
Eagle Point	541-774-6900	Philomath	541-929-6148
Eugene	541-682-5086	Phoenix	541-535-2050
Fairview	503-664-6223	Portland	503-823-7310
Florence	541-997-8237	Redmond	541-923-7721
Forest Grove	503-992-3229	Reedsport	541-271-3603
Gearhart	503-738-5501	Rogue River	541-582-4401
Grants Pass	541-474-6355	Roseburg	541-440-1175
Gresham	503-618-2725	Salem	503-588-6256
Happy Valley	503-760-3325	Sandy	503-668-0880
Hermiston	541-667-5025	Scappoose	503-543-7184

City	Phone Number
Seaside	503-543-7184
Sherwood	503-625-4226
Silverton	503-873-8679
Sisters	541-549-6022
Springfield	541-726-3753
St. Helens	503-397-6272
Sweet Home	541-367-7993
Talent	541-535-7401
Tigard	503-639-4171
Toledo	541-265-4192
Troutdale	503-665-5175
Tualatin	503-691-3040
Umatilla	541-922-3226
Veneta	541-935-2191
Warrenton	503-338-3697
West Linn	503-656-4211
Wilsonville	503-682-4960
Winston	541-440-4284
Wood Village	503-667-6211
Woodburn	503-982-5250
Yamhill	503-662-3511

County	Phone Number
Baker	541-524-2055
Benton	541-766-6819
Clackamas	503-353-4400
Clatsop	503-338-3697
Columbia	503-397-1501
Coos	541-396-2148
Crook	541-447-3211
Curry	541-247-3304
Deschutes	541-388-6575
Douglas	541-440-4284
Gilliam	541-298-4461
Grant	541-575-1519
Harney	541-889-7422
Hood River	541-386-1306

County	Phone Number
Jackson	541-774-6900
Jefferson	541-475-4462
Josephine	541-474-5405
Klamath	541-883-5121
Lake	541-947-3062
Lane	541-682-6796
Lincoln	541-265-4192
Linn	541-967-3816
Malheur	541-889-7422
Marion	503-588-5147
Morrow	541-988-3043
Multnomah	
Gresham	503-618-2832
Portland	503-823-7310
Troutdale	503-665-5175
Polk	503-623-9237
Sherman	541-298-4461
Tillamook	503-842-3407
Umatilla	541-276-7814
Union	541-962-1317
Wallowa	541-426-6227
Wasco	541-298-4461
Washington	503-846-3470
Wheeler	541-298-4461
Yamhill	503-434-7516

State Contact	Phone Number
In Oregon	800-442-7457
Salem	503-378-4133

BCD Field Office	Phone Number
Coquille	541-396-2148
Pendleton	541-966-0266

Chapter 7

Appendix B

Contact Information

Building Codes Division
1535 Edgewater Street NW
Salem, OR 97309-0404
503-378-4133
State Building Codes Hotline: 800-442-7457

Mailing Address:
Building Codes Division
P.O. Box 14470
Salem, OR 97309-0404
www.bcd.oregon.gov

Oregon Building Officials Association
147 SE 102nd Avenue
Portland, OR 97216
503.691.OBOA (6262)
Fax: 503.253.9172
Email: info@OregonBuildingOfficials.com

Appendix C - Structural Permit Application

Structural Permit Application

Department of Consumer & Business Services
Building Codes Division • Pendleton Field Office
700 S.E. Emigrant Ave., #360, Pendleton, OR 97801
800-452-8156 or 541-276-7814, Fax: 541-276-9244
Web: bcd.oregon.gov

DEPARTMENT USE ONLY	
Permit no.:	
Office:	
By:	Date:

This permit is issued under OAR 918-460-0030. Permits expire if work is not started within 180 days of issuance or if work is suspended for 180 days.

LOCAL GOVERNMENT APPROVAL

This project has final land-use approval: Signature:	DEQ approved: Signature:

Flood plain? ☐ Yes ☐ No

CATEGORY OF CONSTRUCTION

☐ Residential   ☐ Government   ☐ Commercial

JOB SITE INFORMATION AND LOCATION

Job site address:

City/State/ZIP:

Project name:

Directions to job site:

Subdivision:	Lot no.:

PROPERTY OWNER INSTALLATION

Name:

Address:

City/State/ZIP:

Phone: - -	E-mail:

This installation is being made on residential or farm property owned by me or a member of my immediate family.

Sign here:

CONTRACTOR INSTALLATION

Business name:

Address:

City/State/ZIP:

Phone: - -	Fax: - -

E-mail:

CCB license no.:

Signature:

Make check or money order payable to Department of Consumer & Business Services. Do *not* send cash.

If paying by credit card, applicant must sign credit card information box.

☐ Visa ☐ MasterCard ☐ Discover   Phone: -   -

Credit card number	Expiration /

Name of cardholder as shown on credit card

Cardholder signature	$ Amount

DEPARTMENT OF CONSUMER & BUSINESS SERVICES

440-2546-PNDTN (5/08/COM)

LOCAL GOVERNMENT APPROVAL

Zoning approval verified? ☐ Yes ☐ No

FEE SCHEDULE

1. VALUATION INFORMATION

(a) Job description: Include occupancy, construction type, square foot, cost per square foot, etc.

☐ new   ☐ alteration   ☐ addition

(b) Foundation-only permit? ☐ Yes ☐ No

(c) Plan review only? ☐ Yes ☐ No

Total valuation:	$

2. BUILDING FEES

(a) Permit fee	$	70711/1195
(b) Reinspection ($19.50/hr) (no. of hours X 19.50)	$	70711/1195
(c) Investigative fee (equal to permit fee)	$	70711/1195
(d) Enter 12% surcharge (X .12)	$	70711/1291

3. PLAN REVIEW FEES

(a) Plan review (permit fee X .65)	$	70711/1212
(b) Fire and life safety (permit fee X .40)	$	70711/1212
Subtotal of fees above:	$	

4. MISCELLANEOUS FEES

Seismic fee (permit fee X .01)	$	70711/1212
GRAND TOTAL:	$	

DCBS fiscal use only:

Appendix D - Example of One Jurisdiction's Inspection Requirements

MARION COUNTY BUILDING INSPECTION DIVISION
555 Court Street NE / PO Box 14500
Salem, Oregon 97309-5036
INSPECTION REQUEST LINE: 503-373-4427

A **ROADSIDE MARKER** shall be placed at the access point with address numbers in a contrasting and highly visible color, not less than three (3) inches in height.

ADDRESS NUMBERS shall be painted or affixed to the front of the dwelling in a contrasting and highly visible color, not less than four (4) inches in height.

THE INSPECTION GREEN CARD shall be posted on the garage passage trimmer or in visible and readily accessible location throughout construction. Work may proceed only at the direction of the inspector.

APPROVED CONSTRUCTION PLANS AND PLAN REVIEW shall be kept on the site of the building at the time of the inspection.

TO REQUEST AN INSPECTION of completed work, call prior to 7:00 A.M. for same day inspection. The following required inspections must be requested by the owner or builder before proceeding with construction. When calling for inspections, you will need the **PERMIT NUMBER** and the **INSPECTION CODE NUMBER**. Post the **ORANGE CARD**, depicting the property address, at the **driveway entrance**.

STRUCTURAL

101	ZONING/SETBACKS: *Stake property lines and call before concrete is placed.*
102	FOOTINGS: *Call before concrete is placed.*
103	UNDERFLOOR POST & BEAM
104	FRAME: *Call when weather tight; chimney and fireplace installed; all backing, fire blocking, stairs and soffits in place. Plumbing, Electrical, and Mechanical must be complete and approved for cover. Truss details are posted on the job. Flood elevation certification has been submitted.*
	INSULATION
105	DRY WALL
106	POLE HOLES: *Call before concrete is placed.*
107	FOUNDATION WALL/REBAR
108	RETAINING WALL (Over 4')
109	MASONRY REBAR: *When required, call before concrete*
110	*is placed.*
111	BRACE PANELS / SHEAR WALL
112	MASONRY FIREPLACE PRECOVER
113	SUSPENDED CEILING
114	ROOF NAILING
115	DEMOLITION INSPECTION
119	MARRIAGE LINE / CONNECTION
121	MHP/RVP GRADING
122	MHP/RVP PAVING
123	BUILDING SLAB INSPECTION
124	INTERIOR BRACE PANEL/SHEAR WALLS
127	DAMP/WATER PROOFING
128	OTHER STRUCTURAL INSPECTION
199	*FINAL INSPECTION: Call when structure is complete, address numbers are posted, all plumbing, Mechanical, and Electrical systems are installed and approved, and building is ready to occupy.*

****

A **REINSPECTION FEE** may be assessed when:
(1) The inspection Record Green Card is not posted on the job site;
(2) the approved plans are not readily available;
(3) for failure to provide access on the date for which the inspection is requested; or
(4) deviating from the approved plans, requiring approval of the Building Official. No inspection will be performed until the re-inspection fee has been paid at our office.

PLUMBING

201	PLUMBING TOP OUT
204	PLUMBING UNDERFLOOR: Call before adding subfloor.
205	SANITARY SEWER
206	WATER SERVICE
207	BACKFLOW DEVICE
209	PLUMBING UNDERSLAB
210	RAIN DRAINS: *May be done with any of the above inspections before the pipe is covered.*
211	STORM SEWER/DRAIN
299	FINAL PLUMBING INSPECTION

ELECTRICAL

301	PRE-COVER
303	UNDERGROUND
304	POOL BONDING
305	SERVICE
306	TEMPORARY SERVICE
307	LIMITED ENERGY/ALARM
308	IRRIGATION PUMP
311	WELL PUMP CIRCUIT
399	FINAL ELECTRICAL INSPECTION

MECHANICAL

401	MECHANICAL PRECOVER
403	MECHANICAL UNDERFLOOR
404	GAS PIPING/TEST
405	COMMERCIAL HOOD TEST
406	WOODSTOVE/GAS FIREPLACE
498	OTHER MECHANICAL INSPECTION
499	FINAL MECHANICAL INSPECTION
509	OVERHEAD SPRINKLER SYSTEM
510	UNDERGROUND FIRE SPRINKLER SYSTEM
514	SPRINKLER ALARM
515	SPRINKLER TEST
599	FIRE SPRINKLER SYSTEM FINAL

SEPTIC

801	SEPTIC SYSETM PRECOVER
808	SEPTIC TANK
809	PUMP
810	DRAINFIELD

Sample Questions

CHAPTER 7

1. **No building or structure regulated by the building code shall be constructed, erected, enlarged, altered, repaired, moved, improved, or converted without first obtaining:**

   ❑ 1. A permit, except for work that is exempt from the permit requirements.

   ❑ 2. An inspection.

   ❑ 3. A permit or an inspection.

   ❑ 4. A CCB permit.

2. **Contractors working on detached one- and two-family dwellings that are three stories or less in height would use which code?**

   ❑ 1. *2014 Oregon Structural Specialty Code.*

   ❑ 2. *2014 Oregon Residential Specialty Code.*

   ❑ 3. *2014 Oregon Electrical Specialty Code.*

   ❑ 4. International Building Code.

3. **A contractor should do which of the following to avoid getting a stop work order?**

   ❑ 1. Try to not have any previous stop work orders.

   ❑ 2. Ask for a special five-day permit exemption from the building official.

   ❑ 3. Make sure he or she has a valid permit and all work and inspections are per the building code requirements.

   ❑ 4. Work on the weekends.

Answers: 1. [1]

       2. [2]

       3. [3]

Chapter 7

CHAPTER 8

OREGON OCCUPATIONAL SAFETY AND HEALTH DIVISION AND SAFETY ISSUES

Objectives

At the end of this chapter, you will be able to:

1. Know where to find Oregon OSHA statutes and administrative rules.
2. Understand the purpose of Oregon OSHA laws and regulations.
3. Identify the rights and responsibilities of a contractor and employees during an Oregon OSHA job site inspection, including enforcement of standards and possible penalties.
4. Understand general safety and health practices, including personal protective equipment, hand- and power-tool safety, and hazard communication on job sites.
5. Explain appropriate job site record-keeping practices and requirements, including procedures for reporting accidents.
6. Identify safety responsibilities and relationships among contractors and subcontractors working on a job site.
7. Understand how Oregon OSHA requirements and services reduce accidents and injuries, thus benefiting the contractor's direct and indirect costs.

Oregon OSHA

Employers in Oregon are responsible for the safety of their employees. Oregon OSHA helps employers provide a safe workplace through the following services:

- Educating employers and employees about safety and health through training, consultation, conferences, and technical assistance. Holding informal conferences to discuss citations, penalties or correction orders, and other safety and health matters.
- Identifying safety and health hazards and bringing them to the attention of employers and employees.
- Inspecting places of employment.
- Issuing reasonable correction orders.
- Issuing citations with a possibility for monetary penalties for violations.
- Granting or denying extensions of the times set by correction orders.
- Investigating worksite accidents, fatalities, and catastrophes.
- Writing and publishing standards for occupational safety and health.

What is Oregon OSHA?

The mission of Oregon OSHA is "To advance and improve workplace safety and health for all workers in Oregon."

Oregon OSHA enforces Oregon's occupational safety and health rules. These rules establish minimum safety and health standards for all industries and outline standards for individual industries such as construction.

Services Provided by Oregon OSHA
Consultation Services

Trained safety and health professionals provide free consultation services to help employers identify and correct occupational safety and health hazards. These services are designed to help reduce work-related injuries, illnesses, and fatalities, and the associated high cost of workers' compensation insurance.

Oregon OSHA consultation provides many no-cost, confidential services, including:

- Safety, health, and ergonomic hazard assessments
- Recommendations to control and eliminate hazards
- Written program evaluation
- Industrial hygiene services, such as noise monitoring and air sampling
- Hands-on training on health and safety topics
- Safety and health program assistance

Oregon OSHA consultants **will not**:

- Issue citations or propose penalties for violations of OSHA standards.
- Provide other businesses with information about your participation, hazards, or business processes.
- Guarantee that your workplace will "pass" an Oregon OSHA inspection.

The Benefits to Business

Improving a business' safety and health program can result in fewer accidents, lower injury and illness rates, decreased workers' compensation costs, increased employee morale, and lower product losses. Oregon OSHA can provide:

- Personal, professional, and relevant assistance specific to a business
- Guidance with establishing a safety committee or improving its effectiveness
- Answers to questions about Oregon OSHA rules and standards

The Consultative Process

The consultation process begins when a business requests the service from Oregon OSHA. The request may be limited to an area of specific need or it could be for a broad company-wide review. Based on the business's request, Oregon OSHA will send the appropriate consultants, trained in workplace safety, industrial hygiene, and ergonomics to the employer's worksite. At the conclusion of the worksite audit, Oregon OSHA's consultant will create a written report for the employer that will help a business reduce lost-time accident costs and show a business how to make a workplace safer by developing comprehensive programs to manage safety and health.

Enforcement

Oregon OSHA's enforcement program ensures that employers follow Oregon OSHA rules. Compliance officers, for example, conduct unannounced inspections of job sites that may result in citations. The Enforcement Section also:

- Provides abatement help to employers who received citations
- Offers pre-job conferences for mobile employers
- Investigates workplace fatalities and serious injuries
- Conducts workplace inspections on referral and complaints of unsafe working conditions

Standards and Technical Resources

The Standards and Technical Resources Section:

- Writes and publishes Oregon's rules for occupational safety and health
- Helps members of the public understand new or revised standards
- Considers alternative applications of specific rules when an employer demonstrates equally effective health and safety measures are being followed in the workplace

- Reviews and acts on requests for innovative safety committees
- Develops brochures, booklets, and guidelines on occupational safety and health to assist employers and employees
- Maintains the Oregon OSHA Resource Center

The Oregon OSHA Resource Center offers publications, video and a DVD lending library, online video resources, and a library that includes books, journals and consensus standards about workplace health, chemical hazards, and safety and health requirements for new businesses.

Public Education

Oregon OSHA offers free, year-round training workshops throughout Oregon as well as online training modules at www.orosha.org. Topics include:
- Working in Confined Spaces
- Ergonomics
- Lockout/Tagout
- Fall Protection
- Excavations
- Safety & Health Management
- Accident Investigation
- Safety Committees
- Job Hazard Analysis
- Recordkeeping

Statutes and Rules

The primary laws governing construction safety in the state of Oregon are: Oregon Revised Statute 654 and Oregon Administrative Rules 437, Division 1 and Division 3. These laws and rules may be obtained by contacting Oregon OSHA at 503-378-3272 or viewing them online at www.orosha.org.

OAR 437, Division 1, General Rules

Division 1 deals with such general subjects as safety committees, employer and employee responsibilities, reporting, recording, and inspections. These rules apply to all employers in any industry. For more information visit: www.cbs.state.or.us/osha/standards/div_1.html.

OAR 437, Division 3, Construction Activities

Division 3 prescribes minimum safety and health requirements for employers engaged in construction work, including demolition, blasting and use of explosives, and power transmission distribution and maintenance work.

Other subjects covered are:
- General safety and health (training, education, first aid, sanitation)
- Occupational health and environmental controls (noise exposure, hazard communication)
- Personal protective and lifesaving equipment
- Fire protection and prevention
- Signs, signals, and barricade.
- Materials handling, storage, use, and disposal.
- Tools
- Welding and cutting
- Electrical
- Scaffolding
- Fall protection
- Motor vehicles
- Excavations
- Steel erection
- Concrete and masonry construction
- Underground construction
- Stairways and ladders
- Toxic and hazardous substances

For more information, visit www.cbs.state.or.us/osha/standards/div_3.html.

For access to the construction rules, letters of interpretation, program directives, hazard alerts, fact sheets, and trainings, select the *Construction* link within the *A-Z Topic List* on Oregon OSHA's website: www.orosha.org .

Inspections

Enforcement

Oregon OSHA's enforcement program conducts unannounced inspections of job sites. These inspections may be regularly scheduled inspections, or special emphasis inspections focusing on particular hazards, such as fall protection, complaint inspections, or accident inspections. When employees are found to be exposed to a hazard, corrective actions and citations may be issued to the employer.

What is an Inspection?

According to OAR 437, Division 1, an inspection is "an official examination of a place of employment by a compliance officer to determine if an employer is in compliance with the Oregon Safe Employment Act."

A compliance officer may inspect a worksite to determine if safe working conditions exist. The employer will not receive advance warning. If the officer finds violations, the officer will cite the employer, listing what rule has been violated and when it must be corrected.

Contractor's Rights During Oregon OSHA Inspections

An **employer** representative and an **employee** representative have the right to accompany the compliance officer during an inspection. The employer also has the right to:

- Attend an opening and closing conference, although if the employer declines to have these conferences, the inspection will still take place
- Protect trade secrets
- Correct violations during the inspection, and by doing so, possibly lessen the penalty imposed
- Present any pertinent information regarding the violation

Violations and Potential Penalties

The Department of Consumer and Business Services (DCBS) has the authority to assess civil penalties for violation of any Oregon OSHA rules.

Appeal

The employer may appeal the violation within 30 days of receipt of the citation. An informal conference will be scheduled with an appeals specialist.

Job Site Safety (Recommended Safety Techniques)

Job site safety should be considered just as important as any other project activity or business responsibility. Determine any workplace risk and decide how to eliminate or minimize that risk.

Contractor Safety Commitment

A company that has a safety and health program shows a commitment to minimizing workplace risks and preventing injuries. The safety program must cover subjects like accident prevention and safety training for workers. All workers must participate in on-the-job safety practices.

Communicating a Commitment to Safety

Businesses that are committed to creating and maintaining a safe and healthful workplace communicate that commitment to employees. Written policies should be prepared whenever possible. Fewer misunderstandings will occur when employees have a written policy to refer to if they have questions.

Employers need to confirm that employees understand the policies. This may be accomplished through testing, role-playing, or demonstrations.

Job site safety inspections, which owners or management should conduct regularly and routinely, help identify safety problems.

Safety Training for Employees

Employers should carefully plan the training, set objectives that are relevant to employees' jobs, use competent instructors, and motivate the employees. Here are some tips:

- Written documents are a good way to start training. Documents give employees a point of reference if they have questions.
- Safety talks given by experienced workers can also help explain the hazards employees may face, how to recognize hazards, and what steps to take to avoid or eliminate hazards.
- Use training to simulate actual tasks as closely as possible. Develop learning activities that let employees demonstrate the skills to do their jobs safely.

Training programs may have to be adjusted if feedback from employees shows that a change is needed.

Oregon OSHA has many training aids to help employers, such as publications, workshops, and videos. Learn more about these training aids by contacting the nearest local Oregon OSHA office or by logging onto www.orosha.org.

Employer Responsible for Leased and Temporary Workers

An on-site or host employer ensures a safe place of employment for leased or temporary workers. When a business contracts with a worker leasing company or temporary agency for construction labor, the business is responsible for the risk or exposure of the leased or temporary workers, not the leasing company or temporary agency. The requirement also applies when a business arranges with another contractor to use his or her employees for work on a project, and those employees are covered by workers' compensation insurance.

The worker leasing company or temporary agency must provide workers' compensation coverage on workers, and extend that coverage to its workers who are leased by a contractor.

Worker leasing companies and temporary agencies are exempt from CCB licensing requirements. The business using the leased or temporary workers must provide adequate training, supervision, and instruction for those workers. They are also responsible for providing appropriate personal protective equipment and for reporting fatalities and hospitalizations.

Direct and Indirect Costs

Safety practices impact workers' compensation claims and costs. When well thought out, comprehensive safety measures are put into practice, fewer claims will be filed, and insurance premiums will be lower.

Because Oregon OSHA has made great strides in reducing work-related accidents, injuries, illnesses, and deaths, Oregon employers now pay one of the lowest rates for workers' compensation insurance in the nation. A safe working environment equals reduced rates for workers' compensation.

According to information obtained by Oregon OSHA, the average 2013 cost in Oregon for a workers' compensation claim involving a disabling injury in the construction industry is:

- **Direct costs:** $35,200. That compares to $21,970 for all industries. Direct costs include:
  - Medical expenses
  - Time loss reimbursements
- **Indirect costs.** These are estimated at two to five times the direct costs. Indirect costs include:
  - Productivity lost from work by injured employee
  - Lost time by fellow employees
  - Loss of efficiency because of break-up of crew
  - Lost time by supervisor
  - Training cost for new replacement worker
  - Loss of production for remainder of the day
  - Damage from accident
  - Failure to meet deadlines

Job site Safety and Subcontractors

Where joint responsibility exists, both the general contractor and subcontractors must enforce workplace practices (Oregon OSHA 1926.16, Rules of Construction, and Oregon OSHA's "Multi-employer Workplace Citation Guidelines" program, Directive A-257).

The rules state:

- The general contractor and any subcontractor may make their own arrangements for job site safety but in no case will the general contractor be relieved of overall responsibility for compliance with the requirements.
- The general contractor assumes all obligations prescribed as employer obligations whether or not he or she subcontracts any work.

- When the subcontractor agrees to perform any part of the contract, he or she also assumes responsibility for complying with the standards for that portion of the work. With respect to the work, the general contractor and any subcontractor(s) have joint responsibility.
- Where joint responsibility exists, both the general contractor and his or her subcontractor(s), regardless of tier, shall be considered subject to the enforcement provisions of the act.

Before contracting work to another independent contractor, find out if that subcontractor has had any Oregon OSHA violations and, if so, what the violations were and how they were resolved. The contractor should also determine whether any workers' compensation claims were filed against the subcontractor.

If the subcontractor has violated Oregon OSHA regulations or has had numerous workers' compensation claims filed against him or her, the contractor may want to test the subcontractor and his or her employees about safety knowledge. This test could lead to requiring safety training before starting the job.

General Safety Practices

Fundamental Job site Safety

Employers and employees must follow Oregon OSHA safety requirements and practices. This can be confusing when the employer is a corporation or other business entity and the owners are directors and employees of that entity.

In a corporation, Oregon OSHA has jurisdiction over corporate directors when they work on projects as supervisors or workers. Even though they are directors or owners who act for the corporation, they are working for compensation and under the direction and control of an employer, which is the corporation.

When an individual works on a multi-employer job site with temporary electrical power, for example, corporate individuals are under Oregon OSHA jurisdiction, and all need to consider others that may be at risk through individual action.

Oregon OSHA jurisdiction is different than CCB's. Oregon OSHA requires job site safety practices for all workers in situations when individuals:
- Work on a job site
- Are paid or compensated for the work
- Work under the direction and control of an entity, like a corporation, even if an individual is the sole or controlling member of the corporation

As of October 2009, Oregon OSHA has changed one of the definitions for administrative rules for an employer to: "Any corporation in relation to the exposure of its corporate officers except for corporations without workers' compensation coverage under ORS 656.128 and whose only employee is the sole owner of the corporation."

Oregon OSHA still has jurisdiction under the Oregon Safe Employment Act; however, Oregon OSHA elects to not issue citations to sole owner corporations having no employees or no workers' compensation coverage on themselves.

Employer Responsibilities
Employers must:
- Ensure that workers are properly trained and supervised in the safe operation of machinery, tools, or similar equipment they are authorized to use
- Ensure that employees work in a safe manner, use all safety devices to safely accomplish their work, and do not remove safety devices
- Inform employees regarding known health hazards to which they are exposed, measures taken to control those hazards and proper methods for utilizing such control measures
- Provide and maintain health hazard control measures necessary to protect employee's health
- Respond to safety committee recommendations in a timely manner
- Provide a realistic schedule for correcting safety problems
- Provide support to safety committee members if scheduling or personnel conflicts arise
- Support activities of safety committee
- Ensure that lines of communication are open and non-threatening

Employee Responsibilities
Employees must:
- Conduct their work in compliance with Oregon OSHA rules
- Promptly report all injuries to the person in charge
- Make full use of all safeguards provided for their protection
- Not use defective tools or equipment
- Not operate machines with faulty or missing guards
- Stop and lockout machinery before oiling, adjusting, or repairing, except when means to prevent the possibility of hazards contact with moving parts is in place
- Not interfere with, remove or destroy any accident prevention device, sign or barrier
- Making sure appropriate precautions have been taken in hazardous work
- Warning fellow employees who are observed working in an unsafe manner

- Notify the person in charge when safety and health hazards are identified
- Suggesting workplace safety improvements
- Following all safety committee procedures and practices
- Communicating with safety committee members when appropriate
- Becoming a safety committee member, if appropriate

Injury and Illness Prevention Plan (non-mandatory)

Each employer should implement an injury and illness prevention plan. The goal of this plan should be to assure safe and healthful working conditions for employees. The plan should include information about how the business will identify and evaluate hazards, train employees, keep records, and comply with the requirements of Oregon OSHA.

General Safety and Health Environment Controls

The employer has the responsibility to initiate and maintain programs that:
- Provide regular and frequent inspections of job sites, materials, and equipment
- Ensure that no machinery, tool, material, or equipment that does not comply with Oregon OSHA requirements will be used
- Ensure that only employees qualified by training or experience operate equipment and machinery

Medical Requirements

Before beginning a project, employers must develop an emergency medical plan to provide emergency care for all employees who are injured on the job or who develop major illnesses on the job. Arrangements must be in place for providing medical services in case of serious injury.

First Aid

First aid is one-time treatment and subsequent observation of minor scratches, cuts, burns, splinters, or similar injuries that do not ordinarily require medical care. Regardless of who provides it, this type of treatment is first aid and can be given by anyone.

All employers are required to provide first-aid supplies and medical care for employees. First-aid supplies must be available for each shift and must be placed in a weatherproof container that is clearly marked, not locked, and easily reached or accessible.

If treatment requires more than first aid, then the employer's emergency medical plan must ensure that medical services are rapidly provided to injured or ill employees.

If the job site is not close to emergency medical services, a person who holds a valid certificate for emergency medical training by American Red Cross (or equivalent) must be available on the job site. Workers must be trained to apply first aid, to properly notify certified medical providers when needed, and to follow the employer's emergency medical plan.

For access to the rule and additional information, select the *First Aid* link within the *A-Z Topic List* on Oregon OSHA's website: www.orosha.org .

Provisions for Serious Injuries

To prepare for serious injuries, the medical plan must provide for communications with emergency medical services and transportation to the nearest medical facility.

The employer must provide either:
- Equipment for prompt transportation of an injured person to a nearby hospital
- A communication system for contacting an ambulance service

If 911 is not available, the telephone numbers of doctors, hospitals, and ambulances shall be conspicuously posted.

If the job site is close to emergency medical services (physician, hospital, or clinic and an ambulance with emergency medical technicians), the emergency medical plan must contain the emergency telephone number of the ambulance, the doctors, and the hospitals. These numbers must be conspicuously posted. If the job site is located in an area with a designated 911 number, then the 911 number can be used and posted instead of the ambulance number.

Transportation must be available to transport injured employees to a point where an ambulance can be met or to the nearest medical facility. These vehicles must be equipped to give appropriate medical care, and they must be available at all times. These vehicles have right-of-way over all other employer vehicles.

In areas where employees handle materials that could injure them by coming in contact with their bodies or splashing into their eyes, the employer must provide emergency showers or eyewash facilities.

Safety and Health Training and Education

Employees need to be trained to recognize, avoid and control unsafe conditions in their work environments.

If employees are required to handle or use poisons, caustics, or other harmful substances, they must be trained in safe handling and use, potential hazards, personal hygiene, personal protective measures required, and first aid procedures in event of exposure.

If harmful plants or animals are present on the job site, employees should be trained on potential hazards, how to avoid injury, and first-aid procedures in the event of injury.

Employees also need to be trained in handling flammable liquids and gases or toxic materials and what precautions to take if they will be required to enter confined spaces.

All employees who enter confined or enclosed spaces must be trained to recognize the hazards, take proper precautions and wear necessary protective equipment.

For access to the rule and additional information, select the *Training* link within the *A-Z Topic List* on Oregon OSHA's website: www.orosha.org .

Poster Requirement

Employers are required to permanently post the Job Safety and Health poster summarizing employer and employee rights under Oregon OSHA. **This poster MUST be permanently displayed at the job site.** This is not a requirement for temporary sites. Posting at the job shack or in the office is adequate.

Receive a free poster by downloading it from the Oregon OSHA's website or contacting Oregon OSHA at 503-378-3272 or 800-922-2689 (Oregon only).

Recordkeeping

Employers generally must report, record, and keep records of employees' work-related fatalities, injuries, and illnesses when it is a new case and falls in one or more of the following categories:

- Death
- Days away from work
- Restricted work or transfer to another job
- Medical treatment beyond first aid or medical removal of an employee
- Loss of consciousness
- Significant injury or illness diagnosed by a physician or licensed health care provider
- Infectious, blood-borne disease

- Loss of hearing
- Tuberculosis

Additional categories may be added so check with Oregon OSHA for the latest requirements.

Note: If your company never had more than ten (10) employees during the last calendar year, you do not need to keep OR-OSHA injury and illness records unless the director informs you in writing that you must keep records.

Accident and Injury Recording and Reporting Procedures

Although small business employers are subject to overall coverage of Oregon OSHA, they are generally not required to keep injury and illness records unless notified by DCBS to do so for a particular year. If your company never had more than ten (10) employees during the last calendar year, you do not need to keep OR-OSHA injury and illness records unless the Director informs you in writing that you must keep records.

Determining and Recording Injuries or Illness on OSHA 300 Forms

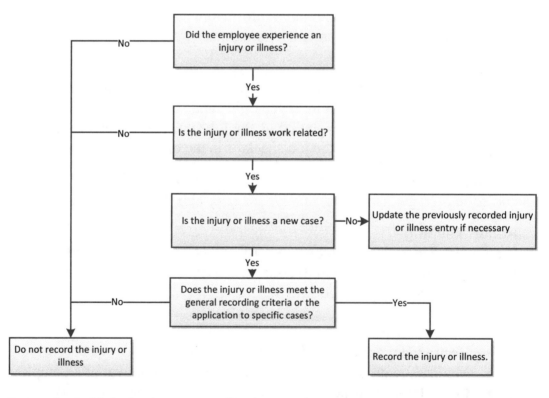

Reporting of injuries is separate from recording. All employers are covered by the reporting requirements. Accidents generally are not reportable if first aid provides sufficient treatment. All fatalities, catastrophes and overnight hospital stays **must be reported** to Oregon OSHA within specific time lines. See Oregon OSHA's

Fact Sheet "Reporting Work-Related Incidents" that is available on their website for details and time limitations.

For access to the rule and additional information such as fact sheets, select the *Recordkeeping/Reporting* link within the *A-Z Topic List* on Oregon OSHA's website: www.orosha.org.

Written Programs

Employers must prepare some written documents such as a hazard communication program, safety committee or safety meeting minutes, lockout/tagout procedures, and a respirator program. However, to protect and inform employees, the employer may also want to prepare additional written documents for training purposes.

Hazard Communication

Companies with employees who use hazardous chemicals, substances, or materials are required to prepare a written hazard communication program.

Oregon OSHA's purpose in hazard communication is to ensure that all chemical hazards are evaluated and that information concerning these hazards is conveyed to employers and employees. A comprehensive hazard communication program includes employee training, container labeling and Safety Data Sheets (SDS).

In 2012, the Hazard Communication standard was revised to incorporate the Globally Harmonized System of Classification and Labeling of Chemicals, also known as "GHS".

For access to the rule and additional information, select the *Hazard Communication* link within the *A-Z Topic List* on Oregon OSHA's website: www.orosha.org.

Written Hazard Communication Program

A good, written hazard communication program shows the employer's commitment to health and safety issues through education of employees and documentation to meet requirements.

The written hazard communication program should include:
- A statement of how obligations for labeling, Safety Data Sheets (SDS), and education will be met
- An up-to-date list of all hazardous chemicals used in the workplace
- Methods of educating employees about hazardous chemicals they will encounter in their work
- Methods of informing employees of other contractors who will work in the workplace

Employer Responsibility

Employers must adequately train their employees, including leased or temporary workers, on the dangers associated with hazardous chemicals, substances, or materials in their workplace. If someone else provides employee training, the employer is still responsible for verifying the training.

Employers may wish to train employees on individual chemicals, or on hazard categories (for example, flammable liquids, corrosive materials, or carcinogens). Some construction activities use materials that release hazardous chemicals during and/or for a time after installation.

These chemicals could be swallowed, inhaled as vapors or fumes, or absorbed through skin or eye contact. Protection is required, and employees must be trained about hazardous chemicals and related safety procedures, such as:

- Health hazards of the chemicals in the work area
- Detecting the presence or release of a hazardous chemical in the work area
- Measures employees can take to protect themselves from hazards
- Details of the hazard communication program

Labeling

Chemical container labeling lets employees and employers know of potential chemical hazards and appropriate protective measures. Labels contain a product identifier, signal word, graphic pictograms, precautionary statements, hazard statements and supplier information displayed on or attached to containers of hazardous chemicals.

Portable containers that temporarily hold hazardous chemicals which are intended for immediate use by only one person and under the exclusive control of that person do not require labels when the contents are used in a single work shift.

Labels and other warnings must be in English. Other languages may be added to assist employees who speak another language, but they may not replace the English information.

Multi-Employer Workplace Policy

Employers who use hazardous chemicals at a workplace must be sure that their hazard communication programs convey the following information to employees of all other employers at their job site:

- Access to Safety Data Sheets (SDS)
- The labeling system used in the workplace
- Any precautions that might need to be taken

Employee Information and Training

Employees must know of any operations in their work areas where hazardous chemicals are present. They must also know the location and availability of the written hazard communication program, including the required lists of hazardous chemicals and the required Safety Data Sheets (SDS).

Employees must know how to read and use labels and Safety Data Sheets (SDS). They must understand and be able to follow appropriate protective measures.

Use of Safety Data Sheets (SDS)

Since the 1980s, OSHA regulations have required employers to obtain, maintain and make available to their employees a product specific document for each workplace hazardous chemical called a Material Safety Data Sheet. These documents in the United States have been widely known by their acronym: "MSDS". MSDSs provided employees with product specific, chemical safety information in a document separate from the container's label.

In 2012, the Hazard Communication standard was revised to incorporate the Globally Harmonized System of Classification and Labeling of Chemicals (GHS) which altered the MSDS format and content. Due to these changes, chemical manufacturers will discontinue the MSDS format, replacing it with a new format known as a Safety Data Sheet (SDS). SDSs will provide employees with a more comprehensive, easier to read, 16-section safety document that explains:
- Why the chemical is hazardous
- How the chemical can harm you
- How to protect yourself from the chemical
- What to do if the chemical causes an emergency

The Hazard Communication standard requires chemical manufacturers, distributors, or importers to prepare the Safety Data Sheets.

The employer is responsible to make the Safety Data Sheets (SDSs) available to each affected employee.

Housekeeping

Employers must keep work areas, passageways, stairs, and areas in and around buildings clear of debris. Combustible scrap and debris must be removed periodically, and a safe means of removal must be provided.

Employers must provide containers for collecting and separating waste, trash, oily and used rags, and other refuse.

Containers containing caustics, acids, harmful dusts, etc. must be equipped with covers. All waste must be disposed of at frequent and regular intervals.

Safety Committees

Oregon OSHA requires every public and private employer, regardless of size, subject to Oregon OSHA jurisdiction, with the exception of sole owners with single employee corporations and members of boards and commissions who do not participate in the daily operation of the company, to establish and administer an effective safety committee or conduct safety meetings.

The purpose of safety meetings is to bring workers and management together in a non-adversarial, cooperative effort to promote safety and health in workplaces. Safety committees and safety meetings are designed with the intent to effectively assist employers in making collaborative recommendations for improvement of their safety and health programs.

Safety Committees vs. Safety Meetings

IF	You Can Have a Safety Committee	You Can Have Safety Meetings
You have 10 or fewer employees more than half of the year (including seasonal and temporary)	Yes	Yes
More than half of your employees report to construction sites	Yes	Yes
More than half of your employees are mobile or move frequently between sites	Yes	Yes
Most employees do not regularly work outside an office environment	Yes	Yes
You have more than 10 employees at a location, and none of the above applies	Yes	No
You have satellite or auxiliary offices with 10 or fewer employees at each location	Yes	Yes

Safety Committee Responsibilities

Safety committee members must:

- Serve a minimum of one year, when possible.
- Be compensated at their regular rate of pay.
- Have training in the principles of accident and incident investigations.
- Have training in hazard identification and conduct inspections at mobile work locations as often as the safety committee determines necessary.
- Establish procedures for conducting workplace safety and health inspections.
- Work with management to establish, amend or adopt accident investigation procedures to identify and correct hazards.
- Evaluate management's accountability system for safety and health, and recommend improvements. Examples include use of incentives discipline, and evaluating success in controlling safety and health hazards.
- Have a system that allows employees to report hazards and safety and health related suggestions.

- Establish procedures for reviewing inspection reports and for making recommendations to management.
- Evaluate all accident and incident investigations and make recommendations for ways to prevent similar events from occurring.
- Make safety committee meeting minutes available to all employees.

Choosing Safety Meetings

Safety meetings are an alternate form of a safety committee designed to meet the special needs of small employers and employers with mobile worksites, such as construction employers.

Safety meetings must include all available employees. Employers must make certain that in scheduling their safety meetings, they do so on dates that will allow the most employees to attend. The intent of safety meetings is that all employees provide input and to make suggestions or recommendations for improvement when appropriate.

The employer must make certain that at least one management representative with authority to make decisions on safety and health issues attends each meeting. Safety meetings must be held on company time and attendees paid at the appropriate rate of pay. For example, if they are on overtime, employees should be paid at the overtime rate to attend the meeting.

Employers with employees engaged in the construction industry must meet:
- At least monthly
- Before the start of each job that lasts more than a week to discuss hazards of that work location

Following these guidelines, there may be some months where only one safety meeting is required and other months where more than one safety meeting is required. Compliance will require some advance planning and estimating the length of jobs.

Safety meetings must:
- Include discussions of safety and health issues.
- Review any accident investigations and suggest corrective measures to be taken to prevent similar accidents from recurring.
- Take meeting minutes and make them available to all employees (written minutes must be kept for three years). Meeting minutes must include:
  - All hazards related to tools, equipment, work environment and unsafe work practices that have been identified and discussed.
  - The date the meeting occurred and names of those who attended.

For access to the rule and additional information about both safety committees and safety meetings, select the **Safety Committees** link within the *A-Z Topic List* on Oregon OSHA's website: www.orosha.org.

Personal Protective Equipment and Clothing

Personal protective equipment does not eliminate an employee's exposure to job site hazards. Personal protective equipment (when properly selected, worn and maintained) reduces the potential for harmful effects when hazards are encountered. Before providing employees with personal protective equipment, employers must first take steps to exclude hazards through engineering controls, administrative controls or by eliminating the chemical, process or task creating the hazard.

When workplace hazards cannot be eliminated, employers are responsible for providing and ensuring that their employees wear personal protective equipment to reduce the risk associated with hazardous conditions.

Examples of some of the personal protective equipment and clothing that might be required are:
- Fall protection
- Electrical arc flash protection
- Head protection
- Hearing protection
- Eye and face protection
- Respiratory protection
- Highly visible clothing worn during exposure to vehicular traffic
- Personal flotation device for work over water

For access to the rule and additional information, select the **Personal Protective Equipment** link within the *A-Z Topic List* on Oregon OSHA's website: www.orosha.org .

Competent and Qualified Person Requirements

The terms "competent person" and "qualified person" are used throughout Oregon OSHA standards such as the following: electrical, scaffolding, excavation, fall protection, and steel erection as examples.

A competent person is one who is capable of identifying existing and predictable hazards in the surroundings or working conditions that are unsanitary, hazardous, or dangerous to employees, **and** who has the authority to take prompt corrective measures to eliminate them.

A qualified person is one who, by possession of a degree, certificate, or professional standing, or by extensive knowledge, training, and experience, has successfully demonstrated his or her ability to solve problems relating to the project or work.

It is important to understand the difference between the roles and responsibilities of competent persons and qualified persons. Additionally, when reviewing Oregon OSHA's regulations, it is important to distinguish between these two designations.

A person may be evaluated by an employer and deemed to be competent or qualified for the purpose of a specific regulation such as fall protection; however, that same person may not have the skills, training or experience to be competent or qualified in another topic such as excavations or electrical.

Hand- and Power-Tool Safety

All hand and power tools, whether provided by the employer or the employee, must be maintained in a safe condition. Hand tools with wooden handles should be free of cracks or splinters. Wrench jaws should not be sprung, and impact tools should be free of mushroomed heads.

Most handheld power tools should be equipped with a constant pressure switch that will shut off the power when released. Certain specific handheld tools may be equipped with a positive on-off switch.

Hoses or electric power cords must not be used to hoist or lower tools.

Power-operated tools that are designed to have guards must be used with the guards in place.

Machinery that is used in a fixed location must be secured to prevent movement Employees who work with equipment that causes the following hazards must be provided with the proper protective equipment.

- Falling objects
- Flying objects
- Abrasive products
- Splashed objects
- Dusts
- Fumes
- Mists
- Vapors
- Gases

Specific regulations on the use of tools are found in OAR 437, Division 3, Subdivision I.

For access to the rule and additional information, select the ***Hand Tools*** link within the *A-Z Topic List* on Oregon OSHA's website: www.orosha.org .

Vehicles

General vehicle safety requirements include the following:

- All vehicles must have a service brake, emergency brake, and parking brake.
- Vehicles must have at least two headlights, two taillights, and brake lights.
- All vehicles must have a working audible device (horn).
- Vehicles with an obstructed view may not be used unless: (1) they have a reverse signal alarm; or (2) the vehicle is backed up only when an observer signals that it is safe.
- Vehicles with cabs must have windshields, and wiper and defrosting devices (in areas where necessary).
- A vehicle transporting employees must have seats and seat belts.
- Tools and materials must be secured when they are transported in the same vehicle as employees.
- A vehicle must have a cab shield and/or canopy if it is loaded with cranes, power shovels, shovels, or other similar equipment.
- Trucks with dump bodies must have equipment to prevent accidental lowering while maintenance is being done. Operating levers for dump trucks shall have a device to prevent accidental starting or tripping. Also, trip handles must be arranged so that the operator will be in the clear.
- Certain requirements exist for fenders, depending on date of manufacture.
- Each vehicle must be checked at the beginning of each shift for absence of specific problem areas.

For access to the rule and additional information, select the ***Vehicles*** link within the *A-Z Topic List* on Oregon OSHA's website: www.orosha.org.

Fall Protection and Prevention

Employers must provide fall protection systems when workers are exposed to a hazard of falling 10 feet or more to a lower level, except for specific situations where fall protection is required at 6 feet. Workers can be faced with a possible fall hazard, at any height, when working over dangerous equipment. Workers also need to be protected from falling objects. In these situations, workers need fall protection and prevention measures such as personal protective equipment and toe boards, screens, barriers, or other acceptable means. Fall protection and prevention criteria and standards are found in OAR 437, Division 3, Subdivision M.

For access to the rule and additional information, select the ***Fall Protection*** link within the *A-Z Topic List* on Oregon OSHA's website: www.orosha.org.

Planning

Before beginning any project, the employer should develop a plan. This plan should identify any fall hazards and the procedures that will be used to control the hazards. This will reduce risks for workers. Careful planning will help maintain an accident-free job site.

Portable and Fixed Ladders

Ladders designed and built in accordance with the national consensus standards listed below, meet OSHA requirements. Employers must provide ladder safety training to all employees who use ladders. There is a ladder setup application on the website. Consult the *A-Z Topic page* under ladders.

Manufactured portable metal ladders

American National Standards Institute (ANSI) A14.2-1982 – *American National Standard for Ladders – Portable Metal – Safety Requirements*.

Manufactured fixed ladders

ANSI A14.3-1984 – *American National Standard for Ladders – Fixed – Safety Requirements*.

Workers can reduce ladder fall risks by frequently inspecting and maintaining ladders, matching the appropriate ladder to the task, setting up ladders correctly, and ascending and descending properly.

Before working with a ladder, use the following checklist to ensure that the ladder is hazard free:
- Check to see that the ladder is in good condition with all rails tight, hardware securely attached, moving parts operating properly, and non-slip feet in place.
- Make sure ladder rungs are clean and free of grease and oil.
- Teach workers not to stand on the top step of a portable ladder and to face the ladder when ascending or descending.
- Portable ladders should extend a minimum of 36 inches above the elevated surface.
- Portable ladders need to be erected to a 1:4 slope to the surface against which they rest.
- Portable metal ladders should be marked with warning signs prohibiting use around electrical equipment.
- Steps, rungs, or cleats of ladders should be a maximum of 12 inches apart.

Holes, Wall Openings, Established Floors, Mezzanines, Balconies, Walkways, or Excavations

Workers must be protected from fall hazards when they are exposed to a fall hazard of 6 feet or more in these situations: holes, wall openings, established floors, mezzanines, balconies, walkways, or excavations *when the excavations are not readily seen because of plant growth or other visual barrier.*

One of the following fall-protection systems are required to prevent fall-related injuries:

- Personal fall-arrest systems
- Covers for holes in floors, roofs, and other walking or working surfaces
- Guardrail systems
- Safety-net systems
- Fall-restraint systems

Roofing and Related Activities

Fall protection is required at heights over 10 feet or more; except for specific situations where fall protection is required at 6 or more feet. These systems include guardrails, safety-net systems, personal fall-arrest systems, positioning-device systems, warning-line systems, safety-monitoring systems, slide guard systems, covers, or protection from falling objects. Fall protection criteria and requirements are found in OAR 437, Division 3, Subdivision M.

Standard Guardrails

Guardrails are vertical barriers that consist of top rails, midrails, and intermediate vertical members. Guardrail systems can also be combined with toeboards, which are barriers that prevent materials and equipment from dropping to lower levels.

- The top edge of a guardrail must be 42 inches, plus or minus 3 inches, above the surface.
- Guardrail systems must withstand a force of at least 200 pounds when applied within 2 inches of the top edge, in any outward or downward direction.
- Top rails and midrails must be at least one quarter inch thick and must be free of anything that could snag a worker's clothing or cut a worker.
- When wire rope is used for a top rail, it must be marked at least every 6 feet with high-visibility material.

Oregon OSHA's requirements for guardrail systems are in OAR 437, Division 3, Subdivision M.

Stairs and Stair Railings

Stairways having four or more risers or rising more than 30 inches, whichever is less, shall be equipped with at least one handrail and stair rail system along each unprotected side or edge.

Stair rails installed **after** March 15, 1991, shall not be less than 36 inches from the top to the tread.

Stair rails installed **before** March 15, 1991, shall not be less than 30 inches or more than 34 inches from the top rail to the tread.

A stairway or ladder is required at any personnel point of access that is 19 inches or more in elevation change and if no ramp or hoist exists.

Fall protection criteria and requirements are found in OAR 437, Division 3, Subdivision M.

Asbestos

OSHA has developed rigorous regulations to deal with the removal of asbestos from existing buildings. These regulations are designed to protect employees and the general public from exposure to airborne asbestos.

Asbestos Abatement Projects

Asbestos abatement includes projects such as demolition, salvage, removal, encapsulation, construction, repair, alteration, maintenance, or renovation of existing structures that contain asbestos (ACM) or presumed asbestos-containing material (PACM). It also covers installation of products that contain asbestos, spills or emergency cleanup, and transportation, disposal, storage, or housekeeping activities involving asbestos.

Small-Scale vs. Full-Scale Asbestos Abatement Projects

Asbestos abatement projects are divided into four categories.

Class I asbestos work means activities that involve removal of thermal system insulation (TSI), ACM, and PACM.

Class II asbestos work means activities that involve the removal of wallboard, floor tile and sheeting, roofing and siding shingles, and construction mastics.

Class III asbestos work means repair and maintenance work that is likely to disturb TSI or surface ACM and PACM.

Class IV asbestos work means maintenance and custodial work in which dust, waste, and debris from Class I, II, and III are cleaned up, but ACM and PACM are not disturbed.

Certification

A competent person is defined by Oregon OSHA as one who is capable of identifying existing asbestos hazards in the workplace and selecting the appropriate control strategy for asbestos exposure with authority to take prompt corrective measures to eliminate them. In Class I and II work, this person must have special training that meets EPA's Model Accreditation Plan (40 CFR Part 763). For Class III or IV work, this person must be trained in a manner consistent with EPA requirements for training of local education agency maintenance and custodial staff.

Recordkeeping

If the work the employer is doing with asbestos-containing material is shown **not** to release particles into the atmosphere, records of the data that was relied upon to reach that conclusion must be kept and maintained for as long as they are being relied upon.

The employer must keep a record of all measurements taken to monitor employee exposure to asbestos. These records must contain:

- Date
- The operation being monitored
- Sampling methods used and evidence of their accuracy
- Number, duration, and results of samples
- Type of protective devices worn
- Name, Social Security number, and exposure of the employees whose exposure is represented

This record shall be maintained for at least 30 years.

For access to the rule and additional information, select the *Asbestos* link within the *A-Z Topic List* on Oregon OSHA's website: www.orosha.org .

Additional Safety Practices for Certain Construction Activities

Excavation

Excavation is any man-made cut, trench, cavity, or depression made in the surface of the earth by soil removal. Guidelines for excavation safety practices are found in OAR 437, Division 3, Subdivision P. In addition, fall protection is required wherever workers are exposed to a fall hazard of 6 feet or more when they are required or permitted to cross over excavations or when the excavation is not readily seen because of plant growth or other visual barriers.

For access to the rule and additional information, select the *Excavations* link within the *A-Z Topic List* on Oregon OSHA's website: www.orosha.org.

Planning

Before beginning any excavations, the contractor must assure that the project and excavation methods meet all applicable standards. Zoning laws, land use plans, and environmental regulations should all be considered. Excavation may have an impact on groundwater runoff, wetlands, water tables, or other aspects of the environment.

Properly Trained Workers

All employees working in excavation must be properly trained. In addition, a competent person is required at all excavation sites for daily inspections, inspections after rainstorms, and to monitor water removal. A competent person is one who is capable of identifying existing and predictable hazards in the surroundings or working conditions that are unsanitary, hazardous, or dangerous to employees. The competent person has the authority to take prompt corrective measures to eliminate predictable hazards.

Trench

All trenches are excavations; however, not all excavations are trenches. Trench or trench excavation means a narrow excavation made below the surface of the ground. In general, the depth is greater than the width, but the width of a trench is not greater than 15 feet measured at the bottom.

Underground Installations - Call 811

Companies must call for locates for any operation where earth, rock, or other material on or below the ground is moved or otherwise displaced by any means. That does not include sidewalk, road, and ditch maintenance less than 12 inches in depth that does not lower the original grade or original ditch flow line. "Excavation" does not include the tilling of soil for agricultural purposes conducted on private property that is not within the boundaries of a recorded right-of-way or easement for underground facilities and does not exceed 18 inches in depth. The estimated location of utility installations such as, sewer, telephone, fuel, electric, water lines, or any other underground installations that may reasonably be expected to be encountered during excavation work must be determined before opening an excavation.

Utility companies must be contacted, advised of the proposed work, and asked to establish the location of the underground utility installations before the start of actual excavation. In Oregon, call the Utility Notification Center, and they will contact all the utilities.

Utility Notification Center	
Portland Area: 1415 SE Ankeny Portland, OR 97214-1471 Phone: 503-246-6699	All Other Areas in Oregon: 800-332-2344

Utility companies have 48 hours to locate their installations. Employees must be safeguarded from underground utility installations while the ground is open.

Access and Egress

A stairway, ladder, ramp, or other safe means of exit must be located in trench excavations that are 4 feet (1.22 m) or more in depth. They must be located so that no more than 25 feet (7.62 m) of lateral travel is necessary.

Emergency Rescue Equipment

Emergency rescue equipment, such as breathing apparatus, a safety harness and line, or a basket stretcher, shall be readily available where hazardous atmospheric conditions exist or may reasonably be expected to develop during work in an excavation. This equipment must be attended when in use.

Water Accumulation

Employees must not work in excavations in which there is any accumulated water unless precautions are taken to protect employees. These precautions vary with each situation but could include special support or shield systems to protect against cave-ins, water removal to control the level of accumulating water, or use of a safety harness and lifeline.

Stability of Adjacent Structures

Support systems, such as shoring, bracing, or underpinning must be provided to ensure the stability of adjoining buildings, walls, or other structures that may be endangered by excavation operations.

Inspections

A competent person must make daily inspections of excavations and protective systems for evidence of possible cave-ins, indications of failure of protective systems, hazardous atmospheres, or other hazardous conditions. These inspections must be conducted before work starts and as needed throughout the shift. Inspections must also be made after every rainstorm or other hazard-increasing occurrence. Employees must be removed from the hazardous area until the necessary precautions have been taken to ensure their safety.

Barriers

To protect employees from falling, walkways that crossover at 6 feet or higher over open excavations must be provided with guardrails. Physical barriers shall be provided around all remote excavations.

Aluminum Hydraulic Shoring

This is a pre-engineered shoring system made up of aluminum hydraulic cylinders used with vertical rails or horizontal rails. This system is designed specifically to support the sidewalls of an excavation and prevent cave-ins.

Shields

A shield system is a structure that is able to withstand the forces caused by a cave-in and thus protect employees within the structure.

Sloping

Sloping protects employees from cave-ins by inclining or sloping the walls of the excavated area away from the excavation.

Electrical

Requirements to safeguard employees from electrical hazards in construction work are divided into four major divisions.

Installation Safety Requirements. Included in this category are electric equipment and installations used to provide electric power and light on job sites.

Safety-Related Work Practices. This category includes hazards that occur because of employees using electricity at job sites or accidentally coming into contact (directly or indirectly) with energized lines. (An example of "indirectly" is touching one end of a conductive object, such as a pipe or ladder, when the other end is touching an energized line.)

Safety-Related Maintenance and Environmental Conditions. All wiring components and utilization equipment in hazardous locations are maintained in a dust-proof, dust-tight, or explosion-proof condition.

Except in special circumstances, equipment shall not be located in damp or wet locations where gases, fumes, vapors, liquids, or other agents can have a deteriorating effect on wire insulation inside or near the equipment. In addition, equipment shall not be exposed to excessive temperatures. Control equipment, utilization equipment, and busways approved for use in dry locations only shall be protected against damage from the weather during building construction.

Safety Requirements for Special Equipment. Unsealed batteries shall be located in enclosures with outside vents or in well-ventilated rooms and arranged to prevent the escape of fumes, gases, or electrolyte spray. Ventilation shall be provided to ensure diffusion of the gases from the battery and to prevent accumulation of an explosive mixture. Racks and trays must be treated to make them resistant to the electrolyte, and floors must be of acid-resistant construction unless protected from acid accumulations.

Face shields, aprons, and rubber gloves must be provided for workers handling acids or batteries. Facilities must be provided for quick drenching of the eyes. Facilities must also be provided for flushing and neutralizing spilled electrolyte and for fire protection.

Battery charging installations shall be in designated areas. Charging apparatus shall be protected from damage by trucks.

When batteries are being charged, the vent caps shall be kept in place to avoid electrolyte spray. Vent caps shall be maintained in functioning condition.

Clearance and Safeguards Required on Overhead Power Lines
Oregon OSHA requires employees working near overhead power lines to de-energize the lines and ground them. Standards for employees working near power lines include approach distance requirements to prevent contact with, or arcing from, energized overhead power lines.

Employees who work on or around vehicles and equipment such as, forklifts, cranes, elevating platforms, and scaffolding, are potentially exposed to contact with overhead lines and must be trained in ways to avoid exposure to hazards.

Oregon OSHA prohibits the following activities if such activities cause tools, equipment, or structures to be moved to within 10 feet of high-voltage lines:
- Operation, erection, or transportation of any tools and equipment
- Transportation or storage of materials
- Moving of any building

Ground Fault Circuit Interrupters (GFCI)

Ground Fault Circuit Interrupters (GFCIs) are required when working on 125 volt, single phase, 15-, 20-, and 30-amp temporary circuits. When working on other than 125 volt single phase, 15-, 20-, and 30-amp temporary circuits, you can use GFCIs **or** establish and implement an assured equipment-grounding program.

Cord sets and other equipment must also be inspected daily before use on the job. More information on this is found in OAR 437, Division 3, Subdivision K.

For access to the rules, letters of interpretation, program directives, publications, hazard alerts and fact sheets on electrical activities, select the *Electrical, Electrical Generation, Transmission and Distribution*, or *Electrical Overhead Powerline Clearance* links within the *A-Z Topic List* on Oregon OSHA's website: www.orosha.org .

Lockout/Tagout Procedures

Lockout/tagout is an Oregon OSHA requirement for protecting employees from hazards, either electrical or mechanical, whenever they perform maintenance or service on machines or equipment. These activities include lubricating, cleaning, un-jamming equipment, and making adjustments. The standard requires written procedures, training, and periodic inspections.

Lockout means placing an energy-isolating device on a piece of equipment. When the device is locked in place, the equipment will not work until the lock is removed. An employee can then safely service or maintain potentially hazardous equipment.

Tagout means placing a warning tag on an energy-isolating device. The tag must be securely attached to the energy-isolating device. It must state that the equipment is being worked on, including service or maintenance, and that the equipment cannot be operated until the tag is removed.

More information about lockout/tagout can be found in the booklet, *Lockout & Tagout, Oregon OSHA's Guide to Controlling Hazardous Energy.*

For access to the rule and additional information on Locout/Tagout, select the **Control of Hazardous Energy** link within the *A-Z Topic List* on Oregon OSHA's website: www.orosha.org.

Sanitation

An adequate supply of safe drinking water must be provided at a job site. Containers used to dispense water must be capable of being tightly closed. Water may not be dipped from containers, and a common drinking cup is prohibited. Water containers must be refilled daily or more often as necessary.

A designated number of toilets must be provided for employees on construction job sites. The number depends on the number of employees. The general contractor must provide flush toilets and washing facilities for all projects over $1 million in value.

More detailed information on sanitation requirements can be found in OAR 437, Division 3, Subdivision D.

For access to the rule and additional information, select the *Sanitation* link within the *A-Z Topic List* on Oregon OSHA's website: www.orosha.org.

Abrasive Wheel Equipment and Grinders

Floor stand and bench mounted abrasive wheels for external grinding must be provided with safety guards. They must also be provided with work rests that are rigidly supported and readily adjustable.

All abrasive wheels are to be closely inspected before mounting to ensure they are free from cracks or defects.

Employees who use abrasive wheels must wear protective eye gear.

More information about abrasive wheel equipment and grinders may be found in OAR 437, Division 3, Subdivision I.

For access to the rule and additional information, select the *Abrasive Wheel Machinery and Tools* link within the *A-Z Topic List* on Oregon OSHA's website: www.orosha.org.

Welding and Brazing

Welding and brazing activities present a wide variety of hazards that must be addressed such as fire prevention, personal protective equipment, hazard communication and electrical safety. Provisions for safe use, storage, and transportation of compressed gas cylinders, regulators and manifolds must be considered on every worksite. Both oxygen and fuel gases have specific safety rules that must be followed to ensure workplace safety. Additionally, personal protective equipment such as respirators and eye protection must be provided for workers engaged in welding or brazing. More information is found in OAR 437, Division 3, Subdivision E.

For access to the rule and additional information, select the *Welding* link within the *A-Z Topic List* on Oregon OSHA's website: www.orosha.org.

Forklifts/Industrial Trucks

Only trained and authorized employees are allowed to operate powered industrial trucks such as forklifts. Loads on forklifts must be balanced and be the appropriate weight for the type of forklift being used. Unauthorized personnel shall not be permitted to ride on powered industrial trucks.

Industrial trucks (forklifts) must have the rated capacity posted on the vehicle, clearly visible to the operator. No modifications or additions that affect the capacity or safe operation of the equipment can be made without the manufacturer's written approval.

All high lift rider industrial trucks must be equipped with overhead guards and meet the applicable requirements of design, construction, stability, inspection, testing, maintenance, and operation as defined in ANSI B56.1 – *1969 Safety Standards for Powered Industrial Trucks*. More information is found in OAR 437, Division 3, Subdivision O.

For access to the rule and additional information on forklifts, select the "*Powered Industrial Trucks*" link within the "*A-Z Topic List*" on Oregon OSHA's website: www.orosha.org.

Blasting and Explosives

A blaster must be qualified through training, knowledge, or experience to transport, store, handle, and use explosives. The blaster must be able to understand and give written and oral orders.

Only authorized and qualified persons are permitted to handle and use explosives. All explosives must be accounted for at all times.

Warning signs must be prominently displayed. Other requirements on blasting and explosives are found OAR 437, Division 3, Subdivision U.

For access to the rule and additional information, select the *Blasting* link within the *A-Z Topic List* on Oregon OSHA's website: www.orosha.org.

Masonry – Block Wall Construction

A limited-access zone must be established before start of construction of the wall. This zone is to be established on the side of the wall that does not have scaffolding. No employees are permitted to enter the zone except for those actively working on the wall.

Masonry walls over 8 feet in height must be adequately braced to prevent overturning and collapse **unless the wall is properly supported**. Bracing must remain in place until permanent supports of the structure are in place. The bracing system must be designed by a professional engineer or follow Oregon OSHA requirements.

More information is found in OAR 437, Division 3, Subdivision Q.

For access to the rule and additional information, select the ***Concrete and Masonry Construction*** link within the *A-Z Topic List* on Oregon OSHA's website: www.orosha.org.

Concrete Construction

No construction loads may be placed on a concrete structure unless the employer determines that the structure is capable of supporting the load.

Protruding reinforcing steel must be guarded if there is the hazard of falling into or on it.

Employees may not apply cement, sand, and water through a pneumatic hose unless the employee is wearing protective head and face equipment.

Workers must be out from underneath overhead loads of concrete.

Specific information is found in OAR 437, Division 3, Subdivision Q.
For access to the rule and additional information, select the ***Concrete and Masonry Construction*** link within the *A-Z Topic List* on Oregon OSHA's website: www.orosha.org.

Demolition

Before employees can start demolition, a competent person must conduct an engineering survey to determine the possibility of any unplanned collapse of any part of the structure.

All utility service lines must be de-energized, capped, or otherwise controlled before work is started.

Before work is started, it must also be determined if any type of hazardous materials were used in the structure. If so, testing and purging shall be performed before demolition is started.

Other requirements on demolition are found in OAR 437, Division 3, Subdivision T.

For access to the rule and additional information, select the ***Demolition*** link within the *A-Z Topic List* on Oregon OSHA's website: www.orosha.org.

Powder-Actuated Tools

Only trained employees may use powder-actuated tools. Tools must be tested each day before loading to make sure that safety devices are in proper working condition. Loaded tools are not to be left unattended. Tools must not be used in an explosive or flammable atmosphere.

Employees must use personal protective equipment with tools not loaded until just before the intended firing time.

Oregon OSHA follows ANSI standards. Powder-actuated tools used by employees shall meet all other applicable requirements of ANSI A10.3-1985, *Safety Requirements for Powder-Actuated Fastening Systems*.

More information is found in OAR 437, Division 3, Subdivision I.

Steel Erection

Employers have a duty to protect employees from hazards while building, altering or repairing single- or multi-story buildings and other structures such as bridges where steel erection occurs.

Steel erection activities include but are not limited to hoisting, laying out, placing, connecting, welding, burning, guying, bracing, bolting, plumbing and rigging structural steel, steel joists and metal buildings.

Information on requirements for steel erection is in OAR 437, Division 3, Subdivision R.

For access to the rule and additional information, select the *Steel Erection* link within the *A-Z Topic List* on Oregon OSHA's website: www.orosha.org.

Confined Space

Confined spaces may be dangerous when entered without proper evaluation and hazard mitigation.

Spaces encountered in the workplace are a confined space by definition if they meet *all three* of the following:
- Large enough and so configured that an employee can fully enter the space and perform work
- Has limited or restricted means for entry and/or exit
- Is not designed for continuous human occupancy

Spaces meeting the criteria of a confined space must be further evaluated to determine if they are also a "permit-required" confined space. Confined spaces need only to meet one of the following four criteria to be classified as a permit required:

- Contains, or has a potential to contain, a hazardous atmosphere
- Contains a material that has the potential to engulf an entrant
- Has an internal configuration such that an entrant could become trapped or asphyxiated by inwardly converging walls or by a floor which slopes downward and tapers to a smaller cross-section
- Contains any other recognized serious safety or health hazard that can inhibit an entrants ability to self-rescue

Employees who enter into confined spaces must be instructed on the hazards involved. They shall also be taught the necessary precautions to take and the protective and emergency equipment required.

More information is found in OAR 437, Division 3, Subdivision C.

For access to the rule and additional information, select the **Confined Spaces** link within the *A-Z Topic List* on Oregon OSHA's website: www.orosha.org.

Working Over or Near Water

When employees work over or near water, where the danger of drowning exists, they must be given Coast Guard-approved life jackets or buoyant work vests. These vests shall be inspected before and after each use. Defective life jackets and buoyant work vest may not be used.

Ring buoys with at least 90 feet of line must be provided and readily available for emergency rescue. The distance between ring buoys shall not exceed 200 feet.

At least one lifesaving skiff must be immediately available at locations where employees are working over or next to water.

Other requirements are found in OAR 437, Division 3, Subdivision E.

For access to the rule and additional information, select the **Working Over Water** link within the *A-Z Topic List* on Oregon OSHA's website: www.orosha.org.

Aerial Lifts

Aerial lifts must be designed and constructed to conform to the applicable requirements of ANSI A92.2-1969 *Vehicle Mounted Elevating and Rotating Work Platforms*. Aerial lifts include the following types of vehicle-mounted aerial devices used to elevate personnel to job sites above ground:

- Extensible boom platforms
- Aerial ladders
- Articulating boom platforms
- Vertical towers
- Any combination of such devices

Aerial equipment may be made of metal, wood, fiberglass-reinforced plastic (FRP), or other material; may be powered or manually operated; and are deemed to be aerial lifts whether or not they are capable of rotating about a substantially vertical axis.

Aerial lifts may be "field modified" for uses other than those intended by the manufacturer. Modifications must be certified in writing by the manufacturer or by any other equivalent entity, such as a nationally recognized testing laboratory, to conform to ANSI standards and be at least as safe as the equipment was before modification.

For access to the rule and additional information, select the *Aerial Lifts* link within the *A-Z Topic List* on Oregon OSHA's website: www.orosha.org.

Traffic Control

Oregon has the following traffic control standards:

Adequate and appropriate traffic controls shall be provided for all operations on or adjacent to a highway, street, or railway. The traffic controls shall conform to the *Millennium Edition of the (FHWA) Manual of Uniform Traffic Control Devices (MUTCD), December 2000.*

Where the term *Manual on Uniform Traffic Control Devices for Streets and Highways (MUTCD)* appears in the administrative rules, it shall mean *Manual on Uniform Traffic Control Devices for Streets and Highways*, Federal Highway Administration (FHWA). If the scope of the operation is three days or less, then employers who follow the most current edition of the Oregon Temporary Traffic Control Handbook for Operations of 3 Days or Less comply with this requirement.

For access to the rule and additional information, select the *Traffic Control* link within the *A-Z Topic List* on Oregon OSHA's website: www.orosha.org.

Slings

Slings used with other material handling equipment for the movement of material by hoisting are covered in OAR 437, Division 3, Subdivision H.

For access to the rule and additional information, select the *Material Handing* link within the *A-Z Topic List* on Oregon OSHA's website: www.orosha.org.

Cranes and Personnel Platforms
Crane Operator Safety Training Requirements

The crane and derrick construction standard outlines new crane operator training, qualifications and/or certifications, qualified riggers, and qualified signal person requirements.

Maximum intended loads, which include employees, tools, and materials, have been developed.

Information on personnel platforms may be found in OAR 437, Division 3, Subdivision CC.

These rules require that employers determine whether the ground can support the anticipated weight and associated loads of hoisting equipment. The employer must assess hazards within the work zone that would affect the safe operation of hoisting equipment, such as power lines and objects or personnel that would be within the work zone or swing radius of the hoisting equipment. The employer is also required to ensure that the equipment is in safe operating condition through required inspections and that employees in the work zone are trained to recognize hazards associated with the use of the equipment and any related duties that they are assigned to perform.

For access to the rule and additional information, select the *Cranes and Derricks* link within the *A-Z Topic List* on Oregon OSHA's website: www.orosha.org .

Scaffolds

A scaffold is any temporary elevated platform (supported or suspended) and it's supporting structure (including points of anchorage) that supports workers and materials. Common types of scaffolds include but are not limited to:

- Fabricated (welded) frame scaffolds
- Ladder jack scaffolds
- Large area scaffolds
- Mast climbing scaffolds
- Mobile (rolling tower) scaffolds
- Pump jack scaffolds
- Two-point adjustable scaffolds
- Tube and coupler scaffolds

Oregon OSHA establishes duties for both competent persons and qualified persons where scaffolds are used. Duties include training of scaffold users, erecting and dismantling of scaffolds, access to and stability of scaffolds.

When scaffolds are used in the workplace, other regulations such as fall protection, electrical and falling object protection must be considered.

More information on scaffolds may be found in OAR 437, Division 3, Subdivision L.

For access to the rule and additional information, select the *Scaffolds* link within the *A-Z Topic List* on Oregon OSHA's website: www.orosha.org.

Appendix A
Oregon OSHA Resources

Some of the Oregon OSHA programs and services available to contractors include:
- Consultative services
- Standards and technical resources
- Video library
- Education and training (workshops and online)
- Conferences
- Employer tool kit

Resources, programs, and names of office directors are available from the Oregon OSHA offices. In addition, Oregon OSHA has field offices across Oregon. Access the Oregon OSHA website at www.orosha.org, or contact one of these offices.

Oregon OSHA Central Office
Salem
350 Winter Street NE, Room 430
Salem, OR 97301-3882
Phone: 503-378-3272
Toll-free: 800-922-2689

Field Offices

Bend Red Oaks Square 1230 NE Third Street, Suite A-115 Bend, OR 97701-4374 Phone: 541-388-6066	**Pendleton** 200 SE Hailey Avenue, Ste. 306 Pendleton, OR 97801-3072 Phone: 541-276-9175
Eugene 1140 Willagillespie, Suite 42 Eugene, OR 97401-2101 Phone: 541-686-7562	**Portland** Freemont Place, Bldg. I 1750 NW Naito Parkway, Suite 112 Portland, OR 97209-2533 Phone: 503-229-5910
Medford 1840 Barnett Road, Suite D Medford, OR 97504-8250 Phone: 541-776-6030	**Salem** 1340 Tandem Ave. NE, Suite 160 Salem, OR 97301-8080 Phone: 503-378-3274

Sample Questions

CHAPTER 8

1. Which is NOT an employer's right regarding an Oregon OSHA inspection?

☐ 1. To attend or refuse to attend the opening and closing conferences.

☐ 2. To correct violations during the inspection.

☐ 3. To be notified before the inspection to prepare for the inspection.

☐ 4. To protect trade secrets.

2. Which is true about hand and power tools?

☐ 1. Machinery that will be used in a fixed location is not required to be secured.

☐ 2. Impact tools must be free of mushroomed heads.

☐ 3. Hand and power tools owned by the employer are held to a higher standard of safety than those owned by the employee.

☐ 4. Hand tools with wooden handles may have cracks and splinters that are no more than 2 inches long.

3. What information about hazardous chemicals is NOT found on SDS?

☐ 1. Chemical characteristics.

☐ 2. The potential for fire and explosion.

☐ 3. Medical conditions that are often aggravated by exposure.

☐ 4. Effective and ineffective protective equipment disposal measures.

Answers: 1. [3]
        2. [2]
        3. [4]

CHAPTER 9
SOUND ENVIRONMENTAL LAWS AND PRACTICES

Objectives

At the end of this chapter you will be able to:

1. Understand environmental regulations that govern construction activities for protecting water, air, and land quality.
2. Identify activities that require special contractor licensing.
3. Identify activities that require an air or water quality permit.
4. Understand contractors' responsibilities and liabilities related to the environment.
5. Describe the benefits of pollution prevention, waste reduction, reuse, and recycling.
6. Describe two or more ways to eliminate soil erosion for preserving water quality.
7. Know how to properly dispose of various environmentally hazardous materials in new and old construction.
8. Understand regulations that govern management and disposal methods of solid waste, hazardous waste, and special waste.
9. Know why proper disposal of solid wastes can prevent environmental problems or hazards.
10. Understand the differences between conventional building practices and green building.

Introduction

History

The Oregon Department of Environmental Quality (DEQ is responsible for water, air, and land quality, including the management of hazardous and solid wastes.

DEQ administers the following federal and state laws:
- Federal Clean Water Act, adopted in 1970
- Federal Clean Air Act, adopted in 1970
- State Solid Waste Act, adopted in 1971
- Safe Drinking Water Act, adopted in 1974
- Federal Resource Conservation and Recovery Act, adopted in 1976 (covers hazardous waste and underground storage tanks)
- Federal Comprehensive Environmental Response, Compensation and Liability Act (or Superfund), adopted in 1980
- Oregon Cleanup Act, adopted in 1987

These laws protect human health, the environment, and the beneficial uses of Oregon's natural resources.

Costs and Benefits of Regulatory Compliance

In the short term, complying with regulations may take more time or money. In the long-term, however, violations often lead to contamination, cleanups, lawsuits, civil penalties, criminal fines, and other costly noncompliance. Construction projects have a direct impact on the environment. General contractors and subcontractors must comply with environmental laws and regulations, and are held responsible for any damages caused by their actions, even if they are unaware that their actions cause environmental damage. Contractors should understand the impact of the project on the environment. They need to know the regulations that apply, train employees and subcontractors, write language in the construction contract that addresses environmental issues, and verify they have adequate insurance coverage.

Enforcement of Environmental Regulations

DEQ duties include:
- Monitoring and evaluating environmental conditions
- Establishing rules
- Issuing permits
- Conducting inspections
- Cleaning up contamination
- Enforcing environmental laws
- Educating businesses and citizens to encourage pollution prevention

The agency emphasizes education and technical assistance. However, enforcement measures, through legally binding procedures, are necessary to quickly correct and clean up environmental problems.

Goals of DEQ enforcement are to:
- Obtain and maintain compliance with environmental statutes, rules, permits, and orders
- Protect public health and the environment
- Deter future violators and violations
- Ensure an appropriate and consistent statewide enforcement program

A DEQ inspector who identifies a violation will send a **Warning Letter** to the alleged violator. Some warning letters notify a person of alleged violations for which formal enforcement is not anticipated while others provide an "opportunity to correct" the alleged violation(s). If the alleged violation(s) are not corrected, a pre-enforcement notice will then be sent. A notice is for more serious violations and provides notice that a civil penalty will be forthcoming. A notice generally will identify the alleged violations, what needs to be done to comply, the consequences of further noncompliance, and the enforcement process that will occur. DEQ always refers the more serious (Class I) violations for enforcement regardless of whether the violator corrects the violation or is cooperative.

Formal enforcement action is taken when a business refuses to comply with the law, repeatedly or chronically violates the law, or when the law violated is especially important to the environment or to the operation of the relevant regulatory program. Under Oregon law, penalties can be up to $10,000 per day for each violation. A monetary penalty is generally payable to the state's General Fund and does not fund DEQ programs.

A **Notice of Civil Penalty Assessment and Order (the Notice)** outlines DEQ's findings of facts, identifies the laws or regulations alleged to have been violated, invites the business to attend an informal discussion, and provides information on how to appeal the penalty. Depending on the violation, DEQ may issue an order. The order may be appealed, along with the penalty, but failure to comply with an order is a violation in and of itself.

After receiving a notice, a business may request an informal discussion with DEQ staff. During this informal discussion, the business presents its position on alleged violations.

More than 90 percent of DEQ's penalty actions settle after the informal discussion. DEQ may recalculate the penalty based on new information, and offer to settle the enforcement action. If no settlement occurs, the alleged violator may choose a contested case hearing. At a hearing, DEQ must prove the violation(s) occurred and that the penalty calculation was accurate according to the rules. The hearing is a semiformal proceeding conducted by an impartial, independent administrative law judge, who is not an employee of DEQ. The hearing includes the opportunity to present evidence and cross-examine witnesses.

After the hearing is complete, the Hearing Officer issues a "proposed and final order" that will become a "final order." The business may appeal the final order to the Environmental Quality Commission within 30 days the date of the proposed and final order. After 30 days, the business has another 60 days to appeal the order (which is now final) to the Oregon Court of Appeals. If the business does not appeal, it must comply with the final order and to pay any civil penalty that was imposed.

See Appendix F, Penalties for Environmental Violations, for actions or activities that cause violations.

Environmental regulations alone do not protect the environment. Individuals and businesses that understand how best to prevent environmental harm by following regulations, protect the environment.

Environmental regulations that apply to contractors are divided into three categories:
- Water quality
- Air quality
- Land quality

Contractor Activities that Require Special Licensing, Permits, or Notices

Contractors must receive a specialty license or certification to perform construction activities described below. The licensed specialty contractor must comply with all applicable regulations. When a contractor is not DEQ-licensed or certified for this work and encounters these site conditions, he or she must notify the property owner or operator. The owner or operator should then contract with a qualified person to determine if the condition is hazardous, and a DEQ-certified or licensed specialty contractor needs to abate or remove the hazard.

Activities that Require Special Licensing, Permits, or Notices

Activity	Special Contractor License	Permit Required	Contact
Underground storage tank removal (UST) and cleanup*	DEQ-licensed business and contractors must remove tanks and perform cleanup activities	30-day notice to DEQ before performing services	Contact DEQ for list of licensed UST contractors
Asbestos Abatement Projects	DEQ-licensed asbestos abatement contractor must abate materials containing friable asbestos	Specialty-licensed contractor must submit notification of abatement project to DEQ	Contact DEQ for information on becoming licensed, or for a list of licensed asbestos abatement contractors
Renovation, repair and painting of homes, child care facilities and pre-schools built before 1978	Lead-based paint renovation certification from Oregon Health Authority plus lead-based paint renovation license from CCB.		CCB See Appendix A
Lead-based paint activities (abatement) apply to inspection, risk assessment, project design, and abatement activities in pre-1978 target housing and child-occupied facilities.	Lead certificate from OHA and individual and business license from Construction Contractors Board (CCB).	Certified abatement contractor must submit a notice of abatement form (NOA) to OHA at least seven business days before the start of an abatement project	Contact OHA or CCB for a list of certified abatement contractors See Appendix A
Clandestine drug lab decontamination/cleanup	OHA.		Contact OHA See Appendix A
Home heating oil tank removals**	DEQ-licensed business and contractors	Local fire department or Fire Marshal may require a permit or notice	Contact DEQ for list of Heating Oil Tank Program Licensed Service Providers
Water Well Construction	Oregon Water Resources Department (OWRD) Licensed Constructors	Notify Water Resources Commission by making a report before beginning work	Contact OWRD, see Appendix A
Monitoring Well Construction	OWRD Licensed Constructors	Notify Water Resources Commission by making a report before beginning work	Contact OWRD, see Appendix A
Onsite Wastewater Treatment System Septic tank construction/ installation, alteration and/or repair Sewage pumping	DEQ licensed sewage disposal service provider	Permit required for septic tank construction/ installation, alteration and/or repair	See Appendix C for listing of governments who issue construction/ installation permits for onsite wastewater treatment systems Contact DEQ for list of DEQ- licensed sewage disposal service providers

Activity	Special Contractor License	Permit Required	Contact
Underground injection control (UIC) system use including disposal of water in dry wells, French drains, etc.	No special license required	Register with DEQ and obtain DEQ approval prior to construction or use	Contact DEQ at 503-229-5263
UIC system closure	No special license required	Notify DEQ at least 30-days prior to planned system abandonment or decommissioning	Contact DEQ at 503-229-5263
Construction activity that disturbs one or more acres of ground	No special license required	DEQ storm water permit required	Contact DEQ regional office, see Appendix B
Open burning	No special license required	Must get a DEQ letter or local agency permit	Contact DEQ regional office, see Appendix B
Construction activity in a natural waterway or wetland	No special license required	DEQ and/or Division of State Lands permit required	Contact DEQ regional office, see Appendix B
Construction washing	No special license required	DEQ permit required	Contact DEQ regional office, see Appendix B
Removal and disposal of polychlorinated biphenyl (PCB) containing lighting ballast	No special license required	If you engage in the transportation, storage, and disposal of PCBs or PCB-containing materials, you must obtain an EPA identification number	Obtain Environmental Protection Agency (EPA) PCB identification number form 7710-53 at www.epa.gov/pcb/pubs/771053.pdf Contact EPA Region 10's PCB Coordinator, Dan Duncan at 206-553-6693
Hazardous waste generators generating more than 220 lbs. a month	No special license required	Registering with and annually reporting to DEQ	Contact DEQ regional office, see Appendix B

*UST services include installation, retrofit, decommissioning, cathodic protection, tank tightness testing, or soil cleanup.
** Heating oil services include site assessments for contamination, decommissioning tanks, or cleanup.

Pollution Prevention

The U.S. Environmental Protection Agency (EPA) defines pollution prevention as:

"The use of materials, processes or practices that reduce or eliminate the creation of pollutants or wastes at the source. It includes practices that reduce the use of hazardous materials, energy, water or other resources, and practices that protect natural resources through conservation or more efficient use."

Benefits of Pollution Prevention

New construction projects that implement pollution prevention practices and use resources efficiently can provide the following benefits:

- Protect the environment by creating less waste, less pollution, and by preserving natural features.
- Use less toxic materials.
- Use less energy for operation and maintenance.
- Use products made from discards, recycled materials, and secondary resources.
- Provide for the safety and health of construction contractors and occupants.

Reduced Costs

Disposal costs for construction and demolition debris are on the rise. Recycling materials such as wood, drywall, cardboard, metals, plastics, leftover paints, and solvents can reduce contractor disposal costs. If salvaged materials can be used on another project, raw material costs can be lowered. Hazardous wastes are more expensive to manage than solid wastes.

Improved Health and Safety

Exposure to chemicals used in the construction industry, such as lead, formaldehyde, pesticides, and wood preservatives, adversely affects people's health. During use and after a project is completed, many adhesives give off harmful chemicals. Switching to less toxic adhesives can be healthier for framers, carpet installers, cabinetmakers, tile layers, vinyl installers, and occupants. Proper ventilation can help dilute exposure to these chemicals.

The most effective control of pollution is to eliminate these pollutants and substitute safer and equally effective products.

Better Marketability

Consumers are pleasantly surprised to see products that are often considered waste transformed into useful and attractive products. They will be very accepting of measures contractors take to enhance the environment. Contractors will benefit by offering products that are competitive and have environmental benefits that appeal to consumers.

Design Considerations

The greatest opportunity for source reduction and overall pollution prevention is in the planning and design of buildings and construction projects. Contractors may have a significant impact on the environment and human health with the type of materials, design, and practices that they employ. By choosing carefully, contractors can select materials to reduce the impact of mineral extraction and minimize energy requirements in manufacturing.

Healthy buildings increase occupant productivity, decrease disability claims, and avoid litigation. Some strategies for constructing healthy buildings include:

- Choosing safe materials and equipment that do not contain or create harmful pollutants
- Providing ways to purify air and water
- Maintaining desired humidity
- Reducing the need for toxic chemicals used in cleaning and maintenance

Contractor Liability

It is important for contractors to understand the responsibilities for environmental damage even if they are unaware that their actions caused environmental harm. Contractors need to know environmental regulations that apply to their project, train employees and subcontractors, be aware of language in construction contracts, and make sure they have adequate insurance coverage. General contractors are often held liable by DEQ for violations committed by their subcontractors and should ensure that subcontractors are fully compliant with the relevant laws.

Contractual Issues

Written contracts will have a significant impact on both environmental responsibility and the extent of liability. Before entering into any contract, it is important to understand how environmental responsibilities, risks, and costs are allocated between the owner and all others involved in the project. Also, visit the job site to identify environmental conditions that may occur during the project and be sure the contract provides for these conditions.

Compliance with Environmental Regulations

Compliance with environmental regulations can protect a contractor from liability claims, civil penalties, criminal penalties, and possible private party lawsuits. Contractors should be aware of all job site activities and also prevent any third party from creating hazards or environmental pollution.

Contracts with subcontractors should address environmental concerns with their trade. Subcontractors should be required to strictly comply with all environmental regulations and identify hazardous materials used or stored at the project site.

Unexpected Site Conditions or Hazardous Substances

Contracts need to state who is responsible if the contractor encounters unexpected environmental site conditions during progress of work, such as heating oil tanks, abandoned dry wells, or hazardous substances discovered on the site. Generally, the contract states that a contractor is not liable for existing environmental hazards. During the job site visit the contractor should evaluate the risk of finding such hazards before signing any contract. If unexpected conditions or hazardous substances are encountered during progress of work, the contract could provide for the contractor to stop work and immediately notify the owner. Together, they could assess the situation and, if needed, the owner could contract with an environmental consultant to determine if the site condition or contamination is hazardous or regulated.

Working at Contaminated Sites

Many sites that have been used for industrial or commercial purposes in the past are contaminated with hazardous substances from spills, leaks, and operating or waste disposal practices. In the job site visit, the contractor can determine if the site has this history. Site assessment or an environmental impact statement may be referenced in the project bid documents.

Responsibility and Liability

A contractor can become liable for cleanup costs by contributing to or exacerbating existing contamination during construction activities. Excavation of soil and construction de-watering can spread contamination to surface soil or surface water and may generate hazardous waste. The Environmental Cleanup law does not specify actions by contractors. However, it is in the contractor's best interest to avoid aggravating existing contamination. The most common unexpected finds at construction projects are abandoned tanks and residual contamination from underground storage tanks.

Practical Options to Improve Compliance

The best way to avoid endangering employees or increasing existing contamination is to determine the site history. The project plan must allow for managing unexpected contamination.

Most property owners conduct an environmental investigation of their site in order to obtain financing for construction projects. Review the report to learn about potential contamination at the site.

DEQ also maintains databases of sites that have or have had environmental permits, or may have been contaminated by past practices. The department's *Facility Profiler* is available with search instructions at http://deq12.deq.state.or.us/fp20. *Facility Profiler* searches all permit databases, underground storage tank databases, and the environmental cleanup database. Not all sites that are contaminated are known to the department or listed in the databases.

The contingency plan should cover:
- Contaminants that are likely at the site based on the operating history
- What signs to look for (odor or discolored soil, for example)
- What actions to take if unexpected contamination is found

The contract should clearly describe the consequences (such as delays or increased costs), and the responsibility for addressing unexpected contamination.

Insurance Coverage

Violations of environmental regulations can be costly if civil penalties, criminal penalties, third-party lawsuits, and/or environmental cleanup activities result from the violation. It makes good business sense for contractors to obtain pollution liability insurance. Insurance usually comes in two forms: endorsement to an existing liability policy or a separately issued policy. Because pollution liability insurance is extremely complicated, contractors should consult with qualified insurance professionals to obtain the coverage that best suits their needs.

Water Quality Regulations and Best Practices

The Water Quality Division of DEQ protects Oregon's public water for a range of uses. DEQ sets water quality standards to protect "beneficial uses," such as recreation, fish habitat, drinking water reservoirs, and natural settings. DEQ monitors water quality by regularly sampling rivers and streams in Oregon.

Contractors should use work practices that prevent sediment runoff and pollution to waterways, and should follow federal, state, and local requirements. DEQ technical specialists can assist businesses in ensuring construction activities near Oregon waters comply with these requirements. When beginning a new construction project, review the scope with a DEQ or city representative to become familiar with the requirements that apply to specific project activities.

The water quality activities and regulatory requirements described in this section are listed in the following table:

Activity	Regulatory Requirements
Protect Drinking Water Quality	Federal Safe Drinking Water Act; OAR Chapter 340, Division 40
Minimize and Control Runoff	NPDES Permit 1200C
Water Well Constructors	Licensed contractors with the Oregon Water Resources Department who follow reporting requirements in constructing new wells, altering or converting existing wells.
Underground Injection Control (UIC) systems (any fluid injection into the subsurface)	Register new and existing systems with DEQ. Systems must be approved by DEQ either through authorization by rule or issuance of a Water Pollution Control Facilities permit otherwise the system must be closed. Notify DEQ at least 30-days prior to planned system closure or conversion.
Construct Subsurface Sewage Disposal System	Permit required. Specialty licensed contractor performs work.
Stormwater Management	NPDES Permit 1200C and erosion control plan when one acre of more is disturbed and have potential to discharge stormwater to waters of the state. (Permit is only required if both conditions are met)
Construction Washing near Waterways	NPDES 1700-B permit.
Construction Activity in Natural Waterways	Section 404 permit from Army Corps of Engineers. DEQ 401 certificate. Removal – Fill Permit from Oregon Division of State Lands.

Potable or Drinkable Water Quality

Many rural Oregonians use ground water as their sole source of drinking water. During construction activities, contractors can protect this water supply and avoid possible contamination by:

- Locating all new sources of private or community drinking water away from potential pollution sources.
- Avoiding the use of old wells and the areas around them as disposal sites.
- Making sure wells have a proper seal.
- Locating septic drain fields at a safe distance from wellheads.
- Installing injection systems properly to prevent any injections and/or contaminants from reaching the aquifer.

Water Well Constructors

Any person who engages in a business or activity that involves constructing new wells or altering, deepening, abandoning, or converting existing wells must possess a license from the Oregon Water Resources Department (OWRD).

OWRD regulates activities to prevent waste and contamination of ground water, including setting and enforcing standards for well construction, and inspecting well construction.

The two types of water well constructor's licenses are:
- Water Supply Well Constructor License
- Monitoring Well Constructor License

Before obtaining a well constructor's license, the constructor must pass a written examination, have the required experience, and pay the licensing fee. Before advertising services or entering into contracts for well construction, the licensed well constructor must provide a $10,000 surety bond or irrevocable letter of credit to the OWRD. This bond is in addition to the surety bond required for the CCB license. Licensed constructors must display their license and photo identification when requested by OWRD personnel. For renewal of the two-year water well constructor's license, constructors must pay a license renewal fee and complete continuing education requirements.

The licensed constructor must follow reporting requirements and regulations administered by OWRD. Before beginning work, the constructor reports certain information about the well to the OWRD. During progress of work, the constructor keeps a log of each well and furnishes a certified copy of a well report to the OWRD within 30 days of completion of work. For more information, refer to OWRD's website at www.wrd.state.or.us or Appendix A on Water Quality.

Minimize and Control Runoff

By using methods that control runoff, contractors limit specific pollutants from being discharged into the water. Erosion occurs when exposed soil is washed away by rain or snowmelt and deposited directly or through a MS3 into surface water and streams. Contractors can minimize soil erosion by disturbing as little land as possible during construction, and using methods that allow stormwater to soak in rather than "runoff" to nearby streams and rivers.

Some of those methods are:
- Using gravel or masonry blocks instead of asphalt for paving projects
- Using grassy swales along roadways to collect water instead of curbs, gutters, or storm drains
- Creating shallow, grassy swales between parking rows instead of pushing up islands
- Using oil-sediment catch basins, compost filters, or similar bio-filters in parking areas

Drainage Systems for Construction Washing

Contractors often wash and rinse buildings, equipment, and large tools at the project site. Pollutants from construction washing can run off into rivers or streams and leach into groundwater.

Contractors can avoid construction washing runoff by:

- Directing the wash water into an oil and water separator (if construction equipment) and washing must be done onsite using a lined washout allowing the water to evaporate and recycling or properly disposing of solids in a landfill
- Never directing wash water to any type of injection system (for example, drywell, sump, French drains, drill hole or perforated pipe)
- Using biodegradable washing detergent since detergents or cleaners containing phosphate are prohibited from washing into groundwater or surface water. 1200c allows vehicle washing under the "authorized non-stormwater discharges" - as long as no detergents or hot water are used
- The onsite use of soaps, detergents, and chemicals is prohibited, unless all water is contained or trucked off by a washing contractor who is approved for disposal of the wash water into the sanitary sewer
- Sweeping paved areas instead of washing with water
- Using absorbents to remove leaks or spills, such as hydraulic fluid from a broken line, and never washing them into storm drains
- Contacting the OHA for information on controlling runoff if washing a building that has lead-based paint

If construction equipment cleaning and washing must be done onsite, check with the jurisdiction for approval to dispose of treated wash water into the sanitary sewer system. If the jurisdiction does not allow such disposal, contractors must obtain a permit to dispose of the wastewater into a ditch or stream. DEQ or a local jurisdiction may penalize contractors who fail to obtain the required approval(s).

Dry Wells, Sumps, French Drains, Infiltration Drains

Contractors can install underground injection control (UIC) systems to facilitate the discharge of fluids, including stormwater and other wastewater, below the ground surface. UIC systems may be used for disposal of fluids when no other means of disposal is available or appropriate. Contractors can also decommission or close UIC systems for site construction, site redevelopment or when an alternate means of disposal becomes available. If not properly managed, disposal practices utilizing UIC systems can pollute groundwater and surface water. UIC system location must comply with required setbacks from drinking water wells as specified by DEQ and the local regulating authority where applicable.

Common underground injection systems in Oregon include:
- Stormwater dry wells and drill holes
- Catch basins with sumps
- Trenches with depth from ground surface that is greater than width
- Soakage trenches (also known as recharge beds, infiltration trenches or infiltration galleries) of any dimension that deposit water subsurface. Any infiltration that has an above ground influent is exempt from permitting or rule authorization
- Trench drains, French drains and perforated piping used to distribute fluids in the subsurface
- Subsurface septic systems with drain or leach fields serving 20 or more people or injecting 2,500 gallons or more per day
- Industrial or commercial process waste disposal systems, for example, cooling water
- Aquifer recharge and aquifer remediation wells
- Geothermal wells

All existing and planned UIC systems must be registered with and approved by DEQ. DEQ maintains a record of UIC systems in a database that is available to the public. If a UIC system cannot receive DEQ approval through authorization by rule, the injection system must be retrofit to meet requirements for authorization otherwise approval must be obtained through DEQ issuance of a Water Pollution Control Facilities (WPCF) permit or the injection system must be closed.

Contractors may encounter sewage drill holes, also known as sewage drain holes, which are a type of prohibited UIC system. Sewage drill holes are drilled, hammered, or blasted boreholes or natural lava cracks or fissures used for sewage or sanitary waste disposal. They may include a septic tank ahead of the disposal well used to dispose sewage, industrial or commercial waste at a domestic or commercial site. Unless one of very few exceptions applies, sewage drill holes must be closed.

When conducting a job site investigation, a contractor must identify all UIC systems in the same manner as underground utilities or underground storage tanks. If the project requires retrofitting an existing UIC system to accommodate new construction or remodeling, the retrofitted UIC system must comply with current regulations including the requirements for injection system registration and approval.

A contractor should submit required registration information for new injection systems 60 to 90 days before use, preferably during the planning stage, to allow time for potential design changes to meet site requirements and obtain approval. For more information on the registration and approval process, contact DEQ.

Decommissioning or abandonment of an injection system requires a 30-day notice to DEQ. DEQ may also require sampling and proper disposal of likely contaminants, such as oils and metals, prior to closure. Forms for registration and notice of closure are available on DEQ's website at http://www.deq.state.or.us/wq/uic/forms.htm.

Onsite Wastewater Treatment System

Contractors who plan to build an onsite wastewater treatment system must receive a license from DEQ prior to performing the work.

Sewage Disposal Service Business Licenses

If contractors plan to perform sewage disposal service activities, they must apply for a sewage disposal service license from DEQ. Sewage disposal services include:

- Constructing sewage disposal systems, including the placement of portable toilets or any part thereof
- Pumping out or cleaning sewage disposal systems, including portable toilets or any part thereof
- Disposing of material derived from the pumping out or cleaning of sewage disposal systems
- Grading, excavating, and earth-moving work connected with sewage disposal activities, including drainfield trenches and excavating for tank placement

When obtaining a license, the applicant must submit the application and fee to DEQ. DEQ requires a bond or other security for sewage disposal services in addition to the license. The licensee is responsible for complying with statutes and regulations pertaining to subsurface sewage disposal.

A requirement to possessing a sewage disposal service license is for installers to have an installer certification card. Installers are required to attend a one-day certification class and pass a written test. The certification is good for three years and over that period 18 hours of approved continuing education must be obtained to recertify. The class, test and recertification program is administered by Chemeketa Community College.

As part of the license, DEQ requires an annual inspection of the pumping equipment, and requires accurate records of septage collection and disposal to be retained.

DEQ requires a Construction-Installation permit or a Water Pollution Control Facilities (WPCF) permit before construction or repair of an onsite sewage disposal system can begin.

Construction-Installation Permit

DEQ or the contract county issues a Construction-Installation permit for residential septic systems and, generally, for septic systems that serve small commercial facilities. Construction of the system must comply with regulations and specific conditions in the issued permit. After installing the system, the installer must notify DEQ or the contract county to schedule an inspection of the system before covering it. Once a contractor properly installs the system, DEQ or the contract county issues a Certificate of Satisfactory Completion that approves the installation and allows use of the system.

Contractors can obtain permits through an application process by contacting the appropriate contract county or DEQ office. The overseeing agency will issue or deny a permit within 20 days of receiving a complete application and associated fee. The permit is valid for one year, but a contractor may renew it. See Appendix C for a list of DEQ agents or county contacts.

Water Pollution Control Facilities (WPCF) Onsite Permits

The DEQ WPCF permit is an operational permit that must be kept in force for as long as the septic system is in use. Since 2005, it is required for:

- Septic systems (a single system and multiple systems serving the same facility) over 2,500 gallons per day
- Systems to serve facilities with high-strength wastewater, such as restaurants
- Sand filters serving other than a residence
- Holding tanks
- Complex treatment and disposal systems

A WPCF permit takes about 90 to 180 days to obtain, and the processing time may take longer if there is considerable complexity to the project or public interest and involvement. DEQ may require a public notice and hearing.

Sewer Hookups into a Municipal Sanitary Sewer

Contractors must have a license and required bonding with the CCB if they intend to construct drain and sewage lines that hook up to a municipal system. Before beginning the project, a contractor should check local requirements as well.

Stormwater Management

Contractors are required to obtain a National Pollutant Discharge Elimination System (NPDES) permit for construction activities that disturb one or more acres or are part of a larger plan that will disturb one or more acres and have the potential for stormwater runoff to reach waters of the state or a conveyance system that discharges to waters of the state (see the permit.) Contractors should also check with the appropriate local government jurisdictions to learn if there are additional erosion and sediment control ordinances in effect.

National Pollutant Discharge Elimination System (NPDES) Permit

DEQ has established a NPDES #1200-C Permit for construction activities such as clearing, grading, and excavation that can result in runoff or stormwater discharges to surface waters of the state or conveyance systems that lead to surface waters. Before beginning a project that will disturb one or more acres of land or disturb less than one acre but is part of a larger common plan of development or sale that will ultimately disturb more than one acre, and there is a possibility that runoff could discharge from the site to surface waters, contractors must apply for a NPDES #1200-C Permit, which is good for all phases of a project and is renewable. As part of the permit application process, contractors must submit an erosion control plan. DEQ, or a local agency under DEQ's jurisdiction, administers the permit and approves the contractor's erosion control plan. DEQ enforces the requirements of the permit by assessing penalties.

The erosion control plan must include:

- A narrative site description
- Site maps and construction plans
- Planned erosion and sediment controls, and an implementation schedule
- Any local erosion control and sediment requirements and identify the erosion and sediment control inspector

Current research shows that new erosion control best management practices (BMPs) are much more effective than outdated ones and can save significant money. For example, compost berms, socks, and blankets (simply a 3- to 6-inch thick layer of finished compost) can replace sediment fences and hydroseeding with less installed costs and little or no removal or disposal costs. They also capture water, turbidity, suspended solids, and bind up pollutants better. For more information, refer to the stormwater website at www.deq.state.or.us/wq/stormwater/nwrinfo.htm. Select *Reports* and *Construction Site Stormwater Flocculation Report*.

Turbidity Water Quality Standard

Turbidity refers to particles in the water that block or reduce the amount of light reaching plants and animals in the stream. High turbidity is usually indicated by muddy, murky, or cloudy water. Construction activities that erode dirt, sand, or silt into the water increase these turbid conditions.

Every site must meet the state water quality standard for turbidity whether or not a permit is required. Contractors should verify the current standard with the appropriate DEQ jurisdiction before they begin construction activities.

Water Quality Requirements for Specific River Basins

The Tualatin River sub-basin and the Oswego Lake area have additional special erosion and stormwater regulations. The requirements of these regulations are similar to the NPDES #1200-C Permit with the exception that they are applicable to all construction projects, not just projects that are one or more acres, and may require permanent stormwater quality control facilities.

Construction Washing Near Waterways

Construction washing near or in state waters is a point source discharge requiring an NPDES 1700- B permit. Similar to stormwater runoff, DEQ has established this general permit for construction washing.

Exemptions

The following activities do not need a permit:

- Washing of buildings when there is no runoff offsite or discharge to surface waters, storm sewer or injection systems (such as dry wells), and no use of chemicals, soaps, detergents, steam, or heated water.
- Washing of roads, parking lots, sidewalks, and other paved surfaces if surfaces are swept prior to washing, and there is no runoff offsite or discharge to surface waters, storm sewers or injection systems.
- Washing of construction equipment and vehicles at construction projects for the removal of dirt when there is no runoff offsite or discharge to surface waters, storm sewers, or injection systems. Cleaning must be restricted to the exterior of the vehicle or equipment.

Special Requirements and Limitations

To protect water quality, both permitted and exempt activities must follow these special requirements:

- Acids, bases, metal brighteners, steam, or heated water are prohibited
- Biodegradable, phosphate-free cleaners with cold water are allowed
- Permit does not cover hydro-blasting activities

Discharge of wash water should be minimized but is permitted if there is no runoff offsite or discharge to surface waters, storm sewers, or injection systems.

Construction Activities in Natural Waterways

DEQ issues "401 certifications" to review and certify that a project meets state water quality standards. In addition to DEQ, other state and federal agencies also regulate activities that affect ground or surface waters, state waters, and wetlands. Some of the activities and agencies include:

- Dredging and filling activities require a Section 404 permit issued by the Army Corps of Engineers.
- Construction activities affecting navigable waters are regulated by the Federal Waters and Harbor Act.
- Prior to removal or fill of material in state waters or wetlands, the Oregon Department of State Lands issues a Removal-Fill permit.

Section 404 Permit (U.S. Corps of Engineers)

Any filling, installation of piling, or construction on navigable waterways or rivers requires a Section 404 permit from the U.S. Army Corps of Engineers. The type of permit depends on the impact the project will have on the waterways. The permit must be approved before construction activities begin.

Oregon Removal-Fill Permit (Division of State Lands)

Any dredging, filling, or alteration of a stream requires a Removal-Fill Permit from the Oregon Division of State Lands. These activities remove, fill, or alter more than 50 cubic yards of material within the bed or banks of state waters. The permit application is jointly processed with the U.S. Army Corps of Engineers. Examples of these activities include removing gravel, replacing riprap, reclaiming land, relocating or altering river channels, and preparing pipeline crossings.

Water Quality Best Practices

Site Preparation

Site preparation is critical to the construction process. Care should be taken to reduce surface water runoff, maintain soil health, and prevent the destruction of natural features such as wetlands.

Preserve Wetlands, Streams, Lakes, Trees, and Meadows

Preserving natural features both maintains good environmental quality and enhances the livability of a community.

A wetlands area is any land where saturation with water is the dominant factor in determining the nature of soil development and the types of plants and animals living in the soil and on the surface. Water may not always be present on the surface of the wetland area.

Wetlands naturally filter water that passes through them and are extremely sensitive to any disturbance. The best method of protecting a wetlands area is to avoid disturbing it or to minimize the disturbance. Contractors should protect wetlands by:

- Obtaining all necessary permits before filling or building on wetlands
- Installing and maintaining oil and sediment traps in storm drains
- Using bio-filtrations, such as bags filled with chips or bales of straw, during construction to control erosion
- Maintaining a vegetative buffer around all surface waters. Buffers provide natural filtration and absorption of pollutants
- Identifying and protecting if not impacting with orange high visibility fencing

If wetlands must be disturbed during a project, the permit(s) obtained may require that the disturbance be balanced by building or enhancing other wetlands areas.

Maintain Soil Function and Existing Vegetation

Natural landscaping that contains healthy, established plants and organically rich soils minimizes erosion potential and reduces landscaping costs to the contractor. Plants that are native to the area are more resistant to diseases and pests. This reduces the need for chemical treatments, which have many potential long-term health effects for plants, animals, and the building users. Contractors should retain topsoil and native plants at construction projects, remove non-native invasive plants, and support any new landscaping required with healthy soils.

The following techniques are some ways to maintain soil function and existing vegetation:

- Clear the minimum amount of land needed for each project.
- Clear grasses/shrubs by hand mowing or cutting instead of removal.
- Fence critical areas, such as tree root zones to avoid destruction.
- Reuse excavated soils in landscaping.
- Minimize use of herbicides and pesticides.

Air Quality Regulations and Best Practices

DEQ's Air Quality Division monitors air quality to ensure air quality health standards are met. The following air quality activities and regulatory requirements are described in this section:

Activity	Regulatory Requirements
Open Burning	Open Burning Letter Permit
Abate Friable Asbestos	DEQ-Licensed Asbestos Abatement Contractors and Certified Workers
Install Wood Stoves	DEQ-Certified Units

Open Burning
Open burning means any burning done outdoors, which includes:
- Fires in burn barrels, outdoor fireplaces, and backyard incinerators
- Burning piles of yard debris or land waste
- Burning stumps to clear land
- Burning construction debris or the remains of demolished structures

Materials that cause dense smoke or noxious odors are considered "prohibited materials" and may not be burned in Oregon. Examples of prohibited materials include: plastic, wire insulation, automobile parts, asphalt, petroleum and petroleum treated products including painted wood and wood treated with creosote or pentachlorophenol; rubber products, tires, wet garbage, industrial waste, and any material that creates dense smoke or noxious odors.

DEQ prohibits open burning of construction and demolition waste within open burn control areas in counties throughout the state, unless authorized by an Open Burning Letter Permit.

Using fire to clear land and dispose of debris is a major source of air pollution and should not be done.

Practical Alternatives to Open Burning
Before choosing open burning, consider:
- Composting or chipping plant materials
- Using curbside yard debris pickup
- Reclaiming used lumber and other building materials
- Taking leaves to community cleanup events
- Recycling or composting materials (see Appendix A, *Recycling Resources*)
- Contacting DEQ's Solid Waste program for the nearest reusable building materials facility

Check with DEQ and the Local Fire Department Before Open Burning

Construction contractors who want to burn land debris or construction waste must adhere to DEQ regulations and local burning ordinances. Local fire departments determine if burning is allowed on a particular day. If a contractor must open burn, these precautions must be followed:

- A responsible person must constantly attend any open burning of construction or demolition materials until extinguished.
- Construction and/or demolition wastes, with prohibited materials removed, must be dry, clean, loosely stacked, and periodically restacked to promote efficient burning and to prevent excessive smoke.

When an Open Burning Letter Permit is Needed

Contractors must have an open burning letter permit for open burning of construction and demolition waste within open burn control areas. Contact the local DEQ office (see Appendix B) to determine if the proposed burn site is located within a control area or at www.deq.state.or.us/aq/burning/openburning/openburn.asp.

How to Obtain an Open Burning Letter Permit

The DEQ is likely to issue an Open Burning Letter Permit when the contractor can show that there are no practical alternatives to burning and presents a letter from the local fire department that verifies:

- The material consists only of woody material
- The burn can occur in three days or less
- The location is more than three miles from any incorporated town
- The location is more than three miles from any air quality special control district
- The location is more than one-half mile from all residences, but not counting the applicants
- The proposed burn is acceptable to the local fire authority

Asbestos

Asbestos is a mineral fiber that was manufactured in more than 3,600 products up through 1987. However, there are still some products manufactured today, such as vinyl floor tile and roof patch, which can contain asbestos. Exposure to asbestos fibers can cause lung cancer, asbestosis, and mesothelioma. Asbestos is a hazardous air pollutant, a known carcinogen, and there is no safe level of exposure. Asbestos was commonly used in building materials that included flooring, wall, and ceiling materials; heating, ventilation, and pipe insulation; and exterior siding and roofing. Most buildings, including residences, still contain asbestos-containing materials in one or more materials.

Unless proper work practice and disposal methods are followed, asbestos fibers can be released into the air and be absorbed into the lungs. Asbestos fibers can stay in the air (breathing zone) for very long periods of time. Contractors must be familiar with the asbestos requirements and use caution when working around asbestos-containing materials.

A list of materials that may contain asbestos is shown below, but keep in mind that this list does not include every product and material that may contain asbestos. More information about asbestos is available at www.deq.state.or.us/aq/asbestos.

Identifying Asbestos-Containing Materials

Prior to beginning any renovation or demolition project, the contractor needs to: consult with the property owner and request a copy of the asbestos survey. An asbestos survey of the building or the areas where the renovation will occur must be performed by an Environmental Protection Agency (EPA) accredited inspector. A copy must be kept at the project site during all renovation or demolition activities. The property owner and/or operator can be held responsible for survey violations. During the survey, the inspector will sample all suspect asbestos-containing material for laboratory analysis. The only way to positively identify asbestos-containing materials is through lab analysis.

Abatement

Both friable and non-friable asbestos-containing materials must be properly abated prior to any renovation, demolition, repair, maintenance, or construction activity. If asbestos-containing materials are identified in the survey and will be impacted by any activity, the contractor must have a DEQ licensed asbestos abatement contractor properly abate all friable asbestos. If non-friable asbestos-containing materials are present, the contractor may remove and dispose of the non-friable asbestos-containing material in a manner that does not render the asbestos friable and is performed in compliance with the asbestos requirements. There are notification, work practice, and disposal requirements that must be met for non-friable abatement.

Extreme caution must be exercised because some materials that are non-friable can become friable during removal and disposal activities. If this scenario occurs, immediately stop work and contact a licensed asbestos abatement contractor.

Exemptions

Roofing products and mastics that are fully encapsulated with a petroleum-based binder and are not hard, dry, or brittle may be exempt. These exemptions end whenever the materials are burned, shattered, crumbled, crushed, run over by equipment, or reduced to dust.

Repair activities limited to handling less than 3 square or 3 linear feet of friable asbestos-containing material provided such repairs are necessary and asbestos abatement is not the primary objective, may be exempt from the licensing requirement. Contact DEQ for further information on this very narrow exemption.

Two Categories of Asbestos-Containing Materials

Friable asbestos-containing materials can easily release asbestos fibers when disturbed or are in poor condition. Examples of friable asbestos-containing materials can include, but are not limited to, the felt-like backing on sheet vinyl, acoustical panel products, wall and ceiling textures, skim coats, furnace and duct insulation, pipe insulation and niccolite roof paper. Only DEQ licensed asbestos abatement contractors and certified asbestos workers can remove and dispose of friable asbestos-containing materials.

Non-friable asbestos-containing materials have a binder that holds the asbestos fibers within a solid matrix (asphalt, cement, vinyl) and will not easily release asbestos fibers, unless mishandled, damaged, or in badly worn or weathered condition. Examples of non-friable asbestos-containing materials are vinyl floor tile, cement asbestos board shingles or panels, and cement water pipe. A person does not need to be a DEQ licensed asbestos abatement contractor or a certified asbestos worker to perform non-friable asbestos abatement. However, the non-friable materials must remain in non-friable condition (predominantly whole pieces) during the removal and disposal process. There are work practice and disposal requirements that must be followed during non-friable abatement. If any non-friable asbestos-containing material cannot be removed in predominantly whole pieces, the contractor must have a licensed asbestos abatement contractor remove and dispose of the asbestos-containing material. DEQ has guidance documents available for the proper abatement of non-friable materials. Contact a local DEQ office or visit the DEQ asbestos web page for copies of the guidance documents.

Asbestos-Containing Materials

The following table lists materials that commonly contain asbestos. One or more of these materials can be found in and/or on most buildings constructed prior to 1988. This list does not include every material that was manufactured with asbestos, only those that are common in most buildings.

List of Materials that May Contain Asbestos

Acoustical ceiling tiles
Adhesives/Mastics
Air-duct cement, tape & insulation
Block insulation
Building insulation (walls, attics – does not include fiberglass insulation)
Caulks and putties
Cement asbestos board (Transite)
Cement siding and roofing products
Cement water pipe
Electrical wiring (encased in black tar-based material)
Fire doors & walls
Flashing cement
Furnace cement
Gaskets (furnaces, boilers, woodstoves)
Interior wall textures, skim & brown coats
Joint compound & taping mud compound
Niccolite roof paper
Paint
Patch compounds
Plaster
Roofing felt, patch and rolled roofing (asphalt or tar saturated)
Sheet vinyl flooring (through 1986)
Spray-applied insulation soundproofing and fireproofing
Spray-applied textured or acoustical ceilings (popcorn texture, orange peel)
Stucco
Tank & boiler insulation
Thermal system pipe insulation (may have a chalk-like appearance or may look like corrugated cardboard and is often called air-cell)
Vapor barrier products
Vinyl floor tile (both 9"x9" & 12'x12") & mastics
Wallboard

Contractor Requirements

Contractors and their employees must follow the DEQ asbestos requirements during renovation, demolition, construction, repair, and maintenance activities on any public or private structure.

Make sure that an asbestos survey has been performed, keep a copy of the survey onsite, and hire a licensed asbestos abatement contractor to abate friable asbestos-containing materials. Contractors who elect to perform non-friable abatement must comply with all notification, work practice, and disposal requirements. DEQ holds contractors to a high standard and expects contractors to know and comply with the asbestos requirements.

Failure to follow the asbestos rules can result in an enforcement action for rule violations and could expose contractors to liability for cleanup costs and civil penalty assessment. Penalties can be assessed for each day of violation. These DEQ regulations are separate from those required by Oregon OSHA.

Oregon OSHA regulations also require building surveys for asbestos, and regulate employee safety and safe work practices.

DEQ Licensing

DEQ licenses all contractors who perform abatement of friable asbestos-containing materials. Licensed contractors must employ DEQ certified asbestos workers and supervisors. Contact the Northwest Region Office for information on Licensing or Certification.

> **NOTE: DEQ Requires Written Notification of all Asbestos Abatement Projects**
> Contractors and/or building owners are required to notify DEQ before all friable and non-friable abatement (handle, removal, disposal, enclosure) of any asbestos-containing material by submitting a *Project Notification Form* along with a fee. The waiting periods for asbestos removal projects are 10 days for friable notifications and five days for non-friable notifications. The waiting period begins when the DEQ Business Office receives the completed notification and the appropriate fee.

DEQ Asbestos Program Contact Information

Copies of non-friable guidance documents, program fact sheets, the list of asbestos abatement contractors, the list of EPA accredited inspectors, and project notification forms and other information can be found on the DEQ web page at www.deq.state.or.us/aq/asbestos. For further information or technical assistance about the asbestos requirements contact a regional program staff:

- Clackamas, Clatsop, Columbia, Multnomah, Tillamook, and Washington counties:
  Northwest Region Office
  503-229-5982 or 503-229-5364

- Benton, Lincoln, Linn, Marion, Polk, and Yamhill counties:
  Western Region Salem Office
  503-378-5086 or 800-349-7677

- Lane County:
  Lane Regional Air Protection Agency
  541-736-1056

- Jackson, Josephine, and Eastern Douglas Counties:
  The Western Region Medford Office
  541-766-6107 or 877-823-3216

- Coos, Curry, and Western Douglas Counties:
  Western Region Coos Bay Office
  541-269-2721 ext. 222

- Crook, Deschutes, Harney, Hood River, Jefferson, Klamath, Lake, Sherman and Wasco counties:
  Eastern Region Bend Office
  541-633-2019 or 866-863-6668

- Baker, Gilliam, Grant, Malheur, Morrow, Umatilla, Union, Wallow and Wheeler counties:
  Eastern Region Pendleton Office
  541-278-4626 or 800-304-3513

Dust and Uncontrolled Emissions

Controlling Dust Emission

Contractors must take reasonable precautions to prevent dust and other uncontrolled emissions from becoming airborne. In processing, handling, and storage activities, the building or equipment is tightly closed and ventilated in such a way that air contaminants are controlled or removed. Some precautions include:

- Using water or environmentally safe chemicals to control dust in the demolition of structures, construction operations, grading of roads, clearing of land, material stockpiles, unpaved roads, or other impervious surfaces
- Where the use of water or environmentally safe chemicals is not a practical solution to control dust, minimize soil disturbance and leave vegetated areas as long as possible Covering all trucks that transport materials likely to become airborne
- Removing all dirt and other debris from impervious surfaces before they become airborne

State Regulations

Regulations for dust and uncontrolled emissions are described in the following table:

Oregon Regulations for Dust and Uncontrolled Emissions

Description	Geographic Area	Standard	Rule Reference
Visible Emissions	Statewide	20 percent opacity for 3 minutes	340-208-0100
	Clackamas, Multnomah, Washington Counties	20 percent opacity for 30 seconds	340-208-0600
Fugitive Emissions	Benton, Clackamas, Columbia, Lane, Linn, Marion, Multnomah, Polk, Washington, Yamhill Counties	Abate fugitives	340-208-0210
	Umpqua Basin		
	Rogue Basin		
	Within 3 miles of any city of 4,000 or more		
Nuisance Rules	Statewide	Abate nuisance	340-208-0300 through 0450

Noise Pollution

Noise pollution at a construction project includes blasting, drilling, sawing, compressor operation, jackhammers, back-up beepers, and heavy construction equipment. Excessive construction noise must be managed to reduce disturbance to property owners. Some measures to reduce noise pollutions are:

- Use mufflers on vehicles.
- Enclose loud equipment for soundproofing.
- Use portable noise barriers and schedule loud activities during less sensitive times of day.

Since local regulations of noise pollution vary, contractors should be familiar with restrictions, standards, or curfews required in an area before construction. Many city and county noise control ordinances contain restrictions and decibel standards, with the exception of emergency work.

Installation of Wood Stoves

Residential wood heating contributes to air pollution and excessive woodstove or fireplace smoke can violate air quality health standards. When a contractor is required to install a woodstove or fireplace insert, the units must be Oregon DEQ-certified or EPA-certified for a building permit. Certified woodstove and fireplace inserts have a permanent label attached that prove the unit has passed federal emissions standards. Oregon's woodstove regulations govern the sale of both new and used woodstoves.

The following stoves are exempt:

- Antique stoves built before 1940 that have a higher than normal resale value. Check with DEQ on the application of this exemption.
- Cook stoves designed solely for cooking, which have ovens and/or separate burning plates.
- Wood furnaces that are part of a ducted central heating system.
- Some pellet stoves.

Refrigerants

Contractors who service, maintain, repair, or install air conditioners, refrigerators, chillers, or freezers must follow EPA regulations on refrigerants. Refrigerants contain chlorofluorocarbons (CFCs) and hydrochlorofluorocarbons (HCFCs) that destroy the earth's ozone layer. Some of the EPA regulations:

- Require service practices that maximize recycling of CFCs and HCFCs during servicing and disposal of air-conditioning and refrigeration equipment
- Prohibit venting of refrigerants to the atmosphere during maintenance, service, repair, or disposing of air conditioning or refrigeration equipment
- Require certification of service technicians

- Require contractor and re-claimer certification for recovery and recycling equipment
- Restrict the sale of refrigerant to certified technicians
- Require the repair of substantial leaks in air conditioning and refrigeration equipment (charge greater than 50 pounds) and recordkeeping on the amount of refrigerated added to equipment
- Establish safe disposal requirements
- Prohibit the sale of containers of CFCs less than 20 pounds to anyone who is not certified

Air Quality Best Practices

Building methods and materials can pollute the air. Contractors should evaluate sources of pollution and identify cost-effective alternatives in construction.

Radon

Radon gas is a radioactive, colorless gas that occurs naturally in the earth, particularly in areas of high granite deposits in the subsurface or subsoil. Radon levels can build to unhealthy levels when trapped indoors. The only way to know if a home has a radon problem is to test. When trapped in buildings, gas concentration can increase and can cause health hazards. Fortunately, radon gas levels in Oregon are low. However, the potential for radon exists. Many contractors incorporate methods to deter radon, control moisture, or increase energy efficiency. In fact, radon-resistant construction techniques are in residential building codes. For more information on radon, visit www.healthoregon.org/radon or call the Oregon Health Authority's Radon Program at 971-673-0440.

Auto Exhaust and Combustion Byproducts

Attached garages are common in residential construction. Car exhaust is a source of indoor air pollution. Residential appliances, such as furnaces, wood stoves, and gas appliances, can produce methane, nitrogen dioxide, carbon monoxide, and carbon dioxide that can accumulate in a residence if not properly ventilated. Contractors should properly seal attached garages, and properly ventilate gas appliances to avoid pollutant buildup inside the building.

Diesel Emissions

While diesel engines are very important for many construction applications, the exhaust from these engines is especially harmful. When idling more than a minute, turn motors off. Idling diesel and gasoline engines add wear and tear on equipment, waste fuel, increase costs, and unnecessarily expose workers to harmful exhaust fumes. Exhaust from idling machines could also impact nearby residents and workers, leading to complaints and nuisance calls. It is better to plan ahead to avoid diesel emissions than to have to take time away from the construction project do deal with these problems.

Diesel emissions can be mitigated by good job site ventilation and conversion of diesel engines to propane.

Ventilation
Diesel exhaust in garages, warehouses, or other enclosed areas should be controlled using ventilation.

Local Exhaust Ventilation
A good ventilation system should include both intake and exhaust fans that remove harmful fumes at their source. Tailpipe or stack exhaust hoses should be provided for any vehicle being run in a maintenance shop.

General ventilation
Uses roof vents, open doors and windows, roof fans, or floor fans to move air through the work area. This is not as effective as local exhaust ventilation and may simply spread the fumes around the work area. General ventilation may be helpful, however, when used to supplement local exhaust ventilation.

Substitution
Where possible, replace diesel engines with propane-burning engines, which burn more completely and cleanly than diesel fuel. Tax credits are available to retrofit diesel equipment and engines with advanced pollution controls.

Land Quality Regulations and Best Practices

DEQ's Land Quality Division protects human health and the environment by ensuring:
- Proper management of solid and hazardous waste
- Timely emergency response to spills of oils and hazardous substances
- Proper removal and replacement of underground tanks and home heating oil tanks
- Clean up of sites contaminated with hazardous substances to safe exposure levels

This section discusses the following solid waste activities and regulatory requirements.

Activity	Regulatory Requirements
Dispose Solid Waste (not clean fill)	DEQ permit
Dispose Mixed Solid Waste	DEQ permit at Mixed Waste Processing
Dispose Construction Waste from Projects with Permit Value of $50,000 or greater	City of Portland requires certain materials or waste separated and recycled

Proper Management of Solid/Nonhazardous Wastes

Construction projects generate solid waste during demolition, renovation, repair, construction, or maintenance of buildings, roads, and other structures. Solid wastes must be collected and stored to prevent conditions that transmit diseases, pollution, dust, or other nuisances.

Non-hazardous construction and demolition debris includes concrete, insulation, bricks, asphalt paving, wood, glass, masonry, roofing, siding, scrap metal, cardboard and other packaging, carpet, plaster, drywall, soil, rock, stumps, boulders, and brush. Hazardous waste generated on a construction project may include waste solvents, pesticides, herbicides, and wood preservatives. Other wastes that may be hazardous include leftover paints and coatings, adhesives, caulks, oils, and greases.

Oregon's policy for waste management follows these priorities:
- Reduce waste and reuse materials when possible
- Recycle materials that are unsuitable for reducing or reusing
- Compost material that is unsuitable for reuse or recycling
- Recover energy from solid waste when it is unsuitable for reuse, composting, or recycling
- Properly dispose of unusable solid waste

Prohibited Disposal

The following materials are prohibited from disposal at any solid waste landfill. These items must be recovered or recycled:

Used oil

Used oil that is not recycled must be managed as a hazardous waste. A used oil re-refiner or processor may recycle used oil.

Home or industrial appliances

"White goods" include water heaters, refrigerators, kitchen stoves, dishwashers, washing machines, and clothes dryers. Scrap metal dealers and most landfills and transfer stations accept these for a fee.

Lead-acid batteries

These may be taken to a retailer, wholesaler, or recycling facility or to a state or EPA-permitted secondary lead smelter. Batteries that are not recycled must be treated as a hazardous waste.

Whole tires

Some transfer stations or drop-off depots will take tires for a fee, and then have the tires recycled or chipped for disposal.

Vehicles

A wrecking yard or scrap metal dealer can recycle auto bodies.

Generally, landfills and other disposal sites prohibit the disposal of liquids.

Clean Fill

Materials that are "clean fill" include clean soil, rock, brick, building block, and old, weathered asphalt paving. DEQ does not require a permit for the disposal or use of clean fill. However, Division of State Lands may require a permit for sites that accept such materials. Mixed construction waste does not qualify as clean fill. Other contaminants, such as spilled oil or lead-based paint on material, do not qualify as clean fill. Contractors who are unsure if the material they have qualifies as clean fill can contact DEQ for a determination and applicable fees.

Solid Waste Recycling and Recovery

Many landfills, transfer stations, and other disposal sites offer recycling to contractors, but some recycling sites accept only a limited list of materials, such as common household recyclables. Most sites accept scrap metal. There may be a charge for certain items that require special preparation or handling for recycling, such as major appliances. Some sites will also accept wood and yard debris at a fee. Two options for recovering materials are:

- Collecting the materials separately onsiteMixing wastes together and sending them to a mixed waste processing facility for sorting

Use of Solid Wastes in Construction Activities

Oregon encourages and permits the recycling of solid waste materials into usable construction materials or products. The intent is to recycle and reuse solid waste appropriate for construction activity.

Example

Glass and ceramic products can be crushed and used for such things as drainage material, utility line bedding, roadbed material, and structural aggregate.

Local Government Requirements

Certain local jurisdictions have additional requirements for managing solid waste from construction. For instance, the City of Portland requires all building projects with a permit value of $50,000 or more to separate and recycle certain materials from the job site. These materials include wood, metals, rubble (e.g., rock, concrete, and asphalt), land clearing debris, and cardboard. The City of Ashland has similar recycling requirements for demolition.

Proper Management of Hazardous Wastes

Hazardous waste requires special handling and disposal. Construction activities often generate small amounts of hazardous waste that could cause environmental damage if not properly managed. Some common examples of such hazardous wastes include caustic cleaners, solvents, oil-based paints and coatings, adhesives, caulks, and pesticides. Proper disposal of hazardous wastes is an important part of the construction process.

The following regulations apply to hazardous waste management:
- Resource Conservation and Recovery Act (RCRA)
- Comprehensive Environmental Response Compensation and Liability Act (CERCLA)
- Superfund Amendment Reauthorization Act (SARA) Title 3
- Oregon Administrative Rules (OAR 340-142) regulating spill reporting and cleanup, identification of hazardous wastes, required reporting and fees, toxic use, and reduction plans

See Appendix D for information on specific regulations.

Determine Which Wastes are Hazardous

A contractor must determine which wastes are hazardous. A hazardous waste is material that can be a solid or liquid with certain properties, such as toxicity, corrosivity, or ignitability and could pose a danger to human health, property, or the environment. Sometimes, a lab analysis must be done to determine if used chemicals or unknowns generated during construction activities produced a hazardous waste. Other important hazardous waste management steps could include checking shipping papers, labeling containers, or reviewing MSDS to identify which products are hazardous.

DEQ provides free, onsite and telephone technical assistance to assist businesses.

Hazardous Waste Generator Categories

If a construction business generates hazardous wastes, the next step is to determine the amount. The more hazardous waste a business generates, the more regulations that apply. A business is placed in one of three categories based on the monthly amount of waste generated.

Conditionally Exempt Generators (CEGs) generate 220 pounds or less of waste or spill cleanup debris containing hazardous waste in one month. Also, a business is a CEG if it generates 2.2 pounds *or less* of EPA acute hazardous waste. A CEG may accumulate *up to* 2,200 pounds of hazardous waste on each project site.

Small Quantity Generators (SQGs) generate 221 to 2,199 pounds of waste or spill cleanup debris containing hazardous waste in one month. An SQG may accumulate *more than* 2,200 pounds of hazardous waste on a project site.

Large Quantity Generators (LQGs) generate 2,200 *or more* pounds of hazardous waste or spill cleanup debris containing hazardous waste. A business is also an LQG if it generates *more than* 2.2 pounds of acute hazardous waste or *more than* 220 pounds of spill cleanup debris containing EPA acute hazardous waste, or if it accumulates *more than* 2.2 pounds of acute hazardous waste on a project site.

Notification of Hazardous Waste Activity

All LQGs and SQGs must notify DEQ of their hazardous waste activity and obtain a site identification number. An LQG or SQG may not treat, store, dispose of, transport, or offer transportation of hazardous waste without a DEQ site identification number. The cost of issuance is $200 and forms are available from DEQ.

A business should receive a site-specific, hazardous waste identification number within 10 days of returning the completed form to DEQ. The number DEQ permanently assigns to a business is based on where the business generates hazardous waste.

Reduce Use of Toxic Chemicals and Hazardous Waste

The best way to minimize hazardous waste generation and potential liability is to reduce or eliminate sources of waste. Contractors can reduce hazardous waste generation through source reduction, material substitution, inventory control, and good housekeeping.

For example, a contractor can:
- Minimize the purchase of raw materials by buying only what is needed for the project
- Use materials before they become obsolete

- Minimize the use of petroleum-based solvents and use alternative products such as water-based paints and coatings
- Use water-based cleaners
- Maintain, wash, and clean vehicles or equipment offsite
- Control access to storage areas and inspect containers for damage during storage and when a new shipment is received
- Properly label hazardous waste containers to avoid mixing incompatible wastes or contaminating clean materials

Reuse and Recycle Hazardous Wastes

Reusing construction materials saves money, extends the useful life of material, and reduces waste disposal costs. Recycling is the best option when a material cannot be used. Some construction practices that reuse products include:
- If possible, using solvents such as mineral spirits and paint thinners more than once
- Combining used and new solvents to extend their useful life
- Using up all paint
- Recycling as many other materials as possible

Dispose of Hazardous Waste Properly

After the project is completed, use the following guidelines to determine the proper disposal method for unused materials.
- Paints may be left with the owner for future use.
- Oils, like form oil, hydraulic gear and engine oils, can be recycled. These cannot be placed in dumpsters, on the ground, in drains, or ditches.
- Sealers may be used for another project.
- A hazardous waste management company should handle paint thinners, pesticides, vehicle batteries, and petroleum products that are not recycled.
- Use a reliable treatment, storage, and disposal (TSD) facility or a hazardous waste management company.
- Check with local solid waste management agency to learn if any hazardous waste collection events are scheduled.

Contractors classified as SQG or LQG are required to complete a hazardous waste manifest before transporting waste offsite. Also, the U.S. Department of Transportation and the Oregon Department of Transportation (ODOT) has requirements.

Annual Reporting of Hazardous Waste

Contractors classified as SQG or LQG must report the quantity of waste generated annually to the DEQ on the agency's Hazardous Waste Reporting System, HazWaste.net. Annual reports are filed electronically and are due March 1.

DEQ assesses a hazardous waste generator fee based on the amount of waste generated and reported each calendar year.

Proper Management of Environmentally Hazardous Materials

Wastes with special management requirements include used oil, universal waste (mercury containing equipment and lamps, batteries, and pesticides), polychlorinated biphenyls (PCBs) found in fluorescent ballasts, asbestos, and lead paint waste.

Environmentally Hazardous Materials

Environmentally Hazardous Material	Construction Material or Activity	Handling or Disposal
Asbestos	Refer to chart earlier in this section for sample list of materials.	Testing laboratory analyzes material to positively identify asbestos. Notify DEQ before handling, removing, or enclosing asbestos. DEQ-licensed asbestos abatement contractors are is required to dispose of material containing friable asbestos at an approved landfill.
Refrigerants Chlorofluorocarbons (CFCs) and Hydro chlorofluorocarbons (HCFCs)	Contractors who service, maintain, repair, or install air conditioning or refrigeration equipment are prohibited from venting "ozone depleting compounds" used as refrigerants. Ozone-depleting compounds include but are not limited to: • Freon 11, 12, & 113, • Halon 1211 & 1301.	Contractors who service, maintain, repair, or install air conditioners, refrigerators, chillers, or freezers are subject to federal regulation. The EPA regulates recovery, recycling, reclamation, and disposal of refrigerants and refrigeration equipment in commercial refrigeration and air conditioning units.
Universal Waste Batteries	Cell phones, computers, and other equipment powered by rechargeable batteries.	Rechargeable batteries may be disposed of at low cost using the industry-sponsored Rechargeable Battery Recycling Corporation (RBRC) recycling services contact them at 1-877-723-1297 (toll free) or at www.rbrc.org. Batteries are managed under universal waste regulations.

Environmentally Hazardous Material	Construction Material or Activity	Handling or Disposal
Universal Waste Mercury containing lamps Fluorescent and high-density discharge (HID) lamps	Change out of fluorescent, neon, high-intensity discharge (HID) including mercury vapor, metal halide, and high-pressure sodium and other specialty lamps often contain mercury in concentrations high enough to exhibit a hazardous waste characteristic for mercury.	Lamps may be disposed of as "universal waste" and must be accumulated in containers that protect them from being broken. Universal waste must be ultimately managed for disposal or recycling at a universal waste "destination facility" or hazardous waste management facility. Universal waste is prohibited from being disposed of as a solid waste at a landfill.
"Universal Waste mercury containing equipment, thermostats and switches"	Temperature control devices containing metallic mercury in an ampule attached to a bi-metal sensing element.	Contractors installing heating, ventilation, or air-conditioning systems are required to dispose of mercury containing thermostats properly, either by using a program established by thermostat manufacturers (the Thermostat Recycling Corp.), or by delivering them to a site that will ensure that they do not become part of the solid wastestream or wastewater.
Universal Waste Pesticides	Site preparation and vector and noxious weed control.	The best practice for pesticides is to use them up for their intended purpose and generate no waste pesticide. Waste pesticide may be disposed of under the universal waste regulations.
Lead	Common component in roofs, tank lining, electrical conduit, plumbing soft solder, lead pipes, and galvanized pipes with lead solder.	Contractors or workers who handle materials containing lead must use a correct and clean respirator, dry protective clothing, proper equipment and appropriate changing facilities. Contractors are regulated by OR-OSHA in minimizing employee risk of lead exposure.
Lead based paint	Buildings constructed before 1978 may contain lead paint on interior/exterior painted wood, siding, window frames, plaster and sheetrock. Today lead paint is banned in residential applications but is used on bridges, railways, and other steel structures because lead based paint inhibits corrosion of iron and steel.	All construction waste, paint chips, dust and debris must be contained and cleaned up. Collect waste and debris and seal in plastic bags. Debris from lead-based paint activities, and renovation, repair and painting of residences, can be disposed of as household waste. Contractors are regulated by OR-OSHA in minimizing employee risk of lead exposure. Contact OHA, OR-DEQ and local landfill for more information on disposal of lead-based paint debris.
Polychlorinated biphenyls(PCBs)	Used before 1979 to insulate electrical equipment like capacitors, switches and voltage regulators.	Before disposing, contractors must determine if fluorescent lamp ballasts contain PCBs. If ballasts are leaking, they must be manifested and disposed by trained personnel in a chemical waste landfill or incinerated in an approved facility.
Used Oil	Used oil is any oil that has been refined from crude or synthetic oil and used as a: ▪ Lubricant ▪ Electrical Insulation Oil ▪ Hydraulic Fluid	Used oil that is recycled is not treated as a hazardous waste and has its own set of management standards for storage, burning on site and disposal.

Environmentally Hazardous Material	Construction Material or Activity	Handling or Disposal
	▪ Heat Transfer Oil ▪ Brake Fluid ▪ Refrigeration Oil ▪ Grease ▪ Machine Cutting Oil	

Used Oil

Used oil must be properly recycled to prevent potential pollution of the air, land, surface water, and groundwater. Used oil can contain cancer-causing agents, metal contaminants, and organic compounds that seep into the groundwater supply when dumped or sprayed as a dust suppressant.

The use of used oil as a dust suppressant (road oiling) is prohibited. Used oil that is recycled for energy recovery is not considered a hazardous waste and has separate management standards for storage, burning, and recycling. If used oil is not recycled for energy recovery, it must be determined as a hazardous waste.

Universal Wastes

Universal waste regulations are streamlined hazardous waste management standards for specific hazardous wastes that are commonly generated. The universal waste rule facilitates environmentally sound collection and increases the proper recycling or treatment. Wastes not subject to universal waste management requirements are those generated by households or conditionally exempt hazardous waste generators.

Types of Universal Wastes

Batteries

Use of batteries is common in construction hand tools, flashlights, radios, cellular phones, pagers, emergency lighting, calculators, and laptop computers. Generally, alkaline batteries and carbon-zinc batteries do not contain significant levels of toxic metals and are not required to be managed as universal or hazardous waste. Some batteries contain toxic metals such as lead, cadmium, lithium, or mercury that are harmful to the environment.

Environmentally Hazardous Batteries

Battery Name	Typical Size	Common Uses	Potential Hazards (Percent by Weight)
Mercury-oxide	Small, various sizes, button type, 9 volt	Cameras, communications	Uses mercury as an electrode. Can contain 35-50 percent mercury.
Silver-oxide	Small, various sizes, button type	Hearing aids, pagers, medical equipment	Can contain 0.4-1 percent mercury.
Zinc-Air	Button type and 9 volt	Hearing aids, pagers, medical equipment	Can contain 0.4-1 percent mercury.
Lithium	C, AA, coin type, button type, 9 volt, 6 volt	Computers, cameras, calculators, watches	Lithium is a reactive metal.
Nickel-Cadmium (Ni-cd)	C, D, AA, AAA, power packs	Cellular phones, camcorders, laptop computers, cordless tools and appliances	Uses cadmium as an electrode. Contains 10-15 percent cadmium.
Sealed Lead Acid	D, battery packs	Camcorders, toys, emergency lighting, power backup	Use lead as an electrode. Contains 50-70 percent lead.

Lamps Containing Mercury

Lamps with fluorescent, neon, high intensity discharge (HID) including mercury vapor, metal halide and high-pressure sodium, and other specialty lamps often contain mercury in hazardous concentrations. Lamps managed as universal waste must be kept in containers and protected from being broken.

Pesticides

Contractors can manage waste pesticides according to the universal waste management requirements. Unused pesticides not managed under the universal waste management standards are hazardous wastes in Oregon and subject to state pesticide regulations.

Thermostats and Switches Containing Mercury

Universal waste mercury containing thermostats are those that meet the definition of temperature control devices containing metallic mercury in an ampule attached to a bi-metal sensing element. In addition, mercury containing ampules that have been removed from thermostats are also subject to the universal waste rule management requirements.

Contractors installing heating, ventilation, or air-conditioning systems are required to properly dispose of mercury containing thermostats either by using a program established by thermostat manufacturers or delivering them to a site that ensures that thermostats do not become part of the solid waste stream or wastewater. This means that mercury containing thermostats need to be managed by the thermostat manufacturing industry-sponsored Thermostat Recycling Corporation (TRC) or a facility that will manage the waste thermostat according to the universal waste management standards. For information on the TRC go to www.nema.org/gov/ehs/trc/.

The installation of mercury containing thermostats in commercial or residential buildings has been prohibited since January 1, 2006.

Disposal

Universal waste must be managed for disposal or recycling at a universal waste "destination facility" or hazardous waste management facility. Universal waste is prohibited from being disposed of as a solid waste.

For information on specific universal wastes review DEQ's Universal Waste web page at www.deq.state.or.us/lq/hw/uw.htm.

Polychlorinated Biphenyls (PCBs)

Before 1979, PCBs were widely used to insulate electrical equipment such as capacitors, switches, and voltage regulators. Studies have shown PCBs to cause cancer and developmental/reproductive defects. PCB containing materials are controlled by federal regulations.

Before disposing, contractors must determine whether fluorescent ballasts contain PCBs. Generally, all fluorescent lamp ballasts manufactured through 1978 contain PCBs.

- If ballast does not have a "No PCBs" label, assume it contains PCBs and dispose of it accordingly. Some ballasts manufactured after December 1998 may not have the words "No PCBs." These ballasts will have a date of manufacture and can be managed as non-PCB ballasts.
- If ballast **does not** contain PCBs, it may be disposed of in a municipal landfill.

- If ballasts contain PCBs in the capacitor only (no PCBs in potting compound or paint), and are intact and not leaking, they may be disposed at a municipal landfill or sent for recycling. This condition only applies if the landfill operator has given permission.
- If ballasts contain PCBs in either the capacitor, the potting-compound (sound insulating material that surrounds the inner workings of a fluorescent lamp), or the ballast paint, and all are intact and not leaking; then they must be disposed in a PCB-approved landfill or sent to a PCB-approved incinerator.
- If a PCB ballast is leaking from either the potting-compound or the oil in the capacitor, the ballast must be removed from service and disposed as liquid PCB's. The only disposal option is a PCB incinerator. All PCB waste and articles that are leaking must be manifested and require the shipper, transporter, and disposal facility to notify the EPA of the PCB handling activities.

A copy of the notification form 7710-53 is available online at: http://www.epa.gov/epawaste/hazard/tsd/pcbs/pdf/771053.pdf. The EPA must be notified and an EPA identification number must be received 60 days prior to offsite shipment for disposal.

If a contractor is involved in a project such as a re-lamping or light retrofit, the property owner must submit a remediation plan to EPA 30 days before the start of the project. The contractor may submit this plan on behalf of the property owner but the property owner must have knowledge of the plan's requirements. This plan will identify the roles and responsibilities of the property owner and the contractor for cleanup and the disposal of any PCBs that may have spilled as a result of leaks from ballasts.

From the time a project begins, there is a one-year time limit for disposing of PCB-containing materials. This one-year period must include time for all handlers of the PCBs in the disposal process, including the final disposal facility.

A contractor who encounters other types of electrical equipment containing PCBs must contact EPA for guidelines. For information refer to the EPA's PCB website at www.epa.gov/epawaste/hazard/tsd/pcbs/index.htm.

Clandestine Drug Labs
Oregon Revised Statutes 453.855 thru 453.912 and OHA rules 333-040-0010 thru 0230 regulate various aspects of the detection, assessment, and decontamination of illegal drug labs. These regulations guide the licensing and certification of contractors for illegal drug lab remediation. Contractors

considering doing this kind of work should contact OHA at 971-673-0440 or www.healthoregon.org/druglab for information on licensing and certification requirements.

Treated Outdoor Wood

Treated outdoor wood, often referred to as pressure-treated wood, is wood that has been treated with a chemical to inhibit wood deterioration from a variety of organisms. The most common types of wood-preserving chemicals used today include creosote, pentachlorophenol, and inorganic arsenicals. Newer treatment chemicals include copper, zinc, quaternary ammonium compounds, and borates. Because of the chemicals used to treat the wood, extra care needs to be taken in managing treated outdoor wood waste. Recommended options include:

Reuse
When suitable, treated outdoor wood can be reused in a manner compatible with its original purpose, such as fence posts, retaining walls, and landscape timbers.

Disposal
Discarded treated outdoor wood may generally be disposed at solid waste landfills that are approved to receive the material. Some landfills may classify treated outdoor wood as a "special waste" and may have additional management restrictions.

Treated outdoor wood must not be burned in fireplaces, wood stoves, or open fires because toxic chemicals may be in the smoke or ash. Treated outdoor wood must not be used as mulch since the chipped wood will release chemicals into the environment at a greater rate than whole wood pieces. When working with treated outdoor wood avoid frequent or prolonged exposure of skin contact and inhalation of sawdust.

For applications requiring treated outdoor wood, contractors should specify, when possible, treated wood protected with alternative products such as ammonium-copper-quaternary (ACQ) or use recycled composite lumber.

Lead (Not Lead-Based Paint)

Lead is a common material in commercial structures, buildings, bridges, and demolition debris. Lead was frequently used in roofs, tank linings, electrical conduits, plumbing soft solder, lead pipes, and galvanized pipes with lead solder.

Before demolishing a structure, a contractor must check for asbestos and remove lead pipe and any hazardous materials like asbestos and mercury containing thermostats. After the structure is demolished, the debris can be disposed at a permitted landfill as long as the lead pipe and other hazardous materials are removed.

Before sandblasting or renovating commercial structures, test for leachable lead to avoid generating a hazardous waste. See Appendix A for DEQ resources.

Lead-Based Paint

Lead poisoning is a serious health problem. It can affect anyone, but young children and pregnant women are especially at risk. Lead poisoning in children can cause behavior and learning problems, as well as damage to the brain, liver and kidneys. In adults, high lead levels can cause high blood pressure, digestive and reproductive problems, nerve disorders, and kidney damage.

Lead is less prevalent in the environment than it was a few decades ago, but many buildings constructed before 1978 contain leaded paint. The Consumer Product Safety Commission restricted the amount of lead that could be added to residential paint in 1978. However, since lead-based paint inhibits the rusting and corrosion of iron and steel, it is still used on bridges, railways, ships, lighthouses, and other steel structures.

Lead contamination can occur during demolition, remodeling, maintenance, and paint preparation activities. Children and people living in older homes can be easily poisoned during remodeling. Nearly half of the childhood lead poisoning cases in Oregon found remodeling or repainting was the source of exposure. Lead abatement workers, renovators, and maintenance personnel can also be exposed to lead and bring it home to their families. To protect themselves, their customers, and their families, they must follow lead-safe work practices.

The U. S. Environmental Protection Agency requires contractors, renovators, and maintenance personnel performing renovation on homes, child care facilities, and schools built prior to 1978 to be certified and follow specific work practices to prevent lead contamination.

Some standard definitions surrounding lead-based paint:

Abatement

Any measure or set of measures designed to permanently eliminate lead-based paint hazards including, but not limited to, the removal of paint and dust, the permanent enclosure or encapsulation of lead-based paint, the replacement of painted surfaces or fixtures, or the removal or covering of soil, when lead-based paint hazards are present in such paint, dust, or soil.

Abatement does not include renovation, remodeling, landscaping, or other activities, when such activities are not designed to permanently eliminate lead-based paint hazards, but, instead, are designed to repair, restore, or remodel a given structure or dwelling, even though these activities may incidentally result in a reduction or elimination of lead-based paint hazards.

Certified and certification

An action by the OHA verifying the successful completion of an accredited training program.

Certified dust sampling technician

A technician who complete a dust-sampling course accredited by the OHA, EPA, or an EPA-authorized program.

Certified renovation firm

A company, partnership, corporation, sole proprietorship, association, or other entity certified by the OHA to conduct renovation under ORS 431.920 or licensed by the CCB under ORS 701.515.

Certified renovator

A renovator who has successfully completed a renovator course accredited by the OHA, EPA, or EPA-authorized state or tribal program.

Child occupied facility

A building, or a portion of a building, constructed prior to 1978, visited regularly by the same child, under age 6, on at least two different days within any week (Sunday through Saturday), provided that each day's visit lasts at least three hours and the combined weekly visit lasts at least six hours, and the combined annual visits last at least 60 hours. Child occupied facilities may include, but are not limited to, day-care centers, preschools, and kindergarten classrooms.

Containment

A process or arrangement of materials to protect workers and the environment by controlling exposure to the lead-contaminated dust and debris created during an abatement or renovation project.

Course completion certificate

Documentation issued by an OHA, EPA, or an EPA-authorized state or tribal accredited training program to an individual as proof of completion of an accredited renovator or refresher training course.

HEPA vacuum

A vacuum cleaner with a high-efficiency particulate air (HEPA) filter as the last filtration stage. A HEPA filter is capable of capturing particles of 0.3 microns with 99.97 percent efficiency.

Lead-based paint

Paint or other surface coatings containing lead equal to or in excess of 1.0 milligram per square centimeter or 0.5 percent by weight.

Lead-based paint activities

In the case of target housing and child occupied facilities, this means inspection, risk-assessment, and abatement.

Lead-based paint hazard

This means hazardous lead-based paint, dust-leads hazard or soil-lead hazard as identified in these rules.

Minor repair and maintenance activities

This means activities, including minor heating, ventilation or air conditioning work, electrical work, and plumbing, that disrupt 6 square feet or less of painted surface per room for interior activities, or 20 square feet or less of painted surface for exterior activities. No work practices prohibited or restricted by OAR 333-070-0090 can be used and work cannot involve window replacement or demolition of painted surfaces. Jobs, other than emergency renovations, performed in the same room within the same 30 days are the same job for determining whether the job is a minor repair and maintenance activity.

Recognized test kit

This is a commercially available kit recognized by EPA under 40 CFR 745.88 as allowing a user to determine the presence of lead at levels equal to or in excess of 1.0 milligrams per square centimeter, or more than 0.5 percent lead by weight, in a paint chip, paint powder, or painted surface.

Renovation

This is the modification of any existing structure, or portion thereof that disturbs painted surfaces. The term renovation includes, but is not limited to:

- Removal or modification of painted surfaces or painted components (e.g., modification of painted doors, surface preparation activity such as sanding, scraping, or other such activities generating paint dust)
- Removal of large structures (e.g., walls, ceiling, large surface re-plastering, major re-plumbing)
- Window replacement, weatherization projects (e.g., cutting holes in painted surfaces to install blown-in insulation or to gain access to attics, planning thresholds to install weather-stripping)
- Interim controls disturbing painted surfaces

Residential dwelling

- A detached single family dwelling unit, including attached structures such as porches and stoops; or
- A single family dwelling unit in a structure containing more than one separate residential dwelling unit, which is used or occupied, or intended to be occupied, in whole or in part, as the home or residence of one or more persons.

Room

A separate part of the inside of a building, such as a bedroom, living room, dining room, kitchen, bathroom, laundry room, or utility room. To be considered a separate room, the room must be separated from adjoining rooms by built-in walls or archways extending at least 6 inches from an intersecting wall. Half walls or bookcases count as room separators if built-in. Movable or collapsible partitions or partitions consisting solely of shelves or cabinets are not considered built-in walls. A screened in porch that is used as a living area is a room.

RRP

The Renovation, Repair, and Painting Rule under OAR 333-070.

Target housing

Any housing constructed prior to 1978, except housing for the elderly or persons with disabilities (unless any one or more children age 6 years or under resides or is expected to reside in such housing for the elderly or persons with disabilities) or any 0-bedroom dwelling.

Oregon's RRP Program

Oregon Program Administration

The federal Environmental Protection Agency created new regulations for contractors working on housing or child-occupied facilities built before 1978. In Oregon, the Construction Contractors Board and the Oregon Health Authority jointly enforce the federal Lead: Renovation, Repair and Painting Rule (RRP) program.

RRP Training

To become a certified renovator, an individual must complete the course titled "Lead Safety for Renovation, Repair, and Painting" that was developed by the EPA and the Department of Housing and Urban Development (HUD). The course must be taught by a training provider who has been accredited by OHA, EPA, or an EPA-authorized state or tribal program.

The initial RRP Certified Renovator Training is a six hour lecture and two–hour, hands-on course that business owners or employees take to learn how to comply with the RRP Rule, and HUD's Lead Safe Housing Rule. Upon completion of the course, the individual receives a course completion certificate.

Individuals who have previously completed an eligible lead renovation training course may take the EPA four-hour RRP refresher course instead of the initial eight-hour training course.

The RRP course completion certificate is valid for five years. To maintain certification, Certified Renovators must take an OHA, EPA, or EPA-authorized state accredited four-hour refresher course taught by an accredited training provider before their certification expires.

A List of Accredited Training Providers offering RRP training in Oregon is available at www.oregon.gov/ccb and www.healthoregon.org/lead.

Who CCB regulates

CCB licenses businesses and contractors who are required to have a CCB license. CCB administers the new "Lead-Based Paint Renovation (LBPR) Contractor License." If a business is licensed by CCB, it is **not** required to be certified by OHA. For more information on the CCB LBPR contractor's license, or to apply for the license, visit CCB's website at www.oregon.gov/ccb or call 503-378-4621.

Who OHA regulates

Oregon Health Authority certifies businesses or agencies (called firms) working on target housing or child occupied facilities that are **not** required to have a CCB license. Examples of businesses or agencies that do not require a CCB license to perform renovation and repair work include:

- Schools or school districts.
- Property managers or maintenance workers.
- Landlords or rental property owners.
- Child care facility maintenance staff.

To become an RRP Certified Renovation Firm with OHA, a business or agency must:

- Complete the RRP Certified Renovation Firm application.
- Submit the application and certification fees to Oregon Health Authority.
- Employ a Certified Renovator to conduct OHA renovation or maintenance activities.
- Follow the standards for conducting lead-based paint renovation activities as prescribed OAR 333-070.
- Maintain all required records for a period of three years.

Certified Renovators

Certified renovation activities must be performed and/or directed by a Certified Renovator. Certification as a Certified Renovator only requires successful completion of an OHA, EPA, or an EPA authorized state or tribal approved training course conducted by an accredited training provider. No application or fee is required to become a Certified Renovator. Instead, the training course completion certificate serves as the renovation certificate. To maintain certification, Certified Renovators must take an OHA, EPA, or an EPA-authorized state or tribal program approved refresher course taught by an accredited training provider, before their certification expires.

Responsibilities of a Certified Renovator

- Be trained by the OHA, EPA, or an EPA authorized state or tribal program approved accredited training provider
- Perform work or direct lead-safe work practices to prevent lead contamination
- Keep a copy of the initial or refresher training certificate on each worksite
- Provide uncertified workers with on-the-job training
- Use EPA-recognized test kits to identify lead-based paint

- Be physically present at the worksite while posting signs, containing work areas, and cleaning work areas
- Be available by telephone when offsite
- Maintain the containment to keep dust and debris within the work area.
- Conduct the cleaning verification procedure
- Prepare and maintain required records

Enforcement

CCB and OHA have enforcement authority under Oregon ORS 431.920 to suspend, revoke, or modify a certification to perform lead-based paint activities or renovation if the holder of the certification fails to comply with state or federal statutes or regulations related to lead-based paint.

Other Lead-Based Paint Regulations

Oregon Department of Environmental Quality (DEQ)

The Oregon DEQ is responsible for managing the proper disposal of potentially hazardous wastes, including lead-based paint debris and waste water. Lead dust and debris from residential properties can be disposed of as household waste and discarded as trash. For information concerning the proper disposal of lead-based paint waste from residential households see the DEQ policy titled, "Applicability of the RCRA Household Waste Exclusion to Wastes and Debris Containing Lead-Based Paint." Or call DEQ at 800-452-4011.

Oregon Lead Abatement and Inspection Program

Lead abatement refers to work done for the specific purpose of permanently removing lead-based paint and lead-based paint hazards from a home. Lead paint abatement services include abatement, inspection, and risk assessment. More about the federal lead abatement rules and regulations can be found on EPA's Lead Abatement web page.

U.S. Housing and Urban Development (HUD)

HUD's Lead-Safe Housing Rule applies to every home built prior to 1978 that receives federal housing assistance where greater than 2 square feet of interior, or 20 square feet of exterior lead-based paint is disturbed during renovation, repair, or painting. If a contractor works in federally-assisted target housing, certain actions are required to address lead hazards and work practice standards that may differ from the EPA's Renovation, Repair, and Painting requirements. HUD's web page www.hud.gov/offices/lead/enforcement/lshr.cfm has more information on the differences between EPA's RRP regulations and the HUD Lead-Safe Housing Rule.

Occupational Safety and Health Administration (OSHA).
OSHA has a Lead in Construction Standard that outlines worker protection requirements for construction workers exposed to lead. The standard includes: requirements addressing exposure assessment, methods of compliance, respiratory protection, protective clothing and equipment, hygiene facilities and practices, medical surveillance, medical removal protection, employee information and training, signs, recordkeeping and observation of monitoring. For information about OR-OSHA's occupational lead standards and regulations visit www.orosha.gov or call 800-922-2689.

Lead-Based Paint Certification (Abatement)
The lead-based paint activities rules apply to all individuals and firms who are engaged in lead-based paint activities (abatement and inspection) as defined in OAR 333-069-0015(38), except persons who perform these activities within residential dwellings they own, unless the residential dwelling is occupied by a person or persons other than the owner or the owner's immediate family while these activities are being performed, or a child residing in the building has been identified as having an elevated blood lead level.

Only person(s) certified by OHA and licensed by the CCB may perform lead abatement activities. The following lists lead abatement activities and who can perform the activities.
- Lead-based paint inspection and risk assessment of target housing, child occupied facilities and schools with children under six years of age: lead inspector and risk assessor.
- Clearance testing: lead inspector and risk assessor.
- Lead abatement projects: lead supervisor and worker.

Work Practice Standards for Abatement Work
When performing any lead-based paint activity described by a certified and licensed individual as an inspection, lead hazard screen, risk assessment or abatement, a certified and licensed individual must perform that activity in compliance with the rules contained in OAR 333-069.

Notice of Abatement (NOA)
Any business or individual conducting lead-based paint abatement activities in target housing or child occupied facilities must notify the OHA at least seven business days before the start date of the project by completing and submitting a "Notice of Abatement" form available from the OHA. The "Notice of Abatement" shall specify the time of day abatement activities will start and the date on which abatement activities will be completed. The

OHA may reject a "Notice of Abatement" form that has not been completed in full and signed by the applicant.

Amendments to or cancellations of the original "Notice of Abatement," including completion-date changes must be submitted 24 hours prior to the original start date. In the event of an emergency, an original or amended "Notice of Abatement" describing the emergency must be submitted within 24 hours of the emergency.

A request for waiver of the 'seven-business day' advance notice requirement must be submitted in writing and granted in writing by OHA before work under the waiver can start.

Occupant protection plan

The abatement supervisor or project designer, together with the building owner, must decide whether the occupants and their belongings need to be relocated. This decision is based upon a risk assessment of health and safety issues of the proposed abatement work and not on cost or convenience. A written occupant protection plan shall be developed prior to all abatement projects. The document shall be prepared by a licensed supervisor or project designer and shall be made available to all occupants and at the job site for inspection at the project site. HUD also requires an occupant protection plan for lead-based paint hazards in publicly funded or subsidized housing built before 1978.

Warning signs

Every job site where lead abatement is being conducted shall bear a sign, readable from 30 feet, warning of lead-based paint hazards. The general public, residents, and especially young children and pregnant women must be kept away from the abatement work.

Scope of work

A scope of work for the abatement project shall be made available for inspection at the project site.

Employee protection

Refer to OR-OSHA requirements for respiratory and personal protective equipment (PPE).

Prohibited work practices
- Do not dry scrape or sand.
- Do not use power sanders or grinders without dust controls or HEPA vacuum attachments.
- Do not use open flame burning or torching.
- Do not use high-pressure power washers without a protective enclosure.
- Do not use paint strippers with methylene chloride.

Safe work practices:
- Contain the work area to prevent dust and debris from spreading.
- Control dust by working wet while sanding or scraping.
- Use HEPA attachments on power tools.
- Close off and seal the work area with materials such as plastic sheeting and duct tape.
- Operate a heat gun only at a temperature below 1,100 F.
- Keep pregnant women, children, and pets out of the work area.
- Cleanup of the entire abatement area must be done every day using wet methods and a HEPA vacuum. Collect waste and debris and secure in plastic bags.
- A final visual inspection and clearance dust sampling must be done by a certified Inspector or Risk Assessor upon project completion and final cleanup
- Lead dust and debris can be disposed of as household waste and discarded as trash. For further information call the Oregon DEQ at 800-452-4011.

Spills and Releases
Reporting
Oregon Emergency Response System (OERS) must be immediately notified of any release of a reportable quantity (RQ) that impacts soil, air, or water. Also, anyone who spills petroleum or hazardous materials in waters of the state, or on the ground that is threatening to enter Oregon waters, must report the spill to the National Response Center (NRC).

RQs for these materials are for:
- Spills of petroleum products
  - Into waters or threatening to spill into waters – any amount.
  - Onto land surface – any quantity over one barrel.
- Hazardous substances – the amount equal to or greater than the reportable quantity listed in Title 40 CFR (Code of Federal Regulations) and ORS 466.

For more regulatory information, see Appendix D. For federal notification, there is no RQ for spills of petroleum materials to land surface.

Cleanup

Despite the amount spilled, all spills must be cleaned up immediately. Trained personnel should perform spill cleanup. A business that does not employ trained personnel should contract with a qualified spill cleanup contractor to manage the cleanup. A business should select a contractor and have agreements in place before a spill occurs. This will improve responsiveness to a spill incident and reduce cleanup time. Less time spent between the occurrence of a spill and the beginning of cleanup often reduces safety risks, liabilities, and cleanup costs.

Anyone who has questions about how to clean up a spill that is less than a reportable quantity should call OERS.

Eliminate Potential Sources of Spills

Identify potential sources of releases and eliminate them or reduce the likelihood of an occurrence by:

- Securely storing containers and keeping them well away from traffic areas
- Trying not to leave tanks and heavy equipment unattended under conditions that lend themselves easily to acts of theft or vandalism
- Having fuel pumps installed in both fuel tanks of semi-tractors and having the crossover line eliminated (crossover line damage is the leading cause of transportation spills)

Underground Storage Tanks

Environmental Issues

Oregon has adopted and modified federal regulations for underground storage tanks (USTs). Tanks must meet specific equipment and operational standards for spill and overfill protection, corrosion protection, and leak detection. The purpose of these regulations is to prevent or detect leaks early to lessen environmental impacts, particularly for groundwater.

DEQ Service Provider Licensing

The DEQ must license businesses and individuals that perform UST services (installation/retrofit, decommissioning, cathodic protection, and tank tightness testing) and soil cleanup. Individuals must take a test before applying for a supervisor license. A business license fee is good for one year. The supervisor license fee is good for two years. Refer to chart on *Activities that Require Special Licensing, Permits, or Notices.*

DEQ Notification of Tank Service

Tank owners/operators and service providers must notify DEQ in writing 30 days before installing, retrofitting, or decommissioning a tank and again verbally three days in advance of the confirmed date. There is an installation fee for each new tank, plus the annual tank compliance fee. DEQ will not issue an Operation Certificate to the tank owner until all required checklists and a report have been submitted. Facilities cannot receive fuel delivery without this certificate from DEQ.

DEQ Contamination Reporting Requirements

Confirmed and suspected spills and releases must be reported within 24 hours. UST service providers must report releases within 72 hours if the tank owner does not.

Heating Oil Tanks

Environmental Issues

Heating oil tanks are usually located close to the home and leaks often spread under the house. In severe situations, homeowners could be exposed to vapors from the oil and groundwater can be contaminated.

DEQ Service Provider Licensing

DEQ must license businesses and individuals who perform "heating oil services" (site assessments for contamination, decommissioning tanks, or cleaning up releases). Individuals must pass a test before applying for a supervisor license. Heating oil tank service providers must have professional liability insurance coverage for $500,000 per occurrence and $1,000,000 total. They must certify that the work they performed meets all technical regulatory requirements. A business license is for a year, and a supervisor license is for two years. Refer to chart on *Activities that Require Special Licensing, Permits, or Notices.*

DEQ Contamination Reporting Requirements

Heating oil tank service providers must report a release to DEQ within 72 hours. The homeowner is also responsible for reporting.

Solid Waste Best Practices

Contractors should try to reduce the amount of waste generated at each job site. Construction of new, single-family homes typically generates between four and seven tons of waste with about half of this being wood, lumber, and composites that may have other uses. Contractors who reduce their waste stream also reduce their disposal fees and construction costs.

Contractors can use the following techniques to reduce the amount of waste produced at a construction project:

- Design to use fewer materials. For example, avoid building headers over interior doors on non-load-bearing walls.
- Use designs that accommodate standard lumber and drywall sizes.
- Estimate and purchase carefully to avoid buying materials that cannot be used.
- Protect materials from weather damage.
- Measure and cut carefully.
- Make subcontractors responsible for their own waste.
- Use alternative products such as structural panels and engineered wood products that can be ordered in the exact size needed.
- Deconstruct and salvage materials for another use.

In 2001, Marion County contractors disposed of about 3,227 tons of construction debris, a drop from 7,800 tons in 2000. Contractors who use waste reduction practices can benefit by:

- Producing less waste
- Using less toxic materials
- Using less energy
- Using more products made from recycled materials and secondary resources
- Reducing liability by producing less hazardous waste
- Creating a safer, healthier workplace for workers and occupants

Create a Plan for Managing Waste

Estimate the types and amounts of waste that will be produced in each project, and determine the best way to manage each. Commonly recovered materials from construction projects include wood, scrap metal, cardboard and other packaging, land-clearing debris and other vegetative wastes, and rubble (rock, concrete, and asphalt paving).

Certain communities can recycle other waste materials, such as some types of carpeting and carpet pads, new sheetrock pieces, asphalt roofing, and ceiling panels. Some wastes will require special handling, including fluorescent lighting tubes, thermostats, creosote or arsenic-treated wood, asbestos, and contaminated soil. Large appliances, lead-acid batteries, used oil, and tires generally may not be disposed and must be recycled.

It is best if the plan for handling waste is in writing. That way the plan can easily be shared with subcontractors and other workers onsite. Having specific goals for recovery (overall or for each material) will help motivate workers to follow the plan.

Communicate the Plan

Once a waste management plan has been created, make sure everybody on the job is aware of the plan and is following it. Put specifications from the plan in all contracts with subcontractors so they will know what is expected and will follow the plan. Include updates on recycling and recovery in any job site or safety meeting. Mark recycling areas and containers well, and include lists of what is accepted and what is prohibited for each material that is separated for recovery.

Deconstruction and Salvage

If a project involves a significant amount of demolition in order to build new structures or remodel existing ones, the contractor should analyze whether deconstruction and salvage of major building components might make more sense than simply wrecking the existing structure and hauling it away as trash. Major timbers, fixtures, appliances, cabinets, doors, windows, moldings, hardware, brick, and wood flooring are just some of the materials that may have significant salvage value.

Some building owners may also be able to obtain substantial tax benefits through deconstruction and donation to nonprofit groups. There are nonprofits in Oregon that will work with contractors to arrange deconstruction and then accept the donated material. Also, contractors might find salvaged materials that can be incorporated into new construction or remodeling projects. Oregon has several businesses and nonprofit organizations specializing in the resale of used building materials. Building owners can then claim the value of the salvaged items as a tax deduction on their federal and Oregon taxes. Additionally, components of the structure being rebuilt can sometimes be incorporated into the new structure.

Separated Versus Mixed Waste Recovery

Generally, separate collection and recovery can result in the highest recovery, the highest value obtained for the material recovered, and the lowest disposal tonnage. However, job site conditions may not allow multiple containers onsite, rental of multiple containers for storage might be expensive, and there might not be enough waste generated to warrant the separate collection of the materials. In these cases, it may make more sense to intermix the wastes and send the entire load to a mixed waste processing facility, or if there are contract requirements for separating waste, contract with another business for these services. See Appendix A for resources in managing solid waste disposal and recovery.

For small jobs with limited space, mixed waste processing facilities might be the most efficient way to handle and recover the waste produced. For larger jobs, segregation of different materials onsite may be cheaper and will usually result in greater recovery tonnage.

Contractors cannot take mixed solid waste back from job sites to their yards for processing and sorting unless they have a mixed waste processing facility permit. However, they generally can separate out materials that are practical to recycle and take those separated materials back to their yards until there is enough material to sell. Materials that are feasible to recycle can be stored this way without a DEQ permit.

Green Building

Green building applies basic compliance with environmental laws and regulations to address a broader set of environmental issues. Through green building, contractors construct buildings that are healthier for living and working, more energy and resource efficient, less expensive to operate, and more durable.

Fundamental Objectives of Green Building

Green building combines fundamental environmental objectives, including:
- Conserving natural resources.
- Increasing energy efficiency.
- Improving indoor air quality.
- Reducing onsite impacts.

The sections below briefly introduce each topic.

Natural Resource Conservation

Conventional building practices consume large quantities of various materials including wood, plastics, metals, cardboard, paper, water, and other natural resources. According to a U.S. Geological Survey, non-renewable construction materials (plastics, paper, oil-based products, etc.) now account for 60 percent of total non-food, non-fuel, raw material consumption in the United States.

The manufacture of some building materials requires considerable amounts of energy and produces air and water pollution. The continued use of natural resources for building materials may harm the environment, and deplete nonrenewable resources.

Builders have an expanding range of green building materials from which to choose. Recycled-content decking, reclaimed lumber, reusable concrete forms and other products typically have reduced environmental impact over their life cycle while improving quality and durability of materials. For example, decking material made out of recycled plastic resins mixed with wood waste fibers can last longer than wood decks and never needs to be treated or painted.

Water conservation is another important issue. Despite Oregon's reputation for rain, water shortages already exist in Oregon communities. Wise water usage reduces the strain on resources while lowering expenses. Today, builders can take advantage of a new generation of high-efficiency appliances and landscape water management systems.

Energy Efficiency

Energy efficiency is a cornerstone of any green building project. Generation and use of energy are major contributors to air pollution and global climate change. Contrary to what many Oregonians may believe, the majority of electricity used in Oregon is generated not from hydropower, but from non-renewable fuels such as coal and natural gas. Improved energy efficiency and use of renewable energy sources are effective ways to reduce the potential of energy supply interruptions, improve air quality, and reduce the impacts of global warming.

The state of Oregon set a goal (HB 3543) to reduce greenhouse gas emissions 75 percent below 1990 levels by 2050. The City of Portland and Multnomah County have adopted a Climate Action Plan that calls for similar reductions. Home energy uses produce about 20 percent of these emissions. Oregon is developing a voluntary Reach Energy Code to guide design and construction of low-energy houses and apartments. Reducing the need for energy while maintaining comfort, health and safety, is an essential part of achieving Oregon's climate goals.

Also, energy efficiency is an economically effective choice for consumers. Lower utility expenses allow homeowners to enjoy financial benefits year after year. Energy-efficiency strategies include orienting the building to maximize solar exposure in winter and shade in the summer, designing the building orientation to utilize natural ventilation (including operable windows) and natural day lighting, exceeding code requirements for insulation, installing double-glazed/low-E windows, installing high-efficiency appliances and lighting, and using solar water heating.

Indoor Air Quality

The EPA reports that the air in new homes can be 10 times more polluted than outdoor air. Poor indoor air quality can be caused by inadequate ventilation and the off-gassing of chemicals found in many building materials, as well as mold and mildew that build up in poorly designed, constructed, and/or maintained buildings.

The building products industry has responded to indoor pollution problems by developing alternative paint, finish, and adhesive products. For example, solvent-free adhesives used in flooring and countertops can eliminate many of the suspected and known human carcinogens used in some conventional products. Paints, varnishes, and cleaners that contain fewer volatile organic compounds (VOCs) are now commonly available from most major manufacturers.

During construction, best management practices can prevent future mold problems. These practices include:

- Material storage to keep interior building materials dry.
- Properly installing all water equipment and checking for leaks.
- Properly installing and checking all penetrations in the building envelope, such as doors, windows, and ducts.
- Properly installing vapor barriers.
- Installing drywall to help wick moisture while avoiding direct contact with concrete.
- Properly applying flashing and caulking.

Other measures contractors can take to improve air quality include:

- Sealing materials that contain formaldehyde with waterproof or water-resistant finishes like paint, wood finishes, counter tops, and floor coverings to prevent moisture entry.
- Reducing exposure to volatile organic compounds (VOCs) by carefully selecting and storing materials, finishes, cleaning compounds, and other chemicals.
- Reducing pathogens and biological contaminants, including mold, mildew, and dust mites.

The contract between the owner and contractor should clearly articulate the consequences and responsibility for addressing unexpected contaminants that compromise indoor air quality.

Reduce Onsite Impacts

New construction can have significant environmental impacts on the local environment of the job site, both during construction and following construction (occupancy). Green building practices include minimizing site disturbance to avoid soil erosion, protecting indigenous vegetation, and planting native and low-maintenance plants for landscaping and managing stormwater onsite.

Benefits of Green Building

There are many reasons to build green. These include a concern for the environment, an interest in building more efficiently, health considerations, and social benefits to a business that is viewed as being environmentally responsible. While green building and its environmental benefits are becoming more mainstream, some green building practices and materials cost more. It is important to understand the added value from green building. Green building can translate to energy efficiency, improved indoor air quality, healthier living and work spaces, more productive work spaces, lower maintenance and operation costs, and durability.

Green Building Certification Options

Green home certification is available for both new and remodel projects. Earth Advantage (www.earthadvantage.org) provides new home certification and technical support. A specialist works with the builder on plan review, materials selection, construction methods, consultations during construction, and performance testing to verify installed measures. A completed home is certified as meeting Earth Advantage standards. Remodels can be certified by a similar process.

Energy Trust of Oregon (ETO) offers the Energy Star New Home certification program, providing financial incentives to qualified energy-efficient homes. The program is available within the service areas of Portland General Electric, Pacific Power, Northwest Natural, and Cascade Natural Gas. Within the ETO area, Earth Advantage incorporates Energy Star standards, so builders of Earth Advantage certified homes also receive ETO financial incentives. More information is available at www.energytrust.org.

Oregon Department of Energy offers builders a Business Energy Tax Credit incentive of up to $12,000 for an Oregon High Performance Home. Qualified homes are 30 percent more energy efficient than if built to state energy code and include solar energy measures. Homes are certified by the Energy Star New Home program. Oregon High Performance Home can be substituted for Energy Star in the Earth Advantage certification.

For remodels, ETO offers Home Performance with Energy Star. Home Performance contractors perform in-depth assessment of a house to identify cost-effective energy saving measures and install and test the package of measures the builder and/or homeowner select. Participating contractors are certified by Building Performance Institute training programs. ETO provides financial incentives to offset the cost of the measures.

LEED-Homes, or Leadership in Energy and Environmental Design for Homes, is a nationally recognized green building rating program sponsored by the U.S. Green Building Council (www.usgbc.org). A LEED-certified home is designed and constructed in accordance with the rigorous guidelines of the LEED for Homes green building certification program. LEED for Homes is a consensus-developed, third party-verified, voluntary rating system that promotes the design and construction of high-performance green homes.

The Oregon State Business Energy Tax Credit Program offers a tax credit for projects built to achieve a minimum "silver" rating using the LEED rating system. In Oregon, Earth Advantage is the LEED-Homes program administrator, providing support services including project registration, technical assistance and certification.

The Green Building Initiative, Green Globes (www.thegbi.org) is another nationally/internationally recognized system for green building certification. For builders who prefer to independently select and install measures to create a green home, the National Association of Homebuilders and International Codes Council have developed the National Green Building Standard ICC-700-2008. The standard, available at www.buildersbooks.com, includes detailed descriptions of construction materials and methods.

Training and Education
Earth Advantage Institute (www.earthadvantage.com) offers green building courses for building industry professionals, including the Certified Sustainable Homes Professional series, which provides participants with technical skills and knowledge required to design and build high performance homes.

Information Resources
METRO and City of Portland (Washington, Multnomah and Clackamas counties) can call the Green Building Hotline at 503-823-5431 to get answers to building-related questions.

A comprehensive listing of current incentives and tax credits is available at the Database for State Incentives for Renewables and Efficiency (DSIRE) website at www.dsireusa.org.

Information and workshops about solar electric and solar hot water systems are available from Solar Now! (www.solarnoworegon.org).

For further contact information and resources, see Appendix A.

Appendix A
Environmental Management Resource List

AIR QUALITY

Open burning

Contact the nearest regional office (see Appendix B)

Dust, odors and other nuisance conditions at construction projects

DEQ Air Quality Division
811 SW Sixth Avenue
Portland, OR 97204
503-229-5359 or 800-452-4011

ASBESTOS

Worker activities, abatement, and proper disposal

Contact the nearest DEQ Regional Office (see Appendix B)
For specific counties, contact:

- Clackamas, Clatsop, Columbia, Multnomah, Tillamook, and Washington counties: 503- 229-5982 or 800-452-4011
- Benton, Lincoln, Linn, Marion, Polk, and Yamhill counties: 503-378-5086 or 800-349-7677
- Jackson, Josephine, and Eastern Douglas counties:541-776-6107 or 877-823-3216
- Coos, Curry, and Western Douglas counties: 541-269-2721 ext. 22
- Lane County: Contact Lane Regional Air Protection Agency , 541-736-1056 ext. 222
- For the area east of the Cascades: 541-633-2019 or 541-278-4626

Regulations and information on employee safety and handling of asbestos

OREGON-OSHA
1225 Ferry Street SE
Salem, OR 97301
503-378-3274

BATTERIES

Hazard identification and proper disposal

DEQ Land Quality Division
811 SW Sixth Avenue
Portland, OR 97204
503-229-5913 or 800-452-4011
The Rechargeable Battery Recycling Corporation (RBRC) at 1-877-723-1297 (toll free) or at www.rbrc.org.
Contact the nearest DEQ Regional Office (see Appendix B)

GREEN BUILDING

U.S. Green Building Council

Leadership in Energy and Environmental Design standards and certification system, at www.usgbc.org/

Oregon Energy Tax Credit

www.oregon.gov/ENERGY/index.shtml or call the Oregon Office of Energy at 800-221-8035

The Green Building Source Guide

A directory of resources produced by the Oregon Housing & Community Services: www.ohcs.oregon.gov/OHCS/DO/docs/gbsourceguide.pdf

Sustainable Buildings Industry (SIBC)

Green Building Guidelines: Meeting the Demand for Low-Energy, Resource Efficient Homes www.sbicouncil.org/displaycommon.cfm?an=1&subarticlenbr=113

Energy and Environmental Building Association (EEBA)

Provides technical resources, case studies and educational opportunities at www.eeba.org

Building Science Corporation

Offers a content rich website with extensive resources and links for builders at www.buildingscience.com

GREEN BUILDING (continued)

Other sources and green building groups:
- www.buildinggreen.com, an independent publishing company providing unbiased information about green building
- www.greenbuildingadvisor.com, a complete source for building, designing and remodeling green homes
- Builder's Guide to Mixed-Humid Climates, www.buildingsciencepress.com
- Green Spec, a comprehensive listing of green building products and materials, www.buildinggreen.com/ecommerce/gs.cfm?
- US EPA Green Homes resources: www.epa.gov/greenhomes
- New Home Construction Guidelines and Home Remodeling Guidelines (Alameda County Waste Management Authority): www.stopwaste.org/home/index.asp?page=269
- GreenPoint Checklist (Alameda County Waste Management Authority): www.stopwaste.org/home/index.asp?page=470
- City of Portland's Green Building Program includes case studies and technical resources: www.portlandonline.com/bps/index.cfm?c=41481
- Landscaping for Stormwater: www.portlandonline.com/bes/index.cfm?c=32142
- Green Globes: www.thegbi.org

HAZARDOUS WASTE

Managing hazardous waste
DEQ Land Quality Division
811 SW Sixth Avenue
Portland, OR 97204
503-229-5913 or 800-452-4011

EPA Oregon Operations Office
811 SW Sixth Avenue, Third Floor
Portland, OR 97204
503-326-3250

Oregon Department of Transportation
355 Capitol Street NE
Salem, OR 97301
503-378-6699

Identification numbers
DEQ Land Quality Division
811 SW Sixth Avenue
Portland, OR 97204
503-229-6938

Spill reporting and cleanup
The Oregon Emergency Response System (OERS); 800-452-0311
The National Response Center (NRC); 800-424-8802

HEATING OIL TANKS

Information on home heating oil tanks
DEQ Home Heating Oil Tanks
1550 NW Eastman Parkway, Suite 290
Gresham, OR 97030
503-667-8414 or 800-452-4011

ILLEGAL DRUG LAB DECONTAMINATION

LEAD

Information on the health effects and sources of lead exposure and how to test for and prevent lead poisoning

Oregon Health Authority
Lead Poisoning Prevention Program
800 NE Oregon, Suite 640
Portland, OR 97232
971-673-0440
www.healthoregon.org/lead

Lead as demolition debris

Contact DEQ at 503-229-5165

LEAD-BASED PAINT

Lead occupational exposure

OR-OSHA
1225 Ferry Street SE
Salem, OR 97301
503-378-3274

DEQ Hazard Notification

DEQ Oregon Operations Office
811 SW Sixth Avenue, Third Floor
Portland, OR 97204
503-326-3250

HUD Lead-Safe Housing Rule

HUD
400 SW Sixth Avenue, Suite 700
Portland, OR 97204-1632
800-767-7478 or 800-569-4287

Training Accreditation and Certification

Oregon Health Authority
Lead-Based Paint Program, Department of Human Services
800 NE Oregon Street, Suite 640
Portland, OR 97232
971-673-0440
www.healthoregon.org/lead

Lead-Based Paint Endorsement and License

Construction Contractors Board (CCB)
700 Summer Street NE
Salem, OR 97310-0150
503-378-4621

MERCURY CONTAINING LAMPS –
FLUORESCENT AND HIGH INTENSITY DISCHARGE (HID) LAMPS

Information on disposal of HID lamps

DEQ Land Quality Division
811 SW Sixth Avenue
Portland, OR 97204
503-229-5913 or 800-452-4011
Contact the nearest DEQ Regional Office (see Appendix B)

MERCURY THERMOSTATS

Information on who collects mercury containing thermostats, prohibited installation and proper disposal

Thermostat Recycling Corporation (TRC) at www.nema.org/gov/ehs/trc/
DEQ Land Quality Division
811 SW Sixth Avenue
Portland, OR 97204
503-229-5913

Department of Consumer Business Services
350 Winter Street NE
Salem, OR 97301
503-378-4100

Annual notice to contractors on prohibiting installation of mercury thermostats

Construction Contractors Board (CCB)
700 Summer Street NE
Salem, OR 97310-0150
503-378-4621

NOISE POLLUTION

Information on noise pollution

Check city and county ordinance

POLYCHLORINATED BIPHENYLS (PCBs)

Information on proper disposal and hazardous notification

EPA Oregon Operations Office
811 SW Sixth Avenue, Third Floor
Portland, OR 97204
503-326-3250

EPA Region 10 PCB Coordinator
Seattle, WA
206-553-6693

RADON

EPA publications

- "Home Buyer's and Seller's Guide to Radon"
- "Building Radon Out," a step-by-step guide on how to build radon- resistant houses

Publications can be obtained from:
Oregon Health Authority
Radiation Protection Services
800 NE Oregon Street, Suite 640
Portland, OR 97232
971-673-0440
www/healthoregon.org/radon

REFRIGERANTS CHLOROFLUOROCARBONS (CFCs)

Information on CFCs that are contaminated in refrigerants and refrigeration equipment

EPA Oregon Operations Office
811 SW Sixth Avenue, Third Floor
Portland, OR 97204
503-326-3250

SOLID WASTE
Managing solid waste DEQ Land Quality Division 811 SW Sixth Avenue Portland, OR 97204 503-229-5913 or 800-452-4011 Contact the nearest DEQ Regional Office
Recycling and deconstruction resources • Check in local phone book under "Recycling" • Check with garbage hauler and drop box companies for their recycling services • In Portland Metro area, contact METRO at 503-234-3000 or go to www.metro-region.org • In Marion County, contact Dept. of Public Works at 503-588-5169 or www.co.marion.or.us/PW/ES/info.htm for "Waste Reduction and Disposal User Guide" and "Waste Reduction Strategies for Businesses"
Online material exchanges Site where contractors can list surplus and others can locate these materials, including clean fill: www.nwmaterialsmart.org/
Construction project waste management information The National Assoc. of Home Builders at www.nahbrc.org/builder/index.aspx, and type "Construction Waste Management" in the search window
Salvage and recycling planning resources Metro Construction Industry Recycling Toolkit is available online at www.metro-region.org/toolkit Contact the nearest DEQ Regional Office

UNDERGROUND STORAGE TANKS (USTs)
Information on USTs DEQ Land Quality Division Underground Storage Tank Compliance Section 811 SW Sixth Avenue Portland, OR 97204 503-229-5913 or 800-452-4011 Contact the nearest DEQ regional office

WATER QUALITY PROTECTION
Water well licensing and construction water supply wells Oregon Water Resources Department 725 Summer Street NE, Suite A Salem, OR 97301 503-986-0900
Well monitoring www.wrd.state.or.us
Sewage Disposal Service Business licensing for installation and servicing DEQ Onsite Program 165 East 7th Ave, Suite 100 Eugene, OR 97401 541-686-7905 or 800-844-8467

WATER QUALITY PROTECTION (continued)

WPCF Onsite permits
Contact Regional DEQ Office

Hookup of subsurface sewage disposal systems (septic)
Construction Contractors Board (CCB)
700 Summer Street NE, Suite 300
Salem, OR 97310-0150
503-378-4621

Department of Consumer Business Services
Building Codes Division
Labor & Industries Building
350 Winter Street NE
Salem, OR 97301-3873
503-378-4100

Hookup to sanitary sewer system
Construction Contractors Board (CCB)
700 Summer Street NE, Suite 300
Salem, OR 97310-0150
503-378-4621

Department of Consumer Business Services
Building Codes Division
Labor & Industries Building
350 Winter Street NE
Salem, OR 97301-3873
503-378-4100

Soil erosion and sediment control
DEQ Water Quality Division
811 SW Sixth Avenue
Portland, OR 97204
503-229-5279 or 800-452-4011
Contact the nearest DEQ Regional Office

Water quality requirements in specific river basins
DEQ Water Quality Division
811 SW Sixth Avenue
Portland, OR 97204
800-452-4011

Underground Injection Control (UIC) system requirements for subsurface discharge of water and wastewater
DEQ Water Quality Division
811 SW Sixth Avenue
Portland, OR 97204
503-229-5696 or 800-452-4011

Construction activities in natural waterways
- **For Section 401 Certification**: DEQ Water Quality Division, 811 SW Sixth Avenue, Portland, OR 97204, 503-229-5846 or 800-452-4011
- **For Section 404 Permit**: Department of Army Corps of Engineers, Regulatory Permits, P.O. Box 2946, Portland, OR 97208-2946, 503-808-4371 or 503-808-4373, www.nwd.usace.army.mil
- **For Oregon Removal-Fill Permit**: Oregon Division of State Lands, 775 Summer Street NE, Suite 100, Salem, OR 97310-1279, 503-986-5200 www.oregonstatelands.us/DSL/PERMITS/index.shtml
- **For Coast Zone Concurrence**: Oregon Dept. of Land Conservation and Development, 635 Capitol NE, Suite 150, Salem, OR 97301, 503-373-0050
- **For Wellhead Protection**: DEQ Water Quality Division, 811 SW Sixth Avenue, Portland, OR 97204, 503-229-5846 or 800-452-4011

Appendix B
DEQ Regional and Branch Offices

DEQ office staff is available to answer questions. Contact the office nearest you directly or call toll-free within Oregon, 800-452-4011.

DEQ HEADQUARTERS

Headquarters - Portland
811 SW Sixth Avenue
Portland, OR 97204
503-229-5696
800-452-4011 (toll-free in Oregon)
Fax: 503-229-6124
TDD: 503-229-6993

Laboratory Division
3150 NW 229th Avenue, Suite 150
Hillsboro OR 97124
503-693-5700
Fax: 503-693-4999
Air Quality Division: 503-229-5359
Land Division: 503-229-5913
Water Division: 503-229-5297

NORTHWEST REGION

Portland
2020 SW Fourth Avenue, Suite 400
Portland, OR 97201
503-229-5263
Fax: (503) 229-6945

North Coast Branch Office
65 N Highway 101, Suite G
Warrenton, OR 97146
503-861-3280

Tillamook
2310 1st Street, Suite 4
Tillamook, OR 97141
503-842-3038

WESTERN REGION

Salem
750 Front St NE, Suite120
Salem, OR 97301-1039
503-378-8240

Eugene
165 East Seventh Ave, Suite 110
Eugene, OR 97401
541-686-7838

Medford
221 Stewart Avenue, Suite 201
Medford, OR 97501
Phone: (541) 776-6010

Coos Bay
381 N Second Street
Coos Bay, OR 97420
541-269-2721

EASTERN REGION

Baker City
2101 Main Street, Suite 207

Baker City, OR 97814
541-523-9097

Bend
475 NE Bellevue, Suite 110
Bend, OR 97701
541-388-6146

Columbia Gorge
Columbia Gorge Community College
400 E Scenic Drive, Building #307
The Dalles, OR 97058
541-298-7255

Hermiston
256 East Hurlburt, Suite 117
Hermiston, OR 97838
541-567-8297

Pendleton
700 SE Emigrant, #330
Pendleton, OR 97801
541-276-4063

Appendix C
DEQ Offices and County Contacts for Onsite Wastewater Treatment Systems

Baker County
DEQ Eastern Region (Pendleton)
700 SE Emigrant, Suite 330
Pendleton, OR 97801
541-276-4063
Fax: 541-278-4063

Benton County
County Health Department
530 NW 27th
Corvallis, OR 97330
541-766-6841

Clackamas County
Water Environment Services
150 Beavercreek Road
Oregon City, OR 97045
503 742-4740

Clatsop County
DEQ North Coast Branch Office (Warrenton)
65 N Highway 101, Suite 202
Warrenton, OR 97146
503-861-3280
Fax: 503-861-3259

Columbia County
County Land Development Services
230 Strand Street
St. Helens, OR 97051
503-397-1501

Coos County
DEQ Coos Bay Branch Office
381 N Second Street
Coos Bay, OR
541-269-2721
Fax: 541-269-7984

Crook County
County Environmental Health Department
Crook Co. Courthouse
300 NE Third Street
Prineville, OR 97754
541-447-8155

Curry County
County Public Services
Curry Co. Courthouse
P.O. Box 746
Gold Beach, OR 97444
541-247-7011 Ext. 229

Deschutes County
County Community Development Department
117 NW Lafayette Avenue
Bend, OR 97701
541-388-6575

Douglas County
Planning Department, Room 106
Justice Bldg., Douglas County Courthouse
Roseburg, OR 97470
541-440-6183

Gilliam County
DEQ Eastern Region (Pendleton)
700 SE Emigrant, Suite 330
Pendleton, OR 97801
541-276-4063
Fax: 541-278-0168

Grant County
DEQ Eastern Region (Pendleton)
700 SE Emigrant, Suite 330
Pendleton, OR 97801
541-276-4063
Fax: 541-278-0168

Harney County
Harney County Planning Department
450 N. Buena Vista
Burns, OR 97720
541-573-8174

Hood River County
County Health Department
1109 June Street
Hood River, OR 97031
541-386-1115

Jackson County
DEQ Western Region (Medford)
221 Stewart Avenue, Suite 201
Medford, OR 97501
541-776-6010

Jefferson County
Community Development Department
66 SE D Street
Madras, OR 97741
541-475-4453

Josephine County
DEQ Western Region (Medford)
221 Stewart Avenue, Suite 201
Medford, OR 97501
541-776-6010

Klamath County
Onsite Sanitation Division
305 Main Street
Klamath Falls, OR 97601
541-883-5121

Lake County
Lake County Building Department
513 Center Street
Lakeview, OR 97630
541-947-6033

Lincoln County
County Public Works Department
Onsite Waste Mgmt. Section
210 SW Second Street
Newport, OR 97365
541-265-4192

Malheur County
County Environmental Health Department
251 "B" St., West, Box 9
Vale, OR 97918
541-473-5186

Morrow County
DEQ Eastern Region (Pendleton)
700 SE Emigrant, Suite 330
Pendleton, OR 97801
541-276-4063
Fax: 541-278-0168

Polk County
County Community Development Department
Polk County Courthouse
850 Main Street
Dallas, OR 97338
503-623-9237

Tillamook County
County Department of Planning & Community
Development
201 Laurel Avenue
Tillamook, OR 97141
503-842-3409

Union County
DEQ Eastern Region (Pendleton)
700 SE Emigrant, Suite 330
Pendleton, OR 97801
541-276-4063 Fax: 541-278-0168

Wasco County
Wasco-Sherman Public Health Department
419 E Seventh Street
The Dalles, OR 97058-2607
541-296-4636

Wheeler County
DEQ Eastern Region (Pendleton)
700 SE Emigrant, Suite 330
Pendleton, OR 97801
541-276-4063
Fax: 541-278-0168

Lane County
Lane County Land Management Division
3050 N. Delta Highway
Eugene, OR 97408
541-682-3754

Linn County
County Environmental Health Department
Courthouse, Room 115
P.O. Box 100
Albany, OR 97321
541-967-3821

Marion County
County Building Inspections Department
5155 Silverton Rd NE,
Salem, OR 97309-1350
503-588-5147

Multnomah County
Bureau of Development Services
1900 SW Fourth Avenue
Portland, OR 97201
503-823-7790

Sherman County
Wasco-Sherman Public Health Department
419 East Seventh Street
The Dalles, OR 97058-2607
541-296-4636

Umatilla County
DEQ Eastern Region (Pendleton)
700 SE Emigrant, Suite 330
Pendleton, OR 97801
541-276-4063
Fax: 541-278-0168

Wallowa County
DEQ Eastern Region (Pendleton)
700 SE Emigrant, Suite 330
Pendleton, OR 97801
541-276-4063
Fax: 541-278-0168

Washington County
County Department of Health/Human Services
155 N First Avenue, Suite 200
Hillsboro, OR 97124
503-846-8722

Yamhill County
County Department of Planning and Development
525 NE 4th Street
McMinnville, OR 97128
503434-7516

Appendix D
Regulations for Specific Topics

To access the Oregon Administrative Rules listed below go to
www.deq.state.or.us/about/rules.htm
Then click on the appropriate division listed below

Topic	ORS's and OAR Chapter 340	Regulation Title	Corresponding Federal Rules (CFR)* Title 40
AIR QUALITY			
Dust, Odors and Other Nuisance Conditions at Construction projects	Division 208	Visible Emissions and Nuisance Requirements	N/A
Licensing and Certification of Asbestos Activities	Division 248	Asbestos Requirements	N/A
Installing Wood Heat Stoves	Regulated in State Building Codes	Residential Woodheating	N/A
Prohibition of Open Burning of Construction and Demolition Wastes	Division 264	Rules For Open Burning	N/A
CLEAN-UP OF HAZARDOUS MATERIALS			
Drug Lab Cleanup	OAR 333-040-xxx	Licensing and certification of individuals engaged in drug-lab evaluation and cleanup	N/A
Underground Storage Tank (UST) Requirements	Division 150	Underground Storage Tank (UST) Rules	Part 280
UST Licensing And Registration Requirements	Division 160	Registration and Licensing Requirements For Underground Storage Tank Service Providers	Part 280
UST Registration and Licensing Requirements for Soil Matrix Cleanup Service Providers and Supervisors	Division 162	Registration and Licensing Requirements For Underground Storage Tank Soil Matrix Cleanup Service Providers and Supervisors	Part 280
Registration and Licensing Requirements for Heating Oil Tank Soil Cleanup Service Providers and Supervisors	Division 163	Registration and Licensing Requirements For Heating Oil Tank Soil Matrix Cleanup Service Providers and Supervisors	N/A
Requirements for Decommissioning a Home Heating Oil Tank	Division 177	Residential Heating Oil Underground Storage Tanks	N/A

Topic	ORS's and OAR Chapter 340	Regulation Title	Corresponding Federal Rules (CFR)*Title 40
ENVIRONMENTAL HAZARDOUS MATERIALS			
How To Handle Fluorescent Light Tubes, Batteries, Mercury Containing Thermostats	Division 113	Universal Waste Management	Part 273
Chlorofluorocarbons	Clean Air Act	www4.law.cornell.edu/uscode/42/ch85schVI.html	Part 82
Polychlorinated biphenyls (PCBs)	Division 110	Polychlorinated biphenyls	Part 761
Lead-based paint	OAR 333-068 and 069 and 070	Certification of individuals and firms engaged in lead-based paint activities and renovation, repair and painting. Accreditation of training programs for professionals engaged in lead-based paint activities and renovation, repair and painting.	Part 745
GENERAL			
DEQ Penalties and Fines	Division 12	Enforcement Procedure and Civil Penalties	N/A
Excess Noise at Construction projects	Division 35	Noise Control Regulations	N/A
HAZARDOUS WASTE			
Identifying Hazardous Waste	Division 101	Identification and Listing of Hazardous Waste	Part 261
Obtaining a Hazardous Waste Identification Number & Requirements Apply to Hazardous Waste	Division 102	Standards Applicable to Generators of Hazardous Waste	Part 262
Hazardous Waste Transport	Division 103	Standards Applicable to Transporters of Hazardous Waste By Air or Water	Part 263
Spills Of Hazardous Materials And Hazardous Waste	Division 142	Spills and Other Incidents	N/A
SOLID WASTE			
Materials Prohibited From Solid Waste Landfills	Division 93	Solid Waste: General Provisions	Part 258

Topic	ORS's and OAR Chapter 340	Regulation Title	Corresponding Federal Rules (CFR)* Title 40
WATER QUALITY			
Protecting Drinking Water Supplies	Division 40	Groundwater Quality Protection	N/A
Special Requirements For Construction Activities For Specific Water Basins	Division 41 Section 455 (3)	Water Pollution Statewide Water Quality Maintenance Plan; Beneficial Uses, Policies, Standards, and Treatment Criteria For Oregon	N/A
Constructing Or Decommissioning Dry wells, And Other Stormwater, Parking Lot Runoff, Washwater Or Wastewater Disposal To Groundwater	Division 44	Construction and Use of Waste Disposal Wells or Other Underground Injection Activities	N/A
Permits Required For Stormwater And Washwater Discharges To Surface Water Or Groundwater	Division 45	Regulations Pertaining to NPDES and WPCF Permits	N/A
Certification Required For Dredging, Filling Or Construction In Any Oregon Waterway	Division 48	Certification of Compliance With Water Quality Requirements and Standards	N/A
Requirements To Site, Construct And Materials Used In Septic Systems & Licensing Requirement For Installer Of Septic Systems, Pumpers	Division 71 ORS 454	Onsite Wastewater Treatment System	N/A
Construction Requirements for Materials Used In Septic Systems	Division 73	Onsite Sewage Wastewater Treatment Systems Construction Standards	N/A
Requirements for contractors hooking up home plumbing to onsite septic systems	ORS 701 ORS 447	Sewer contractor requirements	N/A
Requirements for contractors hooking up home plumbing to sanitary sewers	ORS 701 ORS 447	Sewer contractor requirements	N/A

CFR = Code of Federal Regulation – To access the federal rules go to www.epa.gov/epacfr40/chapt-I.info/chi-toc.htm and click on the appropriate subchapter.
DEQ Oregon Revised Statutes (ORS) can be accessed by going to www.leg.state.or.us/ors/home.html.
Statutes that direct DEQ rules are as follows:
ORS Chapter 183 Administrative Procedures Act; Legislative Review of Rules; Civil Penalties
ORS Chapter 192 Records; Public Reports and Meetings
ORS Chapter 447 Plumbing; Architectural Barriers
ORS Chapter 454 Sewage Treatment and Disposal Systems
ORS Chapter 459 Solid Waste Management
ORS Chapter 459a Reuse and Recycling
ORS Chapter 465 Hazardous Waste and Hazardous Materials I
ORS Chapter 466 Hazardous Waste and Hazardous Materials II
ORS Chapter 467 Noise Control
ORS Chapter 468 Environmental Quality Generally
ORS Chapter 468a Air Quality
ORS Chapter 468b Water Quality
ORS Chapter 701 Construction Contractors and Contracts
OAR Chapter 340 Department of Environmental Quality

Appendix E
Penalties for Environmental Regulations

In addition to any liability, duty, or other penalty provided by law, DEQ may assess a civil penalty for any violation of state environmental statutes, state and state-adopted federal rules, permits, or orders. A written notice from DEQ initiates a formal administrative hearing process on the penalties and the notice may contain separate penalties for each violation and each day of violation. The magnitude and class of each violation determines the amount of any civil penalty. The following schedule generally describes the nature or scope of violations for these classes. Note: Penalty values may have changed. To learn more about penalty calculations, visit www.deq.state.or.us/programs/enforcement/Div12.htm.

Nature of Violation	Matrix	Violation Class	Amount Major/Moderate/Minor
<ul><li>Air quality requirements; open burning of industrial wastes and more than 25 cubic yards of prohibited materials.</li><li>Water quality requirements; violation of ORS 468B.025(1)(a)(b) without an NPDES, NPDES violation by an industrial source, domestic source NPDES/WPCF permittee permitted flow greater than 5 million gallons/day, major vegetable or fruit processor, or a person who installs or operates Class I-V UIC system, except cesspools.</li><li>Underground storage tank requirements; rule, statute, permit or order violation committed by owner, operator or permittee with 10 or more UST facilities, heating oil tank statute, rule, license violation committed by a person who is licensed or should be licensed.</li><li>Regulations governing hazardous waste (HW) management; Violations regarding financial assurance of ships transporting hazardous materials or oil, used oil statutes, rule, permit violation committed by a person who is a used oil transporter, transfer facility, processor, re-refiner, off specification used oil burner or used oil marketer, HW violation committed by a large quantity generator or HW transporter, person who should have a HW treatment, storage or disposal facility permit.</li><li>Hazardous material spill and release requirements.</li><li>Regulations for polychlorinated biphenyls (PCB) management and disposal.</li><li>Rules or orders for environmental cleanup, remediation, or removal of toxic substances and hazardous waste.</li><li>Rules and orders for controlling noise emissions.</li></ul>	$8,000	Class I Class II Class III	$8000/$4000/$2000 $4000/$2000/$1000 $750

Nature of Violation	Matrix	Violation Class	Amount Major/Moderate/Minor
• Requirements for solid waste management and disposal; violation of ORS 459 or other solid waste statute, rule, permit, or order by a person who has or should have a solid waste permit, or a person with a population of 25,000 or more (as determined by the most recent national census).			
• Air quality requirements; Violations of AQ statute, rule, permit or order by a person who has or should have an ACDP permit, except for NSR, PSD, and Basic ACDP permits. • Any violation of an asbestos statute, rule, permit or related order except by resident-occupant. • Any violation of vehicle inspection program statute, rule, permit order committed by an auto repair facility. • NPDES or WPCF statute, rule, permit or order violation with a permitted flow of more than 2 million gallons/day up to 5 million gallons/day. • Water Quality statute, rule, permit, order (WQ violation hereafter)violation for a facility that has or should have a minor industrial source NPDES permit. • WQ violation for person who has or should have a WQ General Permit, except for a 1200-C permit for a construction project less than 5 acres and 700-PM for suction dredges. • WQ violation for a person with a population greater than 10,000 but less than 100,000 who has or should have a WPCF-UIC stormwater system permit or a NPDES MS-4 stormwater permit. • WQ violation for a person who has or should have a WPCF permit for a mining operation involving 100,000 to 500,000 cubic yards other than those using chemical leachate or froth flotation. • WQ violation for a person who owns and has or should have registered a UIC system that disposes of wastewater, except stormwater or sewage. • UST violation committed by a person who is the owner, operator, permittee of 5-9 UST facilities. • SW violation by a person who has or should have a waste tire permit. • SW violation by a person with a population greater than 5,000 but less than 25,000. • HW violation by a person who is a small quantity generator.	$6,000		$6,000/$3,000/$1,500

Nature of Violation	Matrix	Violation Class	Amount Major/Moderate/Minor
• Violations not listed in other categories. • Open burning, excluding all industrial open burning violations, and requirements for burning prohibited materials in a volume greater than or equal to 25 cubic yards • Open burning of more than 15 tires by a residential owner-occupant. • NPDES or WPCF statute, rule, permit or order violation with a permitted flow of less than 2 million gallons/day. • WQ violation for person who has or should have a 1200-C permit for a construction project less than 5 acres • WQ violation for a person with a population less than 10,000 who has or should have a WPCF-UIC stormwater system permit or a NPDES MS-4 stormwater permit. • WQ violation for a person who is licensed to perform onsite sewage disposal services or who has performed sewage disposal services, or other onsite violations, except for violations committed by residential owner-occupant. • WQ violation for a person, except resident owner-occupant, that owns and either has or should have registered a UIC system that disposes of stormwater or sewage. • UST violation committed by a person who is the owner, operator, permittee of 2-4 UST facilities. • HW violation by a person who is a conditionally exempt generator, if the violation does not impact the person's generator status. • SW violation by a person with a population less than 5,000.	$2,500	Class I Class II Class III	$2500/$1250/$625 $1250/$625/$300 $200
• Violations of laws, rules or orders for rigid plastic containers, except for labeling requirements and for rigid pesticide containers, which are subject to Matrix $10,000 and may be managed as solid waste.	$1,000 No civil penalty issued for this matrix shall be less than $50 or more than $1,000 for each day of each violation.	Class I Class II Class III	$1000/$500/$250 $500/$500/$250 $250/$150/$50

Sample Questions

CHAPTER 9

1. **How can a contracting business minimize erosion on a job site?**
   - ❏ 1. Develop an erosion plan and get approval from the local building/planning department where the job site is located.
   - ❏ 2. Remove existing vegetation on steep slopes before construction and replant with native plants after construction.
   - ❏ 3. Remove topsoil during grading.
   - ❏ 4. Use silt fencing and geo fabric to intercept eroded soil onsite.

2. **Which of the following agencies does NOT regulate lead-based paint activities in Oregon residential dwellings?**
   - ❏ 1. Construction Contractors Board.
   - ❏ 2. Oregon Health Authority.
   - ❏ 3. Oregon Division of State Lands.
   - ❏ 4. Department of Housing and Urban Development.

3. **A wetlands area is land:**
   - ❏ 1. That is covered with water more than 50 percent of the year.
   - ❏ 2. Where water saturation is the dominant factor in the type of soil, plants, and animals in the area.
   - ❏ 3. Owned and protected by the Oregon Division of State Lands.
   - ❏ 4. Where more than 50 species of threatened plants and animals reside.

Answers: 1. [4]
2. [3]
3. [2]

CHAPTER 10
OREGON BUILDING EXTERIOR SHELL

Objectives

At the end of this chapter you will:
1. Know the contractor's responsibility to construct a weather-resistant building.
2. Understand the purpose of the building exterior shell.
3. Identify the primary components of the building exterior shell.
4. Understand basic moisture management concepts associated with the building exterior shell.
5. Know the different types of exterior wall assemblies and how they function.
6. Identify key best practices for constructing a weather-resistant building exterior shell.

Introduction

Moisture Problems Increase Housing Costs

Moisture damage due to failures of the building exterior shell is the primary cause of construction defect claims, particularly defects resulting in microbial growth (mold). Such claims cost Oregonians time and money in litigation, damages, repairs, and heightened insurance premiums. While defect claim costs are often covered by insurance and bonds, claims drive the costs of insurance premiums and bonds higher for all contractors – even the ones performing "perfect" work. Through the market, these increased costs eventually are passed on to Oregonians who purchase homes and other structures.

Increases in the cost of housing reduce:
- The number of Oregonians who can afford to purchase homes or make home improvements
- The profitability for Oregon contractors
- Insurance availability and affordability

The Contractor's Responsibility

Oregon law holds construction contractors financially accountable for the work performed by their business, whether the labor is performed by the contractors themselves, or by their workers. Many individuals are now effectively prevented from owning or operating a construction business in Oregon because of the improper work performed by employees who failed to properly apply, assemble, and install construction materials and systems.

Overview of the Building Exterior Shell

The building exterior shell (also known as the "building envelope") includes the outer elements of a building (assemblies, components, and materials), both above- and below-ground, that separate the exterior environment from the interior spaces of the building.

Purpose of the Building Exterior Shell

The major purpose of the building exterior shell is to protect the building at its exterior boundaries and to enclose a suitable interior for occupants. The building exterior shell provides:
- Weather protection (primary focus of this chapter)
- Temperature control and energy efficiency
- Satisfactory ambient interior environmental conditions

Components of the Building Exterior Shell

Many different systems, assemblies, components, and materials work together to make up the complete building exterior shell. For the purposes of this chapter, the building exterior shell has been divided into the following major categories:

- Exterior wall assemblies
- Windows and doors
- Waterproof deck assemblies
- Roof assemblies
- Foundation walls and crawlspaces

Moisture Management in the Building Exterior Shell

Throughout Oregon, there are differing climate zones and environmental factors to consider when designing or constructing a building. The severity and extent of how environmental conditions affect a building can even vary from region to region.

Regardless of location, the construction of the building exterior shell always needs to incorporate methods and materials that prevent or minimize the impact of moisture. Consequently, it becomes very important to understand how moisture can affect the building, as described in the next section.

Moisture Management Concepts and Strategies

Moisture Sources

Water can occur in three different physical states: solid, liquid, and gas (water vapor). Designing and constructing the building exterior shell to control the effects of water differs depending on its physical state. Each form of water poses its own unique design and construction challenges in eliminating common sources of moisture.

Solid Form

Snow and ice can build up on horizontal surfaces. Not only are snow and ice heavy, but they can also accumulate. These elements can cover portions of adjacent walls, doors, and other building components that are not normally designed to withstand contact with such harsh environmental conditions.

Liquid Form

Rainwater

Rain can strike areas not protected by overhangs and then flow down exterior building surfaces. It can also affect wall finishes adjacent to the soil finish grade by bouncing upwards (backsplash). Design and construction of the building exterior shell must take into account the effects of rainwater at many different locations.

Surface Drainage

Improperly graded soil can direct runoff toward the building or into crawlspace interiors, affecting the building above.

Groundwater

Soil can contain a great deal of moisture. The degree of soil saturation depends on many different factors, such as soil type, compaction, slope, duration, amount of precipitation, etc. Depending upon the amount of groundwater and other geotechnical conditions at the construction site, below-grade dampproofing, waterproofing, or even below-grade drainage systems may be required. Individually or in combination, these provisions are installed to prevent moisture from passing through a building's foundation walls and footing (or even up through the floor slab) and causing damage to moisture-sensitive materials.

Saturated Building Materials

Water can be transported into the building through the use of unprotected and wet building materials that have been improperly stored at a job site. Rainwater can also saturate newly installed, yet unprotected construction. If wet building materials are covered up before they have a chance to completely dry, concealed decay can occur.

Gaseous Form

Water vapor transmission

Water molecules can pass through most materials by a process called diffusion. Vapor retarders, along with ventilation systems and strategies, work to prevent excess build-up of moisture in the interior walls and cavities. In Oregon, to prevent water vapor transmission via diffusion through the building exterior shell, vapor retarders are required at the following locations:

- Interior side of the wall (warm-in-winter side of insulation)
- Underneath concrete slabs on grade
- As a ground cover over soil in crawlspaces
- Within ceilings/roof assemblies (when necessary)

Water vapor transport

Water vapor can be transported via uncontrolled air leakage pathways. Common sources include unsealed wall penetrations and air leakage at vent exhaust baffles, window perimeters, and unsealed ductwork. If the right environmental conditions are present, water vapor can accumulate or condense on surfaces and in building materials within wall cavities, resulting in wet conditions that promote concealed decay.

Wall Assembly Types

Different types of building walls feature different construction and weather-resistance strategies. They can be made up of a single material or even multiple materials that, when assembled together, function as a whole system. As a result, each wall type incorporates slightly different moisture management strategies. Some of the more common types of exterior wall assemblies include:

Mass Barrier Walls

Mass barrier walls are designed so that the thickness and properties of the wall materials are relied upon to provide the only barrier from exterior elements. The wall mass itself may absorb rainwater, but moisture permeation to the interior is prevented by the fact that the wall is able to dry out because of its sufficient thickness and absorption capacity.

This type of wall can perform well in Oregon. However, stringent attention to detail is required in order to construct and maintain mass barrier walls so that cracks, holes, and voids are not present. Such imperfections would otherwise allow moisture to migrate to the interior of the wall assembly.

Typical Section – Mass Barrier Wall

Examples of mass barrier walls:
- Cast-in-place concrete walls
- Multi-wythe masonry walls

Face-Sealed Barrier Walls

Face-sealed barrier walls usually comprise several different materials but function in much the same way as a mass barrier wall, and are designed to provide a complete barrier from exterior elements. All joints and interfaces must be sealed to provide a complete and continuous exterior barrier. The wall assembly materials must be considered during the design process, so materials are selected that are able to sustain short-term wetting, as might occur between maintenance cycles of the exterior seals, or from unintended incidental moisture infiltration.

This type of wall system also requires strict attention to detail throughout the design, installation, and maintenance cycles of the wall assembly in order to protect the building exterior shell.

Typical Section – Face-Sealed Barrier Wall

Examples of face-sealed barrier walls:
- Barrier exterior insulation and finish systems (EIFS)
- Some types of pre-cast masonry panels

Concealed Barrier Walls

Concealed barrier walls manage moisture in a slightly different way than the wall types previously described. The moisture management strategy of this wall type relies upon exterior wall surfaces to shed most of the rainwater, similar to face-sealed barrier walls. However, water-resistive materials are also installed behind the exterior wall surfaces to control and discharge an incidental amount of rainwater that might penetrate the exterior surfaces. Discharge of incidental water is accomplished by providing mechanisms to redirect it to the exterior via egress points.

This is the most common wall type used in Oregon. In order to manage moisture, the concealed barrier (including the water-resistive barrier [WRB], metal and membrane flashing, and seals/sealants), must be constructed properly and work with the exterior cladding components.

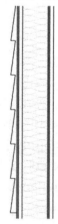

Typical Section – Concealed Barrier Wall

Examples of concealed barrier walls:
- Horizontal lap siding
- Portland cement plaster (stucco)

Simple "Rainscreen" Walls

The moisture management strategy of this wall type is the same as that of a concealed barrier wall, but penetrating rainwater can reach a drainage cavity behind the exterior cladding to mitigate the effects of capillary action. In order to be effective, the drainage cavity must be wide enough so that surface tension does not cause moisture retention, and must be relatively free of obstructions and construction debris. In many "rainscreen" systems, the cavity provides some free airflow as well, thereby aiding evaporation and increasing the drying capabilities of the wall assembly at the same time.

Mid-cycle building code changes in Oregon now require the implementation of a drainage system or mechanism within the wall cavity.

Typical Section – Simple "Rainscreen" Wall

Examples of simple "rainscreen" walls:
- Masonry cavity walls
- Concealed barrier wall types (lap siding, stucco, etc.), but where a drainage cavity exists behind the exterior wall surfaces

Pressure-Equalized "Rainscreen" Walls

The moisture management strategy is the same as that of a simple "rainscreen" wall, but drainage cavities behind dissimilar wall components are compartmentalized into separate areas and a continuous air barrier is maintained behind the exterior wall surface. This wall type reduces the air pressure differentials across the exterior surfaces of a wall, thereby reducing the volume of wind-driven rainwater that must be resisted, drained, or retained by the wall assembly.

This type of wall system has the highest potential for water-resistance and drainage, and drying capacity.

Typical Section – Pressure-Equalized "Rainscreen" Wall

Example of pressure-equalized "rainscreen" wall:
- Simple "rainscreen" wall types where drainage cavities have been compartmentalized and an air barrier has been installed

Best Practices for the Building Exterior Shell

The goal of best practices is to provide optimal weather protection for the building at its exterior boundaries, resulting in work that complies with building code requirements and product manufacturer's installation requirements, and also conforms with industry standards. The following construction practices should be considered to provide optimum weather resistance and moisture management for the building exterior shell.

Exterior Walls

To perform well, exterior walls must be designed, constructed, and maintained to protect the building and its occupants. The diagram below highlights some critical weatherproofing locations on a typical building.

Typical Exterior Wall Assemblies – Critical Weatherproofing Locations

A: Roof-to-wall interface at gutter   F: Projecting trim
B: Window head   G: Door head
C: Projecting trim   H: Guardrail-to-building interface
D: Windowsill   I: Deck-to-building interface
E: Wall-to-finish grade interface   J: Deck surface penetrations

Typical Failures	Causes
• Water leakage at voids or breaches in the wall assembly and at dissimilar material junctions	• Discontinuous wall coverings, unsealed exterior wall penetrations or dissimilar material junctions
• Failure to construct systems to manage moisture effectively	• Moisture transport via uncontrolled air leakage
• Uncontrolled air leakage and condensation(or saturation of building materials)	• Improperly installed assemblies or components
• Decreased energy efficiency and building performance	
• Premature failure of an assembly, system, or component	

Best practice recommendations for exterior walls include:
- All exterior wall materials (concealed barrier and exterior cladding elements) and adjacent components should be constructed so water drains via gravity down and away from the building.
- Exterior cladding and related components should be properly constructed to provide a continuous barrier (no holes or voids) from the elements. Special attention should be paid to moisture management at dissimilar material junctions and transitions.
- The wall assembly should be constructed to provide a continuous and complete air and thermal barrier between the interior and exterior environments. Similarly, vapor-retarding materials should be installed at required locations in order to manage water vapor transmission.
- Exterior seals and sealants should be constructed properly to accommodate anticipated movement and then maintained to provide ongoing protection for the building.
- Wall penetrations should be continuously sealed in order to protect against the elements and uncontrolled air leakage.
- Deteriorated or failed materials should be replaced or rejuvenated at the end of their useful service lives.

Window and Door Assemblies

Windows and doors must be rated to withstand the environmental conditions where they are installed. Additionally, they must be properly integrated with adjacent materials in order to complete the moisture management strategy of the wall type in which they are installed. The diagram below highlights some critical weatherproofing locations for window and door assemblies.

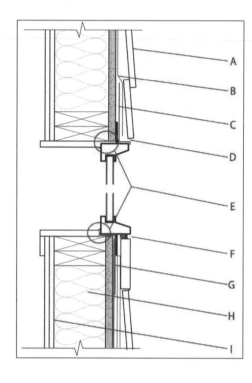

Typical Window Assembly – Critical Weatherproofing Locations

A: Exterior cladding   F: Perimeter sealant joints

B: Concealed barrier   G: Sill flashing

C: Head flashing   H: Insulation

D: Water egress   I: Vapor retarder

E: Interior air seals

Typical Failures	Causes
▪ Inadequate weather resistance or performance characteristics	▪ Environmental conditions exceed weather resistance capabilities of window or door assembly
▪ Water leakage as a result of blocked moisture egress provisions	▪ Improperly placed or constructed wall materials block moisture egress
▪ Water leakage at failed exterior seals/sealant joints	▪ Improperly constructed and failed seals/sealant joints
▪ Uncontrolled air leakage and saturation of wall materials surrounding the rough opening	▪ Inadequate or omitted air leakage control provisions
	▪ Improperly installed wall components and materials fail to manage moisture at window perimeter

Best practice recommendations for windows and doors include:

- Performance characteristics of windows and doors should be appropriate for the environment in which they are installed.
- Windows and doors should be flashed around their perimeter in order to prevent and/or manage rainwater entry.

- All exterior wall materials (concealed barrier and exterior cladding) should be integrated with the windows and doors and constructed so water drains via gravity down and away from the building.
- Windows and doors should be installed to provide a continuous and complete air and thermal barrier between the interior and exterior environments.
- Exterior seals and sealants around window and door perimeters should be constructed properly to accommodate anticipated movement and then maintained to provide ongoing protection for the building.

Waterproof Deck Assemblies

Waterproof deck assemblies represent one of the most challenging areas to construct on any building. Sensitive materials underneath horizontal surfaces exposed to the elements must be continuously and permanently protected in order to prevent moisture intrusion and damage. As a result, selection of materials, design, construction methods, and maintenance procedures must be orchestrated together to protect the building.

The diagram below highlights some critical waterproofing locations for waterproof deck (or balcony) assemblies.

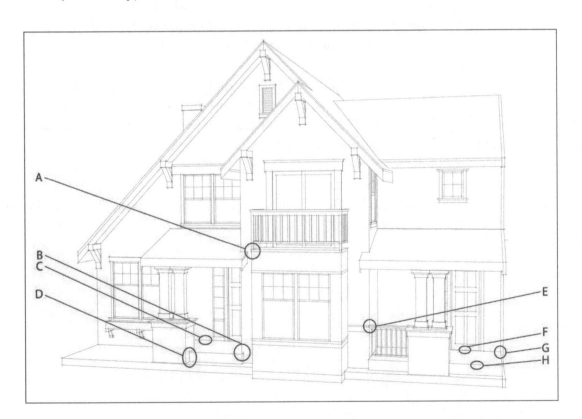

Typical Waterproof Deck Assembly – Critical Weatherproofing Locations

A: Deck penetration E: Deck guardrail penetration
B: Deck corner-to-wall interface F: Door sill
C: Deck-to-wall interface G: Deck corner-to-wall interface
D: Deck corner-to-wall interface H: Deck edge

Typical Failures	Causes
▪ Failed waterproofing materials	▪ Improperly-installed waterproofing materials
▪ Moisture-damaged wall components adjacent to deck surface	▪ Inadequate surface drainage and/or water management
▪ Moisture-damaged wall components below deck assembly	▪ Improper integration of waterproofing systems/materials with adjacent components
▪ Water leakage through deck waterproofing penetrations	▪ Improperly-constructed and failed (or un- sealed) deck waterproofing penetrations

Best practice recommendations for waterproof deck assemblies include:

- Deck materials and related components should be properly constructed to provide a continuous waterproof barrier (no holes or voids) from the elements.
- All exterior wall materials (concealed barrier and exterior cladding) and adjacent components should be properly integrated with the deck materials and constructed so water drains via gravity down and away from the building.
- Runoff should be directed (sloped) to drainage mechanisms (if necessary) in order to protect adjacent wall materials and prevent excess saturation of cladding components below. Special attention should be paid to moisture management at dissimilar material junctions and transitions.
- Deck penetrations should be continuously and permanently sealed in order to protect against the elements.
- Deteriorated or failed materials should be replaced or rejuvenated at the end of their useful service lives.

Roof Assemblies

Similar to exterior walls, roof assemblies must provide a continuous and complete weather and thermal barrier from the exterior elements. As such, they must be designed, constructed, and maintained to provide protection for the building and its occupants. The diagram below highlights some critical weatherproofing locations on a typical roof assembly.

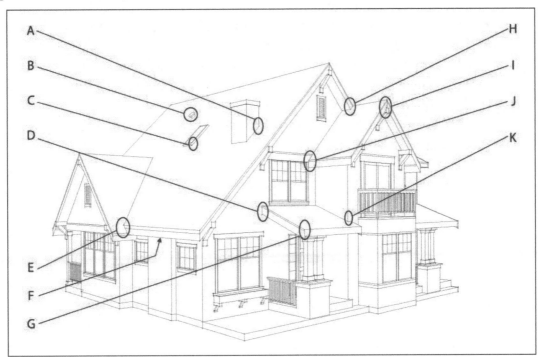

Typical Roof Assembly – Critical Weatherproofing Locations

A: Chimney cricket

B: Ventilation exhaust

C: Skylight penetration

D: Roof-to-wall termination

E: Valley termination

F: Ventilation intake

G: Rake-to-eave flashing

H: Complex roof interface

I: Ridge peak

J: Roof-to-wall termination at gutter

K: Saddle flashing

Typical Failures	Causes
▪ Failed roof assembly materials	▪ Improperly installed roofing materials
▪ Water leakage at voids or breaches in the roof assembly and at dissimilar material junctions	▪ Discontinuous roof coverings and un- sealed roof penetrations
▪ Moisture-damaged wall components adjacent to roof surface	▪ Inadequate surface drainage and/or water management
▪ Moisture-damaged wall components below roof assembly	▪ Improper integration of roof flashing with adjacent wall components
▪ Uncontrolled air leakage and condensation(or saturation of building materials)	▪ Moisture transport via uncontrolled air leakage at unsealed exhaust vents and ductwork
▪ Moisture-damaged components within roof assembly/attic cavity	▪ Inadequate or omitted roof ventilation provisions

Best practice recommendations for roof assemblies include:

- All roof materials, systems, and components must function together and be constructed so water drains via gravity.
- Runoff is normally directed (via drainage slope) to drainage mechanisms in order to prevent excess saturation of wall materials and systems below. Special attention is necessary at the roof perimeters and the ends of roof pitches near drainage components.
- Roof penetrations should be continuously and permanently sealed (or maintained) in order to protect against the elements.
- Roof/attic cavities must be properly cross-ventilated and possess an adequate amount of ventilation, so excess moisture accumulation from interior sources does not occur.
- Deteriorated or failed materials should be replaced or rejuvenated at the end of their useful service lives.

Foundations and Walls

Foundation walls must protect crawlspaces and other interior areas from water penetration, both above and below grade. As such, they require special considerations during design and construction, because soil prevents these components from being maintained following soil backfill along the foundation wall. The diagram below highlights some critical weatherproofing and waterproofing locations for the foundation wall.

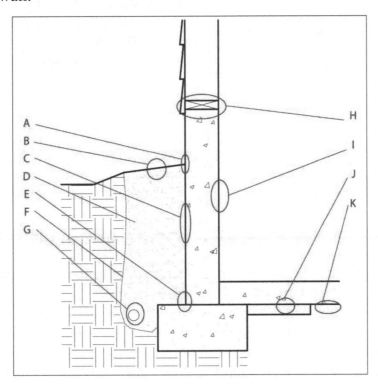

Typical Foundation Wall – Critical Weatherproofing Locations

A: Waterproofing termination

B: Soil slope

C: Dampproofing or waterproofing

D: Drainage backfill

E: Cold joint

F: Filter fabric

G: Below-grade drainage

H: Capillary break

I: Insulation

J: Insulation

K: Vapor retarder

Typical Failures	Causes
▪ Water leakage at voids, breaches, or material failures of dampproofing or waterproofing locations	▪ Improperly-installed dampproofing or waterproofing materials
▪ Moisture saturation of foundation wall at soil Grade	▪ Inadequate surface drainage and/or water management
▪ Water leakage at damaged dampproofing or waterproofing locations	▪ Missing protective mechanism on exterior side of dampproofing or waterproofing materials
▪ Water-leakage at saturated below-grade components (foundation wall, cold joint, floor slab, etc.)	▪ Inadequate below-grade site drainage provisions
	▪ Improperly-constructed or missing vapor retarder and ventilation provisions
▪ Excess accumulation of water vapor in crawlspace and interior cavities	▪ Improperly-constructed or missing capillary break
▪ Moisture-damaged wall components atop foundation wall	

Best practices for foundation walls and crawlspaces:

- Runoff should be directed (via drainage slope) away from the foundation walls in order to prevent excess saturation of wall materials and under-floor crawlspace areas.
- Where below-grade drainage is necessary, materials and components should be installed to direct water toward drainage mechanisms. In many cases, filter materials or systems are necessary in order to prevent blockage from fine soil particles and aggregate.
- Below-grade dampproofing or waterproofing components should be properly installed and integrated with drainage systems and components in order to manage moisture effectively. Along those same lines, protective materials should be implemented in order to prevent damage to the installed components during soil backfill.
- Penetrations through floor slabs and foundation walls should be continuously and permanently sealed (or maintained) in order to prevent moisture entry.
- Insulation should be installed continuously and completely at required areas.
- Crawlspaces typically require proper cross-ventilation and the installation of vapor-retarding materials at required locations in order to prevent excess buildup of moisture from the soil.

Sample Questions

CHAPTER 10

1. The primary cause of construction defect claims is?

❑ 1. Moisture damage caused by failures of the building exterior shell.

❑ 2. Non-delivery of material supplies.

❑ 3. Incorrect building permit issued.

❑ 4. Nonpayment of employee wages.

2. Which is NOT considered part of the building envelope?

❑ 1. Exterior wall assemblies.

❑ 2. Windows and doors.

❑ 3. Roof assemblies.

❑ 4. Heating and cooling system.

3. The goal of best practices for building exterior shell is to:

❑ 1. Ignore manufacturer's instructions.

❑ 2. Provide optimal weather protection for the building at its exterior boundaries.

❑ 3. Warranty workmanship.

❑ 4. Increase labor and material costs.

Answers: 1. [A]

2. [D]

3. [B]

GLOSSARY

ABN: *Assumed Business Name.*

Abatement: The reduction in degree or intensity of pollution.

Acceleration: The advancement of a project ahead of its agreed schedule.

Acceptance of an Offer: Act of a person accepting a bid or proposal as the basis for entering into an agreement for the proposed construction.

Acceptance Period: A period of time, usually referred to in bidding documents, during which the owner may review bids to determine which, if any, are to be accepted. The term usually relates only to public contracts. The owner or agency may hold each bidder's bond or security deposit throughout the acceptance period. After the acceptance period, the bonds are replaced by payment and performance bonds in the case of the successful bidders, and returned to all other bidders.

Accounting: The system of recording and summarizing business and financial transactions and analyzing, verifying and reporting the results, primarily to be used in making economic decisions.

Accounts Payable: The liability arising from the purchase of goods or services on credit. Usually constitutes an unsecured claim for payment by vendors.

Accounts Receivable: The asset arising from the sale of goods or services on credit.

Accrual Method: A method of accounting whereby all income is recorded at the time it is earned, regardless of when it is received. Expenses are recorded at the time they are incurred, regardless of when they are paid.

Acts of God: Highly unusual or catastrophic events (hurricanes, tornadoes, etc.) that cause damages or delays that could not have been reasonably foreseen.

Acute Hazardous Waste: Waste that is acutely toxic. Examples are pesticides and toxic metal compounds. A listing is found in 40 CRF Subpart 201.33E.

ADA: *Americans with Disabilities Act.* Statute that prevents unreasonable discrimination based on personal disability.

Addenda: Modifications to the contract documents issued before the bid date for consideration by the plan holders in preparing bids.

Agreement: A written or verbal contract between two or more parties; an understanding regarding common interests.

Air Pollution: The presence of contaminant substances in the air that do not disperse properly and interfere with human health.

Allowance: Funds set aside to cover the cost of a special item or work activity. The contractor includes in the price and is paid for the item or work at completion alteration, partial construction, and repairs done in and upon an improvement.

Ambient Air: Any unconfined portion of the atmosphere; the outside air.

Ammonium-copper quaternary (ACQ): If using outdoor wood, contractors should specify wood protected with an ACQ treatment.

Annual Employment Certificate: Employers who hire minors must obtain an annual employment certificate. The certificate must be posted in a conspicuous place in the work area where employees may review it.

Appeals Committee: The law creates an Appeals Committee consisting of three CCB board members representing different types of contractors and the public (or composed of the entire board). The Appeals Committee considers written exceptions filed against orders entered by an ALJ.

Aquifer: An underground bed or layer of earth, gravel, or porous stone that contains water. The depth of this layer can vary from a few feet to several hundred feet below the ground.

Arbitration Appeals: An arbitration award based on a CCB complaint may not be appealed to the Appeals Committee. However, a party may request that the arbitrator reconsider the arbitration award. A party may also file exceptions to an arbitration award with a circuit court. The grounds for exceptions to an arbitration award are very limited.

Asbestos: A mineral (magnesium silicate) that has been processed so it is used to fire proof buildings, insulate electrical wires, and make brake linings in cars. Asbestos can cause cancer if inhaled or ingested.

As-Built Drawings: The final drawings submitted by the contractor to the owner illustrating how a project was actually built.

Asset: Resources owned by the company that create value for the business. Assets are divided into current assets and noncurrent assets.

Assumed Business Name (ABN): For the CCB, any name that is not the first and last legal name of the business owner, or that suggests that the business has more than one owner.

Atmosphere: The layer of air surrounding the earth.

Balance Sheet: A financial statement of the financial condition of a business at a point in time that indicates the assets, liabilities, and owners' equity of the business.

Bankruptcy: In bankruptcy, an individual who cannot pay his or her bills may get a fresh financial start. It is a legal proceeding filed in federal bankruptcy court.

Bar Chart: A series of bars plotted to a horizontal time scale used to schedule a construction project. Each bar represents the beginning, duration, and completion of designated work activities.

Best Management Practices (BMP): Erosion Control Best Management Practices.

Bid: An offer to perform a contract for work and labor or for supplying materials at a specified price. In the construction industry, a bid by the contractor is considered an offer to another. The bid becomes a contract after the other party accepts the bidder's offer with all other contractual requirements. (See Contract.)

Bid Bond: A form of security that ensures the bidder will enter into a contract for the amount bid if an award is made to the bidder. (See also Acceptance Period.)

BIN: *Oregon Business Identification Number* (BIN) obtained from the Oregon Department of Revenue.

Biochemical Oxygen Demand (BOD): The dissolved oxygen required to decompose organic matter in water. It is a measure of pollution since heavy waste loads have a high demand for oxygen.

Biodegradable: Able to be broken down into simpler products by microscopic plants and animals.

Bond: An insurance contract by which a bonding agency guarantees payment of a specified sum in the event of a financial loss. Bond requirements depend on the size, risk, and liability of the work a contractor does. In the construction industry, there are different kinds of bonds. (See Bid Bond and Surety Bond.)

Bond Agent (bonding agent): An independent agent, representing bonding or surety companies, who acts as the liaison between the contractor and the surety company.

Breach of Contract: A failure to perform obligations under a contract that results in damages being suffered by another party to the contract. (See Immaterial Breach and Material Breach.)

Break-Even Point: The point where total revenue equals total costs and the business entity begins to realize a profit.

Budget, construction: The sum established by the owner as available for construction of the project. The stipulated highest acceptable bid price or, in the case of a project involving multiple construction contracts, the stipulated aggregate total of the highest acceptable bid prices.

Budget, project: The sum established by the owner as available for the entire project, including the construction budget, land costs, equipment costs, financing costs, fees for professional services, contingency allowance, and other similar established or estimated costs.

Budgeting: A process of developing periodic forecasts of future income and expenses for a fixed period of time. Actual income and expenses are periodically compared to the budget so management is given adequate feedback on the budget's effectiveness.

Building: A structure enclosed within a roof and within exterior walls or firewalls designed for the housing, shelter, enclosure, and support of individuals, animals, or property of any kind.

Building Code: The legal requirements set up by various governing agencies covering the minimum requirements for all types of construction. (See also Codes.)

Building Exterior Shell Training (BEST): The Oregon Construction Contractors Board (CCB) has established that all construction businesses should be minimally trained in the fundamentals of the construction of a weather-resistant building exterior shell. All Oregon construction contractors are mandated to complete training to acquire the knowledge and skills needed to properly assemble building components in such a way as to facilitate a weather-resistant and maintainable building exterior shell. The training includes: sound design and construction principles; reliable, weather-resistant construction; building exterior shell maintenance.

Building Inspector: A representative of a governmental authority employed to inspect construction for compliance with applicable codes, regulations, and ordinances.

Building Official: The officer or other designated authority charged with the administration of a building code, or his or her duly authorized representative.

Building Permit: A permit issued by appropriate governmental authority allowing construction of a project according to approved drawings and specifications.

Building Process: The entire process embracing every step from the conception to the total satisfaction of all building requirements.

Building Trade: Any one of the skilled and semiskilled crafts used in the construction industry.

Business Identification Number (BIN). If an individual or business entity will hire employees, they must obtain an Oregon business identification number (BIN) from the Oregon Department of Revenue.

Business Plan. A business plan is a written document showing where the owner wants to go and how he or she plans to get there. A business plan is an ever-changing document. As the business grows and expands, the plan should be updated. Use it to evaluate problems and find solutions. Then, update it to set revised goals.

Business Trusts. Business trusts are associations engaged in or operating a business under a written trust agreement or declaration of trust and which have beneficial interests evidenced by transferable *certificates of participation*, or shares.

These entities fill out the corporation part of the CCB license application and are treated the same as corporations by the CCB.

Buyer's Right to Cancel: Oregon law contains a mandatory, three-day right of a buyer to cancel a contract solicited at the buyer's home.

Carbon Monoxide (CO): A colorless, odorless, highly toxic by-product of incomplete fossil fuel combustion. It is one of the major air pollutants. Cars give off a great deal of carbon monoxide.

Cash Discounts: The common vendor practice of discounting (often 2 percent to 5 percent) for timely payment.

Cash Flow: This is the inflow and/or outflow of cash in a business or other economic entity. Often used to describe the funds provided by operations of the business.

Cash Method: A method of accounting that records income when cash is received and records expenses when expenses are paid. In this system, a sale on credit is not recorded until the payment is received, and invoices from suppliers are not recorded until the bills are paid.

CEG: *Conditionally exempt generator* which generates 220 pounds or less of waste or spill cleanup debris containing hazard waste in one month.

CERCLA: Comprehensive Environmental Response Compensation and Liability Act. The act provides a federal "Superfund" to clean up uncontrolled or abandoned hazardous-waste sites as well as accidents, spills, and other emergency releases of pollutants and contaminants into the environment.

Certificate of Occupancy: A document issued by the building inspector certifying that the structure conforms to all relevant code sections and is, therefore, safe for use. An owner must obtain a certificate of occupancy before a building can be used. A new building cannot be considered complete until a certificate of occupancy has been issued. In some instances, a partial certificate of occupancy will be issued for portions of the building to be occupied.

Certificate of Substantial Completion: The document issued by the architect when the building, or a portion thereof, is complete to the degree that the owner can use the building, or a portion thereof, for its intended purpose.

CFR: *Code of Federal Regulations*.

Change Order: A document issued by the owner, and signed and dated by both the owner and contractor, acknowledging that the contract has been modified to reflect a change in the scope of work. A change order generally reflects the change in the contract price and/or time that has been agreed upon as a result of the changed scope of work.

Chlorofluocarbons (CFCs): Contractors who service, maintain, repair, or install air conditioners, refrigerators, chillers, or freezers are subject to CFCs regulations.

Claim: A demand, an assertion, a pretense, a right, or title to. An action initiated by one of the parties of a contract against the other party. This action may be in the form of a written letter, a legal document, or some instrument establishing the difference between the two parties.

Clean Fill: Materials classified as clean fill include clean soil, rock, brick, building block, and old, weathered asphalt paving. Mixed construction waste does not qualify as clean fill. Also, contaminants such as spilled oil or lead-based paint on material do not qualify as clean fill.

Code Adoption: A statutory process that authorizes the Building Codes Division to adopt national and international building codes and make those codes usable in Oregon.

Code Interpretation: Responsibility of the building official, and followed by an inspector, during a job site inspection where a code is applied to work activities for compliance.

Codes: Regulations, ordinances, or statutory requirements of a governmental unit relating to building construction and occupancy, adopted and administered for the protection of public health, safety, and welfare.

Collective Bargaining Agreement: A labor contract between an employer and one or more unions, which defines the terms and conditions of employment, such as wages, hours of work, working conditions, and grievance procedures.

Commencement of the Improvement: The time when a contractor actually begins work on the site. Commencement can also begin with the first delivery of materials to the site.

Commercial Improvement: The building, assembly, or other improvements of any infrastructure on a site or sites not used or intended to be used as a residential building.

Commercial Warranties: A commercial general contractor that constructs a new, large commercial structure must provide the owner with a two-year warranty against defects in materials and workmanship that covers the building envelope and penetration components. The warranty should provide that the contractor will annually inspect the building. The warranty does not need to cover failures due to improper owner maintenance.

Compensatory Time: Commonly referred to as "comp time," it is time off instead of paying wages for time worked over 40 hours per workweek. It is only available to government workers. Employers in the private sector are not permitted to use compensatory time in place of the payment of overtime.

Competent Person: A competent person is one who is capable of identifying existing and predictable hazards in the surroundings, identifying working conditions that are unsanitary, hazardous, or dangerous to employees, and who has the authority to take prompt corrective measures to eliminate them. The competent person standard applies only to scaffolding, excavation, fall protection, and steel erection.

Completed Contract Method: An accounting method for earnings recognition in which all revenues and costs on a construction project are deferred until the project is completed.

Concealed or Differing Site Conditions Clause: A clause in a construction contract that allows for a change in price when the contractor encounters differing site conditions. Without such a clause, the contactor must complete the work at the contract price regardless of physical conditions at the site. Site conditions, which differ from those the parties expected when the contract was formed, trigger the clause. Examples of such conditions are the discovery of dry rot during a bathroom remodel or the discovery of rock formations requiring blasting during an excavation project.

Condition Precedent: An act or event that must occur before performance under a contract is required. If the act or event does not occur, the performance is excused.

Conservation: Not wasting, and renewing when possible, the human and natural resources of the world.

Consideration: A promise to perform or not perform some act, or the actual performance of the act, depending on how the offer is phrased. In most construction contracts, the consideration given by the parties is a promise to perform services or provide for the performance of specified work.

Construction: The building or assembly of any infrastructure on a site or sites. This includes improvements, alterations, partial construction, and repairs done in and upon a structure or site.

Construction Agent: A contractor, architect, builder, or other person having charge of construction or preparation.

Construction Contract: A written or oral construction agreement, including all plans, specifications, and addenda relating to activities including:

- Excavating, demolishing, and detaching existing structures and other preparation of land for making and placement of a building or structure.
- Creation or making of a building or structure.
- Alteration, partial construction, and repairs done in and upon a building or structure.

Construction Contractor: In Oregon, anyone who bids or arranges to do or does repairs, builds, alters, improves, or remodels real property.

Construction Contractors Board (CCB): The legislature created the CCB to carry out the legislative directives relating to construction contracting. The CCB is governed by a nine-member board appointed by the Governor and confirmed by the Oregon State Senate. The CCB has seven sections.

Construction Cost: The cost of all of the construction sections of a project, generally based on the sum of the construction contract and other direct costs. Construction cost does not include the compensation paid to the architect, engineer, and consultants, the cost of the land, rights-of-way or other costs that are defined in the contract documents as being the responsibility of the owner.

Construction Lien: A construction lien secures payment of a debt due to a person who provided labor, materials, equipment, or services that were used or consumed in the construction of the improvement, which is located on real property. The construction lien claims a security interest against the real property.

Construction Management: The coordination of a construction project, including the selection of contractors to perform work on the project, obtain permits, scheduling of specialty contractors' work, and purchasing materials. Construction management does not include consulting work performed by a registered engineer or a licensed architect when operating within the scope of that professional registration or license.

Consumer Protection Notice: This notice explains to customers what actions they may take to protect themselves during a construction project. (ORS 701.330(1)). The notice addresses contractor licensing, bond and insurance requirements, warranty requirements, and other information.

Contaminate: To pollute something, or make it dirty.

Contested Case Appeals: If either party disputes the order issued after a contested case hearing, the Appeals Committee will consider the written exceptions filed by either party. The parties are usually allowed an opportunity to provide brief oral comment to the board. Either party can appeal a final order in a contested case to the Oregon Court of Appeals.

Contingency Allowance: A sum designated to cover unpredictable or unforeseen items of work, or changes subsequently required by the owner.

Contract: A mutually understood agreement that has a legal purpose and is made by two or more parties, each party having legal capacity.

Contract Changes: Variations from original contract terms that cause an increase or decrease in time and/or money to the agreed scope of work. If changes are substantial, all parties should sign a change order.

Contract Documents: Documents that define the intent and performance of the parties, which generally include the Agreement, General Conditions, Drawings or Plans, and Specifications.

Contractor: A person who, for compensation or with the intent to sell, arranges or undertakes or offers to undertake or submits a bid to construct, alter, repair, add to, subtract from improve, move, wreck or demolish for another, any building, highway, road, excavation or other structure, building, or improvement attached to real property. Contractor includes general contractors, residential-only contractors, and specialty contractors.

Contractor's Right to Cure Defects: Oregon law now obligates an owner of property to notify a contractor of an alleged construction defect, and give the contractor an opportunity to cure the defect, before starting any other dispute resolution mechanisms.

Corporation: A corporation is a legal entity created under law by *articles of incorporation*. To form a corporation in Oregon, an entity must file its articles of incorporation with the Oregon Corporation Division, Business Registry, together with a required fee. A corporation is owned by *shareholders* who have no liability for corporate debts and obligations. A corporation exists separately from its owners and continues to exist even thought the shareholders may change.

Cost Control: Management procedures that monitor and track project costs for purposes of performing within the estimate.

Cost-Plus-Fee Contract: An agreement under which the contractor is reimbursed for direct and indirect costs and in addition is paid a fee for services.

Covenant: A term of a contract, either expressly stated by the parties or implied by law, in which the parties agree to do or keep from doing a specified deed or action.

Credit: The term used in a double-entry accounting system. To credit is to record an entry on the right side of a ledger account. Credits represent increases in liability, capital and revenue accounts, and decreases in asset and expense accounts.

Critical Path Method (CPM): A planning and scheduling method that uses arrow diagrams to show the connection between work activities or tasks in the construction process. It determines the relative significance of each activity and establishes the sequence and duration of operations.

Current Asset: An asset which can be converted into cash within one year or one operating cycle: cash, accounts receivable, inventory, loans owed to the business, notes receivable, and prepaid expenses are examples.

Current Liabilities: Liabilities that fall due and must be paid within one year in the normal course of business. Examples are notes payable, accounts payable, unpaid wages, payroll taxes, and sales taxes due.

Damages: In context of a construction contract, damages are losses suffered by a party to a construction contract as the result of a breach by another party, for which a court will provide a remedy.

Debit: The term used in a double-entry accounting system. To debit is to record an entry on the left side of a ledger account. Debits represent increases in asset and expense accounts, and decreases in liability, capital, and revenue accounts.

Default: Failure to do that which should be done; a failure to perform a legal duty.

Defect: A deficiency, an inadequacy, or an insufficiency arising out of or relating to the construction, alteration, or repair of a residence; also, includes a deficiency, an inadequacy, or an insufficiency in a system, component, or material incorporated into a residence.

Department of Environmental Quality (DEQ): The mission of the DEQ is to restore, enhance, and maintain the quality of Oregon's air, water, and land.

Department of Human Services (DHS): The department's mission is "helping people become independent, healthy and safe." The department is also in charge of water-quality monitoring.

Depreciation: The amount of expense charged against earnings by a company to write off the cost of an asset over its useful life, giving consideration to wear and tear, obsolescence, and salvage value. The cost of the asset is therefore spread out over its estimated useful life. A portion of depreciation expense is apportioned to each accounting period.

Design-Build (or Design-Construct): A method of organizing a building project in which a single entity does the design and construction of the structure at a set fee negotiated in advance. In a conventional construction contract, an owner hires both an architect and a contractor separately. In the design-build contract, the owner negotiates only one contract with one organization.

Detailed Survey Estimate: An estimating method that consists of listing all items needed and the materials and labor required for each item for a project. A specific price is assigned to each item or function.

Developer: A contractor who owns property or an interest in property and arranges for construction.

Direct Labor Costs: Those basic hourly wages incurred while actually installing, building, or modifying a task item.

Dissolved Oxygen (DO): A measure of the amount of oxygen available for biochemical activity in a given amount of water. Low DO levels are generally due to inadequate waste treatment.

Double Entry: A system of accounting that records each transaction separately using credits and debits that must "balance" or equal each other.

Drawings: Illustrations, or plans, which help define the scope of work and are used in estimating the project to be constructed. The plans communicate the designer's intentions about the structure by showing physical characteristics like dimensions, details, and materials. They include the type, quantity, size, and location of each item included in the project.

Ecology: The study of relationships between living things and their surroundings.

Ecosystem: A community of living things interacting with one another and with their physical environment, such as a rain forest, pond, or estuary.

EEO: *Equal Employment Opportunity Act* of 1972. Provides power to courts to rule against employment discrimination regarding race, color, religion, sex, national origin, or age.

Effluent: Waste material discharged into the environment, it can be treated or untreated.

EIN: Federal Employer Identification Number (EIN), which is issued by the Internal Revenue Service.

Emission: Waste substances discharged into the air.

Employ: To suffer or permit to work. This does not include voluntary or donated services performed for a public employer or religious, charitable, educational, public service, or similar nonprofit corporation, organization, or institution for community service, religious, or humanitarian reasons.

Employee: Anyone who is involved in "work" or its equivalent by physical or mental exertion, as controlled or required by the employer, and done for the primary benefit of the employer and the business. Neither partners nor volunteers are considered employees. An employee generally works under the direction and control of a supervisor or owner, typically for an hourly wage or by piecework.

Employer: Any person acting directly or indirectly in the interest of an employer in relation to an employee.

Employer Identification Number (EIN): If an individual or business entity will hire employees, they must obtain a federal employer identification number (EIN) from the Internal Revenue Service (IRS).

Employer's Breach: Occurs when the employer does not live up to the express, implied, or bargained agreement. This could include such things as not paying an agreed-upon salary, not paying wages in a timely manner, not providing agreed-upon benefits, and not providing workers' compensation coverage.

Entity: A type of business ownership. The choice of a business entity has many effects, including liability, taxes, workers' compensation requirements and other business requirements.

Environmental Protection Agency (EPA): EPA's mission is to protect human health and to safeguard the natural environment – air, water, and land – upon which life depends. The EPA recommends avoiding wetlands or maintaining them as an open space in any land use plan.

Erosion: The wearing away of land surface by wind or water. Erosion occurs naturally from weather or run-off but can be intensified by land-clearing practices.

Estimating: A process of judging or calculating the amount of materials required for a given piece of work; the amount of labor and equipment needed to do the work by multiplying the volume by costs per unit or measurement; and, finally an approximate evaluation of the finished project.

Exempt: An exempt CCB business means the business will not have employees and does not need workers' compensation insurance coverage. In building permits, an exempt item is work that can be performed without a permit. In accounting, a term used to indicate that a particular entity or transaction is excused from a specific filing requirement or other generally imposed rule.

Exempt Work: Construction activities that do not require a permit.

Expense: A cost of doing business, including direct cost, indirect cost, general and administrative expenses, and other expenses.

Extension: Extra time granted to complete the project.

Field Order: A written order effecting a minor change in the work not involving an adjustment to the contract sum or an extension of the contract time; issued by the architect or engineer to the contractor during construction.

Financial Statements: The end product of an accounting system. A set of reports generally consists of a Balance Sheet, an Income Statement, and a Cash Flow Statement.

First Aid: Initial care given immediately to an injured person.

Float Time: In project scheduling, the difference between the amount of time available to accomplish an activity and the time necessary to accomplish the activity.

Foreseeability: The ability to see or know in advance; reasonable anticipation that breach or injury is a likely result.

Friable: Compounds or particles that can be crumbled by hand (often referring to asbestos).

Front-End Loading: The practice of overpricing items of work done at the beginning of a job and under pricing those at the end so that the contractor or subcontractor can receive disproportionately larger payments at the beginning of the contract.

General Conditions: The section of the contract documents that describe the rights and responsibilities of the contracting parties and of others involved in the work, and procedures for implementing the project according to acceptable industry practices.

General or "Original" Contract: The contract between the owner and the contractor for construction of the entire work.

General Contractor: A contractor whose business operations require the use of more than two unrelated building trades or crafts that the contractor supervises or performs. General contractor does not include contractors who perform work in CCB categories of specialty contractors or limited contractors. The general contractor is often referred to as the "prime" or "original" contractor, i.e., a contractor who has a direct contract with the property owner.

General Ledger: An account book in which all final entries of business transactions are recorded. The entries are recorded by account classifications.

General Liability Insurance: A contractual relationship between a contractor and an insurance carrier to reimburse a third party (the customer) for a property damage or personal injury loss caused by the contractor. The CCB requires contractors to provide and maintain the amount of general liability insurance required for their selected license category.

General Overhead: A company's general and administrative expenses that are not directly related to project costs, such as accounting costs, computer costs, rent, utilities, and similar operating costs.

GPD: Gallons per day.

GPF: Gallons per flush.

Gray Water: Water that has been used for showering, washing of clothes, and faucet uses. Kitchen sink, dishwasher, and toilet water are excluded.

Gross Profit: The excess of company revenues over direct costs and indirect costs.

Groundwater: The mass of water in the ground that fills saturated zones of material such as sand, gravel or porous rock.

Hazard: Any condition that may lead to an accident or injury.

Hazardous Material: Any substance that can cause injury or death.

Hazardous Waste: Waste materials that are inherently dangerous in contact, handling, and disposal. They may be toxic, explosive, caustic, or ignitable. Substances classified as hazardous under state or federal law are subject to special handling, shipping, storage, and disposal requirements. Radioactive materials and some biological wastes are also considered hazardous but regulated differently.

HEPA: High efficiency particulate air that applies to specialized exhaust control equipment in capturing particles of lead-based paint debris.

HID (High-Intensity Discharge lamps): HIDs are an environmental hazard that may be found in new and old construction.

HUD: Department of Housing and Urban Development.

HVAC: Heating, ventilation, and air conditioning.

Hydrochlorofluorocarbons (HCFCs): A group of man-made compounds containing hydrogen, chlorine, fluorine, and carbon. They are not found anywhere in nature. Like CFCs, HCFCs are used for refrigeration, aerosol propellants, foam manufacture, and air conditioning.

ICC: *International Code Council.* A code council formed by the ICBO, SBCCI, and BOCA to create a single code in 2000 named the International Building Code (IBCO).

Immaterial Breach of Contract: A failure to perform obligations under a contract that does not significantly lessen the value of the contract for the other party or does not result in significant harm to that party.

Implied Warranty of Good Workmanship: A promise or undertaking by a construction contractor of a structure that such structure is fit for the purpose intended, which exists when the law derives it by implication or inference from the nature of the transaction or situation of the parties.

Improvement: Any building, wharf, bridge, ditch, flume, reservoir, well, tunnel, fence, street, sidewalk, machinery, aqueduct and all other structures and superstructures, whenever it can be made applicable thereto.

Income Statement: Financial statement that illustrates a company's financial status over a given period of time. Sometimes called profit and loss statement, operating statement, or statement of earnings. The income statement reports only the financial condition of the company covered during the accounting period and does not reflect the current financial situation.

Indemnification: To hold harmless against liability. Owners include indemnity or hold-harmless clauses in contracts with contractors.

Independent Contractor: A business entity or individual who contracts to perform a specified activity or project. This entity has the right to determine how the specified work will be done. There are legal requirements, outlined in ORS 670.600, that define an independent contractor for purposes of personal income tax, workers' compensation, unemployment compensation, and licensing with the CCB. A valid independent contractor is required to: (1) be free from direction and control in providing the work; (2) obtain required business licenses; (3) furnish necessary tools and equipment; (4) have authority to hire and fire employees; (5) receive progress payments or payment on a retainer basis; (6) maintain an active license with the CCB; (7) file appropriate business tax returns; and (8) publicly represent that the work is provided by an independent contractor.

Indirect Labor Costs: Those labor costs related to wages or required payroll deductions, such as federal and state withholding, unemployment insurance, FICA (Federal Insurance Contribution Act), and workers' compensation insurance.

Information Notice To Owner About Construction Liens: This notice explains to customers Oregon's construction lien laws and identifies the rights and responsibilities of property owners and contractors under the law. It is required to be given by original contractors on residential projects when the contract price exceeds $2,000. The original contractor must give this notice even if he or she does not intend to record a construction lien. If the *Information Notice To Owner About Construction Liens* is not given when required, the original contractor cannot claim a lien.

Injunction: A legal order to desist an action.

Inspection: An official examination of a place of employment by a compliance officer to determine if an employer is in compliance with the Oregon State Employment Act.

Insurance: Public liability, personal injury, and property damage insurance covering the work of the contractor that is required by the Construction Contractors Board. The contractor's insurance policy covers damage that the contractor might cause as a result of the construction work the contractor performs. For example, a contractor who performs roofing work cannot have a policy that excludes water damage.

Interest Holder: An individual or entity that has an instrument of security interest in the value of real property. A mortgagee is an example of an interest holder.

Job Costing: The process of tracking the costs associated with a work item over multiple projects. Job costing information is used to increase accuracy in project estimating. Includes direct and indirect cost.

Job Log: A daily record of all work, deliveries, accidents, and unusual events that take place at the job site.

Large Quantity Generators (LQG): A business that generates more than 2,200 pounds of hazardous waste or spill cleanup debris containing hazardous waste. A business is also a LQG if it generates more than 2.2 pounds of acute hazardous waste or more than 220 pounds of spill cleanup debris containing acute hazardous waste as defined by the EPA or if, at any time, it accumulates more than 2.2 pounds of acute hazardous waste on a single construction site.

Lead-Based Paint (LBP): Lead paint was commonly used on interior/exterior painted wood, siding, window frames, plaster, and paints. The Consumer Product Safety Commission has banned the use of lead-based paint in residential applications.

Lead-Based Paint Renovation (LBPR): Contractors who perform "renovation" on "target housing" or "child-occupied facilities" are required to hold a CCB LBPR Contractor's License.

Lead: Renovation, Repair and Painting Rule (RRP): An EPA rule requiring contractors, renovators, and maintenance personnel performing renovation on homes, child care facilities, and schools built prior to 1978 to be certified and follow specific work practices to prevent lead contamination. The Oregon Department of Human Services (DHS) and the Construction Contractors Board (CCB) have been authorized to administer the RRP program.

Legal Capacity to Contract: A party to a contract who is 18 years old, has the ability to understand the terms of the contract, and has the authority to enter into a contract on behalf of the licensed entity.

Liability: A legal term signifying legal or financial responsibility.

Liabilities: Debts, or amounts owed to creditors, resulting from current legal, equitable, or constructive obligations of a particular enterprise. Liabilities require the transfer of assets or the provision of services in the future to extinguish the respective debt.

License Endorsements: Contractors required to obtain or renew a license must choose an endorsement as a commercial contractor, a residential contractor, or both a commercial and residential contractor. A commercial contractor must hold an endorsement as one of the following: Commercial General Contractor Level 1; Commercial General Contractor Level 2; Commercial Specialty Contractor Level 1; Commercial Specialty Contractor Level 2; or Commercial Developer. A residential contractor must hold an endorsement as one of the following: Residential General Contractor; Residential Specialty Contractor; Residential Limited Contractor; Residential Developer. To be endorsed as both a commercial and residential contractor, an endorsement from each must be chosen. Contractors may change endorsement at any time during a licensing period.

Licensed Developer: Previously, this referred to a licensed developer who owned property or an interest in property and arranged for construction on that property. This CCB license category was discontinued July 1, 2010.

Lien, Construction: A security interest in real property that secures payment of a debt due to a person who provided labor, materials, equipment, or services that were used or consumed in the construction of the improvement. Under this law, contractors have the right to secure the debt that is owed to them for work on real property by recording a construction lien.

Limited Liability Company (LLC). An LLC is an unincorporated association having one or more members. It is formed under *articles of organization*. To form an LLC in Oregon, an entity must file its articles of organization with the Oregon

Corporation Division, Business Registry, together with a required fee. An LLC can be managed by its members or by a manager.

Limited Liability Partnership (LLP). An LLP is an association of two or more individuals doing business. In this form of organization, the liability of all of the partners is limited. An LLP is formed by a written agreement. An LLP is registered with the Oregon Corporation Division, Business Registry.

Limited Partnership (LP). An LP is a partnership made up of one or more general partners who control the business and who are personally liable for partnership debts and obligations and one or more limited partners who contribute capital and share profits, but who take no part in running the business and incur no liability over and above the amount contributed. An LP is formed by filing a certificate of limited partnership with the Oregon Corporation Division, Business Registry.

Liquidated Damages: A dollar amount stipulated in the contract and agreed upon at the time the contract is formed. The amount intends to compensate for a particular breach of contact, which the owner will recover from the contractor if the contractor substantially completes the project later than the date required by the contract and the delay is not excusable. Liquidated damages are enforceable if they represent a reasonable effort to forecast, at the time of contract formation, the actual damages the owner might incur as a result of the delayed use of the project.

Long-Term Debt: That portion of a debt to be paid later than the current operating cycle or one year, whichever is later. It relates to the principal portion of notes, bonds, or other securities payable and is part of long-term liabilities.

Long-Term Liabilities: Liabilities of a business that are due in more than one year.

Lost Workdays: The number of workdays an employee is unable to work due to illness or injury.

Maintenance Schedule: A contractor that constructs new residential structures or zero-lot-line dwellings must provide a maintenance schedule to the first purchaser or owner of the structure or dwelling. The maintenance schedule must include a description of moisture intrusion and water damage, an explanation how they may occur, a recommended schedule for maintenance to prevent moisture intrusion, advice on how to recognize water damage, and appropriate steps to take upon discovering water damage.

Markup: The amount added to a bid to cover overhead and profit. In an estimate, the markup is often calculated as a percentage of project costs.

Material Breach of Contract: A failure to perform obligations under a contract that causes great harm or substantially lessens the value of the contract for the non-breaching party.

Material Fact: A fact that contributes substantially to the consideration of the contract, or if that fact did not exist, the contract would not have formed.

Material Safety Data Sheet (MSDS): A document that describes the properties and hazards of a chemical.

Material Supplier: Any person or entity that provides materials or products under a construction contract by any contractual means including oral authorization, written contract, purchase order, price agreement, or rental agreement.

Mediation: An attempt by an objective third party to negotiate or facilitate a resolution of a dispute. The recommendation of the mediator is not binding on the parties.

Minor: Any individual under 18 years of age.

Mitigation of Damages: Action taken by a non-breaching party to lessen or reduce the harm caused by a breach of contract.

Mortgagee: A person or entity that has a valid subsisting mortgage of record or trust deed of record securing a loan upon land or an improvement.

Mutual Assent: Two or more parties agree to mutual intentions for a transaction that includes basic elements of performance and price.

National Fire Protection Association (NFPA): The international organization that develops codes to reduce hazards to the quality of life.

National Pollution Discharge Elimination System (NPDES): If a project will disturb one or more acres, the contractor is required to obtain an NPDES #1200-C Permit.

Negligence: Failure to exercise the degree of care that a reasonable and prudent party would exercise under the same circumstances. Negligence occurs when a professional standard of care is not met. An architect's failure to show the existence of an electric power line on a set of plans, which the architect knew was in the construction area, is an example of negligence.

Net Income: The amount of revenues of a business remaining after costs, expenses, and taxes on income have been deducted.

Net Working Capital: The excess of current assets over current liabilities.

Nonconforming Work: Work that does not fulfill the requirements of the contract documents.

Noncurrent Assets: Tangible property used in the operation of a business that does not fall into the category of current assets. It often includes land, equipment, buildings, furniture, and fixtures.

Nonexempt: The CCB business has employees or is allowed to have employees and must have Workers' Compensation Insurance coverage on its employees.

Non-point Source: Water contaminant that cannot be traced to a specific point of origin, but rather comes from many different nonspecific sources.

Nonresidential Structure: See Small Commercial Structure.

Notice of Award: The formal document from the owner informing the contractor that his or her bid has been accepted.

Notice of Compliance with Homebuyer Protection Act (HPA): This notice is required for the sale of new residential property and the remodel or improvement of residential property costing at least $50,000 that is completed within three months of the sale of the remodeled or improved property. The notice indicates the method selected by the contractor to protect the buyer against liens that may be filed or, alternatively, a waiver by the buyer acknowledging there is no protection.

Notice of Procedure: This notice describes the procedures that customers must follow to notify contractors about defective work before compelling arbitration, beginning a court action against a contractor or filing a CCB complaint against a contractor. (ORS 701.330(2)).

Notice of Right to a Lien: The *Notice of Right to a Lien* is a written pre-claim notice given as a as a step in protecting the lien rights of the owner and contractor in a construction contract. It is usually mailed by certified mail, return receipt requested, to the owner of the project.

Notice to Bidders: Also called the Invitation to Bid, the notice to bidders is the formal document that contains information needed to bid on an upcoming project.

Notice to Proceed: Written communication issued by the owner that authorizes the contractor to proceed with work and establishes the date of beginning work. This also applies to a notice from the general contractor to the subcontractor to proceed, although such communication is often a verbal notice to proceed.

Nutrients: Essential elements or compounds in the development of living things. Oxygen, nitrogen and phosphorous are examples.

OAR: Oregon Administrative Rules. As directed by the Oregon legislature, the CCB adopts administrative rules that further carry out the legislative directives relating to construction contracting. The rules can be found at OAR chapter 812.

Occupancy: A time, but limited to, when any of the following events first occur: a majority of furniture and personal belongings is moved in, utility service begins, certificate of occupancy is issued, or resident prepares meals and remains overnight.

Occupation: Any service, trade, business, or industry in which employees are gainfully employed.

ODOT: Oregon Department of Transportation.

Offer: In the construction industry, an offer is most often a proposal, bid, or binding estimate to perform work or provide products or materials in return for monetary or other compensation. An offer is a promise made by one party to do, or not do, a specific act or acts.

Offeree: The person or business entity receiving an offer.

Offeror: The person or business entity making an offer.

Off-Gas: Emission of fumes into the air.

Onsite Waste Water Treatment System: A system of piping and tanks designed to treat and dispose of human waste and household wastewater. The onsite disposal is made to the subsurface soils on the same parcel of property from which the waste was generated. Onsite waste water treatment systems are used in areas where sewers are not available.

Opacity: The measure of how much light is transmitted through an object.

Open Burning: Any burning done outdoors.

Operating Budget: An operating budget is created annually based on information gathered from previous years showing how much it cost to operate the business for a year. Generally, these costs are categorized under general and administrative expenses on the income statement.

Original Contractor: A contractor who has a contractual relationship with the owner.

OR-OSHA: Oregon Occupational Safety and Health Division. OR-OSHA has the primary responsibility for administering the Oregon Safe Employment Act of 1973.

ORS (Oregon Revised Statutes): The Oregon legislature enacts the laws that govern construction contracting. The legislature first created the CCB, then known as the Builders Board, in 1971. The laws can be found at ORS chapter 701.

OSHA: Occupational Safety and Health Administration. A federal agency that regulates and enforces safety in workplaces.

Outfall: The mouth of a sewer, drain, or conduit where effluent is discharged into receiving waters.

Overhead: The portion of the contractor's price that is generally allocated to cover general administrative expenses in operating the construction business. Overhead may refer to project overhead or project "soft" costs, which include indirect costs for constructing a project, such as temporary electricity, cleanup or job site security.

Owner of Residential Property: A person that possesses an interest in a residence or in land that is a residential site or has entered into a contract for the purchase of an interest in the residence of land. "Owner" includes:

- Homeowners association or "association" means the organization of owners of lots in a planned community, which is a subdivision of real property with buildings and improvements for owners to collectively maintain, operate and includes common property.
- Managing entity means the person, who is designated in the timeshare, unit owners, association board, or by the owners to manage all or a portion of the timeshare plan.
- An owners' association, generally a corporation, which organizes an association of timeshare owners in administering, managing, and operating a timeshare plan.
- Any other entity that possesses an interest in a residence or represents owners of a residence.

Owners' Equity: The residual interest in assets that remains after deducting liabilities.

Partnership or Joint Venture (JV). A partnership or JV is made up of two or more individuals, business entities, or a mixture of both. Unlike a general partnership, a JV is normally established for a single, large project. If a partner or joint venturer leaves the business, the contractor must obtain a new license before continuing to conduct a contracting business because it becomes a new legal entity.

Pathogens: Contaminants that include all molds, mildew, and dust mites.

PCBs: Polychlorinated Biphenyls. Widely used before 1979 to insulate electrical equipment such as capacitors, switches, and voltage regulators. Studies have shown PCBs to cause cancer and developmental/reproductive defects. These organic compounds are very persistent in the environment where they accumulate over time. Handling PCB containing materials is controlled by federal and state regulations.

Percentage of Completion Method: A method of recognizing earnings in an accounting system that is designed to match revenues and expenses of a job in the same proportion as the job progresses.

Perfecting the Lien: A lien is perfected by filing a claim of lien with the recording officer of the county in which the improvement is situated and within 75 days after the lien claimant has ceased to provide labor, rent equipment, or furnish materials or 75 days after completion of construction, whichever is earlier. Before filing, the claim of lien must be verified by oath of the lien claimant or some other person having knowledge of the facts, subject to criminal penalties for false swearing.

Performance: The accomplishment of an obligation required in the contract.

Point Source: A stationary location where pollutants are discharged.

Pollutant: A contaminant that adversely alters the physical, chemical, or biological properties of the environment.

Pollute: To make the land, water, or air dirty and unhealthy.

Pollution Prevention: Any activity that reduces or eliminates the creation of pollutants or waste at the source.

Potable Water: Drinking water.

Preparation: An excavation, survey, landscape, demolition and detachment of existing structures, leveling, filling in, and other preparation of land for construction.

Pretreatment: Processes used to reduce the amount of pollution in water before it enters the sewers or treatment plant.

Prevailing Wage Rate Law: The Prevailing Wage Rate (PWR) law is also known as the "Little Davis Bacon Act." Employees on public works must not receive less than the prevailing rate of wage for an hour's work in the same trade or occupation in the locality where such labor is performed. General contractors or subcontractors engaged on a public works project that requires prevailing wage rates must post those rates in a conspicuous and accessible place on the project. The Commissioner of BOLI furnishes these wage rates at no cost.

Preventive Maintenance: Any action or program designed to prevent damage to equipment or machinery.

Prime Contractor: See General Contractor.

Privity of Contract: The direct relationship that exists between parties to the same contract. The general contractor (but not the subcontractors) is a party to a contract with the owner of the property. Since they are parties to the same contract, the general contractor and the owner are in *privity of contract* with each other. Subcontractors are parties to contracts with the general contractor but not the property owner. The subcontractors and the general contractor are in *privity of contract* with each other. The owner and subcontractor are not in *privity of contract* and cannot directly sue each other for breach.

Profit: The excess of total revenue over total expenses.

Progress Payment: Payment for work completed by measuring the work in place and applying a previously agreed unit cost to the measured amount to determine the total payment.

Project Management: Generally, the efficient use of resources to complete a scope of work on schedule and budget.

Project Manager: The individual assigned to carry out and be responsible for construction of all or specified portions of a project; also a representative of the owner who supervises the work.

Project Manual: The manual prepared by the architect for a project, which generally includes the bidding requirements, general conditions of the contract, and the technical specifications.

Project Overhead: Project (or job) overhead includes expenses that directly relate to the project but are not included as construction labor or materials.

Public Agency: A public agency includes the state of Oregon or any of its political subdivisions, or any county, city, district, authority, public corporation or entity, or any of their legal agencies.

Public Improvements: A public works project or "public improvement" is constructed on public property and owned by the local, state, or federal government., Contractors cannot record construction liens against an agency's interest in public improvement projects. Contractors may have rights under the Federal Miller Act or Oregon's Little Miller Act, which are regulated by the respective "Miller Act" and retainage laws. Generally, a successful bidder must execute and provide a bond on a public improvement project and rights under the "Miller Act" are against the bond.

Quantity Survey: Also called a Takeoff. A complete listing of all the materials and items of work needed for a project.

Quasi Contract: An obligation created by law in circumstances where one party receives a benefit from the actions of another, and it would *unjustly enrich* the party receiving the benefit if no compensation was paid.

Radon: Radioactive, colorless, odorless gas that occurs naturally in the earth.

RCRA: Federal Resource Conservation and Recovery Act. Regulates the treatment, transportation, storage, and disposal of solid and hazardous wastes.

Real Estate: Land, including all the natural resources and permanent buildings on it.

Real Property: Ownership of land, buildings, and other improvements on the land.

Reasonable Accommodation: A modification or adjustment that enables a person with a disability to apply for a job (for example, holding a job interview in an accessible location), to perform the essential functions of a position (for example, purchasing an amplifier to allow a hearing-impaired person to talk on the telephone), or to enjoy the same benefits and privileges of employment as other employees (for example, holding a business function in a location accessible to all employees).

Recordkeeping: Organization of information that supports the financial statements, tax returns, and analysis of business operations.

Reliance: A type of remedy in contract damages that returns the non-breaching party to the position he or she would have been in if the contract had not been made.

Remedial Action: Work done at a hazardous waste site to clean up or control the contamination found at the site.

Remediation: The repair or replacement of some or all of the defects described in an owner's notice of defect.

Remedies: The lawful actions that can be taken by a party who has been damaged by a breach of contract to enforce a right or recover for a suffered wrong.

Repudiation: The rejection, disclaimer, or refusal to perform a duty or obligation owed to the other party.

Rescission: A remedy that intends to restore the parties to their original positions before the contract was formed and the contract no longer exists.

Residential Building: A building or structure, including condominiums, floating homes and mobile homes, that is or will be occupied by the owner as a residence and that contains not more than four units capable of being used as residences or homes.

Residential Construction or Improvement: For purposes of the *Information Notice To Owner About Construction Liens*, the original construction of residential property and constructing, repairing, remodeling, or altering residential property that includes, but is not limited to, the construction, repair, replacement, or improvement of driveways, swimming pools, terraces, patios, fences, porches, garages, basements, and other structures or land adjacent to a residential dwelling.

Residential Construction or Improvement Contract: For purposes of the *Information Notice To Owner About Construction Liens*, an agreement, oral or written, between an original contractor and an owner for the performance of a home improvement that includes all labor, services and materials furnished and performed thereunder.

Residential Structure: A residence, including a site-built home, a structure that contains one or more dwelling units and is four stories or less; a condominium or other residential unit; a modular home constructed off-site; a floating home; and a manufactured dwelling.

Residential Warranties: A contractor that enters into a written contract to construct a new residential structure or zero-lot-line dwelling must offer to the first purchaser, or owner, a warranty against defects in materials and workmanship. If a contractor makes a written offer to provide a warranty and, before the contractor and owner have signed a written contract, the owner refuses the warranty, the contractor may withdraw the offer to construct the residential structure or dwelling unit.

Respirator: A personal protection device that prevents airborne contaminants from being inhaled.

Responsive Bid: A bid that complies in all material respects with the request for bid or the request for proposal.

Resource Recovery: The process of obtaining materials or energy, particularly from solid waste.

Restitution: The act of making good or giving equivalent for any loss; restoration of the status quo and is the amount which would put the non-breaching party in as good a position as he or she would have been if no contract had been made and restores to non-breaching party the value of what he or she parted with in performing the contract.

Retainage: The hold back by a property owner or general contractor of a part of the price to be paid for work until conditions specified in a contract are satisfied.

Responsible Managing Individual (RMI): The owner or agent responsible for completing or proving an exemption from the CCB education and testing requirement.

Riprap: A loose assemblage of broken stones or other earth binder erected for erosion prevention.

RRP Certified Renovator: To become an RRP Certified Renovator, an individual must successfully complete the course titled "Lead Safety for Renovation, Repair, and Painting" that was developed by the Environmental Protection Agency (EPA) and the Department of Housing and Urban Development (HUD). The course must be taught by a training provider who has been accredited by the EPA, Oregon Department of Human Services (DHS) or other authorized EPA state.

Runoff: Water from precipitation or irrigation that flows over the ground surface and returns to streams. It can collect pollutants from the air or land and carry them to the receiving waters.

S-Corporation: Generally, a corporation that makes a valid election to be taxed under Subchapter S of Chapter 1 of the Internal Revenue Code. An S Corporation is like other corporations in all aspects except income taxation. There is generally no tax at the corporate level for an S-Corporation. Instead, shareholders are taxed personally on their share of profits, like in a sole proprietorship or partnership, in addition to any salary paid to them by the S-Corporation.

Schedule of Values: A statement furnished by the contractor to the architect or lender reflecting the portions of the contract sum allotted for the various parts of the work and used as a basis for reviewing the contractor's applications for progress payments.

Scope of Work: A thorough and detailed description of the work to be performed that is included in the construction contract. An insufficient scope of work could lead to uncertainty and disputes.

Sediment: Fine particles of soil.

Septic System: A common wastewater treatment system used in rural areas.

Septic Tank: An enclosure that stores and processes wastes where no sewer system exists.

Sexual Harassment: Unwelcome sexual advances, requests for sexual favors, or conduct of a sexual nature (verbal, physical, or visual), that is directed toward an individual because of gender. An employer is automatically liable for sexual harassment when a "tangible employment action" occurs in connection with the harassment. Examples include termination or failure to promote and may include such things as changes in work assignment or schedule. The employer is also liable if the employer knew or should have known about the harassment and failed to take immediate and appropriate corrective action.

Site: The land on which construction or preparation is performed.

Small Commercial Structure: A nonresidential structure with a ground area of not more than 10,000 square feet that is not more than 20 feet tall. A small commercial structure also includes a nonresidential leasehold, rental or other unit that is part of a larger structure with a ground area of not more than 12,000 square feet that is not more than 20 feet tall. A small commercial structure also includes a nonresidential structure of any size if he contract price for all construction is not more than $250,000.

Small Quantity Generators (SQG): A business that generates 221-2,200 pounds of waste or spill cleanup debris containing hazardous waste in one month. A business is also an SQG if, at any time, it accumulate more than 2,200 pounds of hazardous waste on any one construction site.

Sole Proprietorship: A business entity or form of business that is usually unincorporated, owned, and controlled exclusively by one person. The simplest and least expensive business entity to set up.

Solid Waste: Useless, unwanted, or discarded materials with insufficient liquid content to be free flowing. It may be agricultural, commercial, industrial, institutional, municipal, or residential in nature.

Spec Home (Speculative Home): A house built before it is sold. The builder speculates that the home will be sold.

Specialty Contractor: Contractor who performs on a structure, project, development or improvement and whose operations specialize in two or fewer unrelated building trades or crafts for any size residential or small commercial contract. If three or more unrelated building trades are involved, the contract must be for $2,500 or less on any one property. The CCB Specialty Contractor - All Structures license category was discontinued July 1, 2010.

Specifications: Documents that set out the detailed materials and work methods for performing the required construction activities in the scope of work.

Stagnation: Lack of motion in a mass of air or water, which tends to hold pollutants.

Stationary Source: A non-moving source of pollution, such as a factory smokestack.

Stop Work Order: The CCB may order construction work stopped immediately if the contractor was working on a structure and the contractor was not licensed when the work began. A written stop-work order notice issued by the building official and is posted on a job if work is being done without a permit, or if the project is not in compliance with codes, rules or regulations of the code or jurisdiction and other avenues have been unsuccessful in gaining compliance.

Structure: That which is built or constructed, an edifice or building of any kind, or any piece of work artificially built up or composed of parts jointed together in some definite manner, or an improvement attached to real property.

Subcontract: An agreement between the primary or original contractor and a secondary contractor for performing part of the original contractor's scope of work.

Subcontractor: Any person that performed services for the construction, alteration or repair of a residence at the request or direction of a contractor.

Substantial Completion: The time when any of the following events first occur: final inspection is completed, certificate of occupancy is issued, the structure or part of the structure is a habitable or usable condition, or most or all of the completed work has been paid. Work under a warranty provision of a contract, or repair to completed work, does not extend the date of substantial completion. Removal or replacement of completed work may extend the date of substantial completion to the date the replacement work is substantially complete.

Substantial Performance: When a party has made a good-faith effort to perform his or her obligations under a contract and has completely performed all *essential* obligations. A contract may be substantially performed even if minor, nonessential obligations have not been fully performed.

Subsurface Sewage Water System: See Onsite Waste Water Treatment System.

Suitable Position: After an employee returns from an injury, employers are obligated to return that employee to a suitable position when the employee is unable to perform his or her former job but can perform in other position(s). A suitable position is one that is substantially similar to the former position in compensation, duties, skills, location, duration (full or part time, temporary, or permanent) and shift.

Supplier: Any person that furnished or manufactured the systems, components, or materials incorporated into a residence as part of the construction, alteration, or repair of the residence.

Surety Bond: A CCB surety bond is a promise by a bonding agency to provide limited restitution to a consumer if a contractor fails to pay a CCB order or arbitration award. A licensed contractor must provide and maintain a CCB surety bond in the full amount that is required for the license endorsement.

Surface Waters: All public waters, excluding underground waters and wells.

Swale: Land formation that can be used in low-density residential developments to collect storm runoff.

Time Accelerations: An owner may include an option in the contract to direct the contractor to complete the project before the established completion date. In such cases, the contract should specifically state that the owner would pay any additional expenses of the contractor that are a result of accelerating the project.

Time is of the Essence: Phrase that is found in contracts that indicates the completion date or "time is critical" and that time itself has a high value; the phrase establishes that contract dates for performance, rewards, and penalties are strict.

Toxicity: The quality or degree of being poisonous or harmful to plant or animal life.

TSD: *Treatment, storage, and disposal* (facility).

Turbidity: Hazy air due to the presence of particles and pollutants; a similar cloudy condition in water due to suspended silt or organic matter.

UIC: Underground injection control system.

Unemployment Insurance: A tax used for the payment of benefits to unemployed employees.

Unit Price Estimate: A bid that is broken down into several segments or units and assigning costs to each unit of construction.

Universal Waste: Hazardous waste that is produced by a variety of businesses and institutions, not just in traditional industrial settings.

UST: Underground storage tanks.

Ventilation: Atmospheric air circulation determined by wind speed and mixing height. The degree of ventilation is an indication of how well air pollution will be dispersed.

Void Contract: Has no legal force or binding effect. If a contract is void, the law treats it as if it had never existed.

Volatile Organic Compounds (VOCs): Chemical compounds made of carbon, oxygen, hydrogen, chlorine, and other atoms that form gases and easily evaporate into the atmosphere. While found in nature, VOCs are also found in some glue, paint, solvents, and other products. They can react with sunlight to produce ground-level ozone, which may harm our health and even cause cancer.

Volunteers: Volunteers perform duties outside of the employment relationship and must meet the following criteria: (1) the work must be for a public service, religious, or humanitarian purpose; (2) at the volunteer's own initiative; and (3) without any expectation of pay. An employee may not do unpaid "volunteer" work for his or her employer.

Wages: Compensation due to an employee by reason of employment, payable in legal tender or check on banks convertible into cash on demand at full face value, subject to such deductions, charges, or allowances as permitted under Oregon law.

Waste Reduction: Any recycling or other activity applied after waste is generated that is consistent with the general goal of reducing present and future threats to public health, safety, and the environment.

Water Pollution: The addition of enough harmful or objectionable material to damage water quality.

Water Quality: Contractors should be aware of measures that must be taken to avoid contamination of groundwater and ensure that the water supply remains safe for human use.

Water Table: The upper level of groundwater.

Watershed: The area drained by a given stream.

Wellhead: Source of drinking water.

Wetlands: Lowland areas, such as marshes or swamps, that are covered by shallow water, or where the water table is near the surface.

Work Period: The time period from the date a contractor accepts a payment, offers a written proposal, enters into a contract or begins construction, whichever occurs first, until the date the contractual work is substantially completed by the contractor, or if not substantially completed, the date the work by the contractor ceased.

Work Time: Includes both time worked and time of authorized attendance. Generally, does not include lunch breaks unless the employee is required to remain on duty or on-site.

Workers' Compensation Division (WCD): Administers and enforces Oregon's workers' compensation laws.

Workers' Compensation Division Compliance Number: If an individual or business entity will hire employees, they must obtain a compliance number from the Oregon Workers' Compensation Division.

Workers' Compensation Insurance: Type of required insurance coverage purchased by employers for protection in covering payments to employees who are injured in work-related accidents during their employment.

Working Capital: The excess of current assets over current liabilities.

Working Days: Days when work may be performed (not Saturdays, Sundays, and holidays.)

WPCF: Water Pollution Control Facility.

Workweek: Any seven consecutive 24-hour periods as determined by the employer. The beginning of the workweek may be changed if the change is intended to be permanent and is not designed to evade the state or federal overtime requirements.

Written Contract: A contractor who performs work for an owner of a residential structure or a zero-lot-line dwelling must have a written contract with the owner if the contract price is more than $2,000. The contract must be clear and use words of common understanding.

INDEX

Index

V

W